life realized

Elzbieta Pettingill

life realized

Edited by Patrick Pettingill and Katharine Osborne

Visit author's facebook page at **www.facebook.com/LifeRealized**

life realized

I dedicate this book to my loving husband.
You are my biggest dream that came true.
I love you Patrick.

Preface

In her memoir called "life realized," Elzbieta Pettingill depicts her lifelong battle with severe depression, and the steps she took that enabled her to overcome the self-destructive behavior. Finally, after suffering from two major brain seizures, caused by a suicide attempt, she forced herself to look deep within.

Traveling the world while making her living as a high-fashion model did not give Elzbieta the sense of fulfillment or empowerment she had so desperately been searching for. She renounced the superficial lifestyle of modeling, and began her quest for happiness by trying to live a more simple life.

Eventually, the healing sense of empowerment for which she searched her whole life was obtained through her life-changing decision of going to Africa. Completely broke financially, mentally and spiritually, she managed to fulfill her mission of providing land and a house to a group of five children who were homeless when Elzbieta arrived in Kenya.

The author also shares her heartache of losing one of her two beloved German shepherds to a local Hawaiian shelter, while working oversees to provide housing for the homeless children. Back in the United States, she found out that the shelter had adopted her Rex to some strangers, despite the fact that he was identified with a micro-chip. She received conflicting answers from the shelter to her questions, including why her emergency contact person (designated by Elzbieta to care for Rex in her absence), who showed up to retrieve Rex, was not allowed to do so. As she continued to fight for her beloved dog of eight years, the battle unfolded in front of the public eye.

Elzbieta's book also talks about the hardships of growing up in communist Poland. She describes the ordeal of losing her family home, and escaping from the brutal orphanage where she ended up at the age of fifteen. She also writes about what made it possible for her to get her younger siblings out of that dreadful institution, and why it took her six years to accomplish that.

The author also shows how she was finally able to break the cycle of being in unhealthy, often abusive relationships. Tired of constant failures taking place in every aspect of her existence, she finds her own "method" of attracting a Soul Mate.

Throughout her journey, this vulnerable, almost child-like woman discovers strength and courage from within herself. While often paying a high price for a distorted, negative self-image, she eventually learns to accept herself. In the end, she is able to turn her failures into her biggest blessings/success.

Confinement

"Call 911 please," I said to Vivian, slowly, like I was telling her to order a pizza.

"What? Ela, did you take another ecstasy or something?" She didn't look any more alarmed than I did.

"Just call an ambulance, would you? I took a bottle of fucking sleeping pills." My roommate and her boyfriend were now on their feet.

"Oh my God!" I'm hearing Vivian's voice while dialing 911.

The paramedics found their way to the third floor of New York City apartment where we lived. I noticed the astonishment on those young EMT's faces. A police officer was there, too, and making some notes. I was being asked some questions, but shortly they left me alone, and began talking to Vivian and Ron instead.

After that, I remember the hospital bed. I was feeling the sensation of having a round hole on top of my head. The next thing I was feeling was as if some incredibly powerful vacuum cleaner was trying to suck my soul through that hole. I tried to sit up straight to prevent this from happening. I looked at my hands and I wasn't sure if I was hallucinating or if the color of my skin was actually grayish blue. I reached my nose with my fingers and discovered the odor I smelled was like a dead person's body.

"Nurse!" I yelled thinking that I had been left alone to die.

"Yes. How are you feeling?"

"Am I dying?" I asked her.

"No, you're stable. You're OK." I could see that she was trying not to be judgmental.

"But my hands…" I pointed them towards her.

"What about your hands?"

"Can't you smell them? They smell like a dead body." I was talking and probably looking like a child. A lost child.

"No, you're hands are OK my dear. Just try to get some sleep. I'll be here all night. You can buzz me anytime if you start to feel like there's something wrong with you, OK?"

"But I'm afraid that my soul will try to jump out of my body while I'm asleep."

"It's not going to happen. You have charcoal in your stomach that will absorb all those sleeping pills you took, OK? Plus, we have you all connected to this monitor, see? If anything happens, this machine will start to make a sound and all the doctors would come running in no time, OK? So just get some sleep. You had a rough night." She was fixing my hospital blanket and that was such an important gesture for me.

"Get some sleep." I had the feeling that she left the room not only because she had many other patients to look after, but also because it was very overwhelming to see me like this.

I looked at my hands again. They still looked grayish blue to me and I still couldn't tolerate that awful smell. It wasn't really helping much to know that all this was just in my head.

"No! I am not freaking staying here! You don't have the right to keep me here against my will!" I was shouting at a not very attractive female doctor who was sitting behind the desk in her office.

"Miss T-r-e-z-e-ciak. You have tried to kill yourself. I can hold you here for at least seventy-two hours. I have the power to do that. As far as I'm concerned you are a threat to yourself. I will not release you until I make sure that you will not try to harm yourself again." She talked in a very detached and unemotional way.

"I'm not staying in this freaking cuckoo place! This is ridiculous! I'm not a mental case! I'm going to sue you for this if I have to." I realized that in my ugly hospital robe and with my hair all messed up I didn't look intimidating to her, and she wasn't going to take me seriously.

"You're more than welcome to file a request to be released. I have to warn you though that the judge will have to look at it first, and quite honestly, I don't think he will let you go. You'll be just wasting your time and extending your stay here, that's all." She was really getting on my nerves with that self-assured attitude of hers.

"The less you resist and the more you cooperate, the sooner you will prove that you're ready to face the world again. Look, we are trying to help you here. We have a team of the best psychologists and psychiatrists available to you. We will put you on some anti-depressants, which is probably what you need right now. We'll do everything we can but it's up to you to get well." I closed my eyes and I pulled my head all the way back and she paused for a moment.

"Look, I don't know yet what made you do such a drastic thing, but something has obviously happened to you. People feel depressed, this is very common, but not all of them try to kill themselves like you did." I was surprised that her Ph.D.-like attitude allowed her to be more sensitive with me.

"Fine, I'll stay, seventy-two hours and not a minute longer." I got up from my chair and walked to my room.

My room had only two beds. The rest was just the view from the window and a tiny adjacent room that served as a bathroom. It had a shower in it but the small mirror that was hanging above the sink was made of some strange material and not real glass. I guess crazy people can do all kinds of things to hurt themselves or others. Seeing my face in that mirror was like looking at my reflection on a metal toaster.

"What the fuck am I gonna do in this fucking place for three days? Jesus Christ!"

"Dinner time! Dinner time!" I heard the nurses announcing that it was time to feed our bodies.

"Miss T-r-e- chak? Is that how you say your last name? It's time to go to eat Miss Che-chak." A nurse stuck her head in while opening the heavy metal door. I didn't say anything to her. I found the dining room on my own. All the patients were already eating their meals. A fat lady with a face that strangely looked like a five year-old girl was shouting:

"I want more butter! I want more butter! Can anybody please give me some butter? Anybody please. Please." I noticed her voice was high and it sounded as if she was about to cry.

"Here. Take my butter. Take the jelly too. Here, just take all of this, alright?" I handed her my tray.

"Oh thank you, thank you, thank you! I've got my butter! I've got my butter! See?" She was holding the small cube in front of another patient.

"She gave it to me. This pretty girl gave her butter to me. See? I've got butter from this pretty girl." She kept talking. I sat down and started to sip on my orange juice.

"Hi. I'm here because I have schizophrenia. Why are you here?" a guy my age asked me. He had a beard that made him look like Jesus.

"I tried to kill myself." I said.

"I love you, you know?" he replied.

"Scuse me?"

"I love you! Yes, I love you." He was smiling at me the whole time.

"OK." I didn't want to be insensitive.

"I've always loved you. Always. There wasn't a time when I didn't love you." He was staring into my eyes from across the table.

"OK. I believe you." I thought he was crazy but I still thought he was sweet.

"I'll be telling you this all the time. You need to hear me saying it. I love you." He kept smiling and I couldn't tell if that was part of his mental disease or if he could tell what I was thinking.

"OK, whatever makes you happy" I answered, because I wanted the conversation to end. All the other patients were eating their meals in silence. Some had absent looks, some were paying attention to the conversation I was having with the Jesus look-alike. I got up and I went back to my room. In the morning, around 6:00 a.m., the shouting coming from the hole in the door woke me up.

"Medication time! Medication time!" The nurses were shouting while pounding on those heavy, metal doors.

"Miss Che-chack. Good morning. You need to get up to get your pills." The same nurse from yesterday opened the door and stuck her head in my room.

"What pills? I don't take any pills." I turned my body towards the window.

"The doctor prescribed you some anti-depressants. You need to come to the nurses' station to take those pills." She withdrew her head but resumed shouting, "Medication time! Medication time!"

I went to the nurses' station which was right in front of my room. I stood at the end of a line and waited patiently for my turn while watching all the patients in front of me. Some had the same absent look on their faces and some looked very thrilled at the sight of their pills. Some were clapping their hands and smiling at the same time.

"Miss T-chechak. These are you pills. Go ahead and swallow them. Here is some juice." The nurse handed me a small plastic cup filled with apple juice.

"Have you ever taken any anti-depressants before?" She asked me.

"No, not really."

"Well, just so you know; it may take up to three weeks for these meds to kick in. OK? Don't be disappointed if you still keep feeling down, OK?" she informed me.

"Thanks." I went back to my room. I've always been very sensitive to pills. My body seems to respond unusually quickly to anything that I put inside my stomach.

I was still surprised I wasn't able to fall asleep at night. I asked for a sleeping pill but the nurse informed me that I had to first order it from the doctor in the morning, before she could give me one. The night was a nightmare. I couldn't sleep at all and I was feeling a strange feeling of high the whole time. It wasn't making me feel good at all; it was exhausting me instead. I felt edgy. High and edgy.

"What the fuck did they give to me?" I was so mad.

"Why aren't you sleeping yet?" said a nurse who stuck her head in to check why my lights were still on.

"Are you OK?" she asked.

"No, I'm not OK. I feel like I want to smash my head against this fucking window." I told her exactly how I was feeling. She withdrew from the room. A few minutes later she came back with some other people.

"Miss Trzeciak?" A woman that looked like a doctor was talking to me while all the other people were staring at us.

"Miss Trzeciak. I think you're feeling a little uncomfortable. I'm very surprised to see that the medication could have had such an immediate and such strong effect on you. But I have to make sure that you will not harm yourself, OK? I'm going to give you an injection, OK? It will calm you down." She was talking to me in a very soft way. I liked it.

"OK. Whatever you've got to do." I said to her. She gave me the shot and after that the other nurses strapped my arms and my legs to the bed with some special belts. I was falling asleep.

Release

I woke up still tied up to the bed. I had no clue how long I'd been asleep. Time stopped existing for me and I couldn't tell if my mandatory three days had passed yet or not. It didn't matter to me anymore where I was.

What was out there that was so special it would make me want to get out anyway? Which of those people that never came to even visit me, or call me, was I missing the most? I realized how people could be alienated easily, especially when it came to dealing with a person who attempts suicide. Vivian was probably thanking her lucky stars for the help of getting rid of me. She'd been telling me to look for a new place for a while.

The straps were making me feel very uncomfortable and I decided to call for a nurse. The way my limbs were spread on the bed made me feel humiliated.

"Now I understand why they used to crucify people in this position." The staff unstrapped me after making sure that I wasn't feeling violent anymore. The doctor changed my medications and she also prescribed pills so I could get some sleep at night.

The three days passed and nobody was discharging me and I wasn't even thinking about it anymore. Different psychologists, including some young interns were talking to me. It felt as if they were studying my case. A doctor asked me if I was OK with him recording our conversation. He said he was doing some research on the subject of suicide. He was nice to me so I agreed. He sat speechless when I opened up and I told him my life story.

The young intern, who was also a very pretty girl, was nice to me too.

"Hey, why don't you try to take a shower? I know that this is the last thing you're worrying about, but it will make you feel better. You can wash your hair, it will look so pretty. I can get you some makeup, would you like that?" She was sitting on the chair right next to my bed.

"OK." I've always sounded like a little girl when people were nice to me.

"Now why don't you go to the activity room? Today they have a nice woman who does artwork with patients. Do you like to draw or paint?" She was encouraging me to get up.

"I do. I'm actually good at drawing. I drew my roommate and her boyfriend kissing each other, I framed it and I gave it to her as a gift. It was very big, about half size of this door. They loved it and it's now hanging in our apartment." Now I sounded like an excited little girl.

"See? Go then to make some art. I'll come back later with some makeup." She looked happy and she looked proud of herself that she was able to convince me to leave my bed that I was in for I don't know how many days and nights straight.

In the activities room the therapist was admiring the two small paintings I did. One was mostly red and it looked like a rose. In the other one a warm orange color was prevailing and it was depicting a butterfly admired by crowd of people.

"Wow, this is really nice. Did you know what you were going to paint?" she asked me.

"No, not really," I told her.

"We still have some time left. Would you like to do something else?" She asked.

"Yes, I'd like to write a book."

"A book?" She looked surprised. All the patients were looking at me now.

"Yep, I'm gonna write a book. Can I have some paper please?"

She gave me a pile of paper with an expression that said; *Oh poor girl, give her whatever she wants. It may be therapeutically good for her to write her thoughts on paper.* I made holes in the paper and held the pages together with elastics. On the first page that was going to be the cover of my book

I drew the face of a small child sucking on her thumb. I wrote **"Who Am I?"** *by Ela Trzeciak* with the pencil and ***The New York Times Bestseller*** with a red pen. I used the material that was on the table to laminate the cover.

"See? It's going to be a book," I said proudly to the therapist.

"I heard you're writing a book! Let me see."

"Yeah, I'm on page eleven, see?" I was showing my work to everyone with excitement.

"Good job, keep going. Who knows, one day this thing may help other people." At the beginning the nurses looked like they felt pity for me, but now I was actually starting to feel that they liked me. Patients were also nice to me. They were constantly asking me about the progress of my book. One girl offered to correct my grammar. She wrote a poem and she asked if I could include it in my book. And I did.

"This girl gets locked up in a cuckoo house and a month later she walks around this place, with a freaking book that she's writing! Another girl who always acted like she was the toughest cookie in the world, said when I entered the entertainment room.

The book I was writing was giving me hope. I was smiling again and I was even showering at least once a week. I was participating in all the activities.

Most patients looked sad when I was leaving. They were all wishing me good luck. They were reassuring me that they were my family now.

"When I'll get out, I wanna see that damn book in the bookstores, so I can buy it!" It was sweet how much faith they had in me and the story I was writing.

"They let you go?" Vivian didn't look happy at all when she saw me in the living room.

"I know you Ela! You told them some bullshit story how well you've been feeling or something. Why are you back? You're not ready to face the world!" She was getting all hysterical and Ron wasn't being silent this time.

"You should go back to that hospital. You should stay there as long as you can to get well." He was taking his girlfriend's side.

"You need to go back there!" Vivian was pacing nervously.

"I mean; do you have any idea what you put us through?" She kept talking fast.

"Shut up Vivian! Both of you! Get off my case!" I lost my temper from the welcoming I was getting.

"What did I put you through? How many times did you come to visit me? I'm back now so live with it!"

"And how will you pay for the rent?"

"I'll get another job. Now leave me alone."

"You haven't paid for the last month and a half," she kept it up.

"I was in a fucking hospital! Ask your boyfriend to chip in. I'm sure you guys were comfortable here without me."

"I had to pay fifty dollars for that fucking 1-900 number you called to get your fortune told!" She wouldn't shut up.

"So fucking what? Is it that hard to understand that a person who's contemplating a suicide tries any freaking thing in hopes of staying alive? Stop making me feel like you're an angel from heaven and I'm the bad guy! You found a boyfriend, you want the apartment to yourself and now you're looking for excuses to get rid of me. Well, I'm not going. You can move out if you want, but don't expect me to."

"You could not afford this place all by yourself anyway. You don't have any money," she said as if she really wanted to say I was a loser.

"I'll get a roommate. And that's not any of your business anyway."

"You'll be out of here, I promise you that! I'm not leaving this place to you. Come on Ron, let's go out!" She slammed the door hard.

I sat down on the couch. I looked at the new blanket that was covering my sleeping place.

"*Wow, they made themselves nice and comfortable here without me, didn't they?*" I lit up a cigarette. When I was done with it, instead of smattering in the ashtray, I pressed it against the inner side of my left arm. The burning sensation on my skin wasn't painful at all. Seeing the redness that was forming around the butt was actually relieving. In the following days I added six more. I wore long sleeve shirts.

Poland

I remember being five years old. I couldn't wait to reach six so I could attend school with my older sisters and kids from the village. One glorious morning, my mother made four sandwiches instead of three.

"I spoke to the teacher yesterday ..." she said.

My eyeballs bulging from their sockets, she didn't have to finish her sentence for me to know the long days of crying and nagging were finally paying off.

"You're only going there to observe and sit quietly next to your sister!" she shouted from behind the kitchen door, as it slammed shut in my wake.

The students, aged six to ten, attended a small but charming school in Borki, a small village of less than 100 houses in southeastern Poland. Even walking quickly, it took me a good half hour of marching on tiny feet to arrive. I didn't mind the other kids passing me on bicycles because I was too enthralled with the road. It was leading me to sweet destiny.

For me, the road itself resembled a masterpiece by a true artist, referred to by most as the Creator. Walking that road was like being in a painting by Van Gogh.

The footpath leading to school was a labyrinth, curling like a serpent in an asymmetrical S. Walking through its tall fields of grain became my favorite thing to do, particularly when the straw stood above my head. I felt safe surrounded by golden walls.

Over time, the rye and the oats became my closest confidants. Listening to my stories without judging, they didn't have the habit of divulging my secrets or making fun of me like the hateful girls did at school. The grains had an incredibly calming effect on me. Assisted by mighty winds, they showed me their deepest sympathy by bowing their heads respectfully.

The road ended at a small forest, an oasis that produced dainty delights like raspberries and blackberries. But they were nothing as sweet as the school just beyond.

Going to school was like breathing in oxygen — indispensable and effortless. By the time I finally became a full-time student, I had read every textbook for the coming year, cover to cover. My eager attitude was rewarded with straight A's and numerous acknowledgments.

I was a serious type, always surrounded by books. I would do everything I could to avoid doing chores that required physical strength. One day when my mom told us that we had to pick potatoes from the field, I jumped out the window when she wasn't looking and went to school instead. My mother forgave me most of the time, mostly because she knew how much school meant to me, and because she was so proud of my performance. She really believed that she gave a birth to a genius. My siblings, though, weren't as forgiving as she was, and called me a spoiled brat and an evil princess sometimes.

Luckily, I got along with boys quite well. I was ridiculed behind my back on a daily basis by the girls though. I was the "smartass" excluded from girls' social circles, considered ugly with my "big head" and "large nose." My low self-esteem taught me to hate my body. I became obsessed with a tri-fold mirror that stood in a cold and dim corridor of our house. I stared at my teeth, wondering why they just couldn't follow the usual pattern of alignment.

"Why do the gums prevail over my teeth, and spoil my smile?"

In that mirror I saw the refection of a tall and skinny girl with arms too long for the flat trunk from which they hung. When I made myself look deeper, however, I saw hope in her big green eyes, and felt her overwhelming desire to become, perhaps one day, someone even more than beautiful.

My self-centeredness and emotional neediness were overwhelming to almost everybody. My habit of overanalyzing everything contributed to my constant anxieties. My solitude and sadness were perceived by others as weirdness. I cared too much what others thought of me; I desperately, and I mean really desperately, wanted everybody's approval. I felt misunderstood by the whole world, and felt sorry for myself.

My poor mother had no choice but to hear my lamentations.

"Why is my hair so thin, mom? Why? Why mom, why? When will it grow? When will I look pretty? When, mom, when?" I would pull on my sandy hair in frustration hoping the strands would get my message and that for once they would agree with me about altering my appearance by increasing their volume and length.

"Have some patience, my sweet little child. Oh - yo - yo - yo - yoy, my little precious one wants to be so beautiful. My dear Lord, what am I going to do when she finally becomes a star?"

Mom and Dad: Saint and Sinner

In my eyes my mother was a saint — not just any saint, but a beautiful one. She was a tall, full-figured woman rounded perfectly in the right places. Even after carrying nine children, her body managed to look not only beautiful, but sophisticated. Her sweet, feminine smile dominated her prominent facial features, which appeared to emanate warmth not found anywhere else. Her hazel eyes possessed depth beyond measure, leaving you wondering *who could possibly have created this incredible human being?* The sparkles in her eyes reflected her joy of life, and her love for the family she was raising.

But I couldn't figure out where she was getting her strength. She was raising nine children of her own, plus her little brother, while working full-time in a hospital kitchen. On top of that, her husband — my father — was a violent alcoholic, who, when not completely absent, inflicted unimaginable pain.

When he was drunk, my father referred to my mother as "that fucking bitch." He talked about how he planned to kill her, and hang himself afterward. At first those were just verbal threats, but as time went by he attempted to prove he meant every word. He convinced himself he had no other option but to murder his wife.

Dad was a tall and handsome man. If you didn't know he was a factory worker making agricultural equipment and war materials, you'd think he was a famous actor. He had very distinguished looks; his dark hair curled so a single lock would always find its way onto his forehead, giving him a charming yet manly look.

Things were fine when he wasn't drinking. He wouldn't talk much, but when he did it was always funny. I liked how he used to turn everything into a joke, but of course at that time I had no idea this was his way of escaping from the harsh reality of feeling inadequate, and the pain hammering him from within. The resulting disengagement from responsibilities and his lack of accountability were difficult for my mom. He thrived on insulting her, and he thought his sarcasm was hilarious.

She took his verbal abuse the way most women do when they feel like they have no other option. He mistook her submissiveness as weakness, like most men do when they feel like they own a person. His lack of gratitude for meals she prepared and his derogatory attitude towards her were interlaced with his frequent and unexpected bursts of jealousy. He was completely paranoid, constantly accusing her of infidelity, as if that was going to convince her to love him even more than she already did.

Eventually, she started to resent his behavior. She withdrew, at first emotionally, then by committing to daily visits to church. Her unusually strong fascination with religion was her way of distancing herself from the abuse. It was also her way of reaching out for the help and the support she desperately longed for her entire life.

Her absence infuriated my father, and as he continued to threaten her physically and mentally, the vicious cycle of dysfunction perpetuated. It seemed as if nothing could break the pattern. My father was like a lost child, and without my mother, he couldn't function if his life depended on it. The times he felt remorse for his actions were the moments filled with the sweetest tenderness and promises. Oftentimes he would crawl on his knees to her, occasionally sobbing and saying things like:

"I'm telling you, the devil must have got a hold of me, there is no other explanation. Is there? I must be possessed or something."

He would then follow my mother the way a shadow follows its origin. He would come home right after work, sober, and give my mother money. Heck, he would even give us some change to show that he remembered his children. He wanted us to make a big deal out of it, so she would notice it. These were the calmest and the most luminous days of my childhood.

"Go show your mother what you've got," he would say. Her approval was indispensable for his sense of fulfillment. And so we ran to her with our newly-acquired fortune in hand. We could see his contentment, derived from seeing our mother smiling.

"Oh - yo - yo - yo - yoy, my babies are so rich," our mom would play along. "What are you going to do with all that money, and where did you get all this?"

"Mom, dad gave it to us!" we would explain. By then, you could see my father smiling proudly, even though he tried to appear as if it wasn't that big a deal for him.

On rare occasions he would also say nice things to my mother, astonishing her with an occasional compliment.

"How did you get to be so pretty? Look at your mother, children! Can't you see how beautiful this creature is?"

Days such as these he would actually attempt to do some work around the house, but never finished any of the projects. So the TV would never work but at least it would stand there on the table, in the middle of the room, making a false promise to us that one day soon we would be able to watch it. The water would run whenever it felt like, as he ran his experiments with the plumbing system like a mad scientist. He tried to prove that he could fix anything, but fell short more often than not.

My mother was in seventh heaven when he would actually deliver the wood and coal to our small shed. She loved to cook, and since the kitchen wasn't supplied with any electrical equipment (apart from the small refrigerator) her only option was to use a big white stove that ran on combustible materials. My mom's culinary talent wasn't a secret. Her fame was achieved by her impressive catering performances for weddings. She did that in addition to her regular job. She handled each of the catering events by herself, with occasional help from the munchkin brigade. After the events, she came home exhausted and would just go straight to bed. The next day she would wake up at 5:00 a.m. to bustle around the kitchen in order to make breakfast, and catch her bus to work on time. My father still found a way to call her "that lazy ass," and I hated him for that.

His mind was poisoned with vodka and completely washed by our sadistic neighbors who found stirring him up entertaining. Some days he brought an axe with him and swung it around like crazy, cursing us all. I stepped in front of mom and we formed a circle to protect her. In emergencies, I was the hero.

"Who wants to go first, eh? You think you're so fucking brave? I'll show you what you're really made of, fucking whores. I'll kill you all! But first I'll kill that fucking bitch!" He made those threats with the look of true madness in his eyes. Forced to run away, we saw the neighbors gather around, commenting on the spectacle as if watching a sporting event.

My father would yell at us, as if to show the curious bystanders that he was in charge of his household.

"If you hate it so much living here, then get the fuck out!"

He made it clear to me that I was a burden to him. I despised him. I could not forgive him for the hell he was putting us through. I feared, but did not respect him. To me, he was the lowest form of human being. I was consumed by hatred for him. Sometimes I wished he would just die.

Nine of Us

When things got out of control, my mom, my brother, seven sisters and I would have to spend nights away from home. We'd be faced with searching for a friendly family, usually in a different village, that would take us all under one roof. Sometimes our family would have to be split up, and those were my first experiences of separation anxiety. I missed my mom, my sisters and my little brother, and worried about them constantly.

The oldest, Renata, was the one in charge and kept the peace. Renata was my dad's favorite, and she had the biggest influence on him. We were two brick walls, neither willing to give an inch.

Barbara was the second-born, only a year younger than Renata. She understood me like nobody else did. She spoke up for me, and my older sisters would have to go along with it. I loved her for that. She was the first one to console me when I was being made fun of in school. I don't know where she was getting her ideas, but she eventually had me convinced that one day my big lips were going to be an attribute rather than a perceived deformity. Sometimes we talked for hours, until everybody in the house was asleep. She knew how to uplift my spirit.

Next was Bozena, who was one year younger than Barbara. Unlike me, Bozena didn't take things the hard way, and at least to the outside world seemed like she didn't care what anybody thought about her. Every boy wanted her as his girlfriend, and every girl wished to dress the way she did.

And then there was me, Elzbieta, a whole three years younger than Bozena, and five years removed from Renata. I hated that gap between us, and blamed it for causing my painful solitude. But in reality, I was more responsible for my loneliness that I was ready to admit.

There were thirteen people in our two-bedroom house. Since we only had three beds, most of us had to sleep on the floor, or in the barn if weather permitted. Danuta, who was one year younger than me, always slept with grandma because she was her favorite. Sometimes I snuck under their covers, because I loved hearing grandma's bedtime stories. She transported us from our meager surroundings to places of wonder and adventure.

Marta was six years younger than Danuta, and I can still remember the day mom brought her home from the hospital. She smelled so fresh, so new, we all wanted to hold her. Her big blue eyes could steal just about anybody's heart, and her light blond hair gave her the look of an angel. She was as sweet as a child could be. She was our Martoczka.

Just when we thought God couldn't possibly create anyone more astonishing, Monika was born one year later. I was seven years old. I was fascinated by my little sister. I couldn't keep my eyes off her.

It was no secret, though, that our father wanted to have a son, and he didn't hide his disappointment when Monika was born. I think his constant nagging about only having daughters had a lot to do with our ingrained beliefs that girls were somehow inferior to boys. We used to think that he'd be a lot happier and he'd drink less if we had a brother.

The neighbors were starting to make fun of us, particularly of my mother. They used to love to gossip about our family.

"She's good for nothing else but for making babies, and she still can't give him a son!"

Finally, one year after Monika was born, our mother gave birth to a boy, Rafal. We couldn't believe our eyes! My father, after his initial euphoric state had worn off, managed to find flaws with his successor. He didn't like that Rafal's hair was red, and said it was good enough proof that this wasn't his son.

"Take that redneck back to where you got it from! He probably belongs to one of the priests!"

My grandma, just like she did with Danuta, took her grandson Rafal under her protective shield. "You should all be calling him Little King!"

My little brother was a typical boy, full of energy, and full of zest for life. Just like me, he resented our father a lot, but wasn't afraid to let the old man know what he thought of him. Maybe because Rafal was a boy after all, our father tolerated his behavior quite well.

"One day, when I grow big, I'll kick you out of the house!" he used to say to dad.

"And you won't be able to hurt mom anymore! Just watch." Just like the rest of us, he was very concerned about mother.

The youngest child we named Magdalena. She was born two years after Rafal. I remember mom cooking with her right hand, while holding her toddler in her left arm. We used to tease Magdalena what a "mamma's little girl" she was, but in reality we were a little bit jealous of the connection she developed with mom. Most of us never had a chance to spend as much time with our mother as Magdalena did.

Magdalena was also my pupil. She was ten years younger than I, and with that cuteness of hers, she awoke a maternal instinct in me. When I was fifteen and she was five, I'd take her for a walk in the city and while holding her hand, I'd pretend that she was my daughter. I liked to play the role of teenage mom, and she was a very good actress as well.

"Mommy! Mommy! Mommy!" She'd jump on her small feet, while pulling on my hand.

Ela

I have hated my "stupid" nickname for as long as I can remember. It sounded so short, so cold. Ela, Ela — there was no love in it. I wanted to be called my full name, Elzbieta. It sounded more distinguished. Or better yet, I wanted to be called Elzbietka, or Elzunia. These nicknames were endearing terms charged with passion and emotion. I wanted people to have some feeling when they called my name, like they cared.

I've always cared a lot about myself, but not because I thought I was special — simply because somebody had to. Somebody had to tell me I wasn't just the invisible girl who was only good at bringing home straight A's. I told myself that I was going to become a star one day, a big star, so big that no other stars would even be visible in my presence. I was filling my ego with fantasies, but the truth is I needed to nurture myself somehow.

It worked. My fantasy dream helped me to survive when I felt like the times were not survivable. When girls used to laugh at me in school, I used to wonder,

"Why do they have to be so cruel? Is it because I never have any money to go buy a soda with them after school? Is it because I have no bicycle to ride with them? Is it because I don't wear those new jeans that just came into style, all the way from America? Or is it because my legs are bruised from my father's beatings?"

As a young child I had parasites in my stomach and they'd keep me up all night. Whenever my mom was able to get some medicine to kill those monsters, they'd always manage to come back. My mother took me to a mystic woman, considered a witch by the local people. She prayed above my head and told my mom there was very little she could do. She talked about dark forces possessing my mind. She told her to fill a bowl with cold water and add a wooden cross to the bowl, then pour melted wax into it — and all this must be done right above my head.

When I was only three years old, I turned blue and almost died in the ER. Mom told me I scared her to death at the hospital. She said white foam was coming out of my mouth, and she decided then and there to follow the witch's advice. I remember very well her pouring that hot wax once a week. Grandma used to assist her.

I used to suffer greatly from migraines. Many times mom had to call for an ambulance. It was really scary. I would start to lose my vision. My eyes would get very sensitive to light, and I'd often vomit, too. The pain was excruciating. I was afraid to think what would happen if one of these episodes took place while I was in school.

But it did happen. We were in the gym when I started to experience the first symptoms. I ignored them because I didn't want anybody to notice that there was something wrong with me. The girls had enough reasons to gossip, and they didn't need to know that I was tormented by some mysterious illness. When the class was finally over I couldn't hide it any longer. The teacher looked at me and immediately knew something was wrong. The ambulance rushed me to the hospital. The doctor was very concerned, and immediately linked my symptoms with the abuse from my father's hands. He suggested to my mom that she do something about it, but I knew that my mother was scared.

We had called the police on my father many times before. He even went to jail for hitting a police officer who was trying to calm him down. The next day he was back home, drunk and as violent as he could be with us. He was trying to make his point that he was unstoppable, and that it was in our best interest not to call the authorities. He had a point. Our calls were a waste of time, because my father's brother-in-law, our uncle, was the mayor of the region. The fact that he slugged an officer resulted in no consequences whatsoever.

Battle for Home

My grandmother and her son Mietek, my mom's half-brother, knew something — but they kept it secret for a long time.

We lived in a two-bedroom house which was built by my mother and father after the birth of their first three children. When I was born, my parents brought me from the hospital to this brand new place.

The house was built with red brick, and although it was small, to us it was very cozy. The kitchen was the biggest room and the heart of the house. The white cupboard was carefully decorated by my mother with the most beautiful china and crystals she could find. She placed colorful flowers on the window sills, which uplifted the spirit of our home even more. In the corner right next to the cupboard we had a white bookshelf. That was my favorite piece of furniture.

Our home looked like it was from a fairy tale. My mother's garden stood on about half of this small piece of land. The house, two barns and a small shed were surrounded by a wooden fence. The fence stood out from all the neighboring fences because it was the only one that was painted. We had five fruit trees, many flowers, and vegetables. We had a black and white cow, a pig, and plenty of chickens.

The property had an additional five acres of field that extended about a mile from the village where we grew oats and wheat. To work on those fields my father used to borrow his own horse that was boarded on my other grandma's property. Her house and her land were a few miles distant from our place. We didn't get along with her, though. I don't know why but she didn't like us very much. She used to say that we were lazy people. She was even short with my father who was one of her four children. He was her least favorite. She preferred his sisters, my aunts, and especially the one who was married to the mayor.

My other grandma, who used to live with us, had two children; my mom and my uncle. Uncle Mietek was my mother's half-brother and he wasn't that much older than my sister Renata. He grew up with us. Everything was fine until he married a woman who developed a ferocious appetite for the house we were living in. My grandma had given the property to my parents, and my parents had built everything on that land. But the property was in my grandma's name.

When Mietek got married, my grandma went to live with him and his new wife. A short time later they filed a lawsuit against my parents. They wanted all the land, including the house. They won the lawsuit. My grandma testified in their favor, and there was not much our attorney could do.

Just before the judge made his final verdict, my mom decided to perform a strike. She asked us if we were OK with the idea of not attending school until this legal battle was over. And so we did of course stay home with her while protecting our home. My father was then spending more time at his mother's place and we were actually very glad for that. We were even hungrier than before and the house was always cold due to the lack of coal. But at least we had some peace.

School and books (sometimes I read two books per day) were my escape from the reality of life at home. It was very hard on me when my mom told me I couldn't go to school anymore. I was 14 years old and it was going to be my last year. I had already been planning which school to choose for my higher education. I was visualizing what dance night on graduation day was going to look like. Who was going to ask me to dance with them? What dress was I going to wear? In my mind, I was about to be an adult, a grown-up. Well, I did have to grow up, but it was not in the way I had expected. I don't think that anybody could have anticipated what was about to happen.

First Time

Even in the midst of the loss of our home, mom still looked out for me. Any time she had a little extra money, she would give me enough for a bus ticket to visit Barbara. She knew that only Barbara could make me feel as if someone understood me.

On those trips I developed a huge crush on our neighbor, Adam. I was only 15, but Adam was almost twenty. He attended classes with my oldest sister, Renata.

Adam was very tall and never serious. All the guys looked up to him. I liked seeing big smile whenever he saw me walking by his house. When I was in my attic reading books, I could see his window. I fell in love with Adam.

The previous year, at the age of 14, my first period announced I was becoming a woman. My breasts were developing very slowly though, and I hated them for that. I had to steal my sister's bras so I could make them look bigger. My hair reached my waist, and it was having an effect on men. I was delighted that my long, skinny legs were driving them crazy. For the first time, men started to turn their heads and whistle at me. Adam saw that.

One day he was riding his motorcycle when he saw me slowly walking along the road.

"Hop on. I'll take you home," he yelled with a big smile on his face. I was holding on to him like he was the last man on the planet. Adam stopped the engine in the middle of the road. He walked me to the nearest tree while holding onto my hand. He pressed my shaking body against the trunk and leaned forward. He was about to kiss me. I couldn't breathe. Then he finally pressed his lips against mine. I was shaking uncontrollably.

He forced his tongue inside my mouth and I pushed him away. Then he took me home.

I never forgot my first kiss.

"Oh Adam! Adam! I love you!" I fantasized about making love to him for the first time. I really didn't know what an erect penis looked like, and I didn't even know what my own vagina looked like. I was still very bashful, and convinced that I was committing sins with my dirty thoughts. I believed if people knew what I was dreaming about, they would think I was an awful person.

After our first kiss, Adam became surer of himself, and he would wait sometimes in front of his gate to see if I was coming back from my walks. I was so thrilled to see him there, surrounded by all the boys.

"Look who's coming back from her walk!" I could hear them saying to Adam.

"Hey guys." I wanted to sound as casual as I could.

"Hey gorgeous, when are we going to have sex?" Adam thought he was hilarious, with his attempts at juvenile humor.

He then offered to teach me to drive his car. It was a bright red Fiat and it had all kinds of accessories that it made it look like a small race car. What girl my age would turn down this offer? I was very nervous at first but I soon learned how to handle the gearshift.

After a while, he told me to drive off the road, explaining that we needed to turn the car around. I drove along between trees and bushes, and he told me to stop the car. He then forced himself on top of me and unzipped his pants. I told him to stop it.

"Oh come on! Don't tell me you haven't been dreaming about this. You play hard to get but I know that this is what you really want. You want to be fucked!"

"Get off of me! Get off of me, you jerk!" I kept screaming and kicking as much as I could in the confined space.

"You want this! I know you want to feel my dick! Stop pretending that you are a virgin!" He forced his penis inside me, and I thought I was going to die from the pain.

"It hurts! You're hurting me! Stop it! Stop it, you're hurting me!" By now I was crying from the pain. He pulled out after he ejaculated.

My love for him was gone in that moment. I looked at him with disgust and I wasn't even trying to hide my feelings.

"Oh come on! See? You weren't even a virgin. There is no blood on me. I was right, you are a whore. I'm always right when it comes to chicks. People are talking about what a whore your mother is. You're just like her."

At home I had to hide my dirty underwear. I discovered that blood came out after the fact. I hated him, but I told myself that I had to focus on the bright side of all this. I was officially a woman.

At the time, I didn't know that what Adam did to me wasn't just a rape, but a statutory rape, and he would have gone to prison if I had reported him. Typical for a girl my age, I thought I had brought all this on myself. If it happened today (and if I didn't shoot him in the head first), I would make sure he'd rot in prison. This awful experience didn't last only a few minutes in that car.

The trauma stayed with me my entire adult life.

I could not achieve an orgasm, and after awhile I even stopped trying. Each sexual encounter was similar in many ways to my first one.

It was hard to imagine yet how much I would hate men.

Killer Pills

I was suffering from severe depression, without even knowing what was tormenting me. In those times, admitting that there was something psychologically wrong with you was like admitting you were insane or mentally deficient.

At first, I just wished I'd never been born. Then I hoped that God would take me back to wherever I came from. I fantasized about being in a coma, just sleeping my problems away. I couldn't get up in the morning. I wanted to cease existing. Finally, I decided if God wasn't going to do the job, I'd do it.

One morning I took all the medicine pills from the cabinet. While I cried, I swallowed about fifty of them. I was fourteen, going on fifteen, and I really had no clue what the effect on my body would be. I felt relief, which was all that mattered to me then.

I didn't want to think about my mother because imagining her pain was too much for me to handle. I purposely made myself feel angry at the whole world so I could justify my selfish act, and it worked. I kept telling myself all the negative things, everything that had happened in my life. I kept dwelling on how unhappy I was. I kept repeating to myself that I didn't want to live like this anymore and that I've had it with feeling so lonely and misunderstood. I also thought that God didn't give a damn about me, and I couldn't bear that. I hated myself.

A few hours later I began to experience the first symptoms. The skin underneath my eyes and my hands turned dark blue. The room started to spin. Strange voices and noises entered my head. I was hallucinating. My hands shook. I touched my face, and I realized that my body was very cold. I got scared and ran to my mother, admitting to her what I had done. She was terrified, and her shortness of breath made me even more afraid. She said we didn't have time to wait for an ambulance to arrive, and our neighbor agreed to give us a ride to the hospital. She didn't tell him what was wrong with me.

In the ER they were very short with me, as if thinking;

"What kind of selfish girl would do this to her poor mother?" Since I was still conscious, hallucinating but still conscious, they gave me two choices:

"We'll either stick a long tube in your throat, or you'll drink all this water. You pick."

They brought a huge bucket filled with water. They were very short with me the whole time. I could see the judgment in their eyes while I was forcing that water in my mouth. I was very weak and my head was falling to the side. A nurse had to hold the cup for me because my hands were shaking uncontrollably. I finally vomited everything that was in my stomach. They laid me down and they inserted an IV in my arm. I fell asleep.

When I woke up later, I saw my mother's face still looking terrified beyond imagination.

"I'm sorry mom. I'm so stupid!" I started to cry.

"Shhh....Don't talk," she was crying too.

I was still hallucinating, but at least the room wasn't spinning anymore. I was mostly hearing some voices. People were laughing and shouting and I could tell they were in my head.

Eviction

I was not there that fateful day the police arrived to kick my family out of our home. I had to learn about it from the newspaper. It was a front page story, complete with a picture of my mother and my little siblings, with a big headline reading: "**EVICTION TO HEAVEN!**"

The article explained that my uncle Mietek won the lawsuit, and how he came with the police to claim the property. In the chaos of screaming, crying, and yelling, authorities were able to separate the children from my mother. I learned that she had a heart attack and was rushed to a hospital. The small children were placed in an orphanage. I was only fifteen years old, and I became the legal property of that orphanage, but I wasn't going to get caught by them. They sent the police to search all over for me. I learned quickly to turn my head whenever a police car drove by.

When my mother finally recovered from her heart attack, and the doctors were ready to discharge her from the hospital, she didn't have a place to go. My other grandma told her she could stay with her for a while. My father was already living there full-time.

My mom went to visit her small children in the orphanage but I couldn't go with her. I was still on the wanted list. I felt like a hunted criminal, like I did something wrong for wanting to be free.

The people from child protective services convinced my mother that it was in her own best interest if I turned myself in. The judge threatened her with taking her parental rights away if she didn't prove that she had control over me. He put a temporary restraining order on the parental rights of both my parents. I had no choice but to surrender myself. I thought I was going to be strong and that I would watch over my little siblings there.

Prisoner: The Orphanage

The orphanage was about sixty miles from the house we grew up in, and my mom had to take three different buses to visit us. Many times she had to hitchhike. We were grateful when she did come to see us. We would cry a lot, and my heart broke into pieces whenever I saw Magdalena pushing away from our mother. It was her way of saying that she was angry with her, and that she was blaming her for all this.

"Don't worry. I talked to your father and your grandma. They're going to let us stay there, OK? I just need to convince the judge and in no time we're going to be together again, OK?" My mother tried as hard as she could to make this happen, but the truth was that the director of the orphanage was against it.

More than half of my father's salary was going to the orphanage's account, and the director wasn't going to let go of that money. She has arranged it with the judge. The money came to her directly, from my father's paycheck. For six years, my father was left with only enough money to buy a monthly bus-pass, and some cigarettes. It slowed him down on his drinking though; he had no choice this time.

The director was a very fake woman, and talked very nice to my mother. She was trying to fool us all. We didn't buy it, though.

"Mrs. Trzeciak, I understand, but believe me, when it comes to your children being released from the orphanage, it's all up to the judge, not up to me. I wish I could help you but I don't have the power to release your children to you." We knew she was lying. We knew that she was the person the judge was listening to. Six years later I proved that we were right about her, but a lot happened first.

While my mother was away from the orphanage, she spent a great deal of time talking to the judge and social workers. They were short with her, and they all sent her back to talk to the director of the orphanage.

The director enjoyed the torture she put our mother through. I couldn't tolerate her voice or the sight of her any longer. Her big breasts were always pushed up to their maximum with her push-up bras. She revealed her cleavage with low-cut blouses. Her dark, long hair and her makeup were always perfectly applied. She was a once-attractive woman, but she seemed to have no soul inside that body. I knew she would never end this game she was playing with my mother. I knew I had to do something to stop her from destroying our family. The first thing I had to do was to get the hell out of there.

She was keeping an eye on me because she knew I had a rebellious nature. She tried to convince me that she could offer me a lot more support than my mother could. She was trying to play an innocent role with me.

The teachers in school were impressed at how I passed all my exams. They were amazed to know that despite not attending school for a year, I still knew the subjects well. My mind wasn't with my books anymore, however. I was focused on planning how to get my family together again. I was thinking that if I went to Warsaw and became a model, then perhaps I could earn enough money to hire an attorney. There were only two more weeks to finish my schooling, but I couldn't wait any longer. I had to say goodbye to my siblings. They were very understanding but they were also scared.

"Don't worry, I'll be back. It may take me some time, but I will be back to get you, OK? That bitch will never release us to mom and dad, and we know that by now." I was trying not to cry so they wouldn't feel so bad.

"Do you really have to go?" Magdalena was already crying.

"Magda, she'll be back. You have to listen to her," said Rafal, trying to be a big boy while fighting with his own tears. I kissed them all goodbye and turned around so they wouldn't see my tears. The director could tell that I was up to something. She had warned me about the consequences for anybody who attempted to run away. She made it clear that anybody who would dare such a thing would be immediately apprehended by the police and sent to a correctional institution where they kept children locked up.

With all these concerns in my mind, I left the building pretending like I was going to school, with no intention of returning except to collect my family.

Warsaw

I hitchhiked all the way to grandma's house to see my mom. I informed her about my decision and she was supportive of me. On the way, I had made a quick stop in the city where Renata was living with her husband in a tiny barrack while waiting for a real apartment.

I had to come up with a plan. Barbara helped me gather some magazines and we started to look for ads. We found one; a photographer who lived in Warsaw was searching for new faces. We sent him a letter with a picture of me that we took from Renata's photo album. Sure enough, a week later, we got a response.

Renata didn't have a phone then yet, so we had to communicate through letters only. The photographer informed me that I had very interesting looks and that he would love to shoot me. I responded that I wanted to come to Warsaw, but only if my sister could come with me. I was trying to be careful and I was trying not to allow the excitement to affect my thinking. My mom scraped some money together and my sister and I took a train to the capital of our country.

It was a six-hour trip. It was our first time in Warsaw ever. We were thrilled but nervous at the same time. The big city looked very intimidating. The incredibly loud tramways were moving in the middle of traffic as fast as they could. Everything and everybody seemed to move a lot faster here than in our small village. There were people everywhere.

"God, I hope we don't get lost here," Barbara was as nervous as I was. Somehow, we found the studio. The photographer took many pictures of me while Barbara watched us. She was a very old-fashioned girl then, and she wasn't very pleased with him trying to make me look sexy.

"She's only sixteen for God's sake!" She was looking at him like he was a pervert. I could tell that if she hadn't been there with me, the photographer would have made a pass. He was looking at me as if I was a piece of fresh meat, and he'd been fasting for a month.

"Well, you know now where Warsaw is, so why don't you come by yourself next time?" he said to me while Barbara went to use the bathroom. He even offered to let me stay in his place for a while. I wanted to become a model so I could have the money for the attorney, but I wasn't stupid. He was at least fifty years old and he was trying to establish physical contact with me every time Barbara wasn't looking. He had that smile on his face when he'd pretend that he was fixing my hair. Barbara and I realized our trip was waste of time, and that we had to come up with some new plan.

Money, Money, Money

I decided that I'd return to Warsaw and I get a job there. I thought this would give me more autonomy while pursuing my modeling career. Our mother gave me a million zloty that Bozena sent her from Greece. Bozena was working in Athens as a cleaning lady for some rich families. Before she went to live there, she went to beauty school to be a hairdresser, but nobody in Greece would hire a Polish immigrant for anything other than janitorial work. An average employee in Poland made perhaps two million zloty in those days. I was afraid of touching that kind of money.

My sister Danuta and I hitchhiked all the way to Warsaw so we wouldn't have to buy bus tickets. In one of my previous "escapades" to the big city I managed to get a job in a pizza parlor. I was fired the same day I started working there, though. It was one of the first restaurants using computers. I was overwhelmed by all this, and some managers spotted me crying in the kitchen.

"I'm sorry kiddo, but I don't think you're cut out for the life in big city. We're going to have to let you go." He handed me my paycheck.

Danuta and I were walking in central Warsaw, discussing what to do next. The crowd around us was starting to get on our nerves so we decided to just take a train back to grandma's house. I was trying to remember where the Grand Station was. We looked lost. A man in his thirties who was wearing a long jacket was approaching us. His wardrobe made him look like a detective. I freaked out for a moment thinking that the police have sent our headshots all over the country. I realized that it was too late to run away from him. He was charging at us with his sights focused on our faces. For a moment, I couldn't breathe.

"Shit! I think he's after us!" Danuta was realizing the same thing.

"Wait, don't move. I'll handle him." I put my hand on Danuta's shoulder. I was rehearsing in my mind how to convince him that he's got the wrong kids. He opened his jacket and I was certain that he was going to flash his badge in front of our eyes. I was surprised and shocked to see he was holding a gun. With his other hand, he held his jacket so that nobody could see the gun but us.

"Alright kids, give me your fucking money! Everything! Hurry up!" He was talking to us with a crazy look on his face. At first I opened my eyes wide because I couldn't believe what was happening. Then I realized how relieved I was that he wasn't a cop. Finally I couldn't help it and I started to laugh hysterically. When Danuta saw me touching my belly from laughing so hard, she began to laugh with me. Now the man was looking at us as if we were completely crazy. He closed his jacket and turned around. He was gone in no time. We had to sit on the ground because we almost peed our pants from laughing so hard.

Greater Goals

When we arrived at grandma's house, we found out that one of Danuta's girlfriends from the orphanage also ran away. She spent the night with our mom while waiting to hear something from us. She was so happy to see my sister when we got there.

"Hey, the police are looking all over for you guys! The director is super mad at you Ela. She said she's gonna send you to the juvie, and make an example out of you. We need to hide somewhere. Yesterday the cops came to your house. Luckily, we were able to see their car coming when they turned onto the dirt road." She was so agitated and excited at the same time.

Danuta and I were very tired, so I thought we should spend the night there and flee first thing in the morning. We took turns watching that dirt road throughout that night. We thought if they came back for us, they'd do it in the morning, so we felt somewhat secure until then. What we didn't know was that the police drove their car through our grandma's wild forest and approached the house from behind. We had very little time to think when we realized what was happening. We knew that it was too late to run away. We had to hide somewhere and we had to do it immediately. Danuta went inside a tiny barn where the pigeons lived. They never found her. Danuta's friend and I hid behind a pile of red bricks.

"Alright bitches, I know you're hiding there somewhere. Get out before I get really nasty with you!" A fat officer who was in charge was yelling real loud.

"Shhhh… don't move." I was trying to calm down Danuta's friend. She looked terrified.

"I'm getting out." I could tell that she was scared to death.

"Don't. Stay with me and don't worry." I had to hold her because she was starting to get up.

"They'll find us here anyway," she was crying.

"So what? Be quiet." I was trying to whisper without losing the decisiveness in my voice. The police officers found us eventually.

"Get your fucking asses out of that hole, you fucking bitches. I swear you have no idea of what I'm going to do to both of you. Get in the fucking car!"

For a moment, based on the look on his face, I thought he was going to rape us. If he wasn't afraid of talking to us that way, what else wasn't he afraid of? I pulled my arm away from his fat hands, afraid to get in the car. After all, they were going to drive us through that forest, right? I wasn't going to take that chance and seeing Danuta's friend crying like a five-year-old was enough for me. Danuta had told me that this girl was sexually molested by her father, and that's the reason why she lived in the orphanage. The poor girl was shaking the whole time while the fat officer kept yelling in her face. The hatred was shaping his greasy-looking mouth, partially covered by a moustache.

"You like running away? You like that? Let's see what else you're going to like, bitch!"

"Get your fat hands off her." I stood up straight, right in front of his face. I had already grown tall by then and I was looking him straight in his eyes.

"You think you're trying to teach some troubled youngsters a lesson? You're trying to scare the hell out of us! Still, that doesn't change the fact that you're talking to a fifteen-year-old, and you're calling her a bitch. You can bet your fat ass that I will testify against you in court."

"Shut your mouth you stupid bitch! You don't know what I'm going to do with you yet, do you?"

"Oh yeah? Well, you don't know that my uncle is the mayor of this shithole we live in. Say goodbye to your job, mister powerful!" His face changed when I said that to him. He knew my father, and of course he knew who my uncle was.

"You're just bluffing because you're scared to death." He was trying to pretend like he didn't care. The other police officer was looking at him in silence. He didn't look confident at all.

I was shaking inside the whole time, but outside I looked very calm and confident. I learned how to do that when I had to face my aggressive father.

I was convinced by my own words. I believed in every single thing that I was saying to this pathetic excuse for a police officer. I was aware that he knew about our uncle not liking us very much, but I had to pretend like that wasn't true. Anybody could figure out that if the kids were still in the orphanage, then there was something wrong with the whole family. Nevertheless, the fat officer was calming down. When we got to the police station, he even offered me a glass of water.

"Here kiddo, drink some water." I could tell that he was still trying to look mean, but at the same time he wanted me to like him.

"I can't believe how nice they are to you now." Danuta's girlfriend was nearly relaxed by now. She even started to laugh, in a timid way.

"You should have seen his face earlier when you were talking to him. I thought he was about to put those big hands on you." She was now excited with the idea of telling everybody in the orphanage all about this.

"This is more fun than sitting in Peking. I know you're gonna leave again when you get the chance. Promise me you'll take me with you next time?"

"I can't. I'm gonna be in Warsaw next time." I was planning already how to get there. The fat officer took us to another, much bigger police station. He was playing with his moustache while driving. In that station they did some paperwork on us and different officers took us to yet another police station. The last one was the biggest station, as it was the main police headquarters for the entire southeast region of Poland. We were transported in a police van to the orphanage along with handcuffed inmates.

"I can't believe all this! Look what you've got yourself into? To be transported with some criminals like this!" The orphanage director immediately took me to her office.

"Look, I know I have said to you that I would send you to that correctional institution if this ever happened, but I'm going to give you one more chance. I want you to finish school here. I don't want your future husband telling me what an uneducated woman he married. How else will you take care of yourself?"

"I don't need a husband to take care of me."

"That's what you think right now. You're sixteen, my dear. Trust me; no man will respect you if you don't have a formal education. Right now you're pretty but that won't last forever. Plus, didn't you want to become a doctor or something? Come on, you're doing so well in school. The teachers and the principal are so impressed with your work. Don't you remember how they were reading your essay to the whole school? We were trying to see if we could even publish your work for god's sake! Why don't you let me help you? You can become anything you want. You can become a doctor in no time."

"Yes, but now is not the right time. I have my own emergency I have to take care of first. Maybe you do care but I don't think you understand what has happened to me. I can't focus in school anymore. I get good grades because I've read lots of books in the past, not because I'm learning anything new."

"I'm going to do whatever I can to help you. Just give me a chance. I already set an appointment with a psychologist for you. She's going to work with you on that. I trust that you'll make the right decision and that you'll take advantage of this opportunity."

I convinced the psychologist that I would remain in the orphanage. It was easy. I told him what I knew he wanted to hear from me. I was just a lost kid that really needed a direction from a trained professional. He was so flattered when I told him that I was planning on pursuing either psychology or medicine. Well, I wasn't completely lying to him. I wanted to have a doctorate in something for as long as I could remember. I wanted to be everything and to do everything. I wanted to write books and I wanted to know how to heal people. I wanted to be a model and an actress as well. I wanted to fly helicopters and I wanted to shoot guns for real, not just in the movies.

More than anything I wanted to save all the children in the world. I wanted to have power so I could stop the abuse. I wanted to have the money so there wouldn't be any starving children in the world. I wanted to make a difference. I wanted to cure the world from the plague that is expanding everywhere. Getting rid of the indifference from which people are suffering was my goal. Being an advocate for the poorest and most powerless was my mission.

My family was on top of the list of those who needed my help. Of course this was all inside my head, and only a few people had access to my dreams. The professionals the orphanage hired weren't among them.

I told the truth about my intentions of leaving to the second psychologist they made me see. I trusted her. She promised she wouldn't say anything to the director and she kept her word. The director was relaxed and she let me go to school all by myself again. I went to my first class because I knew that she would call the school to make sure I made it there in the morning. I didn't want to be picked up by the police while hitchhiking. Once inside some stranger's car, I felt like I was safe. I was making choices and I was in charge of my life. I was choosing what seemed necessary at the moment. I was choosing a lesser evil for a greater goal.

Losing our home, as well as the separation of the family, was one the most devastating things that I have experienced. It was traumatic and painful. My soul seemed crushed so badly that I thought it may be beyond repair. The term Major Depression could not do justice in describing what I was feeling. My anger towards the world and God was skyrocketing. Every little interest I may have had up to that point had completely vanished. There was no way I could sit and read books like I used to. The only energy left I had was consumed by my obsessing about survival.

The Church

I said my goodbyes to my siblings once again. I asked them to be patient with me. I told the youngest ones that I was practically a model; I wanted them to have hope. I think my own hope was running out because I was feeling more and more depressed. Once again I ran away from the orphanage.

I went to a church to talk to God one day. The church was empty. I kneeled in front of the big altar. I didn't like any religions but I thought that if God was living here, he wouldn't mind.

I hated the fact that people were preaching about humans being brothers and sisters, and yet they would do nothing to help me. I used to come to this church before, during the time I was away from the orphanage. I used to talk to the priests in the hope that they would help my family. The nuns were so touched by my story that they sort of adopted me.

In exchange for my cleaning and waiting the big table where all the priests were dining, they were feeding me with some leftovers. I could see what was on that big table and sure enough it wasn't what I was eating. My meals had a closer resemblance to slop than food. I remained humble though, hoping that I would win their hearts eventually. I would always wear long-sleeved blouses and skirts that were touching my ankles. My long hair was always in a ponytail. I had no makeup and I almost looked like one of them.

They used to call me my full name; Elzbieta. They were the first ones in my life that referred to me this way. I felt so respected. I felt like they were talking to a woman and not to an orphan. I used to have a beautiful voice then and a really good ear for music. I was not afraid of singing out loud with them.

A young priest heard me singing once. He was so impressed. He was thirty-two years old and extremely good looking. He had his guitar and he used to teach all the kids how to sing. He was the church's mascot; everybody loved him, especially the nuns. I suspected one of the younger nuns was completely in love with him. I don't honestly think that they had anything going on, but the way she'd look at him was not completely innocent. She'd look at him as if he was Jesus Christ Himself. He was charming. You could tell he was well-educated by the way he spoke. This wasn't always the case when it came to priests. He was different, and everybody seemed to know that.

His charisma had an incredible effect on everybody. People were always at his door, like they needed something. I hated that. He was trying to teach me how to play the guitar and they were always interrupting us. One girl in particular was getting on my nerves. She was one of his students and she always seemed to need him for something. I was her competition. She couldn't stand me and vice versa. She was jealous that I had one-on-one lessons and that she didn't. The priest had to be very firm with her sometimes because she wouldn't want to leave. I had a good excuse to be there, I was there to clean his room after all.

One day my mom, Barbara, Renata, and I were sitting in my sister's barrack. It was Christmas time and mom and my older sisters were telling me about how my younger siblings were doing in the orphanage. We didn't have any money left, which wasn't uncommon, and we were trying to figure out what to have for dinner. Except for a pickle jar there was absolutely nothing else to eat. I got up from the small table, grabbed my coat and I headed for the door.

"Where are you going? It's snowing outside, you'll freeze!" My mom was concerned.

"I'll be back in no time. I'm gonna get us something to eat." I shut the door behind me. The nuns looked surprised to see me at that hour.

"Elzbieta! What you're doing here in this snow?" I told them that I was hungry and I asked them if they could give me some food so I could take it with me to my sister's place. The nun left me outside in the snow and she said to wait there for her. She came back with two loafs of bread and one piece of frozen margarine.

"Here, Merry Christmas." She handed me the food.

"Merry Christmas to you too, Sister Maria!" I don't think she heard me from behind that door, as she closed it in such a hurry.

Older Men

I went to Warsaw all by myself this time. I didn't have a plan. I thought I'll think about it once I'll get there. While hitchhiking I was thinking where I'd stay. While walking in Central Warsaw I was approached by a man who appeared to be in his late forties. He had thick glasses on his face. He introduced himself to me.

"Hi, my name is Janusz. I work as a photographer for a newspaper. I'm also an artist though, and when I saw you, I couldn't help but to approach you." Janusz was living in a big apartment with his mother. He was divorced and his three children used to stay with him once every two weeks. He was taking pictures of me while I was staying in his place. He was very critical of me.

"My mother who's eighty years old has more energy than you do." I used to hear that a lot. His mother was nicer to me than he was. She used to ask me if I had anything to eat and if I needed anything before she'd go to the store. After almost a year, Janusz was very frustrated with me. He was selling some pictures that he took of me to some health magazines. His frustration though was related to my sexual abstinence. Like most men in my whole life, he would say bullshit things to me, like how much he was in love with me, and how hard it was for him not to have sex with me. In one of those days I gave in under the pressure and I had a quick sex with him. I felt disgusted and I never repeated that mistake again. Not with him at least. I was getting more and more tired of hearing the same crap over and over again and of the constant criticism. One day I finally packed my small bag and I took the city bus to a place where I knew I could hitchhike from. "Where you headed pretty girl?" A man about forty-five years of age stopped his sports car in front of me. There were lots of people trying to get a ride, but the cars always stopped where I was standing.

"Lublin." I answered.

"Pop in then. I'm going all the way to the Ukraine." He was a businessman who was dealing a lot with the former Soviet Union countries. He was explaining to me that now it was still a new market, but how it would soon become very profitable. His name was Alan. He had an American name for some reason. It was maybe because he's lived half his life in Australia and some other countries.

"Aren't you too young to be traveling such distance all by yourself? How old are you?" He asked me.

"Seventeen."

"OK. You're practically of a legal age. Do you have a passport?" He looked like he had some plan.

"I do." I had my passport issued in the hope that I could go to Greece to live with Bozena. Barbara already finished her four years of nursing school, and she was now living in Athens as well.

"Great. Do you want to go with me all the way to Lvov, or you have other plans?" I could tell he liked my company.

"Sure. What the hell!" I answered.

We spent two weeks in Ukraine before he took me back to Poland. He spoke fluently in English, and I was so impressed when I heard him talking on that huge cell phone of his. He knew how to treat me and it wasn't hard for him to seduce me. We had sex indeed and I liked it somewhat. He was married and he had three children. He said that he was almost never home. He was giving me some money while I wasn't with him so I could take care of myself while he was away. He rented rooms and hotels for me everywhere we went so I could wait there for him. I was bored to death for most of the time. He promised that as soon as he'd open his office in Warsaw that he'd hire me as his personal assistant.

To Italy

I was very tired of hiding from the police so my mother finally persuaded the judge to have me emancipated. I was standing in front of the judge and my parents were standing behind me. I told the judge that I was working as a model and that my agency was providing me with place to stay. I was very convincing because she believed everything I said to her. She already had all my school records with her and she kept glancing at the paper. She decided that I was a very responsible girl and she released me from the orphanage. I was seventeen years old and I was emancipated by the court. I was free. No more hiding, no more running away. I could finally go to visit my siblings. The director was never pleased to see me there after that, but I didn't give a crap about her. I still had to find out a way to get the kids out of her evil clutches. I wasn't done with her. She was disregarding me to show me that she has lost her respect for me.

"I hope that you're happy with your life Ela. Just so you know, we would've driven you to Warsaw ourselves if you told us that you wanted to be a model. I don't know why you have to be so stubborn and why you never believe in what I say to you. I am very disappointed in you."

"Yeah, yeah, yeah, you're the Mother Teresa." I was thinking in my head while she was talking to me.

"Look at your little sisters and your brother. You left them behind like they were nothing to you." She was trying to touch my nerves. She was good at it.

"Look, you and I know that it is you who are keeping them here." I would lose my temper whenever she brought up this subject.

"What are you talking about? Your mother has you convinced that I am some evil woman."

"Leave my mother out of this. I have my own eyes and my own brain." I was very sick and tired of hearing bad things about my mother.

"You don't know who you're dealing with. You think that we're just a poor family that has nowhere near the type of influence that you have." I was normally reserved, even shy sometimes, but when it came to defending the honor of my family, I wasn't afraid of anybody. She could say bad things about me all she wanted, but I wasn't going to allow her to make me feel that I was born into a family who deserved less.

"I understand more than you think I do. You're just being defensive. I give you my word that if your parents prove that they can handle raising a family, I will be the first one to have a talk with the judge." Sometimes she almost convinced me that her intentions were genuine.

"Do you really mean that?"

"Of course, what do you think of me, that I'm some type of monster?" She had me really going to the point that I would even blame my mother for inadequate coping skills. I was angry with my mom for not being aggressive enough. I didn't like how she made herself a victim. I still loved her with all my heart, but I was resenting her sometimes. I was thinking that if she didn't go to church every day that maybe my father wouldn't drink as much. Maybe then he would be there to defend us when those assholes came to kick us out. I was even angry with her for putting on so much weight. I thought if she looked as elegant as she used to, then maybe the judge would have more consideration for her. I was so irritated by her sometimes that I couldn't even be in the same room with her.

"Mom, stop making that awful noise. Eat nice for god's sake!" I was so mean to her. The sense of guilt was killing me but I couldn't control myself.

"Why are you feeling sick again? Who's gonna go to talk to that freaking judge? Mom, get up, you'll miss the bus!" My mother was clearly falling into deep depression. I couldn't take this anymore and when Alan's friend told me that I could go to Italy with them, I packed all my stuff and I said goodbye to my mom. I was barely eighteen. My mother was crying so much that she couldn't breathe and it was no different for me.

"Mom, I'm gonna be OK. I promise. They said they already have a job for me there. I will send you some money, OK? Please don't cry."

"I'm not crying baby. I know you have to go. I love you sweetheart. I know you're angry with me sometimes, but I can't really blame you. I will pray for you every day."

"Mom, Renata has a phone now, so I'll be calling her, OK? If you can, please go to her sometimes so I can talk to you over the phone, OK?" I was crying very hard now.

"I love you mom, and I'm sorry that I wasn't able to do anything yet to help. Please take care of yourself."

"I will, don't worry about me, Ela. I'll be fine. You need to think about yourself now. Write me a letter as soon as you'll get there, OK?"

"I promise mom, I will. I'll call Renata and I'll let her know everything, OK?"

I saw my mother's sad face moistened with her tears and I thought I was going to die.

"Be strong. Don't let her see how scared you are." I was talking to myself in my mind. I had to take a bus all the way to Warsaw where Alan's friends were waiting for me. They were a married couple and they drove with me all the way to Italy. They wanted to visit Rome and Sicily, so that's where we went first. We stopped at Florence as well where they had some Italian friends. A few days later we took a ferry all the way to Sardegna. Our final destination was Alghero. The woman explained to me what kind of work I was going to have there.

"You'll just have to talk to the customers and drink with them. They'll be paying for each drink that the waiter will bring every fifteen minutes. All the girls that work there are mostly from Poland, and there are a few from Hungary." She never told me that she was getting one thousand and five hundred milla lira for bringing me there. I found that out later from the other girls.

So there I was, in Italy, working in a nightclub. The owner took me to a police station to arrange for my Permesso di Soggiorno. If any girl was to be caught without this tourist visa, she'd be deported immediately. The police would come sometimes to these places to check on our ID's and our papers. They were all corrupted by the owners of these bars. Nevertheless they had to keep their records of each girl that was working there. This was especially the case after the police found a dead body of some Polish girl. Many girls were trying to marry their clients to get their Italian citizenship. Some of them were actually successful at obtaining their permanent legal status. Once in Italy, nobody wanted to go back to Poland. Who could blame them? I wasn't definitely going to judge anybody. Unfortunately the local people had a different point of view on this matter. They were blaming us that we were stealing their men and their money. If somebody asked you "Where you from?" and you told them that you were Polish, it wasn't a good thing.

"Oh, Polacca!" Oh, Polish. You could see the anger in their eyes. This is why I learned to speak Italian so well. I was so embarrassed of my origins that I wanted to sound like a native Italian. And so when the girls would go out to the beach with the clients they met in the club, I was sitting home on the sofa studying Italian. I kept reading books in Italian one after another. I watched TV and I tried to mimic the actors. At night I engaged in conversations with my customers to practice what I learned. I became so good at my second language, that a year later I could fool anybody with my perfect accent.

La Regina

There were three owners of the first club I worked in. Gian Franco was the youngest and he owned fifty percent of the business. The other two, Salvatore and Tony were at least in their sixties. Every time a new girl arrived it meant huge excitement among the customers. Of course my arrival wasn't any different, except that I became Gian Franco's pupil. He was famous for sleeping with each new girl. He also had a Polish girlfriend, Agata, who knew all about it, and who'd been living with him for three years. Agata was extremely jealous when it came to me. I wasn't having sex with Gian Franco yet, but she could tell that her boyfriend was looking at me in a different way.

"If I find out that you're fucking Gian Franco, I will push you from the window." She would whisper to me while we were in the bathroom. Agata was in her late twenties and her unnaturally black hair combined with her strong makeup made her look like a witch.

In the end, I only had sex with him once, six months later. He took me to the beach at night and I gave in there, which I regretted as soon as he was inside of me. The sand was making me feel very uncomfortable and I realized immediately that men would do and say anything as long as they think that they have shot at sex. I was planning on leaving soon anyway, so I guess I didn't care anymore. Many customers were not satisfied with the fact that I wouldn't let them touch me inappropriately. Some were even aggressive towards me. But before all that, Gian Franco protected me from the horny bastards many times.

"What are you here then for? I'm paying good money so I expect something in return! I don't need to talk, that's what my wife is for." A short Italian man grabbed my ass. I stood up and I slapped him in the face with all my strength.

"Ma va fan culo!" Go fuck yourself! I left my customer who was still clearly in the state of shock. All the girls and their customers were now watching the scene from behind the curtains.

"You ungrateful bitch! Let's see if you'll still have your job after I'll talk to Gian Franco." He was coming to his senses I guess because now he was threatening me. Of course he went straight to talk to the owners who were always standing at the bar, right around the cashier. The unhappy customer was holding his face while explaining to Gian Franco what happened. I was thinking:

"*Screw this, I can get another job*". Then I saw the owners and some other customers laughing hard.

"Vieni qua, Elizabetta!" Come here Elizabetta! Gian Franco was making a hand gesture for me to approach them.

"You see this girl?" He was now talking to my ex-customer.

"She can do whatever she wants and she'll still be my Queen! Be honest with me, have you seen anybody more beautiful than her?" Gian Franco used to smile a lot, apart from the time when he was screaming at people.

"La Regina my ass!" The customer left the club, not without promising that he'd find a new club to spend his hard-earned money. I wasn't allowing the customers to touch me but I was still making good money. I realized that men, when they can't have what they want, they will spend a fortune in an attempt to get it. I had to be very careful with not giving them too much hope. Some of them were more experienced at this game than I was. I changed the club after a while because I couldn't fool them any longer. The new owner was a jackass but his club was more high class and so were some of the customers there.

In the new place I picked up the habit of smoking cigarettes. I was sitting at the bar while killing boredom with the nicotine rush, when I saw that one man in particular was paying attention to me the whole time. He was talking to all the other girls, while observing me closely. He was tall, not bad looking and he was wearing an expensive watch. He looked very mysterious, almost like he was some bad guy. He was definitely sexy. His full lips looked perfidious as if he was up to something. He appeared to be very close friends with the guy that everybody knew was one of the richest guys in the Island. The bartenders and the waiters were bustling around him like they knew him very well. I had never seen him before and I was intrigued. He seemed to have a lot of class and I sure would have noticed him before.

I could tell that I intrigued him as well. He wasn't going to approach me though and it was my policy that I would never approach the customer first. I knew that I was pretty enough that they would always come to me. I wasn't as desperate as many other girls were and my aloofness was sort of my trademark. I learned how to market my inaccessibility pretty well. It was working. This was my way to assure that my customers were somewhat intelligent and that allowed me to engage in conversations. Only those types of people were not intimidated by me.

The owner of this new club wasn't crazy about my tactics, and more than once he'd try to break my attitude. I was contemplating quitting and when he found out about it, he threatened me with "unpleasant consequences". Fortunately one of my regular customers was a cop. The policeman claimed that he was in love with me and he was trying to convince me that I should marry him. I refused to be with him, even though he was a young and not that bad looking of a guy. Later, when I finally decided to leave this type of work behind me, my Romeo in uniform came to my rescue. He talked to his boss at work about me and they sent a restraining order against the owner of the club. They promised him that they would shut down his place in no time, if anybody ever saw him near me. I was very surprised because I knew that some percentage of the owner's money was going towards making some officials somewhere happy.

A waiter approached me with a serious look on his face.

"Come with me dear." He said. The mysterious man was trying not to look at me when we were passing him by. The waiter pointed at one of the private booths.

"There is your bottle of Don Perignon. A gentleman has paid for your entire night, so sit and enjoy your free time. And this is your tip money." He handled me large amount of bills.

This kept happening for the next few days in a row. The owner was kissing my ass every time he'd come to pick up all the girls from our shared apartment.

"How is my favorite girl doing, eh? I see you picked up some rich customers lately. Nice job." He would tell the girls to jump in the back of his car, and to make the room in front for me. He was a very fake man, very materialistic.

I was calling the orphanage these days a lot. While I was talking to my siblings, I knew that the director was standing there listening to our conversations.

"Put the director on the phone for a second, would you?" I would ask them.

"Hello? Ela? How is modeling going for you?"

"Very good. Very good, thanks for asking. How is everything going there? Are we getting any closer to the reunification yet?" I would ask her in a firm way.

"Oh yes, everything looks very promising. Your mother is going to take the kids for the summer break. They're very excited, they can't wait. We're working on it Ela, we're working on it. Just take care of yourself, OK? You have nothing to worry about. Everything goes smoothly here. We're trying to make sure that the kids go home for good by next Christmas." She'd keep lying to me. I believed her and that made me feel relieved.

Romeo

The mysterious man finally decided to join me in my private booth one night. His name was Marco. He was Italian but he was living in Holland. He knew exactly what he was doing. He would never attempt to touch me and he would make me laugh with jokes that he would tell me all night long. This went on for couple of weeks. When I was so comfortable with him that I would even fall asleep on his lap, he decided to ask me out on a date. I said yes of course.

He took me to a boat where he made love to me. I've never knew before how much I really loved having sexual intercourse. His big arms and his tenderness were the perfect combination that made me feel so safe. His kisses were gentle sometimes and aggressive on other occasions. He always knew what mood I was in. Marco read me like an open book. My new boyfriend surprised me one day with airline ticket to Athens. He said that it was time for me to see my older sisters. He insisted that he would fly me over to Holland after that.

I was very happy to see Bozena and Barbara for the first time in few years. They spoke fluent Greek and I was so impressed by them. Barbara took me to Mikonos, where I drove her Greek boyfriend's scooter across the Island. I spent a whole month with my sisters. I was about to fly to Amsterdam, when I decided to clarify one thing with Marco over the phone. Before I left Italy, some girls told me that they saw him walking around with a pregnant girl. I wanted to make sure that this wasn't what it looked like.

"Yes, that's my girlfriend and she's having my baby." He admitted it like there was nothing wrong with that.

"Look amore mio, I still want you to come to Amsterdam. I own a whore house, it's all legal here. You can work here and you can make real money." He kept talking while taking advantage of me being speechless. Barbara and Bozena tried to comfort my broken heart as much as they could. I went back to Italy. I quit my job. "My" policeman helped me to free myself from the club owner's influence. I was free, with some money but with no place to stay. I didn't want to live with my rescuer because I didn't want to be with any man. I walked into a pizzeria to inquire about a job. I knew that they wouldn't hire me without proper papers but I still had to try at least. A young, strong man, good looking, who was a fisherman, engaged me in a conversation. His name was Giovanni.

"You can stay with my parents. I live with them." He offered to me. Giovanni's parents were in their seventies. The father; Giuseppe was a fisherman and he owned his fishing boat. The mother; Antonietta was in charge of the household. They had three other children that were all married, except for Giovanni. They were really hoping that I would return their son's love one day. I couldn't do that and they were respecting me for my honesty. Nevertheless, especially Giuseppe was treating me like his own daughter.

"Elizabetta! Elizabetta! Mangia! Mangia!" Eat! Eat! Don't be afraid of putting some meat on those bones. They all knew my past and they were very understanding. The father sponsored my papers; he "hired" me as a cleaning lady so I could get my work permit. I was unsuccessful in getting any job in this small town though. They were very disappointed when I announced to them, that I was going to search for a job on the other side of the Island.

Porto Chervo was one of the most famous places for tourists in Italy. All the movie stars, and not just the ones from Italy were enjoying their vacations there. The place was unbelievable. I was hired as a waitress in a bar. My new Italian "parents" came to check on me once. They were sad that I left Alghero but they were still very proud of me. Giovanni came with them and he was trying to convince me that I made a huge mistake when I left his family.

"Knock it off, Giovanni! Can't you see that she's trying to be independent?" His father was always taking my side.

"Wasn't she independent with us? She could do whatever she was pleased with. She could go wherever she felt like going. What was wrong with her independence? You guys have treated her better than you've been treating me!" He always challenged his father.

"Basta! Basta! Both of you. We're here to enjoy our time with Elizabetta. We didn't come all the way here to give her a headache!" Antonietta was usually a very quiet woman, but when she did open her mouth, everybody had to remain silent, at least for few minutes.

"Elizabetta! Madonna mia! When will you come back to Alghero to restore our peace?" My Italian "father" was so funny with how dramatic he was.

"Don't forget; you're my Polish daughter!" He used to say that to me at least twice a day. Sometimes his wife would tease him that he better mean that in a not quite literal way.

Danuta's Journey

I worked in Porto Chervo for six months and I met all kinds of different people there. I had a pile of business cards with names of different photographers, talent agents, etc. One of those photographers even took some pictures of me there.

"Why aren't you a model? Why are you waiting on those tables instead?" People were looking at me like there was something wrong with me.

When the season was over, I took a ferryboat all the way to Genova and then I took a train to Milan. The capital of the fashion world was different from what I expected it to be. Modeling as a career wasn't as glamorous as I thought it would be. From all the business cards that I collected, I picked a photographer named Carlo to call. Carlo was also the owner of a very successful photographer's agency and he managed some big names. The work of "his" guys was published in prestigious magazines and they traveled to New York constantly. He was connected in every way. He cared very little about helping me though. He gave me his old bicycle and he told me:

"Go to different agencies and see if they'll like you."

I took his bike and I went to the most known agencies first. I didn't expect anything from Carlo. He was very clear when he said to me that I could live in his place and I could eat his food as long as I was taking care of his Great Dane. He even gave me a small amount of weekly pay for my dog-sitting job. He traveled a lot and he had another model that he was trying to make the next Kate Moss. She was nice to me, even thought she couldn't converse with me because I didn't know English. I think she felt sorry for me. My portfolio had a few pictures from Sardegna and hers was filled with pages of editorial issues and covers of many magazines. Carlo was treating me as if I was a damn brainless girl and I knew that his Great

Dane was the only reason I stayed there. I was the loser and the wannabe model in his eyes. I was always getting on his nerves.

"Where did she go? What a stupid girl!" He'd talk to his model-girlfriend and he'd forget that "stupid" in English doesn't sound that much different from "stupida" in Italian.

The agencies weren't thrilled to see me. Maybe it had to do a lot with me arriving all wet from the rain on that old bicycle. Milan turned out to be a very foggy city and it rained a lot there.

"I'm sorry but you're not exactly what we're looking for. Thanks for coming."

I kept riding that bicycle to all the agencies I could find.

"You need to lose some weight my dear before we can even talk. Your upper body looks OK, but your waist is too big."

"You need to do something about those front teeth. No client will hire you, especially for a magazine cover."

"Are you sure you're 5'9? Let me see. You look much shorter."

"Come back when you get some more pictures in your portfolio."

Each agency had some "good" reason not to sign a contract with me. Each manager of the "New Faces" department thought that I was waste of their time. My spirit was being crushed slowly but surely.

I asked Carlo if I could have Danuta visit me and he agreed. My sister just turned eighteen and the authorities officially took her off the missing children's list. They were no longer after her and she was now free as well. Danuta was more adventurous than I was. I only stood up to people when I felt like I had no choice but she was never afraid of anybody. I was still very insecure and I still believed that I could please everybody if I only tried harder. She had it figured out early that such coping skills never worked and that such methods would only lead to suicidal thoughts.

I sent her some money for a ticket and she was able to get on a bus that was traveling directly to Genova. I couldn't wait to see my sister again. Carlo took his supermodel to one of his trips to Africa, so aside from his assistant that stayed until 5:00 p.m., I had the place all to myself. It was snowing in Milan and I was thinking what a great Christmas I'll have with Danuta. I was concerned that there was not much I could show her or take her to, but I knew that she'd understand. A guy that I barely knew offered to drive me all the way to Genova to pick up my sister. We arrived there three hours early because I didn't want Danuta to have to wait for me. We tried to kill our spare time with some pizza.

Finally the bus, filled mostly with Polish passengers, pulled into the station. I was so anxious and I couldn't figure out why Danuta was taking so much time to get out of the bus. My heart almost stopped when the bus driver told me that there was nobody left onboard. I spoke to Danuta prior to her trip and she was all ready to go. I thought something happened to her. I kept asking all the arrivers if they saw a tall, blonde eighteen year-old.

"Look, is there another bus that arrives from Poland?" I asked the driver.

"Not that I know of. We come here once a week," he informed me. I was panicking.

"I know my sister! I know that something must have happened!"

"Look, calm down. We've already asked everybody. The police officer has her name and your phone number. I think we should just go back to Milan and wait to see if she'll call you." The guy who was my ride looked stressed out as well. Our trip back to Milan was excruciating. I tried not to think of the worst case scenario. I called Renata and she told me that she took Danuta to the bus station herself. I was as scared as I could be. Around 9:00 p.m. the phone rang.

"Hello? May I please talk to Elizabetta?" It was a woman's voice.

"Yes, that's me. Who's calling?"

"Hi, my name is Stefania, and I believe that I have your sister with me."

"Danuta! Is Danuta with you?"

"Yes, yes, she's alright, a little bit tired but she's alright. She only speaks Polish so I can't really understand her very well."

"What has happened to her? Where are you calling from?"

"I'm calling from Switzerland. You're sister is with my husband and I in Geneva."

"Geneva? I was waiting for her in Genova all day long."

"Yeah, apparently the travel agent sold her bus ticket to Geneva in Switzerland, instead of Genova in Italy. My husband and I saw her standing there and looking all lost, and we figured that something was wrong. I think she should stay with us for the night to get some sleep. Poor child, she looks exhausted from sitting in that bus for almost two days. We'll take her to the train station first thing in the morning and you'll be able to pick her up in Milan." I couldn't believe how nice those strangers were. I called Renata to let her know that everything was fine and I asked her not to tell any of this to our mother. I didn't want her to have a second heart attack and Renata agreed with me on keeping our mom unaware of all this.

It was great to have my sister with me but after few weeks Carlo was coming back from his trip, and I knew that she couldn't stay there with me. I arranged for her to visit Sardena before she'd have to go back to Poland. I made sure that she'd get on the right ferryboat. Giuseppe and his family adopted her the same way they did with me. She stayed there for few months and they didn't want her to leave. Giuseppe was taking Danuta on his boat to fish with him, and he even told me that she was more energetic than I ever was. He said that I would always remain his Polish daughter, but he also said that my sister was more fun to be around than I was. I didn't take his comments personally because I knew that he was right, and I liked how we were always honest with each other. We were like a real family.

"She catches fish like a real fisherwoman!" He sounded so excited over the phone that he found somebody who shared his passion.

"You came with us once and you got sea sick. Yeah, I know, you're more delicate type. I'm just giving you a hard time kiddo. I'll always be your Italian papa no matter what."

My Italian family was very upset with me, when Danuta told them that she was going to Greece to live with Barbara and Bozena. I was getting phone calls from Alghero every day.

"Talk to your sister, Elizabetta! Try talking her out of it." Giuseppe sounded like it was my fault that she decided to leave. I knew my sister and I knew that she would do whatever she decided to do. I knew that she was missing our family and even thought I was sad for losing her, I supported Danuta in her decision.

Betty

The big agencies in Milan were getting on my nerves, making me feel so rejected that I finally went to a smaller one. The owner was a really nice woman name Julia and she didn't hide the fact that she was HIV positive. I could tell though, that the entire fashion world was turning their back to her. She tried very hard not to lose her spirit thought she fought a difficult battle to keep the agency going. Despite the small size of her agency, she was able to send me on a casting call for a Giorgio Armani fashion show. The designer himself was sitting among the many people who were interviewing models.

"How tall are you?" Armani was known for not knowing English and he was very surprised when I answered his question immediately, before one of his people would even translate to me.

"I see, you speak Italian. Go ahead and walk for me one more time, would you?" He was looking at my headshots while talking to me.

"I don't know this agency that you're with. OK, that's good for today. Thanks for coming."

I was sitting at the restaurant and I was having lunch with the owner of agency and a man named Antonio who I met recently and with whom I was living with.

"Betty!" The owner of the agency yelled at me with excitement. Julia picked this new name for me, in the hope that clients would mistake me for an American model.

"What?" I wasn't sure if she was choking on her salad.

"Do you know who that was on the phone I was with? Armani's people. You're gonna be in his fashion show!"

"No way! A-a-a-ah!" We were screaming like two little girls. People around us were wondering what was going on. I was hugging Julia and Antonio at the same time. Doing a fashion show for such a big name was something that every model was looking for. Every client would look at you differently if they knew that Giorgio Armani has picked you to represent his collection. This was not even to mention that the pay was above all the small shows I was doing until then. On one of those small shows, the model that was behind me had to push me hard enough for me to move ahead because I was paralyzed from fear. But this was big, this was Armani! Everybody knew that he always picked the finest models. I still couldn't believe what was happening.

"What if he made a mistake? What if he notices that he called for the wrong girl? Oh God, how am I going to hide my wrist when it's time to go to fitting?" By then I was suffering from severe depression again, and I was constantly fighting with Antonio. I had slit my wrist on purpose with some broken glass. The scar was still very visible and I didn't want Armani's people to see that. I was afraid that they would fire me if they knew what a mess I was. I was very lucky because they had me wear two big bracelets. After hair and makeup which was done for us by the best makeup artists, and which took hours to finish, I was finally looking like a real model. I couldn't even breathe, and my shortness of breath wasn't even caused by the hair spray that replaced the oxygen in the room we were in. I was watching some models being interviewed by some journalist. I watched them having pictures taken. Maybe they even took few shots of me, I could not remember if they did, even if my life depended on it. I was flying away into my fantasy world where I was the next super model.

While walking on the runway I was trying to make it look like I had been doing this my whole life. The spotlights and the crowds of photographers and TV cameramen at the end of the runway were giving me a high. I felt like I was on top of the world. I didn't want for this to end, ever. I wanted to remain in that spot for the rest of my life. When the show was over I was dreading the idea of going back to my ordinary life again. I was afraid of living in the darkness again.

"God, I saw the light and I want it back! I don't want to live in my dark and cold room. I want to be bathed with this warm and bright light at all time. I don't want to be forgotten again. I don't want to be unknown anymore!" I was talking to God in my head even thought I was still convinced that I was being hated by whatever force he or she represented.

"Give me a break, please give me a break!" I was getting more and more depressed to the point where I started to feel suicidal.

Facing the Monster

I convinced Antonio that we should go to Poland for few weeks. He agreed and so we found ourselves driving his car on the highway. When I called for my mother she thought that it was one of her younger children that were staying with her temporarily since the summer break. My siblings didn't want to go back to the orphanage and my mother wasn't going to force them. She was waiting for the director to show up with the police like she did the last few times.

"Mom!" I yelled while still outside in the yard.

"What? What? I'm here." She had no idea it was me who was calling her. When she realized her mistake, she ran outside the house as if it was on fire.

"Ela's here! Kids, hurry, Ela's here!" Now everybody was jumping and crying and trying to kiss and hug me at the same time. Nobody even noticed yet that Antonio was standing by his car.

"Oh my God! How did you get here?" My mother was finally calming down.

"With Antonio." I pointed at my boyfriend.

"Well bring him in. Don't let him just stand there like this!"

"Did you bring us anything from Italy?" The kids weren't wasting their time.

"Yeah, we brought you a small TV and you can have all my clothes if you want."

"Is the TV in color?" Rafal asked first.

"Of course it is, you knucklehead!" I rubbed his head.

"We are definitely not going back to that orphanage now!" The kids couldn't wait to see if I wasn't lying about the color TV.

"Mom, what are they talking about? The director told me that they were going to stay with you for good this time." I asked my mother and she explained to me that the director was toying with her the whole time. She told me how this woman kept finding new reasons why she thought that the children were doing better without my parents. She even made Magdalena available for adoption. My youngest sister was spending lots of time in her "aunt's" house. I was infuriated and I wanted to be able to strangle the director with my two hands. I translated to Antonio what was happening.

"You can't let that woman to take your siblings away this time!" He was pacing nervously right with me.

"What am I supposed to do?" I asked.

"Let's go talk to her." He answered.

"And what will I tell her?"

"I don't know, we'll figure something out." He looked really mad as if he really hated the director, who he had never even met before. As we were getting ready to leave, my siblings were getting very excited. It was then when I heard for the first time that some of the caregivers were hitting children.

"They always pick the ones that have no family whatsoever. They even tie them in the bathroom sometimes." Monika was reporting to me. When I translated it to Antonio, he looked like he was going to strangle the director with his own hands.

"There you go. You'll tell that bitch that if she won't release your siblings that we'll go to the police with them. And if those motherfuckers turn out to be corrupted, we'll take the story to the media." I loved how Antonio was taking my family's side. I was wishing that he would treat me this way too.

Antonio and I went to Renata's house first. I haven't seen her for ages and I had to use her phone to call the orphanage. I'm not sure what was more shocking to Renata; seeing me or hearing me on the phone threatening the director.

"Ela, I'm happy to hear that you're in Poland, but I can't see you today. It's Thursday and I'm going away for the next few days. Why don't you come on Monday?" She was talking to me in that fake tone of hers.

"Sure, I can wait until Monday, but I'm more concerned about you, Mrs. Director. You'll be in jail by Monday if you refuse seeing me today."

"Is this some kind of practical joke that you came up with?" Her tone of voice changed immediately.

"No, it's not a joke. I intend to inform the authorities about the child abuse that is taking place in your orphanage. I know that your influence is way beyond the police but you should wait to meet the man that came with me all the way from Italy. He took pictures of my siblings and he can't wait to sell this story to the media." I continued.

"This is blackmailing! Where are you now?" She was very short with me.

"I'm calling you from Renata's house. I don't have anything to hide."

"Can you be here within the next hour?"

"We'll see you in an hour then." I hung up the phone.

"What's going on?" Renata looked like she couldn't believe her own eyes.

"Renata, we'll stop by on the way back, OK? We have to go now."

While driving, Antonio advised me to put my words very carefully in case if the director was going to secretly record our conversation. He told me to be very firm with her and not to be intimidated.

"Don't smile and don't talk about things that are irrelevant. I will put a serious face on as well." I was amazed how Antonio was being supportive. This was actually the first time that I was really glad that I was with him. I was feeling so grateful and I practically forgot all the hardships that he was causing me. We were a team right now.

At the orphanage all the children surrounded our car. I looked at their curious but sad faces and my heart was breaking. I was feeling guilty that I was there to take care of my siblings only. I was feeling bad that I was using these poor children's misfortune to accomplish my goal.

"Betty, I know. But you can't save them all at once. You must think of your family first." Antonio was trying to rid me of my sense of guilt.

"You need to walk in there like you own this world. You need to project the kind of energy that states that under no circumstances you will back up. She needs to not just hear it but feel it from you." I was very impressed with Antonio's motivational speech.

"But what about all these poor children? How can I leave them like this knowing what they're going through?" I looked at the small kids that were trying to see through the windshield, and were trying to find out who was in that foreign car.

"You don't have a choice, Betty. Right now you must think of what you've got and you must play it right. She won't do anything for you if she doesn't get anything in return. You're selling her peace of mind, for now at least. If she knows that what children are saying is true and since she already seems to be scared, then perhaps she will be more careful in the future. This thing with you and your family may scare her enough to force her to control the caregivers from now on. Now let's go and let's face this monster."

"The director is waiting for you in her office." The secretary opened the door for us.

"Ela! What is going on?"

"You tell me. I want you to meet Antonio. He's a well-known photographer in Italy and he took a personal interest in our story. He's here to make sure that you do the right thing this time." I didn't want to make it look like he was my boyfriend. I wanted to look very official.

"Please, have a seat." She had that nice tone again.

"Would you care for some coffee?" She asked.

"No, thank you." I remembered Antonio telling me not to allow her distract me. The director sat down behind her desk. She looked very uncomfortable and she kept waving her hand as if it was too hot.

"How is your modeling going? The kids have shown me some pictures of you in some magazines. I must say, I'm very impressed with you Ela." She said to me and I translated it to Antonio.

"She is shitting in her pants. You've got her in your hands. Go for it." Antonio said to me in Italian and he made his voice sound deep on purpose. I've never seen him being so serious, not even when the two of us were fighting. The director was looking at me as if she was waiting for me to translate.

"Antonio is saying that he didn't come here all the way from Italy to have a chat. We came here to discuss my siblings."

"OK, what is it that you want me to do? You know that it's all up to the judge—"

"And I know that you have the judge in your hands." I didn't let her finish her sentence. I was thinking how to carefully phrase my words in case she was recording all this.

74

"My parents have a house now and they've done everything they could, and more to get their children back. They are more than capable of raising their children and you know it. They raised me, didn't they? I want you to tell the judge the truth, nothing else."

"Well, that's not a problem. We can do that first thing tomorrow morning." She said to me and Antonio asked me to translate.

"I didn't know you spoke Italian so well, Ela." The director was now trying to flatter me. Mrs. Ula, who once used to be my caregiver, and whom I hated with all my heart, entered the office.

"I heard Ela's here. What's going on? You come all the way here and you don't even say hello to anybody anymore?" She was talking while I was looking at her in silence.

"Come on, move your butt Ela. Sit over there, this is my chair." She was touching my shoulder.

"No." I answered.

"What do you mean no? Where did your good manners go? Did you leave them in that famous modeling world of yours? Scoot over!" Mrs. Ula never knew how to talk to people.

"I said NO! Sit somewhere else yourself." I had serious look on my face.

"Mrs. Ula! Sit on the couch for God's sake!" The director lost her temper.

"What on earth is going on here?" The caregiver looked like she was lost.

"Sit down Mrs. Ula. Tomorrow morning I want you to take our driver and I want you to go to Ela's parent's house. You will pick up Ela from there, and you will go to court to see the judge. I will explain everything to you later." I loved the tone the director was using with her employee. I cherished every moment of it.

"One more thing before we leave. Make sure that my father's money goes to his pocket from now on," I said while getting up from the chair.

"Yes, that will be done automatically as soon as the judge gives back full parental rights to your mom and dad," she explained.

"Good, I'll see you tomorrow then, Mrs. Ula. Don't be late." Antonio and I left the office in a way a CEO leaves his conference room.

"Good job Betty. I watched you the entire time. You looked at least ten years older than you are."

"I'll take it as a complement. Let's see what happens tomorrow." I didn't want to get too excited yet.

The next day things went smoother than I could even expect. The caregiver asked me to wait in the hall while she went to talk to the judge. She came outside from that room in no time.

"It's all set. You can take your siblings to their new school in the village where your parents live. The orphanage will send their school records directly to the principal. You father will have his paychecks from his work in the full amount starting from today," she said to me while looking at me in a way as if I was a horrible person and as if I was holding a gun to her head.

I had no doubt that the long six years that my siblings spent in that orphanage were not only the results of my uncle's action, but were also the result of the director's manipulative behavior. I was very happy indeed when a few years later I found out that the director was arrested and that the orphanage was shut down completely. My sister explained to me that she saw everything on TV. The orphanage and the director made big news for some time. Some lady that was trying to adopt a little girl from there, took the orphan to a psychologist, to cure her from what she thought was a withdrawal issue. The next thing she knew was the horrible truth about little girl being sexually molested by some of the caregivers. The woman and her husband knew influential people in TV and of course the whole story reached the media. The justice system was forced to intervene. The director was sentenced to two years on probation and of course she didn't have the orphanage anymore to run. I still thought that she didn't get what she deserved, but I was glad to know that at least she wasn't going to harm any children anymore.

Marta, Monika, Rafal and Magdalena were jumping like some sort of harlequins when I came back from court with the news. They couldn't wait to go to their new school. My mother couldn't breathe very well and even my father was showing some emotions.

"Mom, Ela's a real hero! We tried to warn everybody not to mess with us because we have a famous sister!" The kids were over-idealizing me but I didn't mind that. It was fun to watch them being so happy and so proud of our family. My father gave all the merit to Antonio but I didn't mind that either. The two men were smoking cigarettes and drinking red wine that we brought from Italy. They didn't seem to have a problem with their language barrier. Together they were cutting some wood outside like they knew each other their whole lives.

There was one little problem; the school administration would not accept the children unless they were legally registered under the address they were living in. My father and his mother were the only ones consider legal residents as far as the parish council was concerned. My grandma was refusing to register anybody under her address.

"You are gonna go to that favorite son-in-law of yours, and you're gonna register the kids!" Our father convinced our grandma that he wasn't kidding because finally did what she was asked to do.

"I'm only gonna do that for the little ones that need it for their school. Your wife and your older kids will not be registered." She was arguing with her son.

"Whatever! Don't come back until you'll get that taken care of!" My father knew very well how to look mean; he has practiced that on us many times before. I was glad to see for a change somebody else being his object of attention. I was happy to see him standing up for his children. I actually started to feel forgiveness towards this man. I could actually start calling him dad again.

A couple of years later everybody was registered there. My father's brother-in-law was running for the same position and he wanted all the votes he could get. He lost his campaign though and I was honestly glad to hear that.

Permesso

When I was modeling in Italy, I had to go to police station every three months, to report my legal status to them. They used to issue me a new "Permesso di Soggiorno" each time. This was like a visa or something. I had to submit new pictures of myself each time and I had to pay a small fee with that. I had to prove my residence and that was always a tricky thing. With each new address I had to get a new "Permesso". I was really sick and tired of it. I was tired of being always stopped at the customs on the airports because of my Polish passport.

"Un momento per favore. Dove vai signorina?" One moment please, where are you going Miss? Always the same questions. How much money do you have on you? Where will you stay, who will pay for it? I was tired of always seeing those suspicious looks on guard's faces.

Lascia mi in pace. Give me a break. Leave me alone. I always wanted to say that to them, but I knew that I couldn't. I watched other models with their American passports going through with no problem, and I envied them.

"Oh Americana! Ben venuta al nostro paese!" American! Welcome to our country! I heard them saying that, and I could understand it because I spoke Italian, unlike those American models, who didn't give a crap. They looked at the guard's like, "Whatever, give me my passport back, you Italian prick!"

I hated the fact that I was born in a communist country. I hated that we were being forced to learn Russian in school. I wanted to speak English. I wanted to be like those American girls! I wanted to be all confident and even cocky like them. I couldn't comprehend how they were able to be this way.

"What the fuck are you looking at? What's your problem?" That's what I wanted to sound like! Ma va fan culo in Italian doesn't sound as impressive or as strong as fuck you in English.

"Fuck you! No, fuck you!" I tried to put emphasis on first letter while I was fighting with my boyfriend Antonio; the same guy who helped me to rescue my siblings from the orphanage. He was living near Milan and I was living with him. He chose me for my first editorial job, and he took me to the Dominican Republic to shoot it. He was much older but I really didn't care. He was forty five and I was nineteen years old at the time. In the period of two years that I lived with him, he started to put his hands on me. He was afraid to hit me, but he thought that shaking me violently wasn't going to have any consequences on him. His friends would stare at him in disbelief when they'd see him doing this to me. I put up with it, because my stupid Permesso di Soggiorno had his name on it, as he was my sponsor. His address was my residence, and so he used to take me to that stupid police station to report my legal status.

He said he was madly in love with me, and he even offered to marry me, so I could once and for all get my Italian citizenship, and I almost did. We went to Poland together where we got my birth certificate and all the other necessary papers. When we went back to Italy, all I had to do was to go to city hall, and to say yes, I'll marry this guy. He became so sure of himself, that he started to try to control me even more.

"I told you, you can't smoke!" He'd scream at me even though he smoked cigarettes like he was immune to cancer.

"Get that damn cigarette out of your mouth! You can be better than this! You are my Betty!" That's what he used to call me after the agency decided that my name Elzbieta was too plain. At least I had an American name, right?

"If you don't put that cigarette down, I'll go to that damn police station, and I'll make sure that you won't have your permit to live here anymore!" He was threatening me while trying to shake me so I would get his point more quickly. I finally snapped. I wanted to kill him. I wasn't afraid of him anymore. The adrenaline that was rushing in my body made me feel as if I was Hercules or something. I didn't know what exactly had happened, but all I could see was red blood coming from his mouth.

"Oh my God! I'm bleeding here!" He was talking like he was in shock. He looked like a little boy.

"What did you do to me? I've never put hands on you. What did you do that for? I was just shaking you. I was just trying to wake you up! You can be so much more, you have such a potential. I love you and you know that." He was talking to me while cleaning off his blood. He was looking at me as if he was afraid to realize that I had lost my mind.

"Come on, get up. We're going to the police! Right now!" I yelled at him.

"What for?" He looked like he couldn't understand what was going on. In my mind I was remembering when I was eighteen years old. I was in Poland then, when I got brutally raped by a stranger. I was hitchhiking. The pervert that offered me the ride took me to a forest and I thought he was planning on killing me there. I thought that he was going to leave my dead body there. I thought he was going to cover it with some leaves and branches.

Now I was wishing that I could have done this to that pervert, what I just did to poor Antonio. But I really didn't have a chance then. He was huge and he was pulling on my long hair when I was trying to get out of his car. Apart from being huge in size, he looked like a regular guy. He was wearing nice clothes and he was driving a very nice car. I used to be very careful with whom I would let give me a ride. I used to try to judge people as best as I could before I'd get in somebody's car, but he had me fooled. Once I was inside the car, he locked the doors and he drove off the road like a maniac.

"You fucking bitch! I'm going to rape you whether you like it or not! So stop fucking fighting or I'll kill you." I thought he was going to kill me anyway, so I wouldn't be able go to police and report him. I was praying.

"God! No, no God, I can't talk to God. I know he doesn't like me. Virgin Mary, would you please help me?" I was really convinced that God hated me.

"I know he is going to rape me. I know it's too late for that, but would you please do something to spare my life?" I lost control of my bladder and I was all wet from my own urine. The pervert decided that my mouth was still clean, and he decided to use it instead. He played with his belt around my neck, as if to tell me, that at any moment he could strangle me if he wanted to.

"You fucking whore; you're doing it wrong! Get it together or I'll kill you, you fucking bitch! Don't tell me you've never done it before. I see you're fucking hot. I'm sure all the guys are all over you." He was breathing heavily as he was forcing his huge penis in my mouth.

"Drink that shit! Drink it! Don't even think about spitting it out! Fucking whore!" I was chocking and he had to pull his dick out. My face was all read and I started to vomit. He was laughing at me.

"Don't tell me you didn't enjoy it. Stop pretending like you've never tasted it before. I'm not an idiot, you know? Why would you hitchhike like this, what for? You are probably some professional whore anyway. I've seen girls like you before. Get the fuck dressed. You make me sick!"

I wished I had a gun with me. I tried to visualize how I would shoot him straight in that enormous head of his. No, I'd shoot him in his groin first, to make him suffer. Then I would point the gun to his head, and I'd say to him:

"Prepare to die, motherfucker! You piece of shit, you're poisoning this earth!" I know I would keep pulling on that trigger until I'd run out of ammunition.

"Die motherfucker! Die! Die! Die you asshole!"

Around the World

"Betty!" Antonio brought me back to reality.

"You look crazy! What's got into you?" He continued.

"Shut the fuck up! We're going to the police station right now!" My adrenaline level was still high and I couldn't calm down.

"You're going to tell them that I don't live here anymore, so they can deport me and send me back to Poland. And I'm going to tell them that you've been abusing me, so they can send you to prison." I really meant every single word I said to him, and he knew that. He talked me out of it, and ever since that day, he never dared to put his hands on me. I left him and I went to live in Spain shortly after that. I had just had enough.

"*Screw you and your beautiful but stupid country.*" I was thinking in my head while flying to Barcelona. In Spain I picked up Spanish relatively quickly. I could recognize pictures of me everywhere I went. I had flown to Madrid once before, to shoot for a campaign for cigarettes.

"That's you, isn't it?" The taxi driver was pointing at a few story building. One side of it was completely covered with a billboard that had nothing else but a picture of my face on it. Then he was pointing at all bus stops. I could see my own image on them, right next to the image of Jean-Claude Van Damme. He was selling the movie that he was playing in, and I was selling the fake promise of pleasure that comes from smoking cigarettes.

Barcelona was a beautiful city. Nobody cared there about my Polish passport. Nobody asked me to report to police. I liked it there. I had a cozy place to live, which I shared with a few other models. Most of them spoke in English so I really had a hard time communicating with them. When you don't speak English people sometimes make you feel like there is something wrong with you. So I became friends with the locals instead.

I was vegetarian then, but still, when my friends invited me to go hunting I went with them. At 4:00 a.m. thirty-eight men and two women, including myself, all gathered around the grill. All of us were wearing green and brown clothes that were specially made for hunters. Each of us was armed with a rifle, and even I had one on me. At least a dozen of the hunting dogs were waiting for action to start. Our targets were wild pigs that inhabited the mountains. We had breakfast at an old castle. Some of the people present were very rich, and they owned incredible properties like this one. They were very happy to have me there, and they treated me like one of their own. They were very patient listening to my broken Spanish, and they were very helpful with correcting me.

"We like to see a model like you that speaks our native language. You're a very cool girl, you know that?" They made me feel like I was a princess that owned that castle. When we came back from that mountain, we brought few wild pigs with us. I wasn't able to shoot any of them, and I didn't enjoy the tension of hiding and waiting for them. I had my rifle ready to go the whole time. I was a little bit scared. I was glad that I didn't have any luck and that I didn't have to shoot. I was thinking the entire time:

"What did those poor pigs ever do to me? They've never bothered me. Why would I kill an innocent creature like that?" If I did end up shooting one of them, I'd probably perform CPR, and then I would make a pet out of it.

Later the guys cooked a risotto based on those poor animals. There was nothing else to eat, and so they convinced me that I had to at least try it. I picked out the pieces of meat very carefully and put them aside. I ate the rice and few hours later I wished that I've never had done it. The rice was soaked with the juices from the meat and it made me completely sick to my stomach. I was lying down on grass, ill, in front of that glorious castle, for two hours straight.

The hunters felt very bad for me and they couldn't believe how sensitive my stomach was. After this they'd take me only to events where they'd shoot plastic discs in the air. They made me try to do that as well. I loved it. They were surprised again, this time how good I was at it. They were cheering me enthusiastically as I would break many of those discs with my shots.

"I don't believe you've never held a gun before. You look like a pro." They were teasing me, not without trying to flirt with me.

I was feeling really good. I loved being armed like that. I loved the sense of power that I was feeling while pulling on that trigger. I loved each time I broke that flying orange disc. Enormous relief was coming to my whole body and my mind with each event like this. The cheering was making me feel so good.

"This is the best therapy ever!" I was thinking to myself. And it was. The guys were laughing when I was kissing my rifle, before I had to hand it back to them.

"I've never seen a girl that loves to shoot as much as you do. You're welcome to join us anytime you wish." They made it clear to me that they were having fun with me being there. I felt accepted by others for the first time in my life, but they had no clue about that. They thought that I was a successful model who loves to pull on a trigger. They were impressed by me, and they couldn't wait to tell all this to their buddies.

"You know that girl that you see on billboards everywhere? Well, I went to hunt with her!" They were so funny in telling me what they were talking about at work. They told me that nobody wanted to believe until they showed pictures to them.

Barcelona was the place where I decided to redeem myself. I purchased Anthony Robbins' book, called "Unlimited Power". I read the whole thing, and I started doing everything he was talking about. Every morning I read to myself my list of things I was grateful for. Every day I took the bus to gym, and I swam for hours sometimes. I ate very healthy foods, as every day I'd purchase fresh products from Farmer's Market. I even quit smoking and I did it cold turkey, just like that. I started to feel really good. I think I can safely say that it was the first time in a long time, if not in my entire life that I felt somewhat happy. I still felt lonely but not as bad as before. More than anything else I was missing my family. I couldn't go back to Poland yet, because I told myself that I have to have enough money to build or to buy new home for them. Occasionally I sent them some money from here and there, but I knew that it was not much. Part of the money I made in Japan, went towards the bathroom that my father built in the house my grandmother owned.

Japan was another place where I felt like a princess.

"Oh, kawaii, kawaii!" Oh, cute, cute! She's so cute. The Japanese were in love with my looks. The agency was so happy because I was their number one model and because I was booked almost every day. My lowest fee was one thousand dollars per day. My managers were so happy when they were hearing from photographers and all the crews how professional I was. I was never late to my photo-shoots, and most of them started at 4:30 a.m. I wasn't bitchy and I bowed my head respectfully the way they were doing to me. I loved their culture and I loved the way I was being treated there, like nowhere else in the world.

I was living in Tokyo, in area called Akasaka, and the agency was in Ropponggi. I was staying in a nice hotel and like all other girls I was driven to casting calls by a personal driver. Life was good.

In Tokyo I experienced my first earthquake ever. I thought it was cool how the hotel was swinging, and how the beds were bumping against the wall. I was giggling with another model, when we discovered that it wasn't a ghost that was doing all this movement.

I still didn't know any English then, but some models were from Eastern Europe, so I could easily communicate with them. They were trying to take me clubbing sometimes, but I was always busy with work. I could tell that some of them envied me because of that. I did go out one time, and one time only. I was so amazed how safe it felt to walk in the middle of night in this metropolis. I walked back to my hotel by myself, and nobody bothered me. I thought I could live there forever, if it wasn't so far away from the rest of the world. I made good money and I was about to leave, when the agency told me that they had bad news for me. One of the managers spoke Italian, and she was able to explain it to me.

"I'm really sorry, but we didn't exchange your money to US dollars. The yen has just dropped drastically in its value. You've lost half of your money."

"What?" I was pissed. I was really, really pissed, but unfortunately I didn't know who to talk to about it.

"You know, even with your loss, you still made more money than most girls do when they come here." She was trying to make me feel better. I think she was also trying to cover up the sense of guilt. I was twenty years old, what did I know about money or about markets that fluctuates? Well I learned my lesson and not without paying for it. It cost me a fifteen thousand dollars. I was pissed indeed. This was my first big money that I've ever earned and now half of it was flushed down the toilet for no reason.

Diva

Back in Italy, with each day, I was getting unhappier with my living arrangements with Antonio. Julia let me stay at her place whenever I felt like staying away from my boyfriend. Unfortunately she was forced to close her business altogether and I felt forced to go back to Antonio again. The big agencies were interested in representing me at this point. I chose smaller agency this time as well, because I didn't like to work with fake people. I hated seeing people being nice to me only because of their ulterior motives. I knew that this might not have been the smartest career move on my part, but I honestly couldn't change who I was. I knew that a big agency would turn its back on me the second I'd gain some extra weight for example. I honestly despised the fake world I was living in. The fake smiles and fake hello-kisses were driving me nuts. The "Look who is here!" and the looks on people's faces whenever models would enter the room were getting on my nerves.

"Oh Betty's here!" I'd hear the enthusiasm in a booking agent's voices whenever I was booked for some job. Other times when things were slow, I'd feel like nobody even knew that I even existed. The parties and the "Who's who" and the "Who's with whom" were making me doubt my career choice even more. I eventually stopped attending any of those events and I hid myself in Antonio's cold basement apartment the whole time.

"You're getting depressed again. What is wrong with you? Betty! You could be the next Claudia Schiffer if you really wanted it bad enough. You have the looks, you have the personality, and you're in Milan for God's sake! Do you know how many girls would kill to be in your shoes? Do you know how many girls dream about what you've got? You should be thanking God all day long for all this." Antonio hated seeing me having hard time waking up in the morning.

"Leave me alone! You don't understand me! I'll get up whenever I'll feel like!"

"I'm shooting some models today. They'll be here any moment, you have to get up!" He'd pull the blanket off of me.

"What are you doing? It's freaking freezing here!" I hated him sometimes but I still helped him with his photo shoots. Some models were from Poland, Slovakia or Russia and they only knew their native languages. Most of them were around fifteen years of age. I served as a translator, makeup artist, light holder, and lunch maker.

The intimacy between Antonio and I was fading fast. I was not interested in having sex with him and he was no longer attempting to get any. He still said that I was the love of his life, and so we went back to Poland one more time to get all my papers necessary for getting married. I knew that I wasn't going to marry him and I was just buying some time. I had my agency send me to Greece for work so I could spend some time with my sisters there. Even though I was very happy to spend some time with my family, I was feeling very miserable from within. Japan, Spain, everywhere I went, I was missing something. I could not understand what it was though. I told my agency that it was time for me to go to America. I thought that if I went all the way west that I would find something I've been looking for my whole life. I just wasn't sure exactly yet what it was.

The limousine pulled over in front of some middle-eastern prince's mansion. The palm trees around the mansion were decorated with white Christmas lights. Miami's warm weather was adding a luxurious touch to this already rich environment. All the models, wearing designer evening outfits were making their entrance now. The owner of our modeling agency was there with us. Bringing her best models to places like this one was part of her public relations that she was very good at. The charming and surprisingly young looking prince approached us promptly to welcome his guests of honor.

"Welcome! Welcome! Please make yourself comfortable. Mi casa es su casa." His dark skin, black hair, and his brown eyes looked very sexy against his white attire that was made of cotton. He looked incredibly comfortable in his loose outfit. His bare feet and his wide smile made us immediately feel relaxed. The other guests were waiting patiently for him to finish shaking our hands and kissing us on the cheek. Nobody was chatting anymore and all the eyes were on us. I've experienced this type of attention before and sometimes I felt like it was getting old. I was at the edge of quitting modeling. I wasn't sure what else I could do for living though and I didn't want to end up just marrying some rich guy like many models my age were doing. I was twenty-two years old and that was considered old in this industry. The agency made me lie and say that I was nineteen. People in this business liked young girls that look and act somewhat mature but not vice versa. Unless of course, you were one of the few top models, then that would be a totally different story.

Miami was a fun place to be but I didn't want to work anymore. I lied to the agency that my pager wasn't working and I was going to the beach every day instead. I got a nice tan, and normally it is prohibited for models to get too dark. I love that my skin color turns almost olive when exposed to sun. I just wanted to be myself for once. I felt like nourishing myself with the natural vitamin D, without any restrictions coming from my job. No more dieting and no more putting on a fake smile.

I discovered then that people loved models that were being moody all the time. It made them think that somebody who doesn't give a crap must be somebody who is in demand. A model that works a lot doesn't care as much about anything; hence she can act like a diva if she wishes to. The trick was in not caring, and not just pretending only. For me it was a vicious cycle though, because I honestly didn't care, but that would also mean that I wouldn't work even when I could. Not caring meant not caring at all. "All or nothing" was always my motto through which I lived my life. Being free to do whatever I felt like was more important to me than any amount of money the world could offer to me. Nobody could put a price on my being able to be myself. I was a free spirit and I intended to remain this way until the end, even if I would have to die in extreme poverty. Nobody could capture me and nobody could own me. Nobody could tell me anymore what to think, what to wear, who to talk to, how to talk, how to walk, etc. Nobody could be inside my mind anymore. I was who I was and I was embracing it.

I was now learning how to speak English. The first thing I noticed was how the "I" is being used a lot in this language. "I this", "I that", "I", "I" "I". The one word that I hated the most when I couldn't understand English, and which I thought that was making the speakers sound self-centered, was now my favorite thing to say. I was getting in touch of the real me and this was a dramatic change.

New York

I decided to go to New York City on my own. One of the models that I was sharing the small apartment with on South Beach knew a guy who lived in Manhattan, and he agreed that I could stay with him and his roommate for a while. I had five thousand dollars left in my bank account in Spain, so I wasn't afraid of starving yet. My new roommate Jason was a law-student and he was very patient with me while teaching me how to speak English.

"I – am – going – to – make – us – a – breakfast. What – would – you – like – to – eat?" He spoke very slowly so I could understand him.

"No understand. Que estas diciendo?" I kept helping myself with my Spanish.

"Eat. Breakfast." He made a hand gesture to mimic a person who was eating.

"Aaaaaah, eat, OK, yes, eat."

"In English you say, I don't understand, not, no understand. I, I don't understand." He was very good at explaining it to me.

"I don't understand. I don't understand." He seemed like he enjoyed listening to me practicing my new language.

"Very good. See? You're learning real fast." He never made me feel inadequate.

Jason and I were dining at restaurants frequently. We used to split the tab equally and this was very new to me. Being a fashion model I was used to never having to worry about things like restaurant bills, as those were always taken care of by whoever's company I was in. Things like waiting for a table or standing in line in front of a club were not a part of my reality. VIP treatment was something that I started to miss. Jason would tease me when he'd see a complex look on my face.

"Yeah, that's what regular people do. Regular people like me have to wait their turn." He tried to explain to me how every time he'd go out with me, people would treat him different than when he'd go out with "regular" people. I liked how honest he was with me and mostly how he made me laugh. He wasn't the most attractive guy but he was very funny and very considerate. I tried not giving him any hope but there was little that I could do to prevent him from developing a crush on me.

"It's our first one-month anniversary since we became friends." He looked very disappointed and sad, even though he was trying very hard to hide his emotions from me. Jason looked very disturbed by me not caring about all this. He took me to my favorite Italian restaurant for this occasion. He took care of the bill all by himself this time. I finally decided to stop pretending how indifferent I was, and I pulled out from my purse the gift I made for him. I made him a card that looked like a mini-scrap book. I glued all the pictures of the two of us that we took everywhere we went in the city.

In one month he introduced me to New York City. He took me to Central Park for walks, to the East Village to eat some Polish pierogi. For my twenty-second birthday he took me to Broadway to see "Les Miserables". Jason had a hard time withholding his tears when he saw the card.

"I thought that you didn't care about our friendship as much as I do." He tried not to cry.

"Jason, I- am - no - selfish, no - self-centered - you - think. Not always."

"You're trying to say that you're not as selfish or as self centered as I may think." He laughed while correcting my English.

"That is correct." I laughed with him.

I told Jason the truth that I was slowly running out of money and that I had to go back to modeling. He wasn't very happy when I moved out from his place to live in an apartment that my new agency was renting for models. It wasn't that working as a model meant free board or anything like that. The agencies have always been charging models for anything they could think of. The rent was one thousand dollars a month, while sharing the apartment with sometimes fifteen other models. The girls would usually come and go so you couldn't really get to know anybody that well. My new roommate that I was sharing a small room with was a gorgeous girl from Africa. She was already very established as a model and her name was known at least within the fashion world. I liked her but I don't think that she was a big fan of me though, because she kept complaining about me to the agency.

"Ela, we've been told that you have been crying a lot. What is going on with you?" One of the managers informed me. I knew that my room-mate must have said something. It was the truth though. I tried to be as quiet as much as I could, but especially at night, while in bed, I couldn't cope well with my emotions. I was missing my family and as always I was feeling very lonely. I was feeling turned apart between the desire of being famous, so I could make enough money to bring my whole family here, and my discontentment with the world I was living in. I was a model and I now hated having pictures taken of me. I hated how the photographers made me feel.

"Stay like this. Stay like that. Don't move. Now move." They all made themselves look like they were the center of the universe. Their sig-nificance, their positioning of lights, their directing was responsible for the amazing pictures, not the model they were shooting. It was never the model. It was always the photographers who created the work. Oh, what a geniuses. They were given only some of the most beautiful woman in the world, a whole crew to make some magic with hair and makeup, tons of stylists and assistants, and they were somehow able to make these women to look stunning! Oh wow! Geniuses my ass. I hated how they almost never took the time to ask if I was comfortable while waiting for them to finish their meaningless conversations with the crew. Hey, I'm only wear-ing a winter coat and it's like a hundred degrees on this beach! Or, I'm only freezing in my bikini while shooting on the snow. Usually the only people that showed some concern were the ones who were considered not important themselves. They were the assistants of assistants of assis-tants.

In Spain I fainted once on one of those photo-shoots. I could no longer breathe in the outfit I was wearing and the position they had me hold wasn't helping at all. I scared the hell out of the crew. I think it was the first time then that the photographer actually noticed me. He looked scared too. Apart from the time when I was in Tokyo, this was the first time that I was actually acknowledged at the end of the shoot.

Agencies taking fifty percent of our money, charging us for all kinds of things like head shots, rooms in crowded apartments, airline tick-ets etc, weren't making me feel good either. I wanted out. I just didn't know how to live a life without more practical skills.

Relaxed

I was booked for an editorial job for Marie Claire magazine, and the shooting was going to take place in Jamaica. I already decided that this was going to be my last job as a model. I honestly took that job only because I wanted to spend the whole week on that Island. When we got there I wasn't even trying to hide the fact that I wasn't into taking the pictures. There was another model with us and I was trying to make them to shoot her instead. The model didn't mind that at all but the people cared more about me instead, and they wanted my face especially for the cover. It became crystal clear to me that being nice didn't pay off in life. The bitchier I was the more everybody was trying to accommodate me. They were even scheduling the shoots around and my moods, something that I never have had happen before. I just wanted to lie on the beach and sip on my exotic but virgin drink.

"Come on, one more picture. We promise that this will be the last one." They were trying to convince me and I was really hoping that they were right about it.

Back in Manhattan I was planning on finding a "regular" job. I had to look for a new place soon too, since I wasn't going to be with the agency anymore. Jason was still mad at me for not returning his feelings so I couldn't go back to live in his place.

At some party I met a twenty-nine year-old man named Peter Dabrowski. He was Polish but he was born in the US and only his father spoke my native language. I met his father and I chatted with him few times in Polish, when Peter took me to their mansion in Greenwich, Connecticut. The place was breathtaking. I don't even know how many acres of land there was. It was carefully taken care of by I don't know how many workers. The main house was white and there were many other houses that were built for Peter's older brothers and sisters who were living in their luxurious apartments on Upper East Manhattan. All kinds of workers were bustling around the barns where the most expensive, purebred horses were being kept. Behind those barns there was a special place to play polo. Inside the office-barn, on the walls, there were many pictures hanging. Most of the people on those pictures were rich and famous. I couldn't believe when I was staring at Prince Charles from England playing polo with Mr. Dabrowski.

"What do you do sir to have all this and to know all these people? Weren't you born in Poland like I was?" I couldn't believe what I was seeing.

"Prosze pani…" He was referring to me as Mrs. and I liked to hear him talking in Polish to me. Nobody else could understand us, not even his much, much younger wife, or even his own children.

"I was born ages ago. That's one thing. The other thing, I was very determined to make a better life for myself and to start a family. I fought in War World II and I was a pilot then. After the war was over, I came to United States to start a new life. " He liked when we talked about him and I didn't mind that either.

"To put it in few words, I am now in airplane industry business."

"Sir, are you going to laugh if I tell you that everything you have here, is what I've always dreamed of creating myself?" I asked my Polish war veteran.

"No, prosze pani. You look like an intelligent young lady and I don't doubt that you can achieve anything you set your mind on. By the way, you handle yourself on this horse very well, my dear. I know you're not as experienced and that you've never played polo before, but I can tell that you have it in you. You are what we call natural. I can tell that you love those creatures more than you love people. One day you may have your own horses and your own polo field like this one. I don't see why you couldn't. Peter had been telling me that you used to be a model. You're still young and beautiful. Why did you quit?"

"I hated it. It was making me feel miserable most of the time."

"Well, it's hard to make a real fortune on something that you hate doing. My wife, by the way used to be a model."

"Yes, I know, your son told me."

"You need to believe in yourself and you need to have real passion for what you're doing. Then you just stay focused. What is it, beside the horses that you have passion for, if I may ask? What are you good at, what are your strengths?" He asked me.

"I honestly don't know. I used to love to read books and I was really good at writing. Now I really don't know what I want to do. I want to go within me for a change and find the answers there."

"I said it before and I'll say it again; you may be smarter than what people may think of you based on your looks."

Peter, Mr. Dabrowski's son was also enchanted by me but I didn't want anything special between the two of us. I was OK with hanging out with him and with the occasional sex we were having. We had a very "open relationship" if that's what you could call it. This was why; when he introduced me to his older brother Mark I told him that I was going to have sex with him as well. Peter tried to look like he didn't care, but he did let me know later that it wasn't entirely true. It was too late though, I was completely involved with Mark, to the point that we were even dating exclusively.

Mark was thirty-two years old and he was better looking than his younger brother Peter. The first night I met him was at his house on that Greenwich paradise property. Peter thought I should meet the rest of his family and he thought that I would enjoy the small private parties that Mark used to throw all the time. That night I was wearing khaki pants and a white T-shirt that was made of a very delicate material. I wasn't wearing a bra and it was pretty obvious.

Mark's house was very different from all the other houses. It was made of rough stone and it looked like a monastery. The windows were big and were overlooking the green field of perfectly cut grass. The roses in front of the house that were blooming at this time of the year, were adding a magical touch to this place that looked like it was from a fairy tale. About dozen young women were sitting outside around a fire. They were smoking pot and drinking red wine. Mark was the only man around those sexy girls who were competing for his attention.

"Mark, I want you to meet my friend Ela." Peter introduced me to his brother.

Mark looked at me with surprise written all over his face. I couldn't understand why, since I knew that Peter was known for hanging out with models. The older brother kept staring at me the whole night, while I was lying on the ground in Peter's arms. The girls were keeping him busy with their stories but I still could sense the powerful chemistry that Mark and I had.

"I want to have sex with your brother." I told Peter just like that.

94

"OK. I see him staring at you the way a starved dog stares at a bone." Peter responded with an insecure smile on his face. He told me that he wanted to go back to New York and he left me there.

"I'll come and I'll pick you up tomorrow, OK?" He asked before he left.

"OK".

"Are you going to have sex with Mark?"

"Yes."

"OK, I'll see you tomorrow then." He drove off in his Porsche.

I fell asleep outside in front of the fire. When I woke up in the middle of night I noticed that all the girls were already gone. Somebody had covered me with a blanket. I looked around and I saw Mark getting some wood for the fire.

"Hi," he whispered.

"I didn't mean to wake you up. I thought you were cold and I wanted to keep the fire going for you." He was still whispering. The sexual feelings that were arousing inside of my body were not only hard to control, but were also impossible to describe. The tension and chemistry that was rising between us the whole evening was now about to explode inside of me. He saw that in my face because he took my hand gently but firmly and he whispered again:

"Come." He took me upstairs to his bedroom. We made love the way two lovers do, after they have been separated for years and then reunited at last. His body was big and I wasn't complaining but his male part was more than big. I loved when he was inside of me and I didn't want for him to remove his penis, ever. The sex we were having was unprotected, and I wasn't even thinking about possible consequences. Anything in the world, including my death seemed worth the pleasure I was experiencing. Mark's strong body was holding me in a way as if he was afraid of losing me. His eyes looked like he was trying to tell me; "I just found you. Well, my brother found you for me, and I will not be as stupid as him to let you go."

In the morning my stallion brought me breakfast in bed. He pulled my long and all messed up hair aside and he kissed my neck. He hung around my neck a pendant he bought on one of his trips to South America.

"No stone can ever be as precious as you are." He looked like he meant every single word.

Around noon Peter arrived in his bright Porsche. He looked at me and I smiled. The blissful expressions that Mark and I were having on our faces made obvious to him what took place when he was gone. The three of us went to swim in a heated swimming pool.

"Mark, what did I tell you, isn't she an Angel?" Peter asked his brother while staring at my naked body floating in the water.

"Yes Peter, but she's my Angel now. Thanks for bringing her to my house." Mark swam next to me to put his arms around me.

"She's not just like any beautiful girl. I swear, she has some magical powers in her eyes. I could stare at her like this the whole day without getting tired." Peter was talking to his brother as if I wasn't even there.

"I'm sure you could." Mark looked a little bit jealous of his younger brother. He didn't really know how long I'd been seeing him and whether we had something special going on or not. Peter continued conversing with Mark while looking at me the whole time and even thought he had a smile on his face, I could tell that he was regretting his decision of being OK with sharing me with anybody. After the passionate night with Mark, I didn't want to be shared anymore though. I was sleeping and hanging out with Mark and Mark only. He even stopped inviting those girls and it was just the two of us. Occasionally an engaged friend would show up with his finance, but that was all.

Mark was making the meals for us and I was swinging on the bench that was hanging from the roof. I watched the dears trying to sneak carefully to get some of the best quality grass. I've never knew before what it meant to feel completely relaxed. I was living in the moment, and nothing, including my own thoughts, was able to disturb me.

For most of the time I wore a see-through gown that Mark gave to me. I've never wore shoes, or a bra while I was there with him. We were making love every day, sometimes a few times a day. I'm not sure what I was thinking but I guess I didn't think that I could get pregnant. I've never got pregnant before and maybe I thought that this was good enough reason for me to feel safe. I honestly wasn't planning on having a baby with Mark. Yes, sure, he was handsome, filthy rich, and he was spoiling me a lot. Except that I didn't come to America straight from Poland and I knew a few things about men in general. One moment they're nice to you and the next moment they're not. Besides, if I did get pregnant and had a baby with him, what would happen if for whatever reason I decided to leave him? What would I do if he'd try to take my child away from me? He could hire the most expensive lawyers this country can offer. What about me? What would my public defender say to the judge?

"Your honor, the father is only a multimillionaire and I think you should give the full custody to my client, who's a former model and currently starving."

I couldn't ever give away my child and I wasn't planning now on making this my reality. Pregnancy wasn't something I was thinking about. I wish that wasn't the case though.

A month later I still didn't get my period but I wasn't too alarmed by it. I had irregular periods before and so I thought that there was nothing going on with me. Mark wasn't surprised with my ferocious appetite either. He knew that I enjoyed food and that I loved to eat a lot. Everything looked normal and he kept buying me blueberries which I sometimes swallowed without even chewing first. One evening some girls showed up unannounced. They were "concerned" with Mark. They wanted to know the reason he wasn't seen anywhere anymore. Mark, being a great host, started a fire outside and we all sat around on the pillows and mats. The girls were looking at me with envy. They brought red wine and they convinced me to have some. I've never had a strong drive for the alcohol and so I wasn't really surprised when after two glasses I started to feel sick. Mark was holding my hair the whole time, while I was vomiting in the toilet.

"I'm sick. Something didn't agree with my stomach. I think it was the wine." I was sitting on the bathroom floor and I couldn't even move. I was feeling so weak that Mark had to hold my head. The next morning I woke up feeling fine.

"Good morning sexy." Mark was stretching his arms. We made love like we would usually do after waking up. We were feeling so cozy in bed and we felt like staying there the whole day. Mark started a fire in the fireplace that was right next to this enormous bed. We were making love and I was feeling very frustrated with my full bladder that was interrupting us the whole time.

"I've got to use the bathroom again."

"Again? Are you OK?" Mark looked concerned.

"Yeah, I just have to pee again." Again, frequent urinations were part of my life and so this wasn't making me suspicious at all.

"You know, this reminds me of my sister Renata. When she was pregnant she used to pee every five minutes." I yelled at Mark from the bathroom. As soon as I finished the sentence, it hit me. I climbed the bed with a serious look on my face and Mark was looking at me seriously too.

"I think you're pregnant." He said after realizing that I wasn't going to say a word.

"No, no way. I can't be pregnant. No. Not me."

"Tomorrow we'll go to New York to my office. We'll buy a pregnancy test and we'll know for sure."

"OK. For now let's don't even think about it, OK?" I was a little bit scared but I was still thinking that it was the wine that made me sick and that it was now making my bladder full or something. I was trying to rationalize in my head.

Baby

The next day Mark and I drove to New York City. He stopped at the drugstore and purchased two pregnancy tests. We went to his office which was in a skyscraper. The view from the window that was practically the size of the wall was breathtaking. I was afraid to go to the bathroom and to pee on the stick. I was looking at the city.

"Come on, go ahead and go to the bathroom. I'm here with you." Mark whispered.

I anxiously peed on the pregnancy test. I didn't have to wait very long to see two pink lines forming in front of my eyes. I came outside the bathroom.

"I was right. You are pregnant." I couldn't tell if Mark was happy, in shock, or freaking out. I couldn't talk. The strong emotions that were growing inside of me were overwhelming. Mark was looking at me in silence and his face was now showing the sense of guilt.

"I did this to you." He looked like he was about to cry himself. The thirty-two year-old man in front of me was now looking like a thirteen year-old boy.

"Whatever you'll decide, I'll support you with your decision." He was trying to make himself not as scared as he was.

"I'm gonna have an abortion. I mean, I don't know. I don't know yet for sure, but I don't think I can keep this baby." I looked at Mark to see his reaction and I felt extremely hurt when I saw the sense of relief on his face. He saw the pain in my eyes because he was now trying to fix it.

"You don't have to decide right now. We still have some time. Let's go. I'll take you to my sister. Maybe she could be of some help. She can give you some advice. I think you can benefit from talking to another woman." He really sounded genuine and I was touched. We went to a huge apartment on the Upper East Side of Manhattan. Mark's sister looked like she didn't believe what her brother just said to her.

"Do you have another pregnancy test with you?" She asked him.

"Yes, it's in my car."

"Go get it." She said to him in a cold tone. When Mark came back she made me use her bathroom. She stood in front of me while I was peeing as if she wanted to make sure that this wasn't some kind of scam.

"Yep; she's pregnant." She told her brother who was looking scared again. I realize then that she wasn't ever going to give me any advice or support of any kind. I felt as if she just wanted to make sure I wasn't lying. I started to understand what she was probably thinking of me. I guess I could see why she would think that I was just some ex-model who got pregnant with a rich guy to assure a better lifestyle for a lifetime. Mark and I went back to Connecticut. Before we hit the road, we stopped in the East Village to get some blueberry pierogi for me and the baby that was growing inside of me. At home we made love. It was different this time. Mark was touching my belly and holding me as if he couldn't believe what was happening.

"You know, I feel a lot closer to you this time. Knowing that you are carrying my child makes it that much more exciting to be intimate with you." I loved what he was saying to me, because that was exactly what I was feeling. I didn't know that men could feel this way too. The next few days we tried to relax. Mark was talking to his friends and they were all advising him not to be too involved. He started to distance himself emotionally from me. I couldn't bear his new attitude towards me and I decided to go back to New York.

I stayed on the Upper Westside, with a guy that used to rollerblade with me in Central Park. His name was Daniel and he was living with his beautiful girlfriend Cathy. They were extremely supportive of me. When the Polish restaurant in the East Village wasn't serving my favorite cucumber soup, they were taking me all the way to Brooklyn to satisfy my cravings. They used to take me rollerblading everywhere they went.

"Come on, you need to get some exercise for you and the baby you're carrying." They held my hands and the three of us were zooming across Central Park. Daniel never met Mark before but he was infuriated with him.

"What a schmuck!"

It was very sweet how the young couple was so protective over me. I was getting very depressed. The hormones that were rearranging everything inside me were not helping my already suicidal state. Daniel was hiding all his razors in the bathroom from me, and he was taking turns with Cathy on keeping an eye on me the whole time. He was very concerned and one day he took my cell phone to call Mark. I don't know what he said to him, but few hours later Mark was downstairs waiting for me. He tried to hide it but he still sounded like he was happy that I left. He kept talking about how he has been now taking care of himself and his new business. Mark always wanted to make some money on his own. He didn't like how attachments came with his father's money. He didn't want to be controlled. He was telling me how he was able to open his new store right in the middle of Soho.

He reassured me that he'd pay for the abortion. He even gave me five hundred dollars so I could have some money while I was staying with my friends. While he was talking to me, I could feel how all the intimacy we once shared was now only history. He was looking at me as if he was wishing that he had never met me. I could tell that his niceness was rehearsed. I could tell that his friends and perhaps even his family told him how to behave with me. He looked like he wanted to make sure that I got my abortion done, and until then he was going to try not to piss me off. I couldn't get as mad at him as I was mad at myself. I thought that I knew men by now, and I should have known better. I promised myself that I'd never have sex again until I got married.

Mark came back a few days later to take me to the clinic. He was waiting for me in the lobby. The doctor there asked me if I wanted to see my baby before the procedure. I said yes and she prepared my belly with special gel. The ultrasound was showing the black and white image of my five week-old fetus.

"This is your uterus and there is your baby. See? Right there."

I was staring at the screen.

"Can I look at it for a little bit longer, please?" I asked the doctor.

"Sure." She seemed like she understood the pain I was feeling.

Stranded

"Wake up! Wake up! Your anesthesia should be wearing off by now." The nurse was shouting at me while slapping me gently in my face.

"Wake up. It's over. You can go home now." I looked at a few other women that were lying on their beds in the recovery room. They all looked sad and even depressed. I started to cry like a baby.

"First time?" Some girl asked me.

"Yes, the first time, and the last time." I kept crying until the nurse showed up again.

"Your boyfriend is waiting for you Miss Chechack." She was trying to pronounce my last name.

"I don't wanna get up! I don't want to go anywhere!" I kept crying.

"Come on, Miss Chechak, you're gonna be OK. Post abortion depression is a very common thing. It happens to many women who find themselves in this kind of situation. You're going to be OK. The doctor may prescribe you some anti-depressants. You need to tell her how you're feeling, OK? The nurse in front will schedule an appointment for you."

For the next few weeks I looked like a zombie. I didn't want to shower and I didn't want to eat. Daniel and Cathy were there for me throughout this time. Mark was still feeling guilty. He even paid for a psychologist that he wanted me to see. She prescribed me anti-depressants. I told Mark that I wasn't a hundred percent sure if it was his baby. I explained to him that when I found out that I was five weeks pregnant, there was a slight possibility of Peter being the father after all.

"You know that sperm can live up to five days. Obviously I've got pregnant right when we first met. So I really don't think that there would be a way to find out which of you was the father. Not until later." I don't know why I told him that. I guess I loved torturing myself. Seeing Mark so happy and so relieved was yet another shot of pain that went straight to my blood.

Daniel and Cathy were trying to convince me why it was a good thing that Mark didn't want to see me anymore. I was really glad to have such good friends. The couple took me to Daniel's mom's house for Thanksgiving. They tried very hard to get my mind off of everything that was happening in New York. I had no money left these days and so when the agency called me and asked me to go to Paris, I couldn't refuse their offer.

"We sent your portfolio to the agency in Paris and they absolutely love your looks. They're waiting for you there. I think you will benefit immensely from working in Paris for a month or so. This will boost your career a lot. When you come back, you'll be looked at in different way by everybody." The booking manager sounded very excited. I went to Paris with no money whatsoever. I did have a "Learn French in No Time" guide with me though. I always wanted to be able to speak French. I thought it would look good on my resume right next to Polish, Italian, Spanish, and English. My Spanish was fading from lack of the use though, the way my Russian did after I wasn't using it in school anymore. Nevertheless I was almost excited again. I thought that even if I didn't make good money there, that at least I'd gain some experience. I had to leave United States anyway, because my visa was about to expire, and agency was trying to get me a work permit. They had to submit to immigration office fifteen different samples of my modeling work from Europe and Asia, to prove that I was a real model. They explained to me that immigration likes to give work permits only to people that can't "steal" work from US citizens. Being a model I had better chances at obtaining more permanent legal status since not every US citizen can do my kind of work.

"By the time you come back from Paris, you'll have your social security number and everything." The owner of the agency was explaining to me.

"What's that? What's a social security number?"

"It's just a nine digit number that US residents are given so the government can keep records of their taxes."

"Aaaaaaah."

Paris was what they said it would be: a breathtaking and incredibly romantic looking city. I noticed immediately that it's a lot harder to concentrate on learning a new language if you know English already. Now I had a choice; people could understand me if I wanted to be understood. Most people at least have heard some English before.

I had no money with me so I was completely at the agency's mercy. It is not uncommon for models to be broke, so it's not like it was unusual for agencies to advance some money to them. I wasn't worrying. It wasn't my first time being completely broke and I knew that it wasn't going to be the last time either. C'est la vie! Right? Wrong. After few days, the owner of the agency brought me to his office.

"Ela, right?" He told me to sit down.

"I'm going to be very straightforward with you, so we don't waste each other's precious time." I was getting very nervous from the look he was giving me.

"We made a mistake. You are not what we're looking for. I mean, don't take this personally, this happens sometimes. The agencies send us some pictures, we like what we see, and we ask them to send us the model. Sometimes the model doesn't turn out to be as interesting in person as she may appear in pictures. And I know, we had the Polaroid's of you wearing no makeup and all that. Still, you are not what Paris is about. Paris is about glamour, the best of the best."

"Alright, alright, I get your point. But you'll still pay for my airline ticket back to New York, right?"

"Well, we've already paid for one of your tickets, and obviously we lost on that. I think the agency in New York should pay for you to go back there, don't you think? And, I need you to leave the apartment immediately. We don't accommodate models that don't work for us." He started to shift himself in his chair as if he was late for his next business meeting.

I'm not sure what I was feeling more; the anger towards him or the fear of being stacked on the streets of Paris. He let me use the phone to call New York.

"I'm sorry Ela, we cannot advance you any money. We had to pay fifteen hundred dollars to immigration to have your papers done. By the way you'll have your work visa in few months. You're on your own until then." The manager was very firm with me. I thought I was going to die. The first thing I had to think of was where I was going to spend the night. I remembered then that Cathy went to Paris for six months to study at a university there. I had her number with me, and so I called her from a public phone.

"Come on, pick up, pick up, pick up!" I was shouting out loud knowing that this was the only coin that I had. The wind picked up speed as the sky was getting dark.

"Cathy, pick up!"

"Hello?"

"Oh my God! Cathy! It's Ela. I'm in Paris and I need your help."

"Ela! What are you…"

"Look, I only have one coin so I can't talk. Can you come and pick me up?"

"Where are you now?" She asked. I explained to her that I was in the Centrum of Paris. I described the buildings that were around me.

"Don't move. I'll be right there." I was relieved. I don't think I've ever been so glad to see a friend like I did when I saw Cathy that night. The sky was completely dark by the time she found me standing in the cold with a small suitcase next to me. Cathy decided that we were going to worry about my situation later and that she was going to show me Paris for now.

"Come on, you'll stay with me in the dorm. You came all the way to Paris, so you may as well enjoy it." She was about my age and she was always full of energy. Her roommates were very happy that she brought her friend from US to stay with them. I stayed with them for two weeks.

Finally I called my old agency in Barcelona and I explained to them the situation I was in. They got me an airline ticket to Spain and I had to say goodbyes to my friends in Paris. In Barcelona I was missing New York a lot. I took advantage of being in Europe though, and I flew to Poland to spend some time with my family. Renata and her husband Ryszard came to Warsaw in their tiny car to pick me up. I went to get my driver's license and since I was the one who paid for their mini-Fiat, Renata was more than happy to let me drive it. I had some money I earned in Spain so I took my youngest siblings for tour all over Poland. We drove like crazy everywhere we felt. My nephew Mateusz, few years old, went everywhere with us. Back in Spain I was out of money again so one of my hunting buddies lent me one thousand dollars for the ticket to New York City.

Nightlife

I walked into an Italian restaurant in Soho.

"Good morning Miss. Table for one?" The manager asked me.

"No. I'm looking for a job. I want to talk to a manager," I explained.

"You're talking to the right person then. What kind of position are you looking for?" He asked.

"Waitress, I guess."

"Let's go sit down, shall we?" He took me to an upstairs area where tables weren't occupied.

"Pardon if I may seem too straightforward, but you don't look to me like someone with waitressing experience, but we are currently looking for a hostess though."

"I think that would be too boring for me. And I was once a waitress in Italy."

"Do you speak Italian?"

"I do."

"Oh, nice. Both of the owners are Italian. What do you normally do for living?"

"I used to be a model."

"I was going to say that. You look like a model. Look, why don't you start working as a hostess first, and then we'll see if we can train you to wait the tables? How is that sound to you?" He looked like he wanted me to say yes.

"I would prefer to be a waitress."

"Give me just a second please." He went downstairs to the office and he came back upstairs shortly after that. He brought an application with him.

"So when can you start?" He asked me.

"Right away," I answered.

"All right then. I'll have one of our waitresses to train you. The first table I was serving was where, among other people, the wife of one of the owners was sitting. She was very bitchy and demanding. She was looking at me with apparent discontentment. The manager saw that and he went to explain to her that I was in training. I couldn't stand her. I couldn't stand the way she was making me feel. I wanted to take that plate of pasta I was serving to her, and I wanted to dump it on her ugly face. Of course I didn't do that. I went to the manager instead.

"I quit. I can't do this, it's too hard." I told him.

"Do you want to try hosting then?" He asked and I agreed to it. Standing in the entrance of the restaurant, greeting the costumers and leading them to their tables was extremely boring. I was contemplating on how long I would last. Things got a lot more interesting though when a charming man in his fifties showed up at the door. He was one of the owners. He was single and he owned more than fifty percent of this place. I realized that the manager already informed him that he just hired an ex-model and so the owner was coming to see me.

"What are you doing standing there? Don't you get bored?" He seemed to be reading my mind.

"I'm sorry, I thought I could do this, but I can't. I just don't think I'm cut off for this…" I was giving my resignation for the second time.

"Come with me, please." He took me to the bar where the managers and waitresses were busy doing their work.

"Have you ever tried bartending before?" He asked me while we were walking along the bar that ran the length of the whole restaurant.

"No. I don't normally even drink," I said to him.

"No problem," he said and looked at me as if he had something in his mind. He made a hand gesture to the manager.

"I want you to make this girl a bartender." The manager looked as shocked as I did. The waitresses that overheard what was going on were giving me dirty looks. Everybody knew that the best money came from bartending and here I was being offered the position just like that! I knew that it was going to take some time for them to like me. They weren't even trying to hide their disapproval of me. The busboys were very friend-ly to me though. They were all from Bangladesh and they spoke with heavy accents.

"OK. This is vodka, this is where we keep gin, and all the liquors are in here. When in doubt, just poor whatever you'll find. Most of them won't even notice the difference. Tell me, do you know how to make a cosmopolitan?"

"Do I look to you like I do?" They knew my lack of experience and I wasn't trying to impress anybody. I was just myself and they really liked that.

"OK. Come, I'll show you how to make a cosmopolitan. Many cus-tomers like to drink that."

The bartending was fun job and I was making more money that I would have ever made with waiting the tables. I was in the middle of the long bar and I had two busboys on both sides. The most important thing was that most of my customers were men who were constantly hitting on me, and to whom I could tell to get lost if they didn't like my service. The music was always very loud and of course I wasn't even trying to stop my body from dancing while pouring the drinks. I became a hit very quickly. Mark heard from somebody that I was working there and he came one night. His store was only few blocks away from the restaurant.

"You look good. Sexy, as always." He was trying to smile but he still looked very insecure.

"Yeah, I know." I tried to make myself busy with other customers.

"OK. It was nice seeing you again." He said to me after realizing that I wasn't going to pay any attention to him. I wasn't the same person anymore. I wasn't that girl who wore the see-through gown, who walked barefoot, and who liked swinging on the bench all day long. In front of his eyes he had a girl in tight black leather pants and an even tighter black top. A girl whose eyes were underlined with black eyeliner, and whose eyelashes were more noticeable now. A girl whose blond hair was bright-ened up with the right touch of highlights.

"See you around." I said without looking in his direction.

"*Yes! Go back to your monastery and regret what an immature asshole you are.*" I was thinking in my mind.

"Why didn't you tell me that the guy who just left was Mark? If I've would it known, I'd serve him the kind of drink he deserves!" Vivian was another female bartender hired before me. We used to work together on weekends when the bar was packed. We weren't friends at the beginning thought. She was giving me dirty looks at first, the way all the waitresses were doing for "stealing" their promotion space. Vivian was like them, afraid of me being her competition. She was a very beautiful twenty-two-year-old. She was one year younger than I. Vivian was originally born in Vietnam and her parents brought her to the United States when she was only few years old. Her real Vietnamese name sounded a lot more exotic, but she refused to be called anything else but Vivian. For some reason, and I don't know why, she hadn't became US citizen yet either. I could not understand how a person, who grew up in this country since the age of three, could still function on a green card basis. Vivian was very beautiful indeed. She earned her popularity mostly through her craziness. She never took crap from anybody and she only knew how to shoot straight when it came to conversing with anybody, especially with customers. Her beautiful eyes and her full lips were driving men and women crazy. Her full and natural breasts were very proportionate with the rest of her body. The big tattoo on her back served as a warning sign not to mess with her. Her naturally black hair looked as silky as hair can look. She looked hot.

"I live with another waitress in a small studio downtown. You can stay with us if you want. We can use some help with the rent." Vivian made the offer only because I was staying at the restaurant owner's penthouse for now. He was out of town and she didn't want me to have sex with him once he came back from his trip. The studio was as small as she has promised. There was not much space for anything; the room was filled with clothes that were spread virtually everywhere. Even though the building was two blocks away from the twin towers, the view from the window was practically nonexistent. The neighboring building was blocking any attraction that Downtown could offer. The kitchenette was between "the main room" and the bathroom and it consisted of one table and two beaten up chairs. There were no appliances but there were such "guests" like cockroaches living rent free.

Vivian and I started to get to know each other better. Our third roommate was also our age, a very attractive African American girl. The three of us were having some good times at work and after work. Vivian liked alcohol; champagne was her poison of choice. At work, the managers couldn't bother her habit because they knew that at least one of the owners was OK with the bartender drinking tequila shots with customers. Vivian would get very loud when she was under the influence and all the guys loved that. I had my sparkling water to drink and I was getting high from it. Most people wouldn't believe that my energy wasn't enhanced by recreational drugs. They wouldn't say that to my face, but they did share their concerns with Vivian.

"Some other asshole thinks that you're on ecstasy!" She always had fun in telling me what customers were telling her. She liked how guys were being nice to her and were tipping her good money, so she would set them up with me. She knew how to play games with them.

"Smile, like I'm telling you something nice. That jerk wants to go out with you. Just pretend like you're thinking about it for a second," she'd say to me and then we'd just pretend like we were super busy. Well, for the most part we were.

After work, most of the nights, and especially on the weekends, Vivian and I were going out to Moomba. It was a place where lots of celebrities were attending. The upstairs VIP room was always guarded, but because I used to go there while I was still a model, the two of us were always allowed access. In that VIP room I was drinking my sparkling water nonstop and I wouldn't stop dancing. Everybody wanted to know who I was and which agency was representing me. I didn't care that much about anybody. I just wanted to release my stress.

The Artist

John Stork was a sixty-two year-old, pretty well-known artist. His impressive gallery was right in the heart of Soho, where it was considered the most prestigious area. His days of youth were gone a long time ago, but you could still tell that he was once a good-looking man. He used to come to Moomba and he was always surrounded by beautiful, young women. He also had a young, not bad looking personal assistant name Mohamed that used to follow him like a tail follows a dog. John Stork was watching me enjoy the music. My dancing was always attracting spectators. I usually would close my eyes while dancing and I would forget the whole world. I knew that I was being watched but I was so into feeling my body that nobody and nothing could spoil that. I was getting a high and I was deriving immense pleasure from feeling the music and from following the rhythm. I let my body to do whatever it wished. I didn't think about the moves, I didn't care if I looked ridiculous, I simply let go. I was used to people forming a circle around me and when I'd stop for a moment to open my eyes, I'd often hear what a great dancer I was.

"You look so healthy!" That was John Stork's favorite line to pick up new girls.

"Come, sit with us." He grabbed my hand when I was taking time to drink my water. Everybody on that couch was under the influence of ecstasy, cocaine and God only knows what else. Mohamed's eyes were practically as red as blood itself. Nevertheless I felt very flattered by John's invitation. He had a way of making me feel very special.

"You're the only girl I know that can dance the way you do completely sober." Despite his self-destructive behavior he was very intelligent and he always knew what to say to me.

He used to take me to Cipriani's restaurant a lot. They had the best table always waiting for him and for all the people that were always coming along.

"Esta mujer siempre viene aqui con ese hombre muy feo y muy viejo." This woman always comes here with that ugly and old man. The busboys were talking about me around the bathroom area, totally unaware that I spoke some Spanish. I never said anything to them because I didn't envy them their lives and I didn't want to be mean to them. John Stork became almost possessive of me. He always had me sitting right next to him and he didn't like when other people would engage in conversations with me. He wanted me to devote my full attention only to him.

"God, you look so healthy!" He'd stop whatever conversation he'd be engaged in, to brush my long hair of my face. He had a house upstate where he liked to do his work. He also had a huge loft right across his gallery. He also had a wife and a child but I did not know where the two of them were living. I'm sure it was someplace nice and expensive. John would try to kiss me on occasion and he would totally numb my lips with the cocaine that he was on.

"John Stork! What an honor to have you here!" People looked so thrilled when they saw him.

"John Stork. May I say to you what a big fan of your work I am?" They stopped us sometimes even on the street.

"John Stork! John Stork!" People were kissing his ass all day long. I think what he liked most about me was that even though I had nothing going on, I still remained myself. I didn't expect anything from him. I didn't want him to boost my career, I had none, and I wasn't after his money. I was in the moment, enjoying the company of these crazy, but very creative people. I wasn't demanding like all the other girls and I wasn't high maintenance. I appreciated the smallest things.

"God, I've never seen anybody who'd be so happy from eating an apple!" He was amazed by my simplicity and he loved having me in his sight. He'd often get up and he'd start working as if he was just inspired by something. He never worked alone and besides his inseparable assistant, he always had many people around him. He tried to make me jealous sometimes by chatting with other girls for extended periods of time, but eventually he even stopped doing that. I was pretending like I didn't care and I was always making myself busy with something.

"Get over here!" He'd always find me and he'd bring me back to his work area.

"You're coming back tomorrow, right?" He really looked like he wanted me there the whole time. If I didn't show up, he'd call me on my cell phone.

"What are you doing in Moomba? Get your butt to my gallery right away!" I liked how he seemed to like me a lot. One day we were hanging out in his big loft across the gallery. We were having good time talking about everything and nothing at the same time. I was feeling very relaxed when Mohamed interrupted our conversation.

"You look too cozy together, the two of you. Here, this will make you even more relaxed." He handed John a small pill.

"What is it?" I asked.

"Ecstasy. You should try it sometime." John offered.

"No thank you. You go ahead if you have to, but I'm OK without it." I answered.

"I can't believe you've never tried this shit. I'm telling you, you don't know what you're missing." John was trying to tempt me.

"Come on, I'll give you half of it. It's not like you'll have to take it again if you don't like the way it will make you feel. Come on, I'll take the other half with you." He was being very persistent with me.

"Come on, don't be a chicken. Try it. You'll love it." Mohamed was very supportive of his boss.

"It won't kill you. Worst thing that could happen; you'll have some real good time." Mohamed wouldn't leave me alone.

"Alright, she said no. Now take this money and go see a movie or something." John made it sound like he was on my side. I loved when people did that. I loved when people stood up for me. Usually I had to defend myself, sometimes with my sharp tongue, and I'd melt completely whenever I'd see somebody trying to protect me for a change. I didn't think of John's intentions being less than genuine. He has always respected my decision to remain drug free before. I didn't have reason to believe that this time was going to be any different. John took his half pill and he reminded me that the other half would be there for me, in case if I'd change my mind. He carefully then steered our conversation into a topic related to ecstasy. How it felt good to unwind sometimes, how ecstasy would do no harm to somebody like myself, who wasn't hooked on anything other than smoking an occasional cigarette. How a healthy person like me would suffer no consequences.

"Oh what the hell. Gimme that pill." My curiosity was finally stronger than my common sense. Until then I only smoked pot once or twice and because it made me feel completely paranoid, I promised myself that I'd stay away from this stuff. The ecstasy started to have its effect on me very quickly. I wasn't even completely aware yet that it was the pill that was responsible for the sense of love I was feeling towards everything and everybody. The love I was feeling was so overwhelming that I started to cry like a small baby.

"Are you OK?" John was concerned for a moment.

"Yes, I am. I just....I just have so much love in me! I don't know how to explain this." I was still crying and my tears were dropping on John's chest.

"It's in you. I knew that from the moment I laid my eyes on you. I told everybody you were different. And I was right." John was looking at me as if he was Christopher Columbus and he has just discovered America. He was smiling the whole time. I began to shake uncontrollably. The love and admiration I was feeling for him was beyond the description that any human language could depict. I was even loving and fully accepting myself! No, that wasn't the last thing. I wasn't even mad at God anymore! Now that was a huge deal for me. I was crying out loud to God and John was observing me closely.

"God! I love you, you know? I don't know how I could've been so mad at youuuu. Goooood, I really, really love you!" The tears were pouring down my face like Niagara Falls.

"God never thought little of you because you were mad at him." John must have felt sorry for me because he was trying to make me feel guilt free.

"Really?" I looked at him as if he was God himself.

"Of course. You think anybody could be disappointed with you if they saw how much love you carry in your big heart?" He really knew what to say to me.

"Really? So you think God loves me too?"

"Do I think that? No, I know that for a fact."

"But how can you be so sure?" I still wasn't quite convinced. It still sounded too good to be true.

"Look at you. I've never seen anybody with so much passion and so much love inside until now. And I wasn't born yesterday if you know what I mean."

"But still, how can you tell if God feels the same way about me? How would you know if he's not pissed off with things that I've done or haven't done in my life?"

"God doesn't care about any of that crap. You care about it and so you think that he must do the same."

"You really mean that?" I wanted to believe him.

"But of course. I mean every single word. God doesn't care what you do or what you don't do. God is more than what people made him look like. Think about it, wouldn't a dog, if we'd reverse the word, be a God too?"

"That's right! Dog – goD!" I was super excited that John was so convincing.

"So stop doubting God's love towards you! Keep talking to God. Tell him or her how you feel." He was encouraging me. The crying and shaking felt really good as well as my conversation with God.

"God, I really had no idea how much I love you! I pushed you away from my life because I thought you didn't like me or something. But I feel like I've missed you so much." It felt so good saying these things to God. I felt as if God was responding to me through John's words. Now this was a real ecstasy! Knowing that I wasn't being hated by the force that created me in the first place was like knowing that there was nothing wrong with me.

"I'm not a loser. I'm not insignificant." My tears were the tears of joy.

"I always want to feel this way. I always want to remember that I am being loved!" As soon as I said that, the magic went away. I started to shiver but in a different way this time.

"I'm not feeling good. I feel like I'm getting sick." I didn't look good because John had a concerned look on his face.

"I'm cold. I'm very, very cold." I was crying a different kind of tears this time.

"Come on, get up. I'm going to draw you a hot bath." John looked even more scared as I was feeling sicker with each passing moment. My jaws felt tight and my teeth were gnashing. I was sweating profusely and I was experiencing an immense cold from within me. The feeling of depression and hopelessness were overpowering the state of my mind. My anxiety was so overwhelming, as if some force combined all fear this world has seen, and then gave it to me all at once. The presence of loving God was gone and there was only the essence of a dark spirit in the room. I couldn't walk straight and John had to help me to get in the bath. I couldn't hold myself and so he joined me in the tab to hold my head above the water.

"Wow, you really are super sensitive. Good thing you didn't take the whole pill." His surprise to how my body responded to ecstasy wasn't having a calming effect on me. He saw the fear in my eyes because he started to caress me while pouring the water on my face.

"You're gonna be fine. Ecstasy can bring people down. Not as hard as it did to you, but still, you're gonna be fine. It will pass." He dried my naked body. I looked and I felt like a five year-old. John thought that if I had something to eat that perhaps I would start feeling better. He took me to a small restaurant but I couldn't even look at the food that the waiter placed in front of me.

"Maybe you just need to get some sleep." John was looking like he was getting tired of babysitting me.

"Take me to my apartment please." I said while still trembling vigorously. He did exactly that and he left me there. Vivian and I had moved recently to a one-bedroom apartment on the Upper West Side. It was just the two of us living there, except for the times when her new boyfriend was hanging out with her. Ever since she met Ron, she wasn't spending as much time with me anymore. I could tell that she was glad that John Stork was keeping me busy.

"Ela! What the hell? That bastard made you take ecstasy, didn't he?" Vivian was very good and very fast at estimating the situations. She looked at me lying on the couch, covered in cold sweat.

"I'm taking you to the hospital!" She looked scared and angry at the same time.

"No, I'llll bbbeee fffinnne." My gnashing teeth were making it very hard for me to speak. I somehow convinced her that all I needed was to get some sleep. I didn't want to go to the emergency room even though my heartbeat was not regular.

"I'll cover your shifts. You just rest, don't get up. I'll call you from the restaurant to check on you." Vivian was still not quite sure if it was responsible on her part not having called 911. For ten days straight I could not move from that couch. It was very hard for me to get any sleep and it was exhausting me mentally and physically. Vivian and Ron were bringing me food to eat but I had a hard time with swallowing anything.

"You need to eat. I swear I'll call for an ambulance if this soup is untouched when we come back." Vivian used to puff up her lips whenever she wanted to make clear that she was being dead serious.

116

"I can't believe that he never called you to check on you how you were feeling. What an ass!" Finally, after almost two weeks I seemed to have recovered, at least physically.

Downward Spiral

Mentally I was still feeling very hopeless and very depressed. I had no energy whatsoever. I went back to work only to discover that a lot of big changes took place while I was gone. The same owner that was responsible for hiring me as a bartender was now withdrawing from the business for personal reasons. His business partner was taking over and he was transforming the bar-restaurant into a more conventional place. After working there for four months I was told that the new management decided to let me go. That sucked. When Vivian heard what happen, she quit her job. She didn't do that because she was that much close to me, she did it because she was afraid of being the next employee eliminated. She had her pride.

The two of us found new jobs in a restaurant on the Upper East Side. She was still bartending and I was working as a hostess. I had to make myself swallow my pride and I had to tolerate the boredom that was killing my soul slowly but surely. The money wasn't as good as when I was bartending. This was showing in my shortcomings with my half of the rent. I was sort of pissed why did I have to pay exactly half of the rent anyway if Vivian and her constantly present boyfriend Ron were occupying the only bedroom? Why was my couch in the living room/kitchen worth the same amount as their private love nest? Vivian and I were fighting more frequently over this subject. This was when I overheard her saying to one of her girlfriends how stupid I was and how I had no culture or education whatsoever. I knew very well that the main reason she wanted me out of "her" apartment was that her boyfriend could move in. Like Ron wasn't there every day and every night! Feeling unwelcome and still being very depressed, I started to feel suicidal.

I contemplated ending my life many times before, but the memory of that day in the ER when I was fifteen was still very vivid. Remembering my mother's face was keeping me alive until now at least.

I didn't have a problem with dying per se. What I couldn't stand was pain that my death would cause to my family. But now I was trying to convince myself that it wouldn't be that much different if I wasn't alive anymore. After all I wasn't living with my family and it didn't look like I was ever going to be with them anyway. I wasn't going to go back to where I came from and they weren't probably going to be able to come live with me. Missing them all the time and knowing that not much would ever change was causing feelings of suffocation.

"I want out. I really do." I was convinced that my own death was the only relief I could get. I wasn't crazy about the life I was living or about the person I was. I felt I was such a loser and a powerless victim, something I despised with all my heart. I felt as if I had leprosy, not literally of course, but in a metaphorical sense. How else could I explain the phenomena of being always rejected by everybody? How else could I try to understand why people were getting tired of me so quickly? Being a mental leper was my answer to all those questions. I convinced myself that I was mentally fucked up. Mentally retarded and emotionally messed up, I was a piece of junk that was never going to accomplish anything on this earth. I was a fucked up individual who would always cause more problems than solutions, and that is why this sick individual should die! That is why such person shouldn't be walking around other people and that is why she should have the guts to end her misery. Her absence would bring relief to some human beings at least. She would be forgotten in no time. Those were the type of thoughts that made me pick up the phone.

"Hi Steve. I need you to do me a favor. I need you to get me few ecstasy pills. Would you do that for me?" I wanted to sound as casual as I could to avoid unnecessary suspicion. I knew Steve on an acquaintance basis, but I knew that he could get me my "weapons of self-destruction". I knew that if half a pill had such strong effect on me, that a few of those would definitely stop my heart in no time. And if that wouldn't happen, I knew that I would kill myself while experiencing the inevitable low that comes after the high.

"Yeah, no problem, but how come? You never take any drugs." Steve was asking me questions that I wanted to avoid answering.

"Just bring that damn ecstasy, alright? Stop with the interrogation." I was getting frustrated.

"Alright, alright. No need to be so moody. Where do you live?" I gave him the directions. While waiting for him I was starting to feel very relaxed. The incredible sense of relief I was feeling was convincing me that I was doing the right thing. I was experiencing a strange, euphoric-like sense of high. I tried not to think about my family. I told myself that we all have to die one day and that I will meet them on the other side. I believed in reincarnation at that point of my life and I told myself that I would never come back to earth. I was talking to my soul;

"Whatever you do, do not, I mean under no circumstances try to come back to this crazy world! I forbid you from doing this to me. You failed me, or I failed you. Whatever, this is not the time for blaming. I do not wish to be in a physical body ever again. It hurts too much. It's not worth the pain. Nothing is worth the type of life I've been living. I don't have any hopes left and I don't want to be here anymore. I don't want this to be just a cry for help.

You have no idea how judgmental people are when it comes to suicide attempts. They feel guilty or something so they must blame somebody else to feel less responsible. I hate when people do that. I hate when they talk bad about the victims of suicide. They are even crueler with those who survive such attempts. *"Oh, it's just a big cry for help."* Oh yeah? If you're so smart in diagnosing others then why can't you do something to help that "crying" person? People can be so stupid, so insensitive and such annoying know-it-alls."

The knock at the door announced that Steve found my address.

"Hey," I greeted him as casually as I could.

"Hey. What's up? Gee, you look awful. Is everything alright?" Steve was always full of energy and he always talked a lot.

"Yeah, I'm alright. You have the pills with you?" I wanted my ecstasy and I wanted him gone.

"So this is where you live. How much you guys pay for this place?" Steve wanted to know everything.

"Look, I'm not in a mood for company. Can you just give me what I asked you for?" He was getting on my nerves. He was staring at me with a strange look on his face.

"Steve, if you didn't bring the pills with you then get the fuck out of here!" Now I was getting angry.

"Can I sit down?" He asked me while pointing at my couch/bed.

"I want to talk to you for a moment. And don't worry; I've got everything you need, alright?" He was looking at me with an insecure look on his face while he was making himself comfortable in my small living room.

"Sit down with me please. You make me nervous with this pacing." He was still talking in a careful way, as if he was afraid of pissing me off.

"Steve, you've got the pills or not?" I asked him very firmly while looking him straight into his eyes.

"Yeah, yeah, stop worrying, alright? I need to talk to you about something first." He wasn't giving up.

"Oh God, what is it then? Just get to the point, would you?" I was very short with him.

"You know that I'm bipolar, right?" He looked very serious now.

"No, I didn't know that."

"Well, I am. I've been hospitalized; I've been to rehab, and all that." He wanted to continue.

"Yeah Steve, I'm sorry that your life sucks but I'm not in a mood for more drama, alright?" I couldn't figure out why he wouldn't just give me my pills and why wouldn't he just leave me alone.

"You have depression. Yes, you're like me, you're depressed. You think I can't see that? You think I can't tell that you're suicidal? Do you want to know how many times I cut my wrists? You need help and I'm going to help you!" Now he was practically shouting at me. I remained speechless. Hearing somebody else saying what I was feeling, softened me up. The salty tears were pouring down my face while I was sitting in silence, listening to Steve.

"Look, the girl I'm seeing and I were about to go away for the weekend when you called. My family owns a private cabin on the lake. I'm taking you with us. You need some time off. You need to get away from everything and everybody." Steve always liked me and I knew that he had huge crush on me but I would never allow him to get closer to me. He was nice to me but he was always irritating me and I never cared to know him better.

Conversations with God

The lake was huge. The tall trees that were surrounding the cabin were making this place look very secluded. Steve's date turned out to be a very nice girl too. She didn't make me feel like she was jealous of me being there. The two were making love every time they got the chance. I was staring at the lake from a big window for most of the time. The thunder from a storm was muffling the moaning of lovemaking that was taking place in the next room. The cloudy sky looked as if some heavenly forces were getting very mad. The frequent lightning looked very threatening. The rain was completely amalgamated with the surface of the lake and seemed to be dancing some strange, ritual-like dance. I was feeling sad and yet very peaceful. I was admiring the incredible power that was in front of my eyes. I was feeling the presence of God in every single drop of the rain that was smashing against the big window in front of me.

Why can't I feel this calm and this peaceful all the time, God? Why is it that only nature makes me feel this way, and yet I continue to live in big cities? I love New York City, don't get me wrong. I love how there are people everywhere and how many places stay open all night. I love its architecture and even its busy streets. The endless opportunities that a city seems to offer always attracted me with its sense of hope. How come I seem unable on succeeding in my life? Why do I always have to sabotage myself? When will I stop being so dysfunctional? Why do I feel so powerless? Why am I always so angry and so negative? How come I can't control my own thoughts and my painful feelings that are derived from it? I'm not stupid, or am I? I know that we create our own destinies. I know that we are in charge of our own lives. All those self-help books I've read convinced me of that. So what's wrong with me?

They say that I'm beautiful. I know I'm smart, I'm young, I'm passionate, I'm crazy sometimes, but I don't mind that. My craziness is what

I like the most about myself. When I'm fearless is when I am my biggest fan. Why can't I be all those things without that other stuff that turns me into such a loser? Yeah, yeah, I know; "Conversations with God", which is my favorite book of all times, talks about the opposites and how we couldn't experience something good without experiencing something bad first. All this makes perfect sense God, I'm telling you, I'm with you on that one. I do want to know who I am and so yes, if I have to feel and look ugly in order to know what true beauty feels and looks like, that's fine. But for how long? For how long do I have to experience the lows in order to rise above? And what about the "Communion with God", my second favorite book of all? When will I experience that unity the author talks about in he's incredibly inspiring writings? God, you know I tried to follow everything he talks about, right? *Everything is an illusion.* Alright, fine; everything is an illusion. Nothing in my world is real. Nothing I look at exists, including my own body. All this is simply a projection of the real world that's within me. OK, fine. Everything is within me, not outside of me. I have to tell you, this stuff it's hard to follow without losing your sanity, but, whatever it takes to achieve that sense of unity.

Separation does not exist. Separation is an illusion. OK, fine, we are all connected and the time is here and now. The present moment is the only real time and it never ends. We are all One and we never end. We never stop ceasing to exist, not now and not ever. Physical death is only another form of transition. OK, I can live with that. But you know what? I'm still missing my family. No matter how many times I tell myself that we are all One and that separation is only an illusion, I still feel the sharp pain of being away from my family. Even if it's an illusion, it still hurts!

Need does not exist. Need is an illusion. That one I have a little hard time with. Yeah, I know, we are all One and one does not need anything or anybody. One is self-sufficient. This looks very nice in writing but when it comes to living this new truth is a lot harder, you know? When my stomach is digesting the fat deposits because of lack of food, or when the fear sets in because my roommate threatens me with throwing me out, then its very hard to believe that need does not exist. Yeah, I know, our souls can survive without all that stuff and all that, but why am I then wearing this physical body? What for?

Fear is an illusion too. Fear does not exist. It's all love. Love is all there is. Yeah, this also looks more attractive when written than when somebody tries to actually apply it into life. God, I love that book and you know that I find every single word in it to be true! So why is it so hard for me to live my new truth? Why is this communion with you so impossible? You gave me some glimpses of it briefly, here in New York, after I read those books, but it all went away.

I wanna be with you God. I wanna feel your presence in every single person I encounter, in every single event and in every single moment. In good and bad, in high and low, in day and night, I want to recognize *You*. I want to look at the rock, the flower, the tree, the neighbor, the homeless man who's asking me for money, and I want to know, not just *believe*, but to _know_ that I am looking at myself! Why is this so hard to do? You know I've tried this quiet time, the meditation and all that. You even know that once I practically went into a trance. That felt so good. That feeling that everything is just the way it was meant to be. God, I wanna feel always this way and you know that I haven't been able to reach that state again, despite of all my efforts. Am I not supposed to hope for that euphoria? Gee, God, don't get offended, but you have no idea what's like to be a human being!

Back in New York City I was starting to feel suicidal again. I didn't want to make another attempt on my life so I decided to turn myself into the care of specialists. Vivian and Ron took me to the ER. The doctors kept me there for observation for few days. Steve came to visit me.

"What are you doing girl?" He looked like he was worrying about me.

"Look Steve, I'm not doing anything, alright? I keep feeling suicidal and I couldn't stop it so I came here so I wouldn't do anything stupid, that's all. Maybe being in the hospital will have a cold shower effect on me. At least I'm hoping for that. I don't wanna wake up dead. I don't want my anger to prevail over whatever commonsense I've been left with. More than anything, I don't wanna cause heartache to my family and that is the only reason why I came here, to tell you the truth." I felt like he knew exactly what I was talking about.

The doctors released me upon the promise that I would see a psychologist on a regular basis.

"I have to live. I have to get rid of this demon called Depression, which has possessed my mind." I was repeating the mantra in my mind while rollerblading around Central Park.

Ousted

John Stork was very surprised to see me. He didn't say "You look so healthy!" this time. He heard about what happened. Vivian told everyone that we knew about me taking the sleeping pills and spending almost two month, locked up, at the Roosevelt Hospital.

Mohamed was looking at me like I was crazy. I called Mohamed a few days before and I told him that I was writing a book. I even sent him a few pages I wrote. I was describing him and I was pretty much admitting that I was starting to fall in love with him. Yeah, he was always fucked up on cocaine and he was always following John like he didn't have a life of his own, but I was still enchanted by him. I found him charming, sweet and I loved his looks that originated somewhere in the Middle East. I liked his darker skin and even darker hair that he always used to style with gel. His full red lips looked so sexy. He told me over the phone that he started to date some model and that he was in love with her but she wasn't serious about him. I heard from Vivian that he was hanging out with somebody but I was really hoping that somehow I could have been that model he was talking about. I guess I was totally fucked up from the meds I was taking. I even encouraged the doctor I was seeing regularly on an outpatient basis, to prescribe me some anti-psychotics. She did. She said that Ziprexa that she prescribed me was being used to treat patients with schizophrenia. She explained that it was also used with patients with severe cases of depression. All those meds were giving me high but honestly I didn't like it. I wanted my natural high to come back to me. This new one felt artificial and it was causing many unpleasant sides effects. Sometimes I couldn't sleep but I couldn't do anything useful either. I couldn't focus on my book even though I was constantly trying to write something. I approached a publishing company one day, hoping that they would like my idea and that perhaps they'd buy my book. I was hoping that I could get some advance money for it so I could focus one hundred percent on my project. The receptionist told me that the company only accepted book proposals from literary agents. Vivian kept saying that I was wasting my time with my stupid book and that I was supposed to look for a new place to live instead.

"What if? What if nobody buys your book, then what?" I heard her saying those "what ifs" like a hundred times a day sometimes.

John Stork was at least pretending that he liked my book.

"Well, it's a start. You're warming up. Not bad. You're drawings are pretty good too. Keep doing what you're doing." He said to me. I was glad to hear him saying that. His words gave me some more hope. I sat on the floor in his gallery and I watched him doing his work. As usually there were people everywhere but I wasn't paying attention to anybody. I was thinking about my book and I was trying to picture how much it will change my life. I was trying to visualize how many lives it will touch and how much hope it will bring to the people that have lost it. It was then when I overheard Mohamed saying something about me and my book. I looked in their direction to see John's reaction and I saw them both laughing hard. I felt so hurt that I didn't even want to say anything. I got up and I just wanted to leave without being noticed. On my way out, I saw a red nail polish bottle on the table. I took it with me. I closed the gallery door behind me and using that red nail polish I wrote on the glass door: **FUCK YOU!**

I took the subway to go back to my apartment. When I climbed the stairs I noticed that all my stuff was outside.

"What the fuck?" I said out loud and I tried to open the door with my key.

"They've fucking change the locks! Vivian, open that fucking door! I know you're in there! I'm not leaving until you'll open that door!" I was pounding at the door and my heart was pounding even harder. She opened the door slightly while leaving the safety chain on.

"You can't live here. You've got to go." She was talking like she was afraid that the neighbors could hear her.

"What are you talking about? You can't just kick me out. I'll call the cops."

"And I'll tell them that you're still suicidal. You've got to go. Take your stuff and go." She shut the door. It was late and it was cold outside. I arranged all my stuff in the corner of the staircase. I pulled out my green leather winter coat and I went to sleep. I was scared, tired, cold, lonely, angry, hurt but I was still thinking that Vivian would come to her senses in the morning. I was being delusional.

"*I'm not going anywhere else. This is my place too.*" I was thinking while falling asleep.

"*Where would I go anyway? People live their lives and I don't want to be anybody's burden. God, I'm sick and tired of always depending on somebody. Even when I pay my share I still feel like people are telling me what to do. It's so easy for anybody to manipulate me. Everybody always tries to control me. They love how I always try to explain myself; it makes them feel that they're in charge. When I'm easygoing, they love my company. The moment I say no to something or I withdraw my explanations, the moment I stop saying anything, good or bad, so they can't control me, that's when I become too uncomfortable to them. And then it just takes nothing, like this, to get rid of me.*

Why am I always ending up feeling this way? Is it because I'm stuck in my past? Is it because I'm repeating some old patterns? Does being forced to obey the orphanage regulations at the age of fifteen have anything to do with this? Am I fighting some kind of injustice in my head and by doing so attracting this shit into my life? Even if so, how could I stop this? I'm twenty-four, I'm not a teenager anymore and I should be able to live my adult life as an adult. This regressing into the past doesn't do shit for me. It only opens the wounds that seem to never heal. How can I start a new life? Why does the ghost of my past have to poison all my hopes? I didn't get an airline ticket or a visa for that motherfucker bad spirit to follow me everywhere like this!

If I'll go farther West, like to Los Angeles, will it leave me alone then? Will I then be able to start my life over again? Maybe I'll be more aloof, I'll keep all things to myself so nobody will be able to take advantage of me? What do you think God? Should I go to LA? It's warmer there, that's what I heard. Maybe one day I'll be able to have that dream house of mine. Maybe I'll even have my own horses. Who knows, right? I'll get that German shepherd I've always dreamed of. I'll grow my own vegetables, like I've always wanted to do." I fell asleep with the sweet image in my mind.

"You don't have the right to stay here." Vivian was trying to make herself to look very upset and mean.

"And you don't have the right to change the locks on me, especially without a formal notice." I answered.

"What do you think; you're going to sleep on these stairs forever?"

"And what do you think I should do?"

"I don't know; it's not my problem. Can't you go and ask John for help or something?" Now she was trying to sound somewhat nice.

"Vivian, do you think I'd be sleeping on these stairs if I had other place to go?"

"It's not my problem. We can't help you." She said while opening the door with her new key. Ron was looking at me with a very uncomfortable look on his face. I could see that he was feeling guilty but I could also sense that he was more afraid of pissing off his girlfriend. I went to sleep and this time I put a few sweaters on in advance. I was realizing that my old roommate wasn't such a nice and caring girl after all. She asked me to move in with her the first time because she didn't want me to live in the penthouse with the owner of that restaurant. She asked me to rent this apartment with her because she barely knew Ron at the time and she needed somebody to split the bills with. She was going out to clubs with me because we never had to wait in any line and all the guys were buying us drinks. I was so convenient to her. With my naïve personality it was so easy to manipulate me. So why would it be surprising to me to see how OK she was with me sleeping on the stairs?

"Sister my ass! She's just the same bitch that she was when she was giving me those dirty looks when I first started to work at that restaurant."

Old Soul

The next day I decided to let go of Vivian and the apartment she was occupying. I used my rollerblades to commute the distance between West Eighty Eight Street and Soho. As I was going down through Broadway Avenue admiring the city, I was saying a silent goodbye to all the tall buildings surrounding me. I made up my mind that I'd go to California somehow. I went to Cipriani's, the same restaurant that John Stork used to take me to practically every day. I remembered Franco, who looked more like a bodyguard than a security man who was there in the evenings. He always treated me with such respect and he loved the fact that I spoke Italian so well.

"Hey, I haven't seen you here for a while! What happened to you?" Franco always looked happy to see me.

"Hey Franco. How have you been?" I asked.

"Same old. Sit down, sit down. Are you meeting somebody?" He offered me a tall chair at the bar.

"Thanks. No, actually, I came here to talk to you." I thought the best thing I could do was to be straightforward.

"Me?" He smiled and I could tell that he was flattered.

"I haven't seen you hanging out with John Stork lately. Did you hear what happened?" He asked me.

"No, what happened?"

"I'm not sure exactly but I heard that somebody used some paint to write 'fuck you' on his door, or something," he explained.

"Really?" I was happy inside but I didn't want to show it too much.

"Yeah, I don't know, I guess he pissed off somebody. I'm not that surprised." Franco didn't look unhappy either.

"Yeah, he probably deserved it. Hey Franco, I need some help. I don't have a place to go. My roommate threw me and all my stuff out and I slept on the stairs for the last two nights."

"What? You're serious? For real?" Franco looked like he was in shock or something.

"Yeah, for real." I said.

"Why didn't you come the first day? Why did you sleep on the stairs?"

"I thought she would come to her senses or something. I don't know. I couldn't believe it myself. I was like you are right now when I saw all my stuff outside the door. She changed the locks."

"What a bitch! Yeah, I've seen that girl few times here, drunk and loud like a cheap whore. But we need to get you out of those stairs. Look, you know I would love to take you to my apartment but my girlfriend would kill me. She's very insecure and very jealous. Seeing you wouldn't be a good thing. But I have a partner in my security business. He's married but he has a big house one hour from the city. I'll give him a call. He owes me a favor. But where will you stay tonight?" He was rubbing his big chin with his big hand.

"Thanks Franco. Thank you so much. And tonight I'll just sleep at the stairs again."

"No, you can't do that."

"Look, all my stuff is there. I don't want anything to get stolen, alright? I'll be fine, I mean, one more night, right?"

"Let's hope so. Here, take my number and call me when you wake up. I'll talk to him first thing in the morning. His wife is not the coolest person I know, but he's totally cool. And he owes me so I think they may let you stay there for a while, at least until we'll figure something else out, OK?" Franco looked optimistic.

"Thanks Franco. I really appreciate your help."

In the morning, before I've got the chance to open my eyes, I heard a man shouting.

"What is going on here? What is all this?" It was the neighbor from below. Vivian and Ron opened the door and they started to explain the situation.

"She's leaving. She's not staying here, she's leaving." Vivian looked very nervous and embarrassed.

"She has some mental problems. She spent almost two months in a psychiatric unit at Roosevelt Hospital." Ron was helping his girlfriend in maintaining their innocence in their neighbors' eyes.

"Well, whatever it is, we cannot have people sleeping on the stairs like some hobos." The neighbor was very upset.

"We'll move her stuff today." Vivian was reassuring the upset man.

"You'll better or I'll call the cops. This is outrageous!" The cranky elderly neighbor went back to his apartment.

"We're moving your stuff outside." Vivian started to grab the boxes and Ron was helping her. I wasn't even saying anything because I was going to have to take all this stuff down the stairs anyway so I thought that I might as well use them to carry all that. I was carrying one of my bags outside when I saw a homeless guy taking my green leather coat from the top of the pile.

"Hey, hey, that's my freaking coat! What are you doing? Give me my coat back!" I yelled at him.

"Oh. I thought they were throwing it out. Here." He gave it back to me.

I used the phone from the deli to call Franco. He came with his friend to pick me up few hours later. I stayed in the basement of the house for couple of weeks. I didn't like the wife but I did get along very well with her mother-in-law, who was living there too. She was very straightforward and she liked telling me that she wished that her son would have married somebody like me instead. The two of us were smoking our cigarettes in the garage and sometimes we'd go for a walk. She liked my company and I liked her. She was a very cool, older, but still always such an elegant and classy-looking lady.

"Why couldn't he marry somebody like you? He's my only son, you know? He's good looking, he has a strong body and a big heart. You would have been a perfect daughter-in-law! Eh! Life, eh? What can you do?"

Franco got me a job in a doctor's office. Apparently he knew people everywhere that owed him some favors. It was a small private office with one very nice doctor who specialized in laser treatments. His patients were mostly the ones who wished their unwanted hair permanently removed, but on occasion he had some people who came to him with some serious scars or old, unwanted tattoos.

I got a hold of Steve, the same guy I asked once for those ecstasy pills, and I found out that his girlfriend moved out after a big fight. He said I could come and stay at his penthouse and I didn't hesitate to move to my new place. "My" older lady told me that she'd miss having me at their place. She said that she was happy though, seeing me getting my life together. She even came to visit me once and I took her to Cipriani's for dinner as a thank you gesture. Everybody else, except for Franco of course, thought that I came with my mother. She was a funny lady. She was so elegant and yet she never took crap from anybody. In the short time I lived with her she taught me some valuable lessons. We definitely bonded together. She was very sad when I told her that I purchased a plane ticket to Los Angeles.

"What are you going to do with your knew kitty?" I had recently adopted an orange cat from a shelter.

"Who, Mishia? He's coming with me. I don't have a ticket for him but I will smuggle him in my purse." I explained.

"Are you sure you want to go there? I thought you were happy with your new job and everything."

"Yeah, I know, but I have set my mind already on that trip. Once I decide on something I hardly ever change my mind. I've been here for two years now; I think it's time for some change. I don't know; I've never stayed anywhere longer than two or three years. I just feel like I have to go. I feel the strong urge and I can't help it. I always hope that I'll find true happiness wherever I'm going to. I always think I'll meet new people and that they'll treat me nicer. And yeah, I know true happiness needs to be found within me first and people will treat me nice when I'll start treating myself nice. I know all that, I know. I just can't resist the illusion that somewhere out there something special is waiting for me, you know? I don't even know how to explain this."

"I know; you feel like you have to go. You want to escape from something and you don't even know what it is exactly that you're trying to run away from. You're trying to run away from yourself," she said.

"Yeah, but even being aware of all that doesn't make that much difference." I answered.

"I know. You are an old soul my dear. You're searching desperately for answers. You ask questions that most people don't even bother to think about. The choices you make and your unpredictable life forces you to continue your quest. You're an old soul my child. I get that feeling when I talk to you."

Los Angeles

"Mishia, don't say a word, OK? Be quiet. We've got to get on that plane and I don't have a ticket for you. So just be quiet OK?" The kitty-cat I rescued was the smartest creature I've ever seen and I loved him dearly. I hated so much leaving him at home and I was always missing him so much that I had convinced my boss that it was OK to have a cat in a doctor's office. Patients were always thrilled to see my cat. Mishia was always showing off in front of them with flips that he was so good at doing. The first time the two of us took the subway together, he flipped out at the loud noise of an incoming train. He tried to jump out of my arms and I had a hard time holding on to him. The next day I purchased a nice cat carrier and ever since then he'd always wait at the door when he'd see me putting on my shoes. I took him with me to a gallery opening one day. He was getting more attention than any of the pictures that were hanging on the walls. People were taking pictures of him like he was the biggest attraction and to me he was.

"Oh my God! Is that a cat? No way, it can't be." They looked like they saw E.T or something.

"I think it's so cool that you bring a cat with you. I've seen people bringing Chihuahuas or Yorkies but I've never seen a cat in places like this. Look honey, did you see the cat?" They were pointing at us constantly. They all wanted to pet him and Mishia was thriving from the attention he was getting.

In Los Angeles Mishia and I took a cab to go to a house that was owned by some friend of a friend of Steve. The place was nice. It had a swimming pool and there were some people present there. The friend of a friend of Steve wasn't very thrilled with my arrival. I started to feel very uncomfortable not knowing where I would stay and where I should start to look for a job. Then I got into a conversation with one woman who was sipping white wine in the kitchen. She was in her forties, a single mother of two boys and they all lived in the heart of Hollywood, right by Fairfax Avenue. Her name was Hannah and she had the whitest teeth I've ever seen. Her breasts were very nice too and she told me without hesitating that she had them augmented. Hannah's hair was light brown with some highlights in it. She looked very good and she didn't look her age. She owned a house and few small apartments she was renting out on month-to-month basis. Her tenants were mostly actors-wannabes. She said she'd let me stay downstairs, in one of the small units until I'd figured something else out.

"Hey, you can clean my apartments if you need some cash. I'll give you forty bucks for a day. My cleaning lady is sick. What do you think?" She offered.

"Sure, why not?" I answered not aware of what I was getting myself into. Scrubbing bathrooms, toilets and floors turned out to be a very humiliating experience. It wasn't only the hard work for little money that was making me feel bad. I felt so diminished and so devalued. The looks on people's faces that were coming to visit Hannah were making me feel embarrassed of myself.

"Wait, she looks very familiar." They'd talk to themselves while watching me scrubbing the bathroom floor.

"Yeah, I know, doesn't she? I can't figure out who she reminds me of. THAT'S IT, little orphan Annie! Oh my God, doesn't she look like little orphan Annie?" Hannah was so happy with her discovery.

"Oh God, you're right." Some women with obviously fake boobs were looking at me as if I was a chimpanzee that learned how to clean a house. I had to swallow my pride thought. Hannah was feeding me, she was paying me forty bucks a day when she had a job for me and I didn't want her to ask me to leave that small unit downstairs. But she did.

She said she had to rent it out and that she needed the extra money the new tenant would provide. She found me a hostel and she paid three hundred dollars to cover my monthly stay there.

When I met two Armenian guys, I let them to take me to their friend's house in the Hollywood hills. They told me that I could stay there for a while. Their friend was some kind of a designer and he always dressed in black. He was tall, he looked big and I couldn't figure out if he was homosexual or if he wanted to be perceived as one. Bed-wise he was pretty good at leaving me alone and that was good enough for me. He organized a photo-shoot for me. We used his very futuristic wardrobe and the pictures came out not so bad. I met a Japanese photographer through him and she told me that she'd help me in finding the right talent agency. After a while the designer's enthusiasm was fading and he started to give me bad vibes. He was clearly annoyed with my presence.

"Why are you so boring? Can you be less interesting than this?" He would say to me while wandering around the house, without looking at me. I was afraid that he'd ask me to leave. I didn't want that. I was afraid of being gotten rid of once more. I was sick and tired of the rejections. I was sick and tired of people criticizing me, laughing at me and of not respecting me. I told myself to just be quiet so nobody could get offended and upset with me this time.

"Just be like air; invisible but still there. Don't let anybody close to you. Don't trust anybody. Don't say anything about your past, where you've been or what you've done. Just keep it to yourself." I was withdrawing into my small world which was getting smaller and smaller with each moment. The designer kept giving me cold looks, which wasn't helping my already low self-esteem.

"You're dragging my energy down. I'm tired of you. I called those Armenian guys that brought you here and they're going to take you to a motel. I'll pay for one night, after that you're on your own." He gave them fifty bucks and they dropped me at some motel on Sunset Boulevard. The designer kept Mishia. He said he'd keep my cat for me until I'd settle down. I was really scared. I didn't know what the hell I was going to do.

The next day I took my suitcase and I sat down on the curb of the sidewalk in front of the motel. I lit a cigarette. Some cars were stopping in front of me.

"How much?" Some men were asking me. I was showing them my middle finger.

"Fuck off! Cocksuckers!" I was just as angry as I was scared.

"Hey, are you staying in this motel?" A bold man that could be in his forties approached me.

"None of your business." I answered.

"Look, I have a nice house. You can stay with me if you want?" I looked at him when he said that.

"What do you want? What are you looking for?" I didn't trust him.

"Nothing, just some company," he said but I wasn't convinced. I wasn't saying anything to him so he kept talking.

136

"Look, I have a big house and you probably don't have any money to pay for this motel anyway. Am I right? You can stay in my place for free. What's there to think about? I'm a decent person, you know? I like to help sometimes, whether you believe me or not. Besides, I'm single and I live in an empty house. Who in my shoes wouldn't like to have some nice company? When you get a job, you can pay for your room if you want." I wasn't totally convinced about his intentions but I was feeling so desperate that I agreed to let him take me to his house. It was a nice area and the house looked very clean. He showed me all the rooms and he took me to the master bedroom at the end.

"Yeah, nice." I said without passion and I headed for the door.

"Wait, where're you going?" He tried to stop me.

"What do you mean where am I going?" I looked at him in a serious and sad way. I knew I wasn't going to stay at his house and I was feeling very upset. He wasted my time and I wasn't happy with him trying to take advantage of my situation.

"What? I'm a nice guy, you know? I'm clean, I don't have any diseases. So what if we'd have some fun once in a while? Would it be that hard for you? Did you really think that a man, a normal man, can live with you without trying to sleep with you?"

"Take me back to LA. Now!"

"Hey, chill out, alright? What's the big deal?"

"Take me back to LA or you'll regret that you've ever picked me up from Sunset Boulevard!" I said and I must have had crazy look on my face because he walked me to his car. In Hollywood I asked him to drop me at the designer's house and he did. I opened the gate hoping that I could persuade the designer to change his mind about getting rid of me. I told him that I just needed more time until I'd find a job. He didn't want to listen to me.

"It's not my problem. I don't want you here. I told you I can keep your cat for a while, but that's all." He tried not to look me in my eyes. He escorted me to the front door. I sat down in front of the gate and I looked at the view. The emotions I was feeling were up in my throat. I could barely catch my breath. I reached for my purse and I pulled out all the prescription medications that I brought with me from New York. I read the labels on the plastic containers I was holding: *Zoloft, Neuronten* and *Ziprexa*. I had enough pills to kill half the residents of the hillside I was sitting on. The anger was rushing through my veins. I didn't care anymore about my life and I didn't give a shit about the few things that I had in my suitcase. I didn't want my book to be thrown away though. I knocked at the neighbors' door and I asked the nice looking lady if she could hold on to my book.

"No, no, I can't do that. I'm sorry." She shut the door with an astonished look on her face. I took all the pills I had. I swallowed them fast so I wouldn't change my mind.

"God, what do you want me to do? You want me to fuck some asshole so I can have a place to stay? So I can stay alive? What the fuck is your problem God? Do you really want me to believe that I signed up for all this? Maybe it's true; maybe I am making all those choices. Maybe I am making the wrong decisions. But why do I have to do all this subconsciously? Why can't I live a life in an awaken way? Why can't I be a fucking awaken person? What is wrong with me? I can't God. I can't, I can't, I can't, I can't. I won't. I won't live like this. I can't function in this freaking world, so I'm out of here! Take me back. And don't try to throw me out like everybody else does." I don't know how much time had passed when I saw the Japanese photographer driving up the hill.

"Hey, what you're doing sitting here like this? I brought you something. I found a number to a Polish restaurant. It's in LA. You may be able to get a job there or something." She gave me the piece of paper.

"Shit!" I yelled.

"What's wrong?"

"Nothing. I have to use the restroom." I went inside the designer's house and without asking I went straight to the bathroom.

"Now? Now you're giving me some fucking hope?" I was talking to God in my head. I stuck my fingers in my throat but I couldn't make myself vomit. The designer entered the bathroom.

"What's going on?"

"What the fuck you think is going on? I took the fucking pills!" I yelled at him not without feeling hatred towards him. He called 911. I was still awake when the ambulance arrived. The paramedics were asking me questions.

"What's your social security number?"

"I don't have one." I lied. I remembered when I opened my mouth in New York that I had to go through some serious trouble to clear nearly one hundred thousand dollars in medical bills so that wouldn't go on my credit score.

"Is this your address?" They kept asking.

"No, she doesn't live here. She's been staying here before but she doesn't have a place to live." The designer stepped in.

"Where does she normally live?" The paramedics looked like they were having hard time with figuring out the puzzle they were facing.

"She's homeless." He explained to them.

When we arrived at the hospital I lost control of my bowel. I could not move my body and there was nothing I could do to stop the diarrhea. The nurses had horrified looks on their faces and they were verbalizing their disgust while stripping me out of my dirty clothes. I was half conscious and the last thing I remember was suddenly sitting up straight and catching my last breath.

"What's going on?" I heard the panic in one of the nurse's voice.

"She passed out." The doctors' words were the last thing I heard.

Countrymen

I woke up in a hospital bed and there was a total stranger sitting by my bed.

"Who are you?" I asked him with a weak voice. He looked like he'd been crying and I couldn't understand why he was there or who the hell he was.

"You almost died last night, you know that?" He sniffed his nose while looking at me with the most serious look I've ever seen.

"I'm not kidding. You almost didn't make it." He didn't look like he was kidding. He got up and he left. I didn't know what I was supposed to do. I asked a nurse if I could use the phone to call the Polish restaurant.

"How may I help you?" The woman's voice sounded very warm.

"Hi. Do you speak Polish?" I asked.

"Yes of course. Are you Polish?" She answered.

"Tak." I confirmed in my native language. I broke out and I told her where I was and why. She said that she was going to have a talk with her husband and that she would let me know if they could help me somehow. Later the nurse announced to me that I had visitors who wanted to see me. I wasn't sure who would come to see me. When the door opened I saw a pretty, young pregnant woman and a man that looked a little bit older than her. They were both holding flowers in their hands, some books and chocolates.

"Dzien dobry." I heard good morning in my native language and I knew instantly who my visitors were.

"Ela right? This is my wife Wanda and I'm Tomek Cybulski. And this is our baby that's coming soon." The husband rubbed his wife's big belly with pride on his face.

"Here, I brought you some books in Polish. I thought you must be bored here." Wanda gave me the books and the big box of chocolates. I was still speechless and I couldn't even say anything. I watched her placing the flowers on the small table that was next to my bed.

The couple seemed to like me. The husband said that they were going to take me with them and that I was going to stay in an apartment across from their restaurant.

"My younger brother lives there. You'll share the place with him. He works at our restaurant." Wanda explained to me.

"And until you get a job, we can use your help at the restaurant. We don't need anybody right now, but we can't leave a fellow countrywoman in need without doing something about it." The husband talked in a very loud and authoritative way.

"Are you serious? You're not joking?" I wasn't sure if it wasn't too soon to get excited.

"Hell I'm not joking. I'm gonna talk to your doctor and we'll just take you right now with us." He was excited for me. The doctor didn't like his idea though.

"I know that she's been here for three days now but I don't feel comfortable with releasing her yet." He said to Tomek.

"Look, we're her family and we're taking her with us!" Tomek Cybulski looked so comical with his hand gestures he was making to sound even more determined.

The apartment was very small. Jacek, Wanda's brother, was occupying the bedroom and I had the living room that had a small kitchen in it. It was a very loud place to live in. A gas station was right next to the apartment and the nearby intersection was generating all kinds of noise. The neighbors liked to listen to loud music and were adding their contribution to this chaotic environment. Next door, two angry pit-bulls were barking viciously at anything that moved.

"Shut up! Shut the fuck up! Keep your fucking dogs inside the house or something!" Every morning I had to open the window in Jacek's room to stop the continuous barking. These were not just some dogs that were making occasional noise from boredom. These two mean looking pit-bulls were charging with all their power and jumping against the metal fence every time somebody passed by on the side walk. Their barking resembled the noise from hell. My yelling wasn't intimidating them at all so eventually I started to throw anything I had in my hands straight at them.

"Shut the fuck up!"

"Alright, cool off." I heard man's voice coming from inside the house.

"Get your fucking dogs in order or I'll call Animal Control!" I was so tired from working at the restaurant that I just wanted to be able to get some sleep. If the dogs quieted down for a moment, the music coming from the apartment below would start shaking my floor.

"Hi. How are you? Could you please lower the music a little bit? It's 10:00 p.m." The first time I asked my neighbors to lower the volume they ignored me completely. The second time I went downstairs they were giving me bad looks like I was this annoying white chick who didn't understand what having fun meant. One night, around midnight I picked up the phone and I called the cops. After that my walls weren't shaking as much anymore.

I was missing my cat Mishia a lot. Tomek told me that I could live in that apartment, while splitting the rent with Jacek of course, but only if I'd get rid of my furry friend. I tried to convince him that Mishia wasn't just any cat but he was very firm about it.

"So what's it gonna be; the apartment or the cat?" Cybulski didn't look very friendly when he wasn't getting what he wanted.

"I have to do this, I really have no choice. I have to be responsible for once. I have to let go of Mishia and I have to start taking better care of myself. I cannot end up on the sidewalk once again. I cannot take any pills anymore." I was talking to myself in attempt to convince myself that my landlord was right. I gave Mishia to him and he promised that the little girl he gave my cat to was very happy when she saw her new pet. The second condition of my "rental agreement" was that I could not smoke cigarettes anymore, not in the apartment nor anywhere else. Of course at work I wasn't smoking but at the end of the day, around 10:00 p.m. I'd sneak behind the apartment building to have at least one cigarette.

The job wasn't hard but it was boring. I didn't have to take the orders from the customers. Wanda and Tomek were doing that. I had to make sure that the tables were clean, that the customers had their water and I had to bring their meals to them. In the afternoons when the restaurant wasn't as busy, Wanda and I would sit at our designated table and we'd chat a lot. She was a good listener. She seemed interested to know everything about my family. She shared her upbringing in Poland with me too.

She told me that her brother Jacek liked me a lot and she tried to convince me to go out with him on a date. Both she and her husband were very disappointed when I said that I couldn't do that. Jacek was very optimistic and he wasn't hiding the fact that he wasn't giving up on me yet. He was a very nice guy; tall and not bad looking but most importantly he had a really big heart. He was a really good roommate. The best one I ever had to live with, that's for sure. Jacek was very considerate and funny too. His sister and his brother-in-law brought him to United States so he could work in their restaurant as a chef. He was a real hard worker. Two women from Mexico were hired to help him make all those pierogis. God, those tasted really good! But no matter how good they were, I couldn't eat them every day and since Polish cuisine is based a lot on meat, I stopped being vegetarian. I never had much money to be picky about the food I was eating and the meals at the restaurant were free for the workers. After paying half of the rent, half of the phone bill and a monthly payment I was making to Tomek for the car he helped me get, I was left with virtually no money for anything else.

Swinging

The white Chrysler convertible I got was an old car and it had constant problems with the transmission. Nevertheless it was my first car ever. I had to go to the DMV to get my California driver's license so I could be independent and go anywhere I wanted to. Not that there was much time or money for gas and insurance to go anywhere, but still. On Mondays and Tuesdays which were our days off due to the restaurant being closed, I'd go to Hannah's house to make some extra cash by cleaning. Listening to the radio while driving my car through Hollywood was my way of relaxing. I'd always have the top down. I loved to drive my car and even though it was shaking while I was pressing on brakes, I still enjoyed the sense of freedom it was giving me.

I had to park my car on the street and so bird poop practically became part of the hood. I fought for a parking spot with the manager of the building. She had two cars and because nobody else from my unit had a car before, she felt entitled to an extra space. It took me one year to get my parking space but I eventually got it. After six month of working at the Polish restaurant for forty bucks a day I decided to do something else. I went to an agency that specialized in finding jobs for extras in movies. I told Wanda and Tomek about it.

"I mean, I don't care. As long as you pay your rent on time and you bring your car payment on the first, you can do whatever you want." Tomek had doubts if my new career choice could generate a steady income. I was so happy that I didn't have to work at the restaurant anymore. My new job was providing me with pretty much the same amount of money I was making while bussing tables. With this job at least I got to drive my car to different locations each time.

"Extras! On your vouchers write down; lunch from 12:00 to 12:30 p.m. Do not approach the tables until the crew eats first! Got it? If I see any of you trying to sneak, I'll ask you to take your stuff and you will immediately have to leave the set. Am I clear enough?" The production assistants were shouting at us as if we were bunch of cattle that didn't have brains. Every extra wanted to get into the union as that would mean double the money an extra could make. To be part of the union you had to have at least three union vouchers. To get those you had to have spoken lines in a movie or you had to know somebody who could put your name on a union voucher instead of a simple one. "Regular" extras were always envying union extras and my feelings weren't that much different. The additional money for overtime that we had to do, was compensating for the times when there were days without work. In those days I'd drive my car all the way to Santa Monica or to Venice Beach.

Fiona, who I met in one of the movie studios, would come with me sometimes. She was almost forty years old but she looked like she was thirty. Her mother was from Mexico but she wasn't alive anymore. She has passed away when Fiona was still very young. Fiona's father wasn't her biological father and her half sister wasn't really her sister. My new best friend was a divorcee and she had a teenage son, but he wasn't living with her. She appeared just as lonely as I was. I liked Fiona mostly for how kind she was to everybody. We went out clubbing sometimes and so when she asked me if I'd go with her to a swinger's party, I said; "Sure, why not?"

I had never been to a sex-party before but I wasn't feeling uncomfortable there. It was a little bit shocking to watch some people walking around naked and others having group sex, I admit. However nobody was forcing anybody to take off their clothes or to do anything if somebody didn't feel like doing it. The atmosphere was very relaxing indeed and people were showing full respect to each other.

The wives were usually in charge of picking up the partners for this erotic adventure. Different women were approaching me constantly, asking me if I'd join the love set that those married couples found in one of the many rooms the place had. Each room was decorated in a different style. Some resembled exotic places, some looked like a doctor's office and some had black leather equipment that was supposed to bring pleasure through fetish fantasies. The wives looked very disappointed when I was turning them down, but not as much as their husbands who were staring at me from a distance. The place served free alcohol that was included with the annual membership the couples had to purchase in order to attend these fun events.

"Is she on ecstasy?" As usual, people were asking my friend while watching me dancing with my eyes closed. I never tried to explain to anybody that the sound of music and sparkling water were all that were responsible for the release of endorphins in my brain. Nobody would believe me anyway. People could not comprehend how I could move so freely, where I was getting my energy from and how I could have such a blissful look on my face without even drinking alcohol. How could I have seemed to have forgotten the world around me without some chemical enhancers? They looked at me as if I was from some different world and that much harder the wives were trying to convince me in joining them. I respectfully kept saying; "No thank you though" to them.

That is until one day, during a New Year's Eve party, I let go of my guard a little bit. The people I was having fun with were young and very attractive. The wife wasn't participating as she was busy in some more private room with somebody else. The husband was a really, really, I mean really, good looking man. He could have been thirty years old at the most. He was very tall and his body had just an absolutely perfect shape. His dark hair was bringing out his incredibly intense blue eyes. His two day beard was accentuating his perfectly formed square jaws. God, how hot he was, but the voice; he sounded even sexier that he looked! With his low pitch, he was choosing carefully each word he was whispering slowly into my ear. I was trembling without control. I didn't care that people were watching us while he was caressing my body. He had to literally wipe off my tears that were caused by the ecstasy I was feeling from being this intimate with him. He was so good at controlling both of us.

"Shhhhh…." He was whispering into my ear after noticing that I started to feel as if I was about to explode any moment now.

"Shhhhh…No need to rush. Enjoy every second of this." He was so good at pulling my hair back. He knew exactly how hard to pull on it without making me feel uncomfortable. He was paying attention to me the way no man had paid attention to my body before. He was reading me like an open book and I was so happy that he knew my body language so well. I was moaning and I was making noises that I've never heard before. My breath was in perfect synchronicity with his breath. His full lips seemed as if they had magnet in them. His strong hands knew exactly how to hold my shaking face. His two friends; a guy and a girl who were observing us among other people, approached the big sofa-like bed we were on. I saw "my" guy giving them permission with his look on his face. He looked at me to make sure I wouldn't get scared. I was feeling so safe with him and that was very obvious to him. The other guy started to caress me very slowly as to make sure that I was comfortable with it. The girl was doing the same to me and I pulled back at first. I've never kissed a girl before even though many times they were hitting on me.

This girl was young, attractive enough, and I liked the tattoos she had on her body. She was staring at me as if I was her biggest crush ever. She knew exactly when to touch me and how to touch me. She was making me feel like I was a Goddess that she was worshipping. She was sweet and yet very determined to know each inch of my body. I was shivering constantly. The three of them made me the center of their attention. Everything; every move, every gesture and every word was directed to please me.

"I've never seen anybody like her. She's something else." I was hearing admiration in "my" guy friend's voice.

"She looks like and feels like she doesn't even belong to this world, doesn't she?" The girl was expressing her opinion to her friends while touching my legs. I liked everything that was going on but I was mainly concentrated on my Pierce Brosnan look alike. I was at the point when I was ready to have intercourse with him. I've never done such thing in front of other people but that wasn't relevant at the moment. My thong was so wet by now that it wasn't even funny. I was actually beginning to experience physical pain from the desire that was growing inside of me. My vagina was contracting in such ways that I thought I was going to die if he didn't fill it with his manly part. His body seemed million of miles away as long as he wasn't completely inside of me. I wanted his entire body inside of me, his soul, his mind and everything that was part of him. I didn't want to be separated from him by even a particle. The trembling he was causing to my body was more powerful and felt more ecstatic than the time when I took the ecstasy pill. Everything seemed so magical. I've never been as fully present in the moment as I was when he was touching my face while looking me in my eyes. I knew I could be intense sometimes when it came to sex but this was yet a different level of sexual experience that I've ever pictured in my mind. This was mind-blowing. I lost control and I was begging him to take me. He kept torturing me while showing that he was in charge and that he decided everything. Oh God, kill me now! I was happy and miserable at the same time. I could tell though, that he was struggling with remaining in control as well.

"Oh God!" His eyes were starting to look different and his breath was getting heavier and heavier. He looked almost mad.

"I can't." He said as if it was the hardest thing he had ever said to anybody.

"I can't. My wife and I...we have an agreement....that we wouldn't go all the way. Pheeew....I didn't think it would be...phweeew...so hard to stop. I'm sorry."

"Are you kidding me?" I lifted my head all the way back.

"Oh God! This is so unfair." He was rubbing his face like it was on fire or something.

"I'm really sorry. I should have told you that from the beginning. I honestly didn't think you'd get so excited. I've seen you here few times and I've never noticed you being with anybody. I thought you wouldn't like it. I thought you'd stop me before we would have the chance to get this intense. You know want I mean?" He was apologizing to me with a tender look on his face. He looked like he was contemplating breaking the verbal agreement he had with his wife. He looked around to see if she was anywhere near.

"I can't." He said in an almost angry tone. I was angry at him. I found Fiona and I told her that I wanted to go back home.

The Other Artist

I found some talent agency that was willing to represent me as a model/actress. The office was in Hollywood and the owner looked like a sharp businesswoman. I had some pictures that weren't that bad which she made me use for my headshots. The first thing she wanted to do though was to introduce me to some influential people. She arranged for a dinner in a Japanese restaurant.

"Don't worry; it's not going to be a waste of time. If you want I can pay you for your time. What do you make on those movie sets? I'll give you a check for fifty dollars." She said to me and I accepted her offer. The dinner didn't go well. The man who must have been in his late fifties looked disappointed and the owner of the talent agency was giving him an apologetic look the whole time. A few days later when I tried to cash that check she gave me, the banker told me that whoever gave it to me has stopped the payment on it. I was able to cash the check after I sent an official letter to the owner of the agency in which I informed her that I was going to report her. She believed my threat I guess because she called me and explained to me that she never stopped the payment on it but that simply the account was overdrawn. She was trying to make me feel stupid as if I couldn't tell the difference between bounced checked and the one with stopped payment.

My career in acting/modeling obviously wasn't going anywhere. A few other modeling agencies I decided to visit didn't hesitate to inform me that my days as a model were behind me for good. I began to feel desperate. My car was breaking down frequently and I ran out of all the free triple A assistance. The new used transmission cost me fifteen hundred dollars and that was three hundred dollars more than what I paid for that car in the first place. My sister Bozena rescued me by sending me some money from Greece. After the transmission some other parts were

149

demanding to be looked at. I could not put up with it any longer and I sold the car for three hundred dollars. I couldn't go to movie sets without a car so I decided to get a job somewhere near. Downtown was only few exits from the freeway and so when I heard that there were many Gentlemen's Clubs in that part of LA, I went there and I found a job.

The place that hired me was similar to the night clubs in Italy except that this one was a really low class. With the money I was making from talking to and dancing with customers I was able to rent a small car.

When Wanda told me that one of customers from her restaurant had a modeling job for me, I took his phone number and I gave him a call. Andy was an almost fifty year old artist who had emigrated from Russia and was now living only few blocks away from my noisy apartment. He had a two story house that had a real nice view since it was standing on a hillside. The house looked very empty, almost unfurnished. The small Australian shepherd that was Andy's only companion liked me immediately. The dog looked just as unattractive as the owner did but there was something intriguing about both of them. Warmth, care and loyalty were emanating from these two and it had a very magnetic effect on me. The small but sunny room that Andy used as his studio was downstairs. In this creative work place Bob Marley's songs were filling out the air with love and joy. From some finished and some unfinished paintings that were lying around I could tell that this man had real talent. I was surprised though to see how a full time artist could afford to live in such a big house. Andy explained that he had one rich customer from Beverly Hills and that his orders were pretty much the Russian artist's entire revenue.

Andy was more interested in getting to know me than in my posing for him but I didn't mind that. I enjoyed his company and the one hundred and fifty dollars that he was paying me a day for few hours of sitting still wasn't bad either. The portrait of my face that he painted, he ended up giving to me for my birthday. He gave me some extra money too so I could throw myself a party. It was my twenty-fifth birthday and it was the first time ever that I celebrated the occasion.

The colorful balloons and flowers made my small apartment look a lot cozier and for a moment I was able to forget the sad life I was living. Surprisingly the people that I invited showed up and even more surprisingly everybody appeared to have a good time. For a small fee Wanda provided me with catering from the Polish restaurant. The guests cleared out the dishes filled with Polish Cuisine very quickly. Fiona, Andy, my roommate Jacek and even Hannah from Hollywood were among other guests. Wanda and Tomek brought their daughter Natalie with them. I had even invited one of my customers from the night club in Downtown LA. I was very surprised and pleased to see how everybody was getting along! I was feeling quite overwhelmed. What a feeling it was to see the guests showing up all dressed up nicely to show their respect! And when I was receiving the gifts, no matter what they were, I was enjoying the thought of being on somebody's mind even if just for a moment. I was feeling very grateful towards Andy for sponsoring this small event that had nothing small in the sense of meaning that it had for me.

Andy and I became very close friends and we started to spend a lot of time together even thought I wasn't posing for him anymore. He was giving me some money and when I asked him if he could pay for my front teeth to be corrected, he agreed. After four thousand dollars spent at a dentist's office my smile wasn't crooked anymore. I had to force myself not to direct the corners of my lips downwards anymore. It was hard at first but eventually I learned to smile without any psychologically imposed restrains. What a relief that was; being able to smile without wondering if others would notice my imperfect teeth! For a while I was constantly staring in any mirror I saw. I was smiling at my own reflection but I was still able to see the tracks of sadness on my face and particularly in my eyes.

Satisfaction

Andy was against my new idea of having my nose shaped by a plastic surgeon. He said that he would support me with my decision of getting my breasts augmented and he did later on keep his promise by paying for the procedure and by taking care of me while I was recovering from this painful embellishment that was done to my body.

"Your nose looks just fine. You have a perfect nose. I don't see any need to spend so much money for something so unnecessary." He was arguing with me and I wasn't happy with how stubborn he was. I was convinced that he could never understand what it was like for me to hate the way I saw myself. Andy didn't like to have confrontations with me and so he tried to withdraw himself for the time that he believed was needed for me to get over this absurd idea. He wasn't calling me and I wasn't visiting him either.

I thought I would make the four thousand dollars needed for my rhinoplasty at the night club downtown. I wasn't surprised to see that my old customers moved on to girls who were offering more than chatting and dancing. I was sitting silently near the bar most of the time and I could tell that the owner of the club was keeping an eye on me. It was only a matter of time before I got fired and I knew that very well.

"I am ready to offer you fifteen hundred dollars if you'll sleep with me." An Asian customer who used to be one of my regulars was talking to me while looking me straight in my eyes. I heard him making the same offer to me many times before but I never took him seriously. This time I looked at him in a different way. I was being patient and I let him talk. My half-closed eyes were betraying that I was actually giving some thoughts to his offer this time. The man started to express child-like enthusiasm.

"What the heck? I was thinking in my head. *I've slept with jerks before and I've got nothing in return but the sense of humiliation and the awful sense of being taken advantage of, or I should say, of being simply fucked. This guy seems a lot more respectful than those assholes I've slept with. In this business-like proposition he considers not only his own needs but mine as well. He is not trying to control me the way men have always tried to do. He is straightforward and I like that. He does not make me feel like I'm stupid."*

"Money up front." I finally said to him and he almost jumped.

"You mean...?" His pupils were as wide as they could get.

"Yes. Money up front." I repeated firmly.

"Oh God, yes, of course!" He was probably in his late forties, maybe early fifties, but he looked and acted more like a teenager right now.

While driving to a hotel with my customer I was still wondering if I could do such thing. I couldn't help but to worry that I would hate myself afterwards. The man was sensing my hesitation because he was trying to be very sweet and very attentive as to make sure that I wouldn't change my mind at the last moment. I was very serious the whole time but when we were in the room and we started having sex, I realized that the whole situation was turning me on more than I could have expected. The resulting response of my body was having euphoric effect on my customer.

"Oh God, I knew there was something different about you! This is not sex, this is like making love!" He was looking like a teenager again. I was surprised and pleased to see how much respect he was having for me the whole time. I was sure that I would feel stupid and guilty afterwards and instead I was feeling good! I was actually feeling empowered! All those times I had to ask my boyfriends to buy me something. All that time I was being nice and submissive to them so they would let me stay at their place. And those men made me feel like they were taking me for granted and like I owed them something in return for their "care". And here I was, in this hotel, doing something completely condemned by the society and yet the feeling of being in charge that I was experiencing had a very sweet taste.

I was surprised by all this and I agreed to meet again sometime in the future. My customer was so happy that he mentioned his experience with me to another customer at the club. I turned the man down thinking that the main reason my first time turned out to be less than disappointing was because I got to know my customer while chatting with him during the time I worked at the club. The new client was being very persistent. When he offered me two thousand dollars, I agreed to follow him to his house. The sex wasn't as nearly as pleasant as it was with my Asian friend, mostly because this old rich man was trying to be too controlling. His attitude of "I've got money and I can buy whatever and whomever I wish" was getting on my nerves. Still, while driving back home with my two grand I was feeling the familiar sensation of empowerment and of being in control after all. I met one more time with another client, who was more interested in having company in his nice home, even if just for a day, than anything else. Strangely enough I wasn't regretting any of my "outrageous" decisions. I looked at all this as an experience that taught me a lot about myself. I was actually glad that I did what I did.

Man of My Dreams

I was happy to be able to schedule my appointment with the plastic surgeon. Unfortunately, the long-awaited surgery turned out to be a disastrous experience. Short four thousand dollars, I was left with a nose that felt numb and hard and even bigger in size. The doctor discarded his responsibility by telling me that it would take up to a year for it to heal and that it would eventually "sink" into a proper shape. Well that never happened and by looking at my nose I didn't have to wait that long to see that he simply did a horrible job. I was infuriated but I didn't think that suing him would do anything good. I decided that I would wait a year and that I would find a better doctor next time.

Andy got over the silent treatment he was punishing me with, after he realized that nothing would stop me from getting what I wanted anyway. He offered to pay for my breast implants and he took me to a doctor who had placed an ad in some Russian paper. My new breasts were hurting like hell for a week but it was all worth it. Even though I never had sex with Andy before, I allowed him to massage my perky breasts the way doctor has recommended. Maybe because I was still on pain killers, maybe because he was being so thoughtful and so into me, or maybe because I was feeling so grateful to him for everything that he had done for me, I allowed for the intimacy to take place. I didn't enjoy it but seeing him so happy was somewhat making me feel better. When I told Wanda what happened, she immediately tried to convince me that I should marry this man.

"So he's not one of the most attractive men that are out there, oh well. He's obviously in love with you and he's treating you like a princess. Just think about how much easier your life would be? You'd be an US citizen once and for all." It was hard to argue with her realistic point of view.

"Ela, you're not getting any younger. You should marry Andy and you should have a baby with him. He'd be a good father, I can tell. A woman your age can't be as picky as you are." Wanda's husband Tomek never changed with his straightforwardness. Tomek had a big heart but his nosy and sometimes controlling attitude was getting on my nerves. I liked him but at the same time I wished that I could tell him just to mind his own business. I couldn't make myself say anything because I felt obligated to him.

After all he and his wife did for me, he didn't hesitate to buy yet another car for me, for which Andy was making payments on. The old Buick didn't look nice but it ran well. The couple was always there for me and I didn't want to jeopardize our friendship with my big mouth. For a while, I made everybody believe that I would marry Andy eventually but I knew that this wasn't going to happen.

I still believed that my prince on a white horse was somewhere out there, waiting for me, perhaps to mature a little bit. Like many women I wanted my wedding to be once in a lifetime experience. The idea of walking down the aisle in my beautiful white dress and not feeling my heart beating hard while pronouncing "I do" wasn't very appealing to me. I may have been realistic sometimes but the helpless romantic in me wouldn't allow me to ease my life by marrying somebody for convenience. Not that I thought that there would be anything wrong with that. After all I promised myself that I wouldn't be judgmental about anything. I just honestly still believed that the one and the only one was out there somewhere, wondering who I was and trying to foresee when and how he'd get to meet me. I had the exact image in my mind of the man that I would end up marrying, ever since I started developing crushes on boys. I knew that all my life experiences including my sexual encounters were supposed to shape me into the kind of woman that such man would fall madly in love with. Deep inside I wasn't feeling ready for him and I thought that it was good that I haven't met him yet. I still looked, talked and acted like a girl and the man of my dreams was into women only.

He was a real man and only a real woman could make his heart beat faster. He was the kind of man that had to achieve everything in his life on his own. The only area of his life that he was spoiled with was sex. Women have been drawn to him the way moths are drawn to light at night. He may have even used them but not without being completely honest about his intentions. He's a bad boy but a good man at the same time. He's been through a lot in his life and he had to fight to stay alive more than once. He's an excellent martial artist but he's very modest about his skills and he'd never start a fight unless he'd have to protect somebody. He doesn't like to talk much and he likes to remain mysterious but when he says something it's always something either very profound or something very funny. He is handsome of course and his tall and muscular body is to die for. The scars that reveal his troubled past make him look that much more dangerous and that much more attractive. When he loves somebody, he's not afraid to die for that person. He never pretends to be somebody else, not for his woman or anybody else. He doesn't give a shit what anybody may think of him. In fact, he may have had to spend some time in prison, for whatever crime, guilty or not, and he has carried on with his life. He minds his own business and you would never hear him speaking badly of somebody else. If he has something to say; he'll say it straight to your face. He stays away from any kind of drama, he's not attracted to it. He doesn't try to impress anybody with the money he has made and yet he knows how to enjoy it well. He likes to help the less fortunate and he does it completely anonymously. He loves animals and by the way his horses look at him, you can tell that the love is mutual. He moves in his dirty jeans and his white shirt like he was born in it. He is passionate but he knows how to control his temper. He gives and he never expects anything in return. He does something for somebody and he immediately forgets his charitable act. He's brave beyond limits, but in a smart way. In a dangerous situation, in which he somehow, perhaps due to his dark past, is an expert in, he calculates each deadly move, if necessary. His teeth are as white as the shirt he likes to wear and when he smiles, no woman could ever resist him. His skin, continually exposed to sun, and his dark hair look perfectly harmonized with his tattoos that he got perhaps when he was "away". He definitely knows something about life, he has seen a lot and he's not one of those who'd cry to God for not being fair with him. You'd never see him think or act like a victim even though in his thirty something years on this planet, more than once he was faced with little choice. Nothing ever stopped him from making the best out of what he was presented with. He never got married and he doesn't have any children even though lots of beautiful and smart woman would love to tie the knot with him. He takes the marriage thing as seriously as I do. He'd rather be single for the rest of his life than to be with somebody who doesn't mean the world to him. He's waiting for me...

School

"I need your prove of residence and some bills to show that you've lived in California for more than a year." The woman at the admission office was helping me to fill out my papers for the community college I decided to attend.

"What are you going to major in?" She asked me.

"I'm not sure, maybe psychology." I honestly didn't know what I was interested in most.

It was fun to be back in school even though it was very hard at first, considering that English wasn't my native language. My illiteracy and lack of skills with a computer was costing me a lot. The teachers were slamming on me with their habits of lowering my grades for things like presenting my homework in an old-fashioned, hand-written manner. I had no choice but to get a used laptop and a printer.

It took me a while to figure out the basic things, how to operate my new tools. In my public speaking class I made a few friends with some classmates. The class seemed to like my performances. With my heavy accent and frankness I made them laugh and of course who wouldn't like that. With my hair one day pink, one day black and my new boobs sticking out I was quite a sight to them.

One day towards the end of semester I presented a poem I wrote myself. It was the first time nobody dared to move for a while. They were looking at me as if they just discovered that inside this comical girl there was a profound deepness marked with even a more profound sadness caused by immense suffering. They looked at me as if they were afraid to disturb the silence that followed my performance. In their eyes they had looks as if they were trying to pierce my mind in attempt to find out more about what was going on inside me for real.

"Wow! I don't think anybody expected this." The teacher finally broke the silence and now everybody was following him with applause. Everybody seemed to be eager to comment on what they saw and what they heard. I stood there in front of the class, almost as shocked as everybody else while processing the students' remarks. It was almost ecstatic to feel how touched they were and how so many of them could relate to my topic. My own feelings of inadequacy that I was describing in the poem were very well understood by the majority of them.

"I know that you were talking about your own experience but to me it was more like you were talking straight to me about me, like you knew me very well or something." Even students who were usually less involved were expressing their opinion out loud.

"The expressions you had on your face the whole time, your intonation and that piercing look in your eyes gave me goose bumps on my skin." It felt so good listening to them saying all those nice things to me.

At the end of the semester I took home a B for Psychology, C for Political Science and the Speech classes, D for English 101 and F for Shakespeare course. I was disappointed mostly with the Psychology and the Speech classes. I knew that if I'd followed the instructions from the beginning I could have earn the highest grades for those two courses. Reading Shakespeare was like reading Chinese to me and I wasn't even trying to understand it so I didn't even show up at the finals.

After two years of living there I was starting to feel sick and tired of LA. I couldn't see anything good in there for me. A Russian movie director did become interested in a screen play that I wrote based on my life and he wanted to attempt to make a low budget movie with it but I didn't see it happening for real. As for my acting career, besides working as an extra, my only debut was my appearance in the Blind Date TV show. I've never even watched myself on TV having an awful time with that guy but some people I knew saw me and they were telling me how sorry they were that the producers decided to match me with such a jerk. I don't even remember if he was a jerk to me or not, I was wasted on few glasses of red wine we had for dinner. All I remember was that he had blond hair and I specifically asked them for a guy with dark hair. No matter how ridiculous those kinds of reality shows may be, I still wanted to at least leave a space for the possibility of meeting my soul mate. You never know, right?

With Andy giving me a cold shoulder since I wasn't giving him any answers as far as the direction of our relationship, I ended up meeting with my old Asian customer a few more times. I didn't like having sex for money this time anymore though and I had to end it. The first time it was more like an adventure, an experiment or something, but doing it actually for living was too much for me. That's when I decided that I was going to move to the desert. I just needed to figure out which one, South or North from LA?

Elevated

Fiona and I drove my old Buick all the way to Palm Springs. The desert was absolutely breathtaking. I loved observing the colors of this dry land, with warm orange and yellow textures. Numerous tall palm trees were creating the sensation of oasis in the middle of this empty nowhere.

"What are you going to do here girl? You're crazy." Fiona didn't like my idea of relocating.

"Hey, you'll be coming to visit me, right? I promise I'll let you play poker with my retired neighbors." I laughed and she laughed with me.

"But honestly I don't see myself living here." I said.

"Good. I was beginning to worry; I've seen how unpredictable and how stubborn you can be." She looked relieved.

"But I do see myself living north from LA, in the Mojave Desert area." With a single sentence I killed her hopes again.

"Where? In Palmdale? Are you going to live among those red-necks? You are crazy." She was staring at me with that funny, snobby look on her face and I couldn't control my giggling any longer.

"Look, it's only an hour from LA so you'll be able to visit me there often. I'll come to visit you at least once a month too, you know. I like it there. I'm not sure what it is but I feel like I'm being drowned there by some invisible force. Besides, I've seen that they have horses up there and I'm planning on getting a job on one of those ranches." I told her even though I wasn't being entirely honest with her. The complete truth was that I was hoping not to only settle down in the desert, but I was also hoping that I would end up meeting that dream man of mine there and that I would settle down for good this time.

I was twenty-six years old and even though in my opinion I wasn't a "real" woman yet, I was getting sick and tired of being only an auntie or a godmother to other children. I began to wonder what it would be like to have my own little Ela sitting on my lap for a change, as opposed to watching everybody else's kids growing big. I've always loved children and they've always loved how silly I was letting myself be with them but this time they were almost getting on my nerves. It was probably because I could not predict when I would have my own child and that uncertainty wasn't making me feel good.

Agua Dulce was in the geographical area that was considered high desert. This small town was about sixty miles away from Los Angeles and it was on the way to Palmdale and Lancaster. Farther north, following freeway 14, there was a small town called Rosamond with a military base. Only few miles from there, you'd find yourself in the Mojave Desert. Panoramically speaking this part of world was simply breathtaking. You'd see different view every mile. You'd see mountains covered with short bushes, so typical for Southern California, and then it would seem to you as if those beautiful hills were stripping in front of you. You'd see less and less vegetation until you'd see what Mother Nature looked like completely naked. One moment you'd see Mother Earth wearing orange, almost golden in color and then you'd see a practically red spread of land disappearing in distant horizon. Occasionally you'd notice different rocks in different shapes that were adding a magical tone to this already incredibly spiritual passage. Joshua Trees were spreading for miles sometimes, forming unique, cactus-based forest.

While driving through the Desert I was more calmed and more in tune with my own feelings that I could ever be in the big city. The new surroundings were giving me sense of belonging, almost as if I had returned home after a very long journey. I could see myself having a horse ranch one day here. I could even see myself finally getting married and raising a family. I was trying to imagine if my parents and my siblings would like it here, despite the threat of encountering poisonous rattlesnakes. I was wondering if they'd love living here with me one day.

Agua Dulce was a great place to live in but it was very expensive as well. Being only approximately an hour away from Hollywood, it was a place where many "movie" people and other rich families liked to call their home. Each neighbor owned at least few acres of land that was usually separated with a white wooden fence. Horses wandering within the imposed limits were the most noticeable characteristic of this small town. There was one gas station, one liquor store, one restaurant, one real estate office and a market place that was the latest addition to this Old Western looking corner of the world. Let's not forget a small but very well maintained airport that was not only convenient but that was also pride of the community.

Aah the airport. How much I wanted to learn how to fly! To earn a private pilot license you had to have forty hours of flying and then you had to take a written and practical exam. One hour of floating between clouds with an instructor cost one hundred dollars. Before I moved to Agua Dulce, while still living in LA, I brought Fiona once to this place. I paid the one hundred dollars and the two of us were told to wait for the instructor to come. He was flying all the way in from the Venice airport. In the meantime, since there was nothing else for us to do, we played pool even though neither of us had any prior experience in poking colorful balls on a green table. We were still enjoying it, giggling the whole time, when a cowboy pointed out the window.

"Your instructor's here," he said. We couldn't hide our excitement. I was about to sit in front on a small airplane! There was one tiny problem though. The instructor turned out to be not even close to what we were expecting. Instead of a middle-aged, perhaps with only a little hair left and excess fat around belly, the aviation office matched me with a young and very good looking pilot.

"Oh no Fiona, look! This is not fair. I came here to learn how to fly and how am I supposed to do that while sitting right next to this James Bond? How am I supposed to concentrate?" I was being honest but she was laughing hard.

"I'm glad my dilemma can be so entertaining to you." I said to her and I tried very hard not to burst into laughter myself. In the air Fiona freaked out when "James Bond" who was wearing a black leather jacket and dark sun glasses, announced to me that he was ready for me to take over.

"What? You gonna let her fly all by herself? You're kidding, right?" She looked very sexy in those big ear pieces but the horrified expression on her face was making me laugh this time.

"Don't worry; I'm here with you guys. It's not that much different from learning how to drive a car." The instructor was smiling while explaining to Fiona how safe we were.

"Yeah, but have you seen her driving a car? She's a maniac! She drives like she owns the road. Ask her how many times she had to go to traffic school for speeding tickets." Fiona's panicky reaction was now entertaining us. She calmed down eventually after she noticed how much into navigating I was. I felt as if this small airplane that was carrying us above the mountains was not just some pieces of metal welded together, but that it was an extension of me. It was part of me and just like all of us it had a soul. Its white wings were now my white wings. Its loud engine was now my source of power. Its free spirit was now in perfect union with my free spirit. Oh what a sense of freedom and a sense of elevation I was experiencing!

Fiona was very happy when the sexy looking instructor finally took back control of the plane and when we landed on the runway without any turbulence. She was flirting with the pilot while I was saying a silent goodbye to my white mechanical bird. I flew one more time after this, but I asked for a different instructor this time. The woman in the aviation office had a strange look on her face when I answered her question as to why I wasn't happy with the one they gave me. But I was being serious. I was very interested in learning how to fly and I didn't want any distraction that could potentially hold me back from reaching one of my dreams.

The Ranch

The job with horses that I initially got didn't turned out to be a good solution for me. The owner of the ranch I was living on, an elderly cowboy, made me feel like I was a piece of his property. I didn't mind playing cards with him but what I did mind was the illusion that he created first in his mind and then in the community that I was his girlfriend. I left and I got a new job on a different and much bigger ranch. The old cowboy was very upset with my decision and he attempted to stop me by trying to convince me that I could own all his land and water business he had, if I agreed to be his lady.

"By turning my offer down, you're giving up on your dream of owning a ranch. Whatever suits you, but you'll never have what you could have here." He was getting on my nerves with comments like this for some time and I couldn't take it anymore.

I was very happy and relieved when I was hired at Johnson Ranch. The ranch was spread on three hundred acres and you had to drive for more than a mile on a dirt road to get there. The dust that was generated by vehicle wheels temporarily but completely obscured the view behind. There were more than one hundred horses of different breeds for sale and few pet donkeys and lamas. The big, two-story main house was always empty, as the owners were living in the big city. The main barn had an arena inside, where two young girls were exercising the animals that were waiting to be sold to good homes. All the other buildings, including a guest house, were serving more as storage than anything else. A few trailers that were occupied by families of immigrant workers from Mexico were all the way in the back of the property.

The Latino boys were busting their butts all day feeding the horses, then cleaning the stalls, then feeding the horses again. Despite the harsh conditions they were working in, they still had the energy to be nice to me. Once they understood that I could communicate in their language the chatting would never stop. The Mexicans were very nice to me, but one in particular, Jose, was really helpful in giving me tips on how to scoop dirt with the least amount of energy and still with best results.

The owner, Larry, hired me first as help to those "feeding" boys and for the first four weeks he paid me "under the table" the same amount they were making, which wasn't much. I was living at the barn, inside a small unit that besides a small kitchen, tiny bedroom and small bathroom also had cockroaches and even maggots. The disgusting white crawling creatures were falling down from a ceiling composed of long wooden boards which had extra spaces in between. They were landing on my bed and I was afraid to go to bed at night. The underlying cause for all this was mess and neglect that this otherwise splendid ranch was subjected to. Pigeons and their poop were everywhere. I found their nest right above my living quarters. The dead birds were incubating the creatures that were falling from the ceiling.

The first thing I did was to clean and disinfect all the living spaces including Larry's office, bathrooms and the room that was used as a dining area by the two teenage girls that were working in the arena. After that I asked for some supplies to build a net around those buildings to prevent the birds from accessing this area. Larry was very skeptical about my whole project but because he was so enchanted by me, he let me do whatever I said that was needed to be done. Jose helped me with cleaning and getting rid of all those dead birds. The dust that we generated by moving all the things that were up there, obscured our working area. At the end of the day, our faces were as dark as the night that was upon us.

"Gracias Jose. I can't even imagine how I could have done all this without you." I was shaking Jose's hand and all I could see was his eyeballs and his teeth. I couldn't help but to burst in laughter.

"You look like a devil, you know that?" I was teasing him always in Spanish because he didn't know any English.

"Oh yeah? Wait until you'll see yourself in the mirror." Jose was a hard worker with the biggest heart ever and most of the time he looked defenseless but when it came to jokes, he liked to have the last word. There were rumors among the workers that he was in love with me but he never made me feel uncomfortable and I've always enjoyed working with him. All the workers from Mexico treated me as if I was one of their own. They liked to tease me about anything and everything. They loved how I moved comfortably in my constantly dirty jeans and worn out boots, how I smiled and giggled with them while riding on the back of utility truck while feeding the horses in distant pastures. How while scooping horse manure, we made fun of those two young girls who were always treating us like we were nothing else but some illegal and underpaid immigrants.

"They like giving us orders like they are self-proclaimed managers of this place." Even the actual manager was from Mexico himself and he didn't like their snobby attitude. The two girls didn't like me from the beginning but unfortunately for them, everybody knew that complaints about me to Larry were fruitless. Ever since the day the owner hired me, he wasn't just showing up to work every day but he was also always on time for a change and it wasn't a secret that my presence had something to do with it.

Larry was in his early fifties, unhappily married and he was known to be unfaithful to his much younger and very pretty wife. Their troubled marriage and the affairs on both sides were everybody else's business and were always open for discussions. He was a spoiled son of rich parents who always tried to run his life. The Johnson Ranch and the few million dollar house in the city were their way of keeping him out of trouble.

Larry always dressed like a cowboy even though around the horses he looked as if he was afraid of them. I never saw him riding a horse, not even once. He only knew how to buy horses at auctions in Texas and how to sell them for ridiculously high sums on his ranch in California. He always bought the best looking and ninety-nine percent the most troubled animals. Then, the job of the "training" girls was to ride those horses in the arena and make them presentable to the buyers.

He was a sad individual with emptiness in his heart and yet he knew how to be charming if he wanted to. He had a bad habit of yelling at people in front of everybody if things didn't go his way but he never dared to raise his voice at me. He was extremely selfish and very immature but he knew how to hide it well as long as he had a motive. For a while I was his biggest motive. He was trying hard to be very nice to me. The girls were speculating that I was sleeping with him and were spreading rumors but I didn't care. I had the full respect of my Latino crowd and they were very impressed with the work I did to the ranch in just a month.

The net that I successfully installed around the roof was doing its job and it even looked as if it was professionally done. I've always cared about aesthetics. The exterminator that Larry had to hire after I insisted that I would not work or live in such conditions took care of the pest problem. A small water pond that I cleaned up looked very refreshing. Roses that I trimmed and I took the time to water every day were starting to bloom and were making the place look a lot less deserted. Getting up when it was still dark outside to feed the horses and working for ten hours a day made me lose whatever extra pounds I was carrying. My jeans looked like they were sliding off my nonexistent butt and the only place where I seemed to have some meat left on me were my breasts. But I felt good. I was full of energy and full of ideas on how to transform this place that had such potential. I loved my job even though I was resenting being underpaid.

Then one day a girl that was running Larry's ranch in Texas came with a load of new horses. She was my age, she was originally from Australia and she was a real cowgirl. She knew horses like she knew the back of her hand. She seemed to like me immediately and she showed me more respect than she did to the other two girls. Because Larry's business could not function without her, she knew that she didn't have to explain herself to anybody. When she asked me to buckle a horse and to go with her on a trail ride, I didn't turn down her invitation.

"I don't care what the girls are saying about you. They may have more experience riding horses than you do, but you are a natural. You seemed to understand these creatures more than they ever will. They just pretend like they know what they're doing. If you want, I can show you few tricks while I'm here."

"Are you serious? I would love that! But do you think Larry won't mind that I'm riding horses on my work hours?" I hesitated.

"Girl, those poor horses need to be ridden. Those two girls are doing nothing but riding the same ones over and over again. They're afraid of getting on the new ones and that is not fair to those poor animals that are standing in those stalls all day long. Don't worry, after I'm done with you, your job will be in the arena. It will be up to you though to convince Larry about that. I'll say a word to him but you'll have to be very persistent. The thing is he's gonna have to increase your pay, since you'll be officially on the payroll like the other girls are. You have what it takes and you should take advantage of this opportunity, I'm telling you." She sounded very convincing and I was getting very excited.

With the cowgirl from Australia I was naming the new horses based on feelings they were giving me while riding them.

"This one I'd like to call Breeze. She's riding so smooth that she's giving me the sensation of a breeze in the summer." I was petting a beautiful white quarter horse.

"Ha- ha! I told you; you had the way with them. Breeze is off of the girls' riding list because they're afraid of her." She was laughing.

"Are you serious?"

"Yeah, I'm serious. Don't let those two fool you. They act tough to prove that they know what they're doing and the only reason they get away with that is because most people here are amateurs when it comes to horses. Didn't you notice that most of the clients are parents who decided to buy a new pet for their kids?"

I was very impressed with her confidence and her judgment.

"Come on, I want you take Breeze inside the arena and I want you to show them how it's done. It'll be fun. Besides I want Larry to see it for himself. He knows that neither one of the girls wants to ride her because she's too "difficult" and too "dangerous" to be managed. They constantly cry how he puts their lives in danger by getting such cheap horses with such bad habits. Yeah, they're not all free from behavioral issues but the truth is that those horses crave to be ridden." The cowgirl convinced me and I did what she told me to do.

"Very nice. Very smooth. See? I told you; you need to go for it. You need to get this job." I was listening to her when I saw Larry coming out of the office.

"Hey, is that the white horse that we were going to get rid of on the next auction?" He asked her.

"Yeah, that's right. Ask your new girl how she named her?" She pointed at me with *I told you so look* on her face.

"She named her B -r -e -e -z- e. She said riding her is as pleasant and as refreshing as feeling a breeze in the summer." She didn't wait for me to answer and she was clearly enjoying her triumph over our boss. Larry looked impressed as he kept watching me riding the horses that were on the blacklist as far as the two teenage cowgirl wannabe were concerned. The "feeding" boys were whistling at me showing me their approval.

"Andale! Andale!" They were cheering me and I was feeling a little bit self-conscious but I was still enjoying my performance that attracted so many spectators. Some of the horses were very stubborn and their attempts of bucking me off were creating an entertaining atmosphere.

"She has no fear that girl!" Larry looked very surprised. He was smiling but he was still looking for the approval in the Australian girl's eyes as to make sure if this was safe.

A thoroughbred took me by surprised and I found myself on the ground. It was my mistake. I wasn't as alert with this horse since my new mentor told me that because of their height these kinds of horses weren't known for trying to buck people off. I got up, I undusted my aching butt and I jumped back on the horse. My new job was going to be a lot more exciting and I wasn't going to give up on it.

In the office, Larry agreed that he was impressed with me but he was also insisting that he didn't need another horse exerciser.

"Look, it's either that or I'm out of here." I said to him and I was trying to read his face. I was very glad to notice that he didn't want me to leave.

"Fine, fine, OK then. You've got the job. I'll tell the office people to put you on the payroll," he said and I would have jumped up if I wasn't already standing on my feet. Just to think that I was going to make two thousand dollars a month, before taxes of course, but still for doing something I had a passion for! My life was beginning to make some sense for a change.

The Fall

Larry insisted that I should go with him and the Australian cowgirl all the way to Texas to get some new horses. He promised that my paycheck would wait for me in the office on our return and that I had nothing to worry about. On the trip and in Texas he was as charming as he could be. Hearing things like; "You are one of the few, most beautiful women in the world that I've ever seen" was very flattering. His words and his attention were inflating my ego which wasn't well-fed since the days of my modeling days. I felt flattered, wanted and protected in his presence. Most importantly, my feelings of loneliness seemed to have vanished. It felt good to be desired even by somebody like Larry.

When we arrived at the ranch in Texas, he wanted me to stay in the master bedroom. At night, when he kissed me, I didn't try to resist him. We had sex, and even though strangely I don't remember any details, almost as if I wanted to erase it all from my memories, I do recall Larry being very affectionate with me the next morning. He seemed very happy that we had been intimate with each other and I wasn't regretting anything yet either. But when he left me all day long by myself at the ranch, I began to experience intense anger towards him. I was craving the attention and the courtship and I hated the feeling of boredom that was stealing any excitement that was left in me. In this new place that was distant from town, without my car or even TV to watch, I had lots of time to let negative thoughts pile up in my mind.

I was missing my sense of freedom and my sense of busyness that I left back in California. Not having many options and having to deal with feelings of being trapped, I let my emotions to take over me. I was regretting now that I have agreed to this trip and I was feeling stupid for having had slept with my boss, who's true colors were just about to be revealed to me. I was feeling powerless and hurt, and at the time, inflicting sense of guilt on Larry by remaining silent seemed to be the only choice that I had. His reaction to my subconscious mental manipulation was that of a jackass. He shifted all his attention and his tenderness towards the Australian girl, and she surprised us all with her receptiveness.

Her boyfriend, who was also living at the ranch, seemed to be the only one who was feeling bad for me. I was trying to understand this girl's motives of stabbing me in the back like that and I couldn't come up with anything other than guessing that she herself was missing a father figure in her life.

She'd been working her ass off for Larry for few years now and this was the first time that he was talking to her like he cared about her. She didn't look like a serious cowgirl anymore; she looked more like a little girl who was excited from the birthday surprise that her daddy has secretly organized for her. I was feeling betrayed by both of them and even though Larry was trying to patch things up by letting us purchase some new riding clothes, I wanted to return to California as quickly as possible. I wanted to forget this trip and everything that had or hadn't happened on it.

The long hours of waiting at the horse auctions were excruciating. Watching both of them being sometimes nice, sometimes completely disregarding towards me was a torture that I just wanted to end. On the way back, in Santa Fe, New Mexico, Larry seduced me again. I fell for his crappy explanations that he wasn't himself while we were in Texas and that the pressure of getting new horses got the best of him.

Back in California I started to feel like myself again. I was riding ten different horses a day and I gladly stayed busy even after work hours were over. There was always something to do. There were horses that craved companionship, there was a big rose bush that nobody seemed to care how thirsty it looked, and sometimes there were some customers that got lost and found the place after business hours. Larry was giving me a cold shoulder again and I decided not to pay attention to him, even thought it wasn't easy considering how disrespected he made me feel. I blamed myself for everything and I promised myself that I would stick to my job since it was the only thing in my life that was somewhat predictable and consistent.

It was then when I got my first German shepherd. I named him Rex. He was seven months old and he was already huge in size. He weighted ninety pounds. Rex was handsome, alert and super eager to please me. He was full of energy too. The black and tan colors of his coat were just perfect. The intelligent and sweet look in Rex's brown eyes melted my heart completely since the day I got him. Perfectly erected long ears and the two dark beauty marks on both sides of his face were revealing his pure-bred origins. I had dreamed of having such a gorgeous German shepherd since I was a little girl but as I got older I thought that I wasn't ready for such responsibility that comes with owning a dog. But when my neighbors told me that some strange dudes were sneaking around the barn I was living in, I really got scared. I shared my concerns with a guy I knew and he convinced me to borrow a gun from him. Late in the evenings, as I would go back to the ranch, I would get out of my car while holding the loaded gun right in front of me, sort of in a James Bond's style. I wanted for the possible intruders to see that I was armed and that pissing me off wasn't the smartest thing to do. I'd open the door to my living quarters in an exaggerated manner learned from watching too much TV. Then with the gun sometimes in front of me, sometimes next to my right cheek, other times next to my left cheek, I'd inspect each corner before I'd decide that it was OK to relax. At nights the gun was always underneath my pillow, always fully loaded. The windows didn't have any locks on them and so I wasn't able to get good sleep since I'd wake up frequently to check on the status of the situation I was in. The owner of the gun was worrying about me.

"Girl, you really need to get a dog. Get a big one. See here? They're selling German shepherds in Palmdale." He pointed at an ad in the newspaper that he bought for me.

"I'm telling you, you've got to get this dog. Didn't you always want to have one of these anyway?" He insisted. Even thought I felt like I wasn't ready for such commitment, I also felt like I had no choice, but to follow his advice. I couldn't keep his gun forever. Besides I didn't want to get arrested, in case if I'd get pulled over by highway patrol. It's not like you can just drive around with a loaded and unregistered gun. I wanted Rex to be with me all the time and so whenever I'd go on a trail ride with another girl, I'd take him with us. The two girls never really warmed up to me but because it was a safety policy that none of us could take any horse beyond the arena by herself, we had no choice but to take them to the mountains together. That day I chose an appaloosa to be my ride. She was returned to the ranch by some unsatisfied customer and I was feeling bad for this poor mare that was standing in her stall without a purpose. The morning was beautiful and the sun was promising a quiet day. After having had carefully brushed and then saddled up my horse, I was ready to join my coworker who was already steering her horse towards the gate. Rex for some unknown reason didn't look very excited about the idea of following us this time. I was already in the saddle and I didn't want to leave my dog alone on the ranch.

"Rex, come on, let's go. What's wrong with you?" I've always tried so desperately to control the outcomes and by insisting that my dog would follow us was my way of making sure that he would have some fun with us. I've always hated being this way, so controlling and so tense, but I didn't know a better way then. Like in my childhood I just wanted everybody to be happy and like my childhood I always thought that it was up to me to make that happen. The appaloosa must have sensed my tension and my frustration because all of a sudden she spooked and she sent me in the air. I still didn't think it was a big deal and in those few seconds, since it was too late to hold on to her, I was just trying to imagine what would be the best way of landing on the cement.

The appaloosa apparently kept kicking me while I was falling down because I woke up on the ground and I couldn't move. My terrified coworker called Larry and the two were now explaining to the paramedics what had happened. I had two hoof prints on my skin, one in the middle of my chest and one on the side of my stomach. The back of my head was bleeding and a piece of broken bone was sticking out from my left arm.

"I don't wanna go to a hospital. I don't have a health insurance. I don't wanna pay for medical bills and I don't want those bills to go on my credit." I was mumbling without realizing that my body was in shock.

"What are you talking about? You have Worker's Compensation Insurance. You're on payroll, remember? Don't worry, you're covered. You won't have to pay a dime for anything." Larry was trying to calm me down but he looked like he was the one who needed to be comforted. The paramedics and firefighters were looking at me as if they were afraid of touching me.

"What is your name? Do you remember your name?" One of them was kneeling in front of me.

"Ela." I answered.

"Ela, can you tell me how old you are?" He continued to question me. I didn't know. I didn't know how old I was.

"Do you not remember how old you are?" The paramedic's face was expressing concern.

"I…don't…know. I can't remember. Maybe… twenty… twenty-one?" It was so frustrating not knowing such basic thing.

"That's OK, don't worry. Try not to move, OK?"

"She's twenty-six." Larry explained.

"Yeah, she's slipping away. She's bleeding in the back of her head and I'm suspecting internal bleeding too. Her altered mental status wor-

174

ries me." The paramedic's voice sounded more and more distant. I woke up tied up to a gurney. The helicopter I was in had just landed and medical personnel were rushing in to receive their new patient. I was out again.

"I wanna go home. I need to go back to work." I said to a doctor that was preparing to insert me into an MRI machine.

"You can't right now. You have an open fracture and a surgeon is scheduled to repair your left arm. He's gonna have to put some metal and some screws in it but it's gonna be fine. I'm more concerned about your spleen."

"What's wrong with my spleen?" I asked.

"The horse has kicked you right in your spleen and the organ is still bleeding. We were hoping that it would stop on its own though. It looks like it might. But we need to watch you closely." The doctor explained to me.

Back at the ranch, with my left arm immobilized in a cast, I was getting very eager to go back to work. I grabbed a rake with my right arm and I started to even up the surface of the arena.

"What are you doing? You can't work right now." Larry came out from the office when he saw me through the window.

"I can't sit still. I'm bored to death. I wanna go back to work. I have to do something." I continued raking the sand.

"If somebody sees you doing this and they report you, the Worker's Comp will stop paying you your disability paychecks. You know that, right?" He looked like he was mad at me.

"Just get some rest, alright? There is not much you can do with one arm." I could tell that he felt bad for me but also that he was irritated by the whole situation. I was so not in a good mood either. Larry was avoiding me and I was trying to do the same but this time it was very hard with so much free time on my hands. I hated the situation I was in. Everybody was getting on my nerves and I eventually withdrew myself in my small barn-apartment. I was getting very depressed. I was trying to meditate every day to escape from the world. Instead of helping me to calm down, my attempts of remaining still were aggravating the hell out of me. The anger inside of me was growing in intensity and I felt absolutely overwhelmed by it. Driving my ugly car to the store was my only way of venting my unwanted emotions.

On that dirt road, I saw few paragliders that were landing nearby. After engaging in a conversation with a man who happened to be an instructor, I agreed to visit him in Santa Barbara and for him to teach me how to paraglide. I've never thought of myself as being capable of jumping off the cliff with nothing else but some equipment that was supposed to be picked up by the wind. I surprised myself when I jumped not once but five times. Even with my arm being still in the cast I was able to steer the paraglide while pretending that I was a big bird in the sky. I was smiling again. Then one day, shortly after my trip to Santa Barbara, while driving my car, I lost control of the steering wheel and I drove over a big rock that was at the edge of the dirt road. The impact created a very loud noise and poor Rex vomited in the back seat. Later the mechanic told me that it would cost me a lot to repair the engine but instead of trying to fix it, I gave my car to Jose.

"You can have this piece of junk. If you can somehow fix it, you'll have something to drive around. And don't worry; I'll get another used car." I gave him the keys. He was hesitating at first but eventually he accepted it. I was stuck on the ranch, with a broken arm and without transportation.

Teddy

About six months from the day I was hired at the Johnson's Ranch, I got into an argument with Larry. My arm was cast free then but because of the surgery and the metal plate that was installed; I still had to go through physical therapy before the doctor would release me back to work. My arm still hurt when I tried to lift things but all I cared about was to regain my full independence through work. The two-thirds of my regular paycheck that the Worker's Comp was paying me, wasn't enough for my expenses. I had been trying to convince Larry that I was ready to return to work, thinking that doctor's approval wasn't something that I needed. When I realized that my boss was using this pretext as excuse from keeping me away, I snapped at him.

"I wanna go back to work!" I yelled at him knowing that he was trying to get rid of me.

"We don't need anybody right now. So why don't you just keep taking your disability checks?" He looked very old and ugly and I couldn't understand how I could have ever had found him charming before? I despised him and he could tell that.

"Well, you're fired and so you don't have a job to go back to!" He said to me.

"You can't fire me while I'm on disability, that's illegal." I informed him.

"Well, I just did. You're fired. And I need you to move out of the barn." He walked away towards the office in a way as if he was very proud of himself.

My lawyer encouraged me to file a law suit against Larry.

"He's gonna have to give you at least ten thousand dollars in penalty charges for firing you while you were still on disability. There is a law against this kind of discrimination to protect employees who find themselves in this kind of situation." The attorney didn't hide the fact that this was going to be an easy case for him. He filed the papers, but shortly after that I withdrew the law suit. After moving away from the ranch, I was so relieved from not having to see that awful man anymore and I just wanted not to have to deal with him in the future ever again.

Paul's small house became my residence. He was a friend of a girl that I met in town and he was very happy when she told him that I needed a place to stay. He insisted that Rex and I could stay with him for as long as we needed to. I was still collecting my disability checks and from what my lawyer told me, it would take a while before the insurance case would get settled. Until then I could not work anywhere. One evening Paul and I were sitting in his living room, chatting about something trivial when we heard a knock at the door. It was the same girl who introduced me to Paul. She had with her a four year old boy named Teddy. He wasn't her son but she has been taking care of him for the last six months. Teddy was Paul's grandson.

"Hey guys. How's it going?" She greeted us like she was in a hurry.

"Hey Carrie, what's going on?" Paul got up to hug his grandson.

"Hi grandpa." The boy looked scared and confused.

"I don't have time to explain things." Carrie said to Paul and then she looked at me.

"Can you watch Teddy for me?" She asked like she expected me to say yes.

"Sure. No problem." I answered. The boy was wearing jeans, a long sleeve shirt and cowboy boots. His face was serious and his big brown eyes were wide open. He instantly gave me a feeling of an incredibly smart and sharp child. I was looking at him while trying to figure out his short life story. I only knew that his parents were two teenagers and that his father, Paul's son, had some issues with illegal drugs. I knew even less about his mother, who according to Paul was manipulating everybody and using Teddy to get what she wanted. I wasn't sure what it was that she was after. Regardless of all that I couldn't help but to feel as if I was responsible for this child. I kept staring at him as if I was in shock. It wasn't even a question *if* I was going to take care of him; it was more of a question *how* I was going to assure his happiness?

"I'll just treat him the exact way I wanted to be treated when I was four years old. I'll talk to him in a way I wanted to be talked to. I will not use any sort of punishment to discipline him but instead I'll take time to explain things to him. Everything I'll do to him will be what I'd like to have done to me. I will put myself in his small shoes. He is a child and he doesn't have many options and I have to remember that." I was thinking in my mind and I was feeling excited and worried at the same time.

New Mommy

"Teddy, don't spit it! Keep the soap in your mouth! This will teach you not to disobey!" I heard Paul's voice coming from the bathroom. I rushed in to see what was going on.

"We're trying to put him to bed. He hates that and he doesn't understand that it's his bedtime." Paul and Carrie were looking at me as if there was absolutely nothing wrong with what I was seeing.

"OK guys, its fine, its fine. You can go now Carrie, I know you're in a hurry. I'll put him to bed, don't worry." I took Teddy to bed and I shut the door.

"Hey big guy, I'll stay with you until you'll fall asleep, OK?" I smiled at him on purpose to distract his thoughts.

"Here, I'm gonna cover you so you don't freeze at night. Is that better?" I was trying not to show him how sad his terrified face was making me feel.

"Yeah, eh- he, that's much better." He sounded like he would do or say anything to make sure that I wouldn't leave.

"OK then. See? It's not that horrible to go to bed. We all need to get some sleep so we can have some fun tomorrow. You know what we're gonna do when you wake up? You and I, we're gonna jump on this bed like crazy!"

"We will?" He asked in disbelief.

"Of course we will! That will be the first thing we'll do when you'll open your eyes. But now you need to get some rest so tomorrow you can have l-o-o-o-t-s of energy to jump v-e-e-e-r-y high. Like this high." I pointed my arm towards the ceiling.

"I'll jump t-h-i-i-s high!" He stretched his arms above his head.

"Yep. But now what do we need to do?"

"We need to get some sleep." He answered like he was happy to understand what was going on.

"That's right silly boy." I smiled at him happy to see that there was no trace of sadness on his face.

"Are you gonna be my new mommy?" He shocked me with his question. I hesitated for a moment, not sure what was I supposed to say to him. He was staring at me with his big eyes wide open.

"Do you want me to be?" I finally asked him.

"Yep. I want you to be my mom. My other mommy's not here. But you can be my mom too, you know?" He was so cute in his attempt of explaining to me my new role.

"OK. I'll be your mom then and you'll be my son." I said to him and I started to feel as if my heart was about to melt completely.

"Goodnight baby." I kissed him on his forehead.

"Goodnight mom." He said to me and I just remained speechless.

The next morning Teddy woke up early. His face looked uncertain when he looked at me. He looked like he wasn't sure what was it that he was supposed to do.

"Good morning. Why are you still standing there? Aren't you supposed to jump on the bed?" I smiled at him. I turned the CD player up to its maximum volume. He got up and he started to jump and I started to dance on the floor. He giggled and laughed and screamed and I did the same. Paul walked in the house and he stood in the bedroom door.

"What is going on?" He wasn't sure if he was supposed to be happy or concerned.

"Grandpa! Grandpa! Look how high I can jump!" Teddy was shouting as hard as he could. I gave Paul a look as to say to let him do whatever he was doing.

"Oh boy," Paul mourned but I knew that he was still glad watching us having so much fun.

"I'm going back to work. You guys are gonna be OK?" Paul asked me.

"Yeah, yeah, we're fine, don't worry." I answered while still admiring the little boy that was so amusing to me.

"OK then. You know where the truck's keys are if you need to go to town or anything, right?"

"Yeah, yeah, I know, thanks Paul."

"Bye grandpa!" Teddy looked and sounded as if he has forgotten all his troubles.

"OK, let's make the bed and then we'll brush our teeth and we'll eat something and then we'll take Rex and we'll go to explore those mountains, OK?" I said to Teddy.

"OK." Teddy's lack of any resistance was a surprise to his grandfather but not to me. In the following days I could notice that Paul was a little jealous for the strong bond that his grandchild and I developed. The only way Paul knew how to interact with Teddy was to being controlling and very critical of him and I was very against this kind of upbringing. I knew that he loved his own flesh and blood very much and that he was feeling very guilty for the situation he was in. Paul was trying to resist my child-raising tactics by constantly reminding me that I was spoiling his grandson.

"Even if so, so what? Somebody has to do it." I was very protective over Teddy and Paul knew better than to try pissing me off. The good and the bad thing was that this man was falling in love with me. His growing affection towards me was very useful when it came to decision making regarding Teddy, but it was hard for me to deal with on my personal level. It was exhausting to hear from him jokes with hidden meanings, and I was tired of telling him to knock it off. It was flattering to hear what a perfect woman and a wonderful mother I was, considering my living arrangement thought, this wasn't making me feel comfortable.

Nevertheless I wasn't alone anymore and I had a child to think about now. Even though I could not tell the future, the one thing I was very certain about was that I was committing for a lifetime to this little boy. I was ready to give him everything that he needed. I wanted to love him the way he deserved to be loved. It seemed easy considering how amazing he was. Teddy was not only full of life and full of bright ideas but he was also very obedient and much attached to me. He loved to tell other people that I was his mom and he looked very proud when he was saying it. Just like he loved to let everybody know that Rex was *his* dog. He was always trying to ride him like a horse and I was amazed to see how much patience Rex had with him.

He talked constantly and I just could not comprehend how a four year-old could posses such reasoning. His thoughts were always clear and original and were always coming straight from his heart. He was always bringing me present into the moment. He was my little Guru, my Little Angel and my Savior. I was so grateful to God for bringing him into my life. I was feeling so lucky to have him with me.

Paul on the other hand was getting more and more critical of me, the more he realized that I wasn't going to reciprocate his feelings. His frequently negative attitude towards me was very hard to deal with and it wasn't the first time in life that I felt trapped. But as long as I had Teddy with me I felt like I could withstand anything. I focused entirely on him. I called his mother and I encouraged her to visit her son. I convinced her to write and sign an authorizing letter so I could take Teddy to a doctor's office to get his vaccination shots. I also made arrangements with Paul to enroll the boy in a private preschool.

Mary, Teddy's mother seemed relieved that somebody was taking good care of her son but she didn't seem emotionally available to him. It was painful to watch him looking angry and distant when she was there. I was trying to be very nice to her but her attitude towards me as if I was nothing more than her nanny was irritating the hell out of me. Nevertheless I insisted that I would drive Teddy once every few weeks to her boyfriend's house in the city so the two of them could spend some quality time together. Sometimes she was there, waiting for him so happy and other times the door remained locked and nobody was answering it when I was pounding on it. The next day when I'd call her, I'd hear her saying that she was sick and that she wasn't feeling well.

"OK, well, I understand. Teddy was very upset but I told him that we'll come to see you soon for Christmas. Is that OK with you?" I tried not to sound like I was judging her or like I was thinking of myself as a better person.

"Yeah, that would be great."

"OK, well, we'll see you next week then." I really thought that it was important for Teddy to know that he was being loved by everybody.

Unwelcome

The next week Paul and I did some Christmas shopping and so armed with some colorfully wrapped gifts, Teddy and I headed for the city. He was excited about the idea of unwrapping the presents with his other mommy. I was excited for him too. In a little less than an hour we were standing in front of an apartment's door, but nobody was answering. I was feeling furious with Mary and guilty for making such a promise to Teddy. I was feeling stupid and used.

"Come on baby, let's go back home." I took Teddy's hand and he followed me without resistance. In the car, at first he was very silent which was very unusual for him. I couldn't even tell him how sorry I was because I was boiling inside. Then he started to make a nonsense noise that he used to make every time he'd see his mother. He was being loud and disobedient as if he was trying to distract his own thoughts and feelings. Paul used to hate seeing him this way and he used to say that Mary was turning his grandchild into a monster. While driving on the freeway I was trying to keep my eyes on the road.

"Teddy, just be quiet! Shut up!" It was the first and the only time that I've ever raised my voice at him like that. He looked stunned and I immediately regretted my reaction.

"OK, you know what? Let's do this." I turned on the radio and I found a rock station.

"Let's just scream like crazy! Ready? A-a-a-h!" The two of us started to scream as if the car was on fire or something. After I don't know how long we paused completely exhausted. We were laughing now and everything was back to normal again.

For six months Teddy was in my care. Paul was getting on my nerves with his negative attitude.

"Teddy, I told you to sit up straight when you eat! And stop playing with your food!" He was talking to him with so much anger and frustration in his voice. Paul's jaws looked like they were locked. At the time I had no clue that he was on crystal meth. I chalked up his odd behavior to dissatisfaction with my lack of involvement with him.

"Paul, he's a child, give him a break." I didn't want to aggravate things but I could not watch him treating Teddy this way.

"You're spoiling him too much. He needs some discipline. What he needs is a spanking, that's what he needs." Paul's voice was completely slurred but again, I thought it was due to his dentures that perhaps weren't fitting very well in his mouth. Paul knew that I would never let him hurt the child physically but he also knew that there was very little I could do to protect Teddy from the emotional and psychological harm that he was enduring. More than once I was contemplating taking Teddy and just moving somewhere else but I knew that Paul would not allow me to take the boy with me. I tried to distract Teddy as much as I could. I thought that buying him toys could somehow compensate for the life that he had to live. The first battery operated car I got for him was a green John Deer. Paul still found a way to disapprove how I was spending my own money.

"He doesn't need expensive toys, he needs love." I let him talk while he was assembling the toy car. When Teddy woke up and saw the car, he had an expression on his face that was priceless to me.

"If you behave, you'll get to ride this car." Paul made it sound like the gift was from him and I didn't even want to say anything.

"Is that my new car?" Teddy's wide open eyes were expressing emotions that were rushing through him.

"Yeah, that's your new car. But wait, wait, we need to charge the battery first. You have to wait until it's ready." I could tell that Paul was enjoying the little boy's reaction.

"Thanks mom. Thanks for getting me the best car ever!" Paul and I were both surprised to see how Teddy knew everything. I loved watching him driving it on the dirt road and sandy pasture that was in front of the house. He'd put all kinds of rocks in the back and he'd drive around as fast as the car would allow him to.

"Mom, I'm going to work. I have to go make some money." He'd say to me completely seriously.

"OK. Make sure you make a lot of money." I'd be very serious too.

"OK. I will. Rex, come on, let's go!"

"Oh keeey." It was impossible not to smile at him. I felt so peaceful when I watched him playing in the plastic house that I had to get for him to match his car. He liked to use his plastic phone to call me and to let me know that he was coming to visit me. The more fun I was having with Teddy though, the more Paul was being unreasonable with his criticisms towards his grandchild. I felt like he was doing that on purpose to get to me. Constantly drunk, Carrie also started to show up at the house and she tried to provoke me with her negative remarks. She acted like she was entitled to Teddy.

"Don't call her mom, she's not your mom. Her name is Ela. Call her by her name." She was talking to Teddy in her loud voice. Her dead serious face was having an intimidating effect on the little boy. Things were getting very chaotic and I decided that it was time for me to move out. I rented a car and I wanted to find a room for rent as well. I packed all my stuff even though I wasn't sure yet exactly where I was going to stay. Joy, a girl that I met at the ranch, said that I could stay with her and her parents until I found a room for rent. It was painful for me to leave Teddy where he was but I felt like I had no choice. I was secretly hoping that perhaps after a while, I'd come back to visit and that Paul would let me then take his grandchild with me. The man was very upset at my decision of leaving and he was venting his frustration on the little boy. Paul had once revealed to me that he has served some time in prison for possession of drugs but as naïve as I still was then, I blamed myself for his nervousness. It didn't even cross my mind that he was under the influence of meth. The evening that he was expressing violent behavior towards Teddy, I thought he was crossing the line.

"Teddy, come. Come stay with me in my room." I looked at his terrified face and I tried to smile so he wouldn't feel so scared.

"You stay out of it. He's not your child! He's my grandson so don't forget that! Teddy, get over here! I told you to get over here!" Paul's face was red from shouting. Teddy hugged my legs afraid to move.

"Paul, he's scared. Just leave him alone or I'll take him with me somewhere else right now." I was trying to be calm but this was nearly impossible considering the fury that was growing inside me.

"Where does she think that she's taking him now?" The drunken Carrie stepped in the room.

"Give me Teddy right now! Come on Teddy, come to Carrie." She was approaching us and the boy was trying to hide behind my legs.

"Carrie, he doesn't wanna go to you. Just leave him alone. Go back to whatever you were doing." I said to her and she started to call me different names. I tried to ignore her but when she put her hands on me I stepped back and I grabbed the cordless phone.

"You touch me one more time, and I'm calling the cops." I put my finger on number 9, ready to dial the emergency number.

"Scared of me? Go ahead, call the cops. What you're gonna tell them?" Seeing both of them approaching me and Teddy I dialed 911. Before I heard the operator's voice, Carrie pulled the plug from the outlet.

"There! What are you gonna do now? Smartass!" She had a hateful look on her face.

"Alright guys, that's enough." Paul looked like he was afraid of the police coming in to check what was going on.

"Carrie, go sit down on the couch, let's not make big deal out of nothing." He tried to make it sound as if he was the mediator. Shortly after that we heard a strong knock at the door.

"Police! Open the door!" Paul got up to unlock the door.

"Good evening sir. We were dispatched here because there was an interrupted 911 call from this address." The officer looked very serious. Paul looked insecure as he was trying to explain to both men in uniforms that this was nothing but an argument. The policeman in charge grabbed my wrists and he pointed his flashlight on them.

"Don't worry. I'm just checking for any bruises. I don't believe a word this man is saying." He looked like he was concerned about me. After good half an hour the police were ready to leave.

"Are you sure you feel safe staying here?" The officer really looked like he felt bad for me.

"Yes, thank you. I'll be moving out first thing in the morning. I'll be fine until then." I said to him.

"Here, take my business card. If they cause you any trouble, don't hesitate to give me a call. I'll be glad to put them where they belong." He wasn't even trying to hide his disgust towards Paul and Carrie. The next day I phoned Mary, Teddy's mother. I told her what's been going on and that I was leaving. I thought she would take her son to her mother's house but instead she made it sound as if I was blowing things out of proportion.

"No, he's OK. He's gonna stay with Paul for now. I don't think there is anything to worry about. I know Paul's not perfect but his doing his best." I could not believe what I was hearing.

"I know how much Teddy likes you and I wouldn't mind if you kept visiting him, if you want." She added.

Full House

I stayed for two weeks at Joy's parent's house while she was helping me to find a room for rent. It was hard to find anything considering that I had a dog that weighed a hundred pounds. Luckily, I convinced a Mexican lady in Lancaster that had room for rent for three hundred backs a month, that Rex and I would not cause her any troubles. The twelve hundred dollars that I was still getting from the Worker's Comp wasn't much but I managed to live off it somehow. My landlord's son helped me to get a used but in very good shape SUV.

Lancaster was only half an hour drive from Agua Dulce so I was visiting Teddy quiet often. Paul was still mad at me for leaving but he seemed glad that I was keeping in touch. Teddy was calling me by my first name now but he was always more than happy to see me. It was very hard for me to answer his questions why he couldn't live with me. I didn't want him to know that his grandfather wouldn't let me take him with me. I've never said anything bad about his relatives to him because I didn't think that this would have a positive effect on his developing mind. I was missing Teddy and the sense of meaning he brought to my life when he was with me. Without making him happy my life seemed extremely empty. In an attempt to fill out that void in my heart, I went to a charitable organization that was helping youth "at risk". The man in charge was looking at me in a very suspicious way while I was trying to convince him that I was very eager to become a volunteer. Finally, because he looked like he was hesitating, I told him that I was once in an orphanage. I wanted to convince him that despite my appearance I could relate to those kids. His face changed and in a still hesitant way he explained to me why he was so cold with me.

"I'm sorry, don't take it the wrong way, but I was convinced that the government hired you to check on our organization." I looked stoned when he said that even though it wasn't the first time in my life that somebody accused me of being a spy. The man was apparently still not convinced about my motives because every time I called to check if I could do something to help, they told me that there was nothing to do. I've got tired of it and I decided that I was going to start my own non-profit for underprivileged children.

I was sitting outside Barns & Nobles, discussing my new ideas with a homeless guy, when for the first time I saw Sean. He was sitting at a nearby table, pretending like he was completely taken by his book. He was tall and handsome even though he was carrying some extra weight. He joined our table after a while, under the pretense of being interested in petting Rex. I was almost twenty-seven and he was almost thirty-four years old. Sean was working as a site manager on the air force base and he was renting a house in Rosamond where he moved about a year ago. He was originally from Florida. He was boring but he gave me the feeling of being a good man. I agreed to go out with him that night.

"OK, I'll meet you at that bar then." I said to him and I went home to pick up few blankets for the homeless guy that was sitting and chatting with us. I was disappointed that Sean limited himself to only buying few drinks for him. I perceived him as a middle-class stuck-up guy. I thought that if he knew how broke I was, that he would had never asked me on a date. At the bar I got so drunk that I thought that I was going to pass out when I stood up. My date had to escort me to his truck. Once inside the vehicle, I barely opened the window in time and I vomited all over the door. Surprisingly, Sean kept calling me and he kept asking me on dates. Two weeks later he kissed me for the first time. I was at his house, sitting on the patio and I was crying my eyes out because I hadn't been able to see Teddy.

"Carrie has moved in with Paul and she's been locking the door every time she sees my car." Sean was listening patiently to my story. When he saw my tears rolling down my face, he leaned forward and he kissed me. It was a gentle and brief kiss. A month later I moved in with him and one month after that we had sex for the first time. Before we slept together he told me that I was the love of his life and he cried actual tears when I told him that I wasn't in love with him.

"Sean, I'm just being honest with you. I don't even know what love is. I've never really been in a real and serious relationship. I've never really had a real boyfriend. All I can tell you is that I am intentionally trying to keep my heart open to any possibility. I guess the time will show whether or not I feel something special towards you. Believe me, in many ways my life would be a lot easier if I'd just married you now. I just think it will be a lot better if we'll just wait and see what happens." I was sitting on the bed and Sean was sitting on the edge by my feet.

"Can you really be that sure that what you feel for me is love?" I asked him because he wasn't saying anything. His tears and his shaking lips were making me feel guilty.

"The moment I saw you walking with your dog towards Barnes & Noble, I said to myself; this is the woman that I will marry one day." He paused to wipe his tears.

"I've never felt about anybody they way I feel about you. I've never came even close to telling any woman that I loved her," he continued.

"Sean, I'm not going anywhere. We have all the time in the world to fall in love with each other." I couldn't understand why he was being so sentimental. He wasn't the exact description of the man of my dreams. There was nothing mysterious about him; he didn't serve any time in prison and he was against tattoos, but still, I liked the way he treated me. He had more respect for me that anybody ever had before. Because of him I learned what being truly considerate meant. He was caring and very attentive to my needs. He loved to surprise me and he was good at it.

"Oh no, baby!" He called me once from the master bedroom.

"What?" I yelled across from the kitchen.

"Oh God, look what the cat did in the bathroom!" He sounded extremely stressed out which was very unusual for him since he was always so calm.

"What? What did he do now?" I was marching through the long hall, trying to think of an idea that would keep me from getting mad. I entered the master bedroom and I stood there speechless. I looked around and everywhere I looked I saw brand new clothes hanging like in a department store.

"B-a-a-y-b-e-e-e." I was touched and at the same time I was still mad for the mess that I was expecting to see.

"Do you like it? Do you like your new clothes?" Sean was paying close attention to the expression on my face.

"Of course I do! Thank you baby! I can't believe you did all this. I can't believe you went to buy all these clothes for me." I was hugging and kissing him and he was smiling the whole time like he won a lottery or something. I wasn't still ready to admit that I was in love with him but I was sure glad to hear the garage door opening when he was coming back from work.

"Hi baby. How was your day? How are my babies doing?" He'd try to make his way through Rex so he could hug me.

"What did you do today?" He always seemed very interested to know about my daily activities.

"I went to see Teddy."

"And?"

"He's here. He's in the backyard playing on his swing-set. His mother let me take him for few days. She didn't say when she wants me to bring him back. I'm just really hoping that he'll just stay here with us for good. I already made him a room, come see. We went to a store and we bought all this new furniture." I was very excited and I was talking very fast hoping that if I'd hear my thoughts out loud, I'd convince myself that nobody would take the boy away from me.

"Baby, I just don't want you to get your hopes too high. I'm happy for you but do you remember how much you cried last time when they didn't let you see him? I just don't want you to go through this again, babe." Sean was very protective of me.

"I know babe, but this is Teddy we're talking about." I didn't even want to hear anything hoping that everything would work itself out. Teddy liked Sean immediately. The next morning, when he woke up, he asked me with seriousness on his small face.

"Where is dad? Where did he go?"

"A-a-h, I don't know Teddy." I felt very uncomfortable thinking that he was asking me about his biological father. I was surprised because he has never talked about his father before.

"Did my dad go to work?" Teddy persisted with his questions and then I realized that he was referring to Sean. I was touched to see how much this child was longing to have a normal family.

"Oh yeah. Yeah, your dad went to work. He'll be back later. Come on, take Rex and teach him how to jump on your bed." I was so happy and I couldn't believe that this was my life. I was twenty-seven years old and it seemed like the bad luck I had all my life until now, was gone for good. I was living in a four bedroom house with a wonderful boyfriend. I had all kinds of animals and I had a garden that was keeping me busy and now I had Teddy too. How did all this happen? How did I manage to attract such blessings to my life?

While Sean was busy working, I was busy with rescuing all the animals that I could. Somehow our house became a drop off point for all the creatures that found themselves lost in the hot and not so friendly desert.

I've always liked treating animals like children. When I brought my first goat home, I would put diapers on him, because I thought that I could potty train him. I had to use a duck tape to firm the diaper on him so the tiny round balls of poop wouldn't come out while he'd jump around. When Sean came back from work that day, he asked me:

"What on earth is that noise and where is it coming from?"

"Meh, eh, eh!" Rampy wanted to meet his new daddy.

"Wholly molly! What on earth is this thing and what is it doing in my house?" He would stare at him as if Rampy was from outer space.

Sean was concerned with our white carpet, and he never made peace with the goat being inside the house, but I really didn't care about that. My animals have always been like kids to me, and no man could come before them, ever. He knew that very well. When Sean was at work; Rampy was always in our living room, watching TV with me. Oh how he loved doing that, particularly when I would have Animal Planet on! His head would tilt to the side then, and his mouth would never stop moving, as he'd continue chewing on his invisible food. I would just sit there while staring at him and I'd laugh hysterically. My goat would follow me everywhere. His favorite thing was when I was in the kitchen preparing something to eat. While standing on his posterior legs, he'd support himself with his front feet, by placing them on the kitchen counter. With his dexterous tongue, he'd lick everything he could reach. Rampy thought of himself as being a dog. His identity crises could have a lot to do with the fact that I used to take him on walks with all of us. How much he loved walking in that desert! All of the neighbors knew us very well. The kids especially loved joining us on those walks. Rampy would never listen to me, and he would always pull very hard on his leash. He was always trying to stay in front of everybody. He was as stubborn as any goat could be. His next favorite thing was being chased around the house by Rex. The house, beside the front door, had two different doors that led to the backyard. They'd just run in circles like crazy, followed by the Chihuahua that my neighbor found, who'd make a lot of noise, to overcompensate his miniature size. I really had a good time watching them. My goat used to cause me all kinds of trouble though; he just wanted to play with everything that moved. He thought for example that the tortoise Don Piero was his toy, and he constantly tried to flip him over with his horns. I had to watch them very closely after I found the poor guy lying on his back one time.

One day, my girlfriend Joy called me on the phone, saying that she had an emergency.

"Girl, I found twelve homeless kittens! You've got to help me with them; you know I don't have room anymore in my house." She shouted on the phone.

"Are you serious? Well, bring them here then, you know where I live. But you'll have to help me with finding new homes for them. You know I can't just keep them all here, right?"

"Yeah, yeah, I will." She hung up the phone.

The next thing I knew, I had twelve felines that were only a few weeks old crawling around my house. Rex was absolutely in love with them. He used to carry them in his big mouth and he used to lick them with his huge tongue. Rampy didn't know what the heck to think about those tiny creatures that were crying so loud. He was strangely intimidated by them. Together with Joy, we gave them baths with special shampoo, to get rid of all the fleas. The kitties were as cute as they could be, and it wasn't hard at all to find new homes for them. The hardest part was to be separated from them, after feeding them for several weeks with syringe, and after feeling the joy of living in a full house. Rex didn't like when people were showing up at our house, to pick up their newly adopted pets. He'd follow them all the way to the door, and he'd keep sniffing them as to say:

"Where the hell do you think you're taking my baby to?"

Over the week, as all this was taking place inside the house, I had been hearing some crying that was coming from beneath the cars that were parked on the street. I didn't really pay attention to it, since I knew that it was very common for people to leave their unwanted pets in this area. But one day I heard knocking at my door. It was my neighbor's seven year old daughter; Sierra, who used to come to my house almost every day. She was holding a white cat that looked scared to death.

"I've got your kitty! I found your kitty cat Elzbieta!" She was so happy, because she thought that this cat belonged to me.

"Oh, look!" I couldn't turn him down. He was in an awful shape; he was bleeding from his mouth, where apparently he was bitten by some dog. Fleas had infested his dirty fur and were visible to a naked eye. They were stuck to his mouth, and I had a real hard time in getting rid of them. I named him Milky Way because after the bath, his white fur reminded me of the Milky Way in the sky. I thought,

"I'll just find him a new home, just like I did with the rest of the kittens." I soon found out that nobody wanted him. Maybe it was because he turned

194

out to be deaf, or maybe because he was so skittish. Well, I thought that I'll keep him for a while, until I come up with something else. With the time passing by, Milky Way grew on me. He was still hiding all the time, but he started to jump on my bed at nighttime while I was sleeping. Once he allowed me to pet him, he became totally addicted to it. He'd just flip himself on his back, and he'd start making that funny noise that was supposed to inform me about his demand. If that wasn't working, he'd jerk his head in a funny way that to me looked like he was trying to say:

"What are you waiting for? Can't you see that I need some loving here?"

He was strange sometimes. He would still run away from me at home, but he was very comfortable, and he even looked very confident whenever I took him out in my bag. He didn't mind people petting him, as long as I was the one that was holding him. His favorite thing became sleeping on top of my books, while I attempted reading on my bed. He would lie there like he owned the whole place and he looked like he wanted to make it clear, that he didn't want to be disturbed. His fear of other people though made me become overly protective of him. Sometimes I'd feel like I was paranoid of losing him.

My female German shepherd was already two years old when I first got her. Rex was a year older than Nel so he was already three when she joined our family. One day I found out about a local GSD puppy mill that was facing bankruptcy. The owner was desperately trying to find permanent homes for her unlucky pups that never sold and so she was giving them away free of charge.

Nel was living among several dozens of German shepherds that were being bred and raised there. She was locked up in a kennel that was maybe five feet wide and five feet long and she was sharing her cell with another dog. All the canines were jumping and barking like crazy when I got there and the smell of feces lying around was absolutely unbearable. Nel's fur and her paws were spotted with her own running stool. Her long and fuzzy looking coat made her look almost as if she was half German shepherd, half bear. She was the least aggressive and the most submissive dog that this awful place had. My heart was breaking to watch all these gorgeous and so intelligent creatures jumping inside their crates and barking hysterically as we were walking away.

Nel wasn't completely free from behavioral issues, and it took me quite some time to gain her trust. At first she was super shy and extremely nervous. She always looked scared and confused. Her posture then hardly ever had the shape of that typical proud German shepherd. When she'd get nervous or excited she'd keep running in a circle like crazy. She didn't want to come inside the house at first, and when I tried to encourage her by pushing her gently, she would bite my hands strong enough to get her point across. Nel immediately developed a very strong bond with Rex and so to train her I'd focus on giving my commands to him knowing that she'd do exactly what the big boy would do. Over the period of time she completely overcame her nervousness altogether. Only then her real personality started to shine through. She was all about being silly and goofy as if she understood that taking life too seriously was a waste of time. Her devotion towards me showed me a totally new meaning of loyalty. The pure admiration in her eyes when she'd stare at me always warmed my heart.

Teddy was calling me mom again even though I've never said anything to him. He was just being himself again; full of energy and full of bright ideas. He loved to play in his small plastic swimming pool that I got for him. The entire backyard was designed to entertain him. I was building him a play house from the monkey bars that were there.

"This is gonna be your kitchen and here is gonna be your living room and right here you gonna have your bedroom." I was explaining to him what was it that I was trying to do.

"And the upstairs? What's gonna be upstairs?" He pointed at the ladder.

"That's gonna be your office. That's where you'll go to work. And right there, by the goat's house I'll build you a garage for both of your cars, so you can park'em there at night." I was as excited as he was. I was driving back and forth to Home Depot to get building materials and Sean was concerned how much money I was spending but I didn't really care. I was almost as excited as if I was building a real house for myself. I wanted everything to look as real as possible. I got real shingles for the roof but at the end I covered it with a more modern looking metal shield. All the sliding windows were made of transparent plastic material that looked like glass. The wooden floor that was extending all the way to the porch on both sides of the house, I painted with a transparent lacquer to make it look shinier. The bedroom's floor I covered with a white carpet. The walls I painted white of course. My neighbor, the mother of a little girl who played with Teddy, and who also became my friend, gave me a small plastic bed that had a real mattress and a plastic kitchen set that her daughter wasn't using anymore. I painted the kitchen all white and the appliances like a refrigerator, stove and microwave I painted all silver. It looked really realistic after I was done with it. The garage had two doors and the roof that was matching the roof on the house. On the side, it had space for the

196

hay that I was feeding my goat with. The kids from neighborhood were watching me pounding on nails and drilling screws while trying to keep balance on top of the roof of my new project. I let them in sometimes so they could play but most of the time I wanted to stay focused. I wanted to finish my work in case Mary would call me to tell me that she wanted me to pick up Teddy again.

She took Teddy back and there was nothing that I could do about it. I finally told her that she could stay with us rent-free but I knew that she wasn't going to like that idea. Paul was pissed off too that she took Teddy to live with her teenage boyfriend who wasn't the father of the child.

"I'm telling you, she took him because welfare people must have checked on her. Without a child she can't keep getting money." Paul was telling me his version of what must have happened to Mary that changed her mind about keeping Teddy. I was devastated, but I didn't know what to do. Just like I still didn't know that Paul was using drugs, I had no idea then that Mary and her boyfriend were taking crystal meth too. Teddy's mother let me visit with her son. It was heartbreaking for me to see what effect the chaotic environment had on the little boy.

He was neurotic and confused again. I hated seeing him this way. I hated the sense of powerlessness that I had to deal with. I couldn't stand Mary and I don't even know why but I felt like I wanted to kick the shit out of her immature boyfriend. Both of them made me feel that the only reason I was allowed to see Teddy was because I was bringing toys and money with me.

Eventually I stopped driving to the city but I kept sending checks and toys to them. I could not bear the idea of Teddy being hungry. Sean was of course very much against all that and so I had to do it without his knowledge. He knew that he couldn't control my disability checks but he was trying to control the money that he was giving to me. He was buying the groceries because he knew that if I went to the store, I'd come back with no food but with all kinds of toys instead. Still, because of his frequent work related trips that took him out of state, I was able to scramble enough money together for Teddy.

Sean would call me every day, always concerned if I had enough food in the fridge. With my boyfriend being gone most of the time, I kept working on the play house, hoping that one day Mary would let her son live with me. She only let me pick up Teddy when she was fighting with her boyfriend. A few days later she always demanded for me to bring him back.

I tried to keep myself busy with all the paperwork that I had to do to start my nonprofit for children. I hated doing it but a year later I was proud of myself to have had incorporated a tax-exempt organization. I did it all by myself with a help of Nolo's law book that I purchased from Barnes & Noble. Sean was almost never home. If he wasn't at work, he was in school working towards his degree, and if he wasn't studying, he was at work doing overtime. I was mad at him for neglecting me. I was sick and tired of waiting for that garage door to make that sound when it was being opened. I was sick and tired of glancing at Rex to see whether his ears were going rigidly erect at the faintest sound of Sean's arrival. The self-help work books on how to manage my anger weren't doing much for me. The psychologist and anger management case worker, which I asked for help voluntarily, weren't doing much for me either. I was in pain physically and mentally. I couldn't sleep at night and I had no energy during the day. My medical doctor diagnosed me first with chronic pain disorder and then with fibromyalgia.

Family

"It's a chronic muscle pain disorder and there is no cure for that." Kelly; my neighbor, and the mother of little Sierra, became my close friend since I told her about my health issues. She had the same health problem ever since she was in a serious car accident.

"I don't wanna live like this Kelly. This is a nightmare." I was crying sometimes to her, glad that there was somebody who at least tried to understand what I was going through.

"I know Elzbieta. If I didn't have my children, I don't know if I'd continue to live like this." Kelly was very sweet and very compassionate person. Ever since I moved out of Paul's house, I was introducing myself to everybody with my name the way it was written on my driver's license. I decided not to try to accommodate anybody anymore and I thought that if I made all this effort to learn a different language, I was entitled to expect people to pronounce my name, no matter how difficult it sounded. No more Ela, no more Betty, and definitely I would not let anybody to even try to call me Elizabeth!

"My name is Elzbieta." I learned how to love my name hoping that one day I would learn how to love myself as well. It was much harder though to learn how to accept myself. It seemed virtually impossible to stop being my own biggest enemy. I could not stop beating myself up no matter how hard I tried. I worried constantly about everything and my mind was constantly filled with negative thoughts.

I blamed Sean for not being affectionate with me the way I wanted him to be. I was hurt that he wasn't interested in having sex with me. I was lonely. When I took sleeping pills, Sean freaked out and called an ambulance. He calmed down a little bit in the ER. He realized that my intentions weren't to kill myself but rather to gain relief through the high that was caused by my thoughts of dying. I was missing Teddy and since I realized that nothing was ever going to change, I convinced Sean that we should open our home to a foster child.

We went to an agency and we did everything that we had to do in order to become certified foster parents. After criminal background checks, income verification, child-proofing the house and parenting plus CPR classes that we had to take, we were finally authorized to foster children. Kelly was being very supportive of me. Since she knew that Sean and I were asking for a little girl with the possibility of adoption, she threw me a baby shower. All the neighbors showed up with their kids and they brought all kinds of gifts. It was then that I realized that I was falling madly in love with my boyfriend. I loved having this strong and stable man by my side. I was so thrilled to know that he was OK with the thought of spending the rest of his life with me. I felt loved by him. I told myself that he'd be more affectionate with me once we'd get married. I told myself to be patient with him the way he'd always been patient with me. When I got the call from the agency I was more than thrilled but the woman told me that she needed to talk to me first.

"I know you've asked us to call you when we'd get a girl who is only a few years old, and we are going to do that. But I have a fifteen year old girl here that needs a home right away. Do you think you could take her until we'll be able to find her a more permanent home? This is sort of an emergency, and I'd really appreciate your help even though I'd totally understand if you'd say no."

"Hmm, sure, I'll come pick her up." I said to her not knowing what else could I have done.

"Do I need to bring anything with me? Does she need anything?" I asked.

"No, no. She's all set. She's been waiting to be picked up. Her name is Vanessa." The woman sounded much relieved.

"OK, I'll be there in fifteen minutes." I hung up the phone. Vanessa was one of nine children who were removed from their home after their mother was arrested for selling drugs. She had a twin sister named Brenda that I agreed to bring her home with us as well. I didn't want them to be separated. They were going through enough challenges already. The two teenage girls were being moved from foster home to foster home and after having them in my house for two months I was able to understand why. They felt powerless and obviously they were trying to resist their situation. Every foster parent, including myself, felt bad for them at first, and the girls were given some slack for the first month or so. Listening to the girl's story I was very touched and I shared a little bit with them what it was like for me when I was their age. Honestly I was freaking out about the idea of parenting those two teenagers but my heart would not let me turn them down. When Vanessa told me that their fourteen year-old brother Eliot ran away from another foster home, I agreed that we would drive my car around to look for him.

"Look, I talked to the social worker and he told me that if we find Eliot, he can stay with us. I want you guys to promise me though that when he's here, you'll help me to handle him. Do you think you can do that? Do you think you can make him follow the house rules?" I asked the girls.

"Oh yeah, yeah, he'll listen to us. He's just been acting out because he hates that they always put him in a different foster home with a bunch of other kids. But he'll listen to us, we promise, he's not gonna cause you any trouble." Vanessa was always the one that liked to take charge. She was the one that wanted to rescue her whole family and I could relate to her on so many levels.

"OK well, let's just go then. Let's see if we can find him." I said to them. We drove around the neighborhood where the girls grew up. It wasn't a nice or safe neighborhood. I was uncomfortable when the girls were asking some grownup friends about Eliot.

"I think we need to get out of here." I said to Vanessa and Brenda when I saw group of guys that looked like gangsters, approaching our car.

"What are you looking for?" The tall and muscular teenage boy asked us.

"We're looking for our brother Eliot, have you see him?" Vanessa was sticking her head out of the car.

"No I haven't. Do you need help finding him?" The boys were laughing and trying to jump on the car and I realized that we needed to zoom out of there.

"OK, get off the hood or I'll run you over." I locked the doors and windows and I stepped on the gas even though the guy that was sitting on the hood was obscuring my view. He jumped off when the car was already in motion, leaving a big dent on my SUV. I was pissed but I was still determined to find Eliot.

"We're not gonna find him here. Can you think of anybody that could give you a hint where he could be?" I asked the girls.

"Maybe we can drive to our uncle's house. He may know where Eliot is hiding." Vanessa looked like she really wanted to find her brother before the cops got a hold of him. The uncle did confirm that he heard from Eliot. He's nephew wasn't at his house but he told us where we could find him. The teenage boy had slept behind some liquor store and he looked like he didn't trust me a hundred percent when we went to pick him up.

"Come on moron, you gonna stay with us at Elzbieta's house. She's our foster parent but she's cool." I could tell that Vanessa's anger was caused by her worries.

"You need to behave so you can stay with us and no more running away, you understand that?" She continued scolding her younger brother like she was his mother. I could tell that the family meant everything to this young girl.

Runaways

I really wanted to help this family somehow. When their oldest sister who was married and had her own kids, asked me over the phone if she could visit her siblings, I invited her to my house. Once I week I was driving my foster kids to a park where they had supervised visitations with their mother. She was a young and strong woman but I didn't like how she acted like she was entitled to everything. Even though I could hear the kids telling her that they liked staying at my place, she was still looking at me like she didn't trust me. In her eyes I was just another person who had no right to meddle with her life. At the park all the foster parents were sitting on one side and the families were always trying to get away from everybody. The social worker was trying to kill the boredom by chatting with us.

"So how is everything going? I must tell you, I didn't think that they would last so long with you. They've never stayed anywhere for more than a month." He liked talking to me.

"Yeah, it hasn't been an easy ride but we're hanging there. I took them to school and we talked to the principle and they are now enrolled in a special program. So looks like they'll be able to continue their education there."

"Good, good, they'll have to catch up with a lot of material. You really seem like you care about those kids." The social worker looked surprised and pleased to see how seriously I was taking my new role.

"Isn't that what we have to do?" I asked.

"Yeah, but you'd be surprised to know what kind of people I have to deal with sometimes. I hate to say that but some people really do this just for the money. It's refreshing to see somebody who puts the children as their priority, that's all I'm trying to say."

The three teenagers weren't easy to handle. Sean wasn't helping me very much with them since he was absent most of the time. On Sundays he was taking them out for ice-cream and since he wasn't participating in disciplining the kids, he was viewed as the cool one and I was of course the bad guy. I was infuriated by the lack of understanding and support from my boyfriend. I felt betrayed every time he took the girl's side that I should go easier on them. Vanessa and Brenda in particularly began to act very disrespectfully towards me. In their opinion Sean was in charge of the household and they weren't afraid of telling me that they wouldn't follow my stupid rules.

I was very tired of Vanessa's passive aggressive way of destroying everything around. I was tired of her getting in my face every day to the point where she'd make verbal threats. Teddy was staying with me again and I didn't like how the three foster kids were mean to him. Finally, after a social worker sent by the agency intervened, Sean understood more what I was going through. He promised that he would never let the teenagers manipulate him and that he would always stand by my side. He kept his promise but the kids didn't like it.

The first one to run away was Eliot. The two sisters didn't come back from their walk later that evening. I informed the agency and a few hours later the police knocked at my door. They had Vanessa and Brenda in the car. Even though the girls told the police that I was beating them up and that I wasn't feeding them, I still agreed to keep them in my house. They were being difficult but I couldn't just send them back to the agency. They were making my life hell but once I made a commitment I wanted to stick to it. I felt bad for their lack of stability and somehow I wanted to make a difference in their life.

The twins wanted to attend church, so I made arrangements with people from some religious organization, which would come and pick them up every Sunday. I thought that this would be good for their sense of independence which I knew that they were longing for. At the church they were able to attend the mass with their mother who was still on probation. Then one Sunday people from the church organization told me that the girls managed to run away. I was so sick and tired of all this that when I called the foster agency to inform them, I told them to look for a different home for Vanessa and Brenda. Teddy wasn't with me anymore either, because as usual, Mary took him away from me after a week. She was calling me regularly to ask for money until one day I said no to her.

"Mary, if you're in trouble then you can stay here with us but I won't give you any money anymore, I'm sorry. I can come and pick you up if you want me to. You know that I would do anything for Teddy and that I worry a lot about him. And if you don't wanna stay here, why won't you just let him stay here then?" I was heartbroken when a month later I discovered that she left Teddy at Paul's house.

I was driving frequently to Agua Dulce again and I was insisting for Paul to get a legal guardianship this time. I was sending him emails with information on where he'd have to apply for it. I was so mad that nobody wanted to do the right thing. I was feeling very bad and it was the hardest decision that I've ever had to make but I finally called child services. Paul was granted temporary guardianship after Mary tested positive for methamphetamine. Since I knew that Teddy couldn't be with me and I wanted him to enjoy the playhouse that I finished building, I took the whole thing to Agua Dulce. Sean and our neighbors helped me relocate the mini-house. It was hard to do so and it took us couple of days to move everything. The guys had to unscrew everything apart and then my boyfriend and I had to reassemble everything once we were at Paul's house. Teddy kept jumping and talking to us as if somebody had injected him with a high dose of sugar. Seeing him so happy made me feel like the happiest person in the world.

I was still hoping that somehow he'd be with me one day. I was so eager to make him feel appreciated and loved unconditionally. I wanted for him to wake up every day in a safe and clean environment. It was excruciatingly painful for me not to have any control over his destiny. I could not stand Paul and the way he was with his grandchild and the only reason I was trying to be civil with him, was so I could go and visit them to make sure that Teddy was OK.

Sleep

Sean and I were fighting more often about our future together. I had been living with him for two years and I was feeling like I was ready to start a family with him but he was feeling very reluctant about it. He wouldn't say no but he wouldn't say yes either about the idea of us getting married. He was comfortable with the way things were between us. Sean liked to make me believe that such step was still ahead of us. When I was planning our wedding out loud he was smiling in a charming way as if he was pleased to see me so into it.

"I still have to propose to you." He was looking at me as if my actions were depriving him of the surprise factor.

"Fine, then hurry up because I already decided that my twenty thousand dollars from the insurance I will spend on airline tickets for my family. I want everybody in our wedding." I felt like I couldn't wait for my dreams to come true. I was convinced that Sean was my soul-mate and that his lack of affection toward me was only temporary. I really believed that even though I wasn't sure about it from the beginning, that I had met the man I would spend the rest of my life with. He still kept saying that I was the love of his life and I could never think that he was capable of hurting me. He kept distancing himself thought especially after I told him that I did not want to move to New Mexico with him where he was being relocated.

"I'm buying a house there and I want you to come to live with me in Albuquerque," he said.

"You won't marry me but you want me to follow you everywhere, just like that." I was arguing with him.

"Baby, what are you going to do here without me? You don't receive your disability paychecks anymore and you know that I will have to move out of this house. I can't afford to have a mortgage and a rent on two houses."

"Don't worry about me. I will move to San Francisco." Ever since I took Vanessa and Brenda for a few days trip to San Francisco, I had been thinking about moving to the Bay area. I did not want to follow Sean to New Mexico. Since he didn't want to marry me or even to get engaged, I wanted to be as far as possible from him. I wasn't quite sure what I was going to do for a living there. Even though my nonprofit was ready to receive donations, I wasn't working on fundraising since I had to worry about my own existence first.

I tried to start an internet business but that wasn't going very well. I was trying to sell fashion jewelry on a website that I built. I spent hours and hours on submitting my website to all search engines and all kinds of directories. I doubted the whole thing and so I decided that it was time to finish writing my damn book.

I picked a name for a publishing company and I registered it with the county. I was going to publish my book by myself and this step was supposed to motivate me. After reviewing my old material I decided that it was all nothing but trash. I had to start all over and I couldn't do it. I could not make myself write about my life since I hated every aspect of it. I did not feel like telling everybody things that I have done or things that I haven't done. Besides I didn't believe that anybody would be interested in reading four hundred pages about somebody else's misery. I managed to type one page on my laptop and that was all that I could squeeze out of myself.

"Forget it. I'm not writing that stupid book!" I closed the laptop and I went to sleep. I was doing a lot of that lately. I was numbing all my pains through my addictions to food and TV. My depression took over me once again and one evening, after arguing with Sean, I went to the master bedroom and I swallowed a whole bottle of prescription sleeping pills. I knew that to Sean it would look as if I was just asleep. I was still afraid of dying but I thought that once unconscious I wouldn't have much say on it.

I liked how the pills were making me sleepy and how they were calming me down. When everything in room started to spin, I grabbed a piece of paper and I wrote things that I could not even make sense out of. I went unconscious. When Sean came to bed he found me lying in a strange position. Apparently while I was still writing, my body could not resist the effect of pills and I fell asleep on top of the piece of paper. Sean thought I was just tired but he didn't like how uncomfortable I looked and so he moved me a little bit. He saw the wrinkled paper and he glanced at it from curiosity. The nonsense that was written on it alarmed my boy-friend and so he tried to wake me up. I didn't respond so he pulled my eyelids and he saw that my eyes were completely red. The paramedics forced a tube through my nose but fortunately I didn't have to feel that. At the ER the doctors told my boyfriend to sit in the waiting room while they were trying to save me. He sat there for four hours worrying if I was going to make it. He cried while talking on the phone with his mother.

Born to Lose

When I woke up, I first heard the doctor's voice.

"She's stable now." He touched Sean's shoulder and then he left us alone. It was the first time in a while that my boyfriend looked fully present with me. The remorse on his face was making me feel guilty but at the same time I was glad to see that he cared about me. I didn't have the strength to say anything and judging by Sean's shaking lips, he didn't have it either. He looked overwhelmed and so did I. He sat there next to me the whole night. The next day all my neighbors and friends from the church showed up at the hospital. Everybody looked very concerned and I was very embarrassed.

"Why did you have to tell everybody?" I asked Sean.

"I didn't. They saw the ambulance and the paramedics sticking a tube in you. They came here by themselves. They're concerned about you," he said. At the hospital I had to talk to a psychiatrist who talked and walked like he thought of himself as nothing less than a God. There was nothing humble about that man and his obvious judgmental looks were at the very least unprofessional. He talked to Sean in the privacy of his office and he strongly advised him not only not to marry me but to move away from me. He told my boyfriend that I was a manipulator and that he was enabling me as long as he was with me. Sean told me all about it while we were arguing.

"Even that doctor told me not to marry you. He's convinced that you're trying to manipulate me." I knew that my boyfriend was asking his mother and his best friend what to do with me, but hearing this was just too much. When my lawyer from the insurance claim sent me the copies of all my medical records, I found a paper where that psychiatrist described me. Everything that Sean told me was written there on that piece of paper. My rage was rising inside me when I was reading my diagnosis: "*Born to lose.*"

"That fucking asshole who thinks that his PhD makes him superior to everybody else, he thinks that he can just go ahead and call losers anybody who's not like him!" I was talking to myself while drinking wine straight from a bottle and swallowing sleeping pills. I felt like such a loser all my life but seeing it actually written on a paper by some doctor was unbearable.

"Who gave him the right to condemn me like that? Is it that unethical to do what he did?" I was talking to myself but no matter how much I wanted to blame him for everything, I was really blaming myself because I believed him. I believed that he was right about me. After all, he was a respectable doctor who was working at the hospital, and I was just a twenty-nine year-old woman who wasted her life and with whom nobody wanted to have anything to do with. Sean was shouting at me this time when he came back from his trip and he saw me.

"What if I didn't come home? What if the plane was delayed? What would have happened to you? Why are you keeping on doing this?" He shouted while dialing 911.

In the hospital the same psychiatrist looked at me with that same judgmental look on his face.

"Why did you do it again? I thought you said that you'd go to San Francisco and that you'd start your life there?" As usual besides the judgment in his eyes, his face was deprived of any emotions.

"And you said that I wouldn't make it there. I read my medical records. You wrote that I was born to lose." I said to him without any emotions either. His face changed and his attitude towards me was different. I didn't enjoy it since I knew that the change wasn't caused by the concern about me. He was afraid that I was going to sue him and I could tell that. He even called me at home, once I was discharged, to offer me free consultations.

"No thank you, I'm OK. I'm moving to San Francisco." I said to him, imagining how relieved he must have felt knowing that I didn't intend to be a threat to him. Sean was asking our neighbors to keep an eye on me while he was at work. I didn't mind that too much because all my neighbors were very friendly and I was getting along with them. They were having tea at my house and sometimes they were bringing me some homemade cookies. I liked that neighborhood and I knew that I was going to miss everybody once I'd move to Northern California.

Debt

I wanted to visit Teddy one more time so I could say goodbye to him. Since all three battery operated cars I got for him had since vanished, I stopped by Wal-Mart to get him another one. The toy wouldn't fit in the small car I was leasing so I had to ask my friend Ron to drive me in his truck. Ron was working as a firefighter for LAFD and for years he used to work as an undercover cop for LAPD. My friend and I headed to Agua Dulce. Paul pulled in his big truck shortly after we got to his house. Ron told me then that clearly Paul seemed to be under influence. He was very disturbed to see Teddy riding with the old man who was in such dangerous state of mind.

"If I were you I'd report this man. You can use my testimony if you need to. He's putting this poor kid in constant danger. I can't believe what I'm seeing. I can't believe that social services would not let you have this kid because you're not blood-related to him." Ron was very convincing and I decided to do what he suggested. I called social services and I told them everything. Then I called the social worker who was in charge of Teddy's case and I asked her if I could be his foster parent. At first she didn't even want to talk to me, saying that it was all confidential, but once I explained to her my involvement with Teddy, she promised that she would place the child with me. I didn't want to wait for her to call me and I hired an attorney from whom I found out that Paul tested positive for crystal meth. She was unable to tell me where they placed Teddy and I just assumed that Mary's mother took him. My attorney told me that the judge was giving six more months for Mary to get her act together and that until then we couldn't do anything but to wait.

"This has been going on for more than two years now. She refuses to go to rehab and she keeps testing positive for crystal meth. How can they just let her do that to her child?" I was telling to my attorney and she looked like she understood my frustration.

"I know you want to adopt him but it's gonna be very hard. I'll do what I can, just keep in touch with me. Call me and leave me your new number once you'll settle in San Francisco," she said.

I asked Sean if he would be willing to try adopting Teddy with me. Only to find out that he had no intentions to support me on that or in any other way.

"OK, whatever, I just wanna know one thing; I want you to tell me the exact reason why you don't wanna marry me? Is it because I'm crazy? Is it because I tried to kill myself several times? What is it? I think after living together for two and a half years I have the right to know that, don't you think? Tell me exactly why?" I looked straight into his brown eyes that I used to adore so much.

"It's not that, I mean, you're crazy but that is actually what I love about you." I could tell that he was trying to avoid answering my question.

"Then what is it?" I was being impatient with him.

"Babe, I wanna marry somebody who can be my partner. I mean I wanna marry somebody who makes at least close to a hundred thousand dollars a year like I do," he said.

"Are you serious? So all this is about the money?" I couldn't believe what I was hearing.

"Babe, I was debt-free when I met you and now I have credit card bills that I don't even know how I'm going to repay. You drove me almost to a bankruptcy. I can't say no to you and you know that. I don't wanna live my life like this. I want my wife to be financially free. I'm used to a certain lifestyle and I don't want to have to compromise that." He continued.

"But you don't have a problem with me living with you. You want me to move to New Mexico to your brand new house and yet you're saying that if we were married you could not stand the financial burden that I'd bring to you. Make up your mind Sean because this does not make any sense."

"I wanna get married when I'm not in debt like I am right now."

"Whatever." I was hurt and angry and I just couldn't wait to get away from him. I felt betrayed and mislead. A week later, in the evening when he was supposed to fly back home from a business trip, I went to the kitchen and I started to break all his dishes against the sink. As the pieces of broken porcelain were sputtering around, I felt huge relief. When I was done destroying the whole set, I went to bed and I fell asleep. Ryan woke me up few hours later demanding an explanation.

"Fuck you!" I yelled at him and I went back to sleep. He knew he had to leave me alone because I've never used such language with him before.

I called my friend Julia, who I had recently met at a seminar and who happened to live in Northern California, near Napa, in small town called Glen Ellen. She agreed that I could stay with her and her boyfriend for a couple of weeks, until I'd find my own place. The insurance finally paid me off twenty thousand dollars so at least for a while I didn't have to worry too much about money. I rented a U-Haul which Sean ended up driving while I was following him in my car. Besides some furniture I took with me all my animals; my two German shepherds; Rex and Nel, my deaf cat Milky Way, my tortoise Don Pierro, two love birds and of course my goat Starla. The other goat Rampy was no longer with us. He became too aggressive, constantly trying to break everything around, trying to prove his suitability to Starla I guess. He was taken by a man who ran a petting farm.

Two weeks later I rented a three bedroom house with a very big yard where I could keep my goat. The house was a mess but the owners promised that they would make huge improvements in the next couple of months. The rent was seventeen hundred dollars a month and I knew that I had no choice and that soon I'd have to rent at least one of the rooms to somebody.

I wanted to keep one room empty in case if Teddy was going to stay with me. Sean flew from New Mexico to visit me once. My heart was still beating fast when I saw him pulling over in his rental car while I was digging in my garden. I was hoping that he missed me enough to rethink the marriage thing but Sean kept insisting that he didn't believe in a long distance relationship. When he left the next day, I was very unhappy and I sent him a very long email, basically saying to him that I did not wish to keep in touch with him unless we'd move our relationship to next level. He emailed me back saying everything that I had heard before and that he was sorry. I had no choice but to get over him and to do that I asked him not to ever call me again. I missed him the whole time and there was not a single day that I wouldn't think about him. Nevertheless I restrained my-self from talking to my ex-boyfriend.

Firehouse

The house looked a lot nicer once it was painted inside and out and fenced all around. The colorful flowers and my vegetable garden looked very beautiful against the yellow walls of the house and its green roof. In the small shed that was also renovated to match the house, I made an extra guest room. Starla had a very big, fenced space next to the shed where she could jump and run around without endangering my flowers or the tomato vines that I planted everywhere. Digging in my yard and looking for signs of life coming from tiny seeds was very relaxing. The elderly but very energetic mother of my landlord, who liked my passion for gardening, visited me often. She was always bringing flowers from her own garden and she always gave me useful tips on how to take care of them. I shared with her my heartache of not being able to adopt Teddy. Her daughter and her son-in-law who both happened to be retired lawyers, advised me to file with court a petition for placement.

"You have the case number and you qualify as a de facto parent since he was in your care before. Don't wait for anything. File the petition yourself. They have placed children in different counties, even in different states before." My landlord and her husband sounded very convincing. I did what they told me to and I waited anxiously for response. A few weeks later I got a letter from court saying that the case was moved to different county. The letter was advising me to re-file my petition with the court in Orange County. I did what I had to do but I wasn't getting any response this time. When I finally called the court, the clerk explained to me that the case number was different this time and that without it, they could not accept my petition. None of my pleading was going to make any difference. They refused to talk to me.

I was beating myself up for not filing the papers sooner, when Teddy was still living under LA County's jurisdiction. The more I was blaming myself, the more depressed I was getting. I wasn't getting along with my new roommates either. The young couple that rented out the two rooms was very messy and inconsiderate. They had two dogs and their pit-bull was tearing my flowers out while they were at work. They were getting on my nerves with their attitude that this was their house. They acted like they were annoyed with my nagging that I liked my kitchen sink to be empty. They were leaving a big mess sometimes on purpose to make point that this was their house too and that they were entitled to do whatever they wished. I was tired of this young boy's arrogance and the frequent arguments that he always loved to win. I finally told my roommates that they had to find a new place. They started to act like they were hurt by my insensitivity but my mind was made up; I wanted them out.

While they were still looking for a new place, I was very depressed and I withdrew from the world. My internet business wasn't bringing me any money at all. I was staying in my bed sometimes the whole day. I was once more feeling suicidal and I took sleeping pills again. This time I got very scared when I started to experience an increased heartbeat and difficulty breathing. While afraid that I would pass out any moment, I knocked at my neighbor's door and I told her to call 911. Because I was experiencing shortness of breath, I decided to run barefoot to a nearby fire station. I sat on the grass in front of the firehouse because I was feeling very weak. A young firefighter approached me and asked me what was wrong.

"I took sleeping pills." I said to him. I began to stop grasping for air as all my muscles felt as if they were relaxing completely. I could still hear the firefighters talking on the radio and the sirens of additional fire engines and an ambulance coming. I did not know that my body was convulsing or that I was having brain seizures, I found out about it later. My body was shaking uncontrollably and my eyes rolled all the way back leaving only the whites visible. When I woke up in the hospital I was bleeding from my lips.

"Why do I have blood on my lips?" I asked the doctor who was standing next to my bed.

"Your overdose on sleeping pills caused you to have two grand brain seizures," she explained to me in a tender way.

"Is it true that you were in the orphanage?" She asked me.

"Who told you about it?" Now I knew why she was looking at me in such a motherly way.

"We tried to contact your family, and your friends and neighbors told us that you live alone." She explained.

My landlord's mother came to pick me up from the hospital.

"My daughter asked me to tell you that she's gonna use your deposit to cover your next month rent, so you don't have to worry about anything but to get well. Everybody's worrying about you, you stupid, stupid girl," she said that in an angry and yet very tender way.

"Look at you. You're like a human-sized Barbie. You're gorgeous, you care about people, you love your animals, you're talented, and you're good at so many things. You can't just throw all this away. People need you, we need you." She was afraid to look me directly in my eyes so I wouldn't see how red they were getting. In the next few weeks she was checking on me daily and she was bringing me homemade food.

"Enough of that raw food diet of yours! You need to eat some real food." In her sweet and loving way she was bossing me around like she was my mother. Due to the brain seizures I was having problems with my memory. My mind felt like it was in a fog and I could not remember anything I said or did just a few hours before. All my neighbors were being very nice to me and they were inviting me to chat and to eat with them as well. My roommates who were about to leave were concerned about me too.

"Are you sure that you're gonna be OK all by yourself?" The girl asked me.

"Yeah, of course, don't worry about me. This isn't the first time that I've tried to kill myself. I'm addicted to it or something. Every time I tell myself that I'll never do it again and every time I hope it's the last time that I do such thing."

"I know. Sean told me," she said.

"What? When did you talk to him?" I asked.

"Don't get mad at me but I was very concerned about you. I was feeling so guilty that I didn't see this coming, and so I used your cell phone to call your ex-boyfriend." She looked like she wanted to apologize with her eyes for meddling in my personal life.

"That's OK, don't worry, no big deal. What did he say?" I asked.

"Well, you know what; you did the right thing moving away from him. He didn't say nice things about you. He was trying to warn us about you." She hesitated to tell me the truth.

"What do you mean? Come on, tell me everything. I'm over him anyway so I don't care what he has to say about me." I tried to sound very casual.

"He said that my boyfriend and I are very lucky that we're leaving. He said that if we'd stay, you'd bring us to a bankruptcy like you almost did with him. I'm really sorry, I mean, he sounded like a jackass." My roommate sat down on my bed to give me a hug when she saw the hurt in my eyes.

"Did you tell him that I didn't have your deposit money anymore?" I asked her.

"I did, I'm really sorry," she said.

"Don't worry. I have the money for your deposit like I said I would. I told you that you wouldn't leave before I would give it to you. But it's OK, now I know what Sean thinks of me and it will be that much easier to forget him," I said to her and she looked at the same time relieved and guilty for not trusting me.

I placed an ad on Craigslist for a roommate and I met Jeff. He was twenty-nine years old, one year younger than I was, and he was working in San Francisco as a mechanical engineer. He was cute too and I liked him instantly. Jeff and I were laughing like crazy when we were sharing each other's failures. I even told him about my recent intentional overdose. Jeff seemed nonjudgmental and even intrigued by me. He seemed to like my honesty and my ability to laugh at myself. My sense of humor, even though entertaining to him, was really the result of my desperation. I was almost thirty years old and I didn't know what to do with my life.

Shortly after the recovery from my overdose I went to the fire station and I asked if I could join the volunteer firefighter academy. I decided that if I wanted to stop being always part of problem, I had to become part of solution then. The two firefighters that were standing behind the desk were looking at me in disbelief.

"You don't remember us, do you?" The captain finally asked me.

"No." I hesitated.

"Did you come to that other fire station when I overdosed?" I asked.

"Yes, we were dispatched there." The captain informed me.

"Sorry I didn't recognize you and thank you, thank you for being there for me. I came here because I'm really serious about joining the fire academy," I said looking at them as convincing as I could.

"Well, the next academy doesn't start until the end of March which means that you're gonna have to wait six months for that. Come back in

February, we'll give you more details. Then you are gonna have to interview with our chief first. It's up to the chief who joins our fire department." The captain was very formal with me and I could tell that he didn't believe that he would see me again.

When I told Jeff about my intentions of becoming a volunteer firefighter, his face expressed that same doubt that the captain's face did, but I didn't care. I knew what I was going to do and I knew that the only person who could stop me was me, nobody else.

Sex with Jeff was a typical rebound sex. I knew that Sean was still calling Julia from time to time to check on me and I knew that she would tell him everything about my new sexy boyfriend. It was my way of getting even with him. Jeff was paying all my bills and I didn't have to worry about anything. When I told him about Teddy, he was very supportive and he gave me some money so I could go all the way to Southern California. The people that worked in the Orange County Court were refusing to talk to me. They were saying that without a case number my petition could not be accepted. I kept knocking on different doors on different floors and finally by the time my eyes were completely red from crying, some woman asked me to sit down. After hearing from me everything that I had to say, she told me to wait for her and that she'd be back with some information for me. She came back and she gave me Teddy's new social worker's name and her phone number.

"This is all I can do for you. I suggest you call this Mrs. Evans and you tell her everything you told me. If anything, maybe she can arrange some visitations for you." She gave me the piece of paper and she looked like she really wished that there was more that she could do.

"If I were you, I'd go back home. Social workers are in the field most of the time working with children, and it may take few days before you'll hear from her," she added as if she knew what I was thinking.

I finally got the call from Mrs. Evans few days later. She had a very unpleasant tone like she was annoyed with me. She told me that since Teddy's mother did not wish to stay in touch there was absolutely nothing that she could do for me. I was slowly giving up the idea that I'd ever see that little boy again.

The Firefighter

For Christmas and New Year's Eve, my house was full of people. Jeff invited his parents who came all the way from Michigan and I had visitors from Italy, Antonietta and Giuseppe. My Italian friends were very happy to see me and I was very glad that they stayed with us for five weeks. Everybody was getting along and I think that the tasteful Italian food prepared by Antonietta and Giuseppe had a lot to do with it. All the neighbors, including Julia and her two sons who were close in age to Teddy, visited frequently and our house was full of Christmas spirit. The firewood that was constantly burning in the fireplace was creating a sense of coziness and a sense of romanticism. The Christmas tree and Christmas lights on the roof of the house were adding a magical touch and were lighting up the whole neighborhood.

All this was over when Antonietta and Giuseppe went back to Italy. The house was empty again and Jeff was missing the excitement that I alone wasn't generating for him anymore. Even though he told me that he was moving closer to the city because he was tired of the long commute, I knew that in reality he was tired of me. He did ask me to move in with him but I knew that he didn't mean it. It looked like he was trying to protect my feelings but in reality he was trying to protect his own. He did not want to think of himself as a cold and insensitive guy. It was hard when he left. I was scared. I was afraid of getting depressed again and I had to fight the dark thoughts that were crawling into my head. At night I was petting Milky Way, reassuring him that we were going to be fine. In reality I was trying to reassure myself while trying to overcome the shortness of breath caused by anxiety.

Luckily I was able to find a part time job in San Francisco. On the weekends I was driving to the city to teach young girls at an expensive modeling school. The girls liked me a lot and were telling their parents how fun and beautiful their new teacher was. The director was happy to have hired me, but I could not help but to feel like the whole thing was a scam. I felt that those young girls and their loving parents, who would do anything to make their offspring happy, were being exploited. Still, I needed my paycheck and I needed it badly. My bills were piling up and even the additional rent money from my new roommate wasn't enough to cover even half of the total expense. I was constantly stressed out and constantly afraid of losing the house. I was eating very little, mostly feeding myself from the products that came from my garden. I had no social life and the internet was my only way of staying in touch with people.

I don't know how he found me but one evening I received an instant message from a guy named Dean. I kept denying his invitation to join my friends list and he kept sending me invites with messages.

"Don't be afraid to add me to your list, I'm not a psychopath. I just want to get to know you." Dean was typing while I was clicking on the deny access link.

"Who are you and why do you keep bugging me? Why don't you leave me alone? I don't know you." I finally sent him a message back while still blocking him from my list.

"That's what instant messaging is for, to get to know people. Just add me to your list so we can chat. There is nothing to be afraid of," he'd respond. The messages went back and forth and after a week or so I found myself looking forward to them while starting my laptop. I was impressed with his perseverance and I was feeling somewhat flattered. I still knew very little about instant messaging and if it wasn't for Sean who once installed Yahoo Messenger on my computer, I wouldn't even know what this new way of communication was about. I finally clicked the accept invitation link one day.

"There you are! I've been looking all over for you." Dean was very happy for the chance I gave him.

"Who are you? And why on earth have you been looking for me?" I could not understand what he was talking about. From what I understood he saw some picture of me online and ever since he wanted to know who I was. Dean was a forty year-old businessman who lived in South Africa and who traveled a lot to Europe. He was separated and he had children so he couldn't be my soul-mate but I enjoyed chatting with him. Soon enough I was addicted to our online conversations. Dean was "listening" to me telling him about my first day in the firefighter academy. He was there for me when I was crying and doubting myself. He was encouraging me and always knew what to say to me. He became my friend and I finally agreed to use a web camera so we could see each other.

"Wow, you're more beautiful than you are in pictures." Dean was staring at me as if he couldn't believe his eyes. I liked Dean's attention. I liked how eager he always was to chat with me. I liked how he was showering me with complements. And I really liked how from time to time he was wiring me some money so I could pay my rent on time. Since the academy was taking place also on Saturdays, at least for a while I had to give up my teaching job and I had to find something else.

I got a job at the gas station as a cashier girl. The job sucked but I needed it. The ugly apron I had to wear, which color-wise resembled a milk laden coffee, made me look awful. The customers were mostly unhappy people who were very angry that to get to their jobs, the first thing in the morning they had to do was pump expensive fuel in their vehicles.

"Scuse me. I want to know why my receipt says a different amount from the one that's on the gas meter outside." This was the complaint that I heard every day.

"Ma'am, you must read the sign that's on every gas pump. Right there, you see? If you use your credit card instead of cash, the surcharge fee will be added automatically to your bill." I had to explain to them how their convenience was costing them more money.

"Oh, this is outrageous! Who does business like this? You will not see me here ever again! There are plenty of other gas stations in this town." Many of the customers were trying to take it out on me in their attempt at venting their frustration. I was ignoring them by pointing at the manager's phone number. Luckily for me I had my firefighter academy spicing up my life enough to forget my boring job. There were some other girls in the academy but I could tell that many viewed me as some kind of a mistake.

"What is she doing here?" That was the look on people's faces when I showed up on my first day. My permanent make up and my dyed hair gave them the impression of a spoiled girl whose rich parents sent her to a boot camp to keep their only child on a straight path. My cobra tattoo on my right shoulder must have scared them enough because nobody seemed eager to be my training partner. I was looking forward to experiencing brotherhood and sisterhood and the thrill of teamwork and yet I was feeling like I was back in elementary school.

My lack of physical strength in my shoulders and my fear of heights were not making my life any easier. I was having troubles with raising the twenty-four foot ladder all by myself. My strong determination seemed like it wasn't enough to pass that obstacle that was going to be included in the final exam. The only thought of giving up was burning my eyes like hell and I was more than embarrassed when I couldn't stop my tears from rolling down my dirty and sweaty face. The fire captain, who was the instructor for that particular task, was looking at me as if he was thinking that he would never have to see me again. People were looking in silence while I was struggling with the heavy ladder with its long end shivering uncontrollably in the air.

Everybody remained silent when despite the rule I slammed the ladder against the wall. I had no strength left in my body and the heavy gear I was wearing wasn't helping me either. I was embarrassed, frustrated and angry all at once. After the class was over I went to the firehouse in my town and I asked for help the two firefighters that knew me from my overdose emergency. Captain Shone and firefighter Mason, were the only career firefighters in that station, which meant that they worked full time and they were being paid for it. Everybody else, including chief, was dedicating their time and their skills on a volunteer basis. Many of them had worked as career firefighters in different stations. Chief Murray himself was a retired fire captain for one of the stations in San Francisco. His grandfather was once a fire chief for San Francisco Fire Department. Captain Shone, Mason and even the chief were determined to help me in overcoming my weakness.

"Look kiddo, it's not as bad as it may seem. The strongest parts of you are your legs and you need to learn how to use them to leverage this thing. You're skinny but you're also tall and that is your advantage and you need to learn how to use it in this kind of work." Chief's convincing attitude was very helpful. Captain Shone and Mason practiced with me until I was able to raise the ladder all by myself.

"You're gonna be just fine." Mason patted me on my shoulder. He was very good at explaining things to me. He had a real talent at making things look less intimidating. Being a strong firefighter himself, he never made me feel like he disapproved of what I was trying to accomplish. He never made me feel as if my intention of becoming a firefighter was posing a threat to his macho-hero image.

"Look, I see you running with your dogs every morning. Why don't you ask chief if you can use our gym? You're in the academy now, I'm sure he'll let you use it." Mason said to me and I followed his suggestion. Every day when I wasn't at work, I was at the firehouse doing my cardio and lifting weights. In the academy I was more determined than ever to finish what I started. I did not miss a single day in the three months of training. I loved getting on my knees and searching in complete darkness for a manikin. I loved dragging that hundred and fifty pound thing out in the open while avoiding all the obstacles set by the instructors. I had so much fun cutting cars open, smashing windshields, and in the final day, putting a fire down. Cutting a roof open for ventilation purposes wasn't my favorite thing, but of course it had to be done too. I loved how dirty and how exhausted I was at the end of each class. I liked myself in this new role so much that I didn't want it to end. Ever! My confidence and my self esteem were boosted so much and everybody who knew me noticed it. The respect I was getting for my hard work and dedication was making me feel very good.

"Look who's here! Come, come to my office." Chief always looked like he was happy to see me.

"I've got here your test results. Well, you've passed written and skills exam with flying colors. You've also got a type of comment from the academy coordinator that I haven't seen in years. It says here that Elzbieta did an outstanding job and that it was a true pleasure to have such highly motivated individual on the team. Congratulations! Here's your diploma." Chief shook my hand while handling me the piece of paper.

"Thank you. Thank you so much." I was shaking his hand.

"You did it. I knew you would and you proved I was right. This is something to be very proud of. Now, we're gonna have to send you to a doctor to get a special physical exam and if everything is the way it should be then captain Shone will give you your pager. Now you know that for the first year, before you'll get your badge, you'll be on probation, which means you'll be like a trainee. But you know all that already. OK then. Welcome a board! You're part of this family now."

"Thank you chief! I'm so grateful for this opportunity."

"Continue to work hard as you've been doing so far and you'll be fine. Shone told me that you're taking some classes at the community college. What classes are you taking?" Chief asked me.

"I'm taking a First Responder course, Fire Technology and another class that's a prerequisite for the firefighter academy that the college offers." I explained to him with enthusiasm as if he was my father asking about my grades.

"Well, that's fantastic. But keep in mind that you don't need that academy even if you want to be a career firefighter one day. Every department that hires new recruits puts their new firefighters through their own academy. What you may wanna do, you may wanna take an EMT course. Today, most of the departments require their firefighters to be licensed EMTs." Chief was very good at giving me the sense of direction.

He was like a father to me. He liked my enthusiasm and my dedication. In every occasion he'd tell me how proud he was of me and how glad he was that I was part of his team. In times when I looked tired and insecure he'd take me to his office to have a chat with him.

"Look kiddo, you're gonna be a hell of a firefighter that much I'm sure of. I know you want it very badly and you've proved to yourself and to all of us that you've got what it takes. You belong here just like everybody else does. You're earned the right to be here, so don't be so harsh on yourself. Don't beat yourself up." He always seemed to know when I doubted myself and my performance.

At the end of the semester I got two A's and one F for the classes I took. I didn't pass the prerequisite class that was necessary to join the academy that college was offering. I failed in the last day of the skills exam. That day I felt devastated. I was the only one in class who failed to finish the task on time.

In the next few days I was ignoring the sound of my pager.

"Bee-pee-pee-pee-pee-peep, k-shhhh… Thirty-two eighty-one; respond to traffic collision on Highway 12 and Arnold Drive. Repeat; reported car accident on intersection of Highway 12 and Arnold Drive." I'd listen to dispatcher's voice and I wouldn't even move from my bed. Normally I'd jump in my car and in no time I'd be at the firehouse donning my gear and jumping on the engine with other firefighters. Or I'd be at the firehouse already, working out in the gym or following Mason like a shadow in an attempt to learn as much as I could. My few days' absence was noticed by chief because one morning I saw a red rescue truck pulling into my driveway.

"Chief, what are you doing here? Is everything alright? Is my house on fire?" I was surprised to see him because I didn't think he knew where I lived.

"No, no, everything is fine. I came to talk to you." He laughed while sitting on the bench on my porch.

"How're you doing? Look, I know what happened the other day. I spoke to your instructor from your class and he told me everything. There is nothing to be embarrassed about; if you did your best, and knowing you, I know you did your best. I know how much this meant to you but I've got to tell you this, you don't need that academy sponsored by that community college. You can still be the best firefighter you can be. You passed our academy, didn't you? I believe in you, I always did and you've constantly been proving to me that I was right about you. "

"Thanks chief, it means a lot to me." I said to him while regretting not to have brushed my hair or even washed my face earlier.

"You can still do it. You can still become what you want. Take that EMT course instead. Not only it will give you more confidence but it will also jump your reimbursement check from five dollars and fifty cents to six-fifty per call. You'll be getting a whole dollar more for your time." He laughed and I laughed with him.

The EMT class turned out to be a lot more fun that I would have expected. We all had to purchase and wear dark blue uniforms that were identical to the ones the firefighters wore. Apart from studying in class, we were practicing our skills in created and organized scenarios. The mandatory internship included rides along in actual ambulances, with real EMTs and Paramedics. I never knew before how satisfying it would be to see somebody in desperate need and to be able to do something about it. For the first time in my life I wasn't feeling as powerless as I did before. I surprised myself with the sense of calmness that I was feeling while responding to 911 calls that my pager was alerting me about. I was quick, alert, and yet almost relaxed.

Even though I was technically still a trainee and I didn't have my badge yet, most of the firefighters understood my eagerness towards learning. They were letting me to step in. I soon understood that patient interaction was my favorite thing to do. I loved how my smile and the look on my face like I knew exactly what I was doing were having relaxing effect on everybody. I loved how some patients would joke that if they knew before that I was going to be the one to rescue them, that they would have called for help a lot sooner.

"She's gonna take my blood pressure? Oh boy, the numbers are gonna be through the roof!" Some male patients couldn't stop being funny and everybody would just burst in laughter. I liked my life and I didn't want for things to change. I desperately tried to hold on to my house since living in the firehouse proximity was required in order to be part of the department. When my landlord told me that she put the whole property on the market, I wasn't happy to hear that. She told me that she wanted a more financially stable tenant to be renting her house, in case a potential buyer was interested in buying and then keeping the house rented out for income. Needless to say, she wanted me out.

Heartbroken

Forced to give up the house, I went through a brief period of intense soul-searching. The painful emotions of losing the sanctuary called home, which obviously kept resurfacing throughout my whole life, were making me very angry. I was feeling beyond tired of constantly being on the move. The regular inconveniencies of relocating were getting on my nerves but not as much as the feeling of luck of safety. Even though I was trying to convince myself that I was a strong woman, I was still more than upset at Sean for abandoning me. That's what it felt; abandonment and rejection on his part. The pain could not be numbed no matter how much I tried ignoring it throughout this whole year without him.

Trying to reason that I've survived without Sean before and that I would make it this time again wasn't very soothing either. Even though he'd never really say that to me, I resented him for making me feel that he questioned my intentions towards him. It was clear to me that he wondered sometimes whether I'd still be with him if I had a real place of my own. I hated that feeling. That sense of urge of having to prove myself to everyone. To my defense I tried imagining whether he would remain with me if I was, for example, less attractive? The hurt caused by Sean's decision of not marring me had a bigger impact on me that I was ready to admit. As with each smite and each blow beneath the belt in my life; I dealt with it by trying to suppress my anger the best way I knew how. Pretending like it never happened seemed to be a defense mechanism that my brain had set on automatic. Minimizing things so they wouldn't hurt so much was yet another coping "program" my mind liked to use in its sweet attempt of protecting me. The final stages of this healing process were always run by thoughts typical to "after the break up" ideas.

"*Well, he wasn't that great either. And he was a workaholic. He'd rather spent time with his coworkers than with me. Who wants to live like that? Well, he'll never find someone like me. I'm better off without him anyway.*"

Sean and I had recently started conversing again. It was like two high-school kids trying to play cool with each other.

"She's trying to convince me that I'm still in love with you." He'd try to sound innocent while complaining to me over the phone about his new girlfriend.

"Sean, you've been sitting in the parking lot of the hospital, while she's been waiting for you to visit her, and instead you've been chatting with me for over an hour. Of course she's right about that and you know it." I tried not to sound too excited but it was hard. He'd complain some more about her, trying not to make it sound like he's been thinking a lot about me. Since Sean obviously was never going to "man up" enough to fight for us and our love, I decided to take matters in my own hands. I figured that his new girlfriend knew my name. I was suspecting that she had been checking on my myspace profile. I didn't know who she was so I couldn't write to her directly. So instead I added to my own online profile a photo of Sean and me. I added a "spicy" description to it. I wrote:

"That's right; I'll always be in his heart!" My sweet girlfriend Kelly, my former neighbor, commented on it:

"Oh Elzbieta, he sure truly loved you the way he'll never be able to love anyone else. You were the love of his life, that's for sure." My intuition was right and Sean's girlfriend apparently was stocking me on the internet because she saw the picture of Sean and I as well as the comments. Sean called me later infuriated.

"You have no business to meddle in my love life like that!" He was shouting on the phone. I was shouting back at him:

"What the hell are you talking about? So she saw the picture, eh? It's my freaking space and I will do with it whatever I feel like! Who the hell asked her to visit my profile? What is she doing that for anyway?"

"I don't wanna ever talk to you again!" He continued with his outburst.

"Well then don't! But instead of being such a stubborn ass why don't you just freaking admit that you're still in love with me? Why don't we both stop acting like such morons? In fact, you know what? I'm done with this bull shit. I'm just gonna pack my stuff, take all my kids and, like it or not, and we are coming to New Mexico!" I yelled.

"No, you can't come here! She lives with me."

"Well too bad. You know just as well as I do that you don't really love her."

"Don't come over here! Stay where you are. I'm telling you the house is gonna be locked! You won't be able to come in."

"Well then I'll just have to break the window, won't I?" I wasn't giving up.

I started to pack. Most of my furniture was gone already since the big garage sale that some of my class mates helped me organize. My landlord surprised that I was leaving not just the house but the state altogether agreed to watch over Starla for some time. The tortoise and the birds have been on the loose for some time enjoying their freedom since they had run away. Now it was just me, Rex, Nel and Milky Way. The goat would have to be shipped to New Mexico later; she could not fit in the two-seated car.

"OK. Rex, Nel; are you guys comfortable? Good. How about you Milky Way? Don't worry; we will be with daddy in no time." I put the gear in the reverse.

"Bye Starla! I know, I know! Don't worry; we'll be shipping you to New Mexico too!" I shouted towards the fence through which Starla tried to squeeze her sad looking face. She never liked when we would leave the house without her. I always felt guilty for leaving her alone. I used to take her with us to a dog park that was near the house. She loved running there with all the dogs but I had to stop taking her there after one of them attacked her.

With the top opened and the music blasting from the radio we entered the Sonoma Highway. I was feeling excited to see Sean again after such long time. The sweet memories were passing across my mind the way the pastures of green vineyards were passing us by. The feelings of warmth and tenderness were making me comfortable from within. How great was it going to be with Sean again! How great was it going to be to have my life make sense again! I smiled widely while remembering the "incident" with pierogies. I made those Polish dumplings once when Sean had to travel to Texas for work. I made them with blueberries. I rapped a dozen of them in some plastic bugs and paper-towels, placed them in a box and shipped them to him via UPS. He was touched. He called me immediately when he received the package.

"I'm not sure if you love me that much or if you hate me so much that you just want me dead?" He was joking.

"What do you mean I want you dead?" I couldn't understand.

"Babe, are you sure these pierogies are still eatable after spending a couple of days in the UPS truck?" He hesitated.

"Of course they are! Don't be a woos. Eat my damn pierogies. I spent a whole day making them." I laughed. He ate them and he was fine. Sean enjoyed telling everyone what a crazy girlfriend he had. Everybody had to know that he had practically a zoo in his backyard. He seemed happy with how much diversity I was bringing into his stable, to the verge of being boring life. He seemed to enjoy taking care of me. Sean's level of maturity and how responsible he was is what I admired the most. He made me feel safer than anyone ever did in my entire life. I never really knew how relaxing life could be until I met him. I never felt as much loved until then. He always talked slow with calmness present in his tone. I loved his manly deep voice. It was so soothing. As far as I could remember, he never really raised his voice on me, even though there were times when I would try to provoke him on more than just one occasion. He never seemed to get mad at me or even wanting to get mad at me. Normally I would have a hard time with expressing my feelings towards him but I did love doing so through the numerous letters I'd sent to Sean when he had to travel. He'd sent some cards to me as well. I liked how he kept all my letters in the shoe-box. I liked how he cherished them.

"Hello?" I answered my cell-phone while driving fast. I wanted to reach New Mexico as fast as I could and I still had a couple of states to cross.

"Hey Tomek. What's up?" I was surprised to hear from my Polish friend from LA. Since I moved to Northern California I wasn't keeping as much in touch with his wife Wanda anymore. Tomek and I hardly ever called each other. After a few horribly long minutes later I understood the reason behind that call. It was beyond humiliating to listen to Tomek's reasoning why I should turn around and go home. Apparently Sean called my Polish friends to have them help him with convincing me to remain in California.

"He's over you. You'll make a fool of yourself if you show up at his house. Don't you get it? He got engaged." Tomek's words were like sword cutting through my heart.

"And he said that he will file a restraining order against you if you break into his house. I'm telling you girl, you need to turn around and go home. Don't embarrass yourself like that." The torture continued until I promised Tomek that I'd turn around and we hung up.

I pulled over on the edge of the road. The tears that I wanted to smother were burning my eyes as if they were not made of water but acid instead.

"Engaged? Since freaking when? What? Did he forget to mention that to me when we were chatting? Or did he just run after her with a ring in his pocket right after that myspace picture that I posted? Most likely that's what happened." The acidic-like tears were scrolling loosely down my cheeks. The saltiness in my mouth could be compared to the bitterness I felt about my life.

"How could he freaking hurt me like this? How could he do this?" I could not wrap my mind around the simple thought of Sean being capable of hurting me this much. I felt humiliated, betrayed, abandoned, rejected and I was hurting like hell. I went back to the house that I knew I was gonna have to give up for good in a matter of few days.

Virginia's Ranch

It was hard to accept the fact that I would no longer be part of the fire department since I would no longer be a resident of this small town. The fire department of city of Santa Rosa did not have a volunteer program hence "transfer" wasn't an option either. I knew that I would miss not only responding to calls but that I would also miss the events that our department organized from time to time. I liked how every Thursday evening it was mandatory for all firefighters to attend trainings. These people became my extended family and I didn't want for that sense of belonging to end. Chief still expressed his hope that I would be back one day. Nevertheless I had to be responsible and I had to make a decision to live someplace where I could afford living.

Glen Ellen and its beautiful vineyards was way above my financial limits. The new place I found was on mountainside in Santa Rosa. It was a small trailer parked on property called Virginia's Ranch. Virginia and her husband were the owners of this neglected piece of land and they were using it for their nonprofit for children they were running. They were living in a big house that desperately needed all kinds of repairs. The numerous horses the couple had were being used to teach youth responsibility while having some fun. Virginia had a white van in which she used to pick up kids whose parents signed them up for this program. I offered her my help and she made a deal with me saying that in exchange I could stay in the trailer for free.

"I can't do more than two days a week though because I have to go to school for my EMT class and I just applied for a new job." I told her when she asked me how many days I could work with her.

"What kind of job did you apply for?" She asked me.

"I went to that Assisted Living with Alzheimer Home and I applied for a caregiver position. They called me and I had an interview and it looks like after my criminal background check comes back, I'll be able to work there." I explained to her.

"So, when can you start? When can you move in?" She asked me.

"Well, there is one more thing. I have two dogs, a cat and a goat and I don't want to get rid of them." I looked at her afraid to see her reaction.

"So? What's the problem? Just bring them here. Your goat can stay with our goats, no?" I was finally able to relax. Before I moved to Virginia's Ranch I had brief bit of hope in seeing Teddy. While getting rid of most of my things I found the phone number to Teddy's grandmother. She knew who I was since she met me few times while her grandchild was in my care. After talking to her for at least an hour, I learned that the boy was living with her. She explained to me that the Social Services had placed him in a foster home where he spent two months until she intervened. I told her what I had been trying to do to get him and she seemed like she understood my grief. She agreed that I could come and visit him but only after she talked to her daughter Mary about it first. The next day she wasn't answering my calls, obviously ignoring the messages that I left. I was heartbroken once again and once again I promised myself that I would stop thinking about Teddy.

In my new care-giving job I was making ten dollars per hour before taxes. The facility had more than one hundred elderly residents and only a few caregivers in charge per shift. The job was extremely demanding but it was also in some ways fulfilling. Apart from changing adult dippers and listening to the constant nagging of dissatisfied residents that suffered from dementia, there were moments of actual joy. There was singing that the facility organized a few times a week by bringing in some talented volunteers who knew how to play different instruments. There was a bingo game that the same groups of residents were attending each time.

I was working full time and pretty soon I was picking up extra shifts as well. The caregivers were constantly calling in sick and knowing the kind of workload they had, nobody could really blame them. Every week when the new schedule was being posted in the office there would be a note from the manager; please, extra shifts need to be covered. I'd sign my initials in those boxes agreeing that I would work double shifts those days. I'd go straight from school to work and then I'd do my job for sixteen hours straight. I could barely walk and my back was killing me but still there were people who needed to be showered and others who needed to be moved to their wheelchairs. Every resident had an alarm in their room which they loved to pull on for any reason. I realized that their cry for attention was the only tool they had left. I also realized that in order to keep my sanity I had to stop feeling sorry for these people. I had to face the fact that I was simply a human being and not a saint. The senior citizens were like big children who were competing for our attention which came through the care that we had to provide.

The work with kids at Virginia's Ranch was taking any free time that I had left. There was no time for me and I was feeling guilty for neglecting my animals. I had to remind myself that what mattered was that I could keep them with me at least. But one day Starla got sick. My goat's jaw was swollen and she had real hard time breathing. The vet that came to see her left me with shots of antibiotics and she instructed me on how to feed my goat through the syringe. Virginia became very hostile with me accusing me that I was neglecting my animals and that if I wasn't so busy my goat would never have gotten so sick. I could not understand this woman's negative feelings towards me but considering that I was living in her trailer I felt like I had to put up with her criticism.

"You need to do something about Rex. He's wandering around all day and I'm scared that he'll eat my chickens." She informed me in an authoritative way while I was giving shots to my goat. Rex of course would never do such thing but, I didn't feel like I was in a position to argue with her.

"OK, I guess I'll just have to tie him to the trailer when I'm at work." I said to her. I felt real bad for leaving Rex on a leash all day but I didn't have much choice. Nel didn't have to be tied since she would never leave Rex's site. The two of them were inseparable.

A few days later when the vet told me that Starla wasn't improving, I decided to take my goat to UC Davis hoping that they would save her there. I borrowed a truck from Julia's boyfriend and I put Starla in the back. At the hospital I watched people shaving my goat in preparation for the surgery that she would have to undergo in the morning. The very nice veterinarian told me to go home and she assured me that she would call me the next day, right after the surgery. At the ranch Virginia was waiting for me. She had anger written all over her face.

"Because of you and your goat some people called animal control on us. The animal control officer called and I told him that it was you that he needed to talk to, not me. This is his number, you have to call him or otherwise they'll send some people here. I don't need this. I don't need animal control on my ranch. This is all your fault, you and your busy schedule." She was getting all hysterical.

"Calm down Virginia. I will call the guy and I'll deal with him. Just calm down, you're being unreasonable." I was tired and I tried my best not to lose my temper with her. I called the officer who sounded like a nice guy. I gave him the numbers to both veterinarians who were treating Starla and he told me that he'd have to have a talk with them. He called me back later saying that according to both professionals there was absolutely nothing that I did wrong and he informed me that he was closing this case. The next day I got a call from UC Davis. The same nice vet that I met the day before informed me that my goat suffocated prior to surgery. I could not believe that my two year old goat was dead. I had her since she was so small that she looked very clumsy when she was walking on her skinny legs. When I first went to pick her up, my foster kids were holding her on their knees in the back seat of my car. I named her Starla not only because she was all white like a star, but also because she appeared to be smiling like a diva. It was very painful to lose her like this. I worked a double-shift that day, trying not to think about anything and then I went back to my trailer, hoping to get some sleep.

Glen Ellen Again

"Come on guys. Let's go. Let's go inside. Let's get some freaking rest." I took Rex off the leash and I climbed the poorly installed stairs. Rex and Nel were wagging their tails happy to see me. They were making that usual funny noise from excitement that resembled whining.

"I know, I know. It's been a long day. I-I-I know." I spent few minutes scratching their heads.

"K, let's go!" I clapped my hands and the two of them lined up in front of the stairs ready to come in. I opened the door. The floor was submerged in water. Everything on the ground, from the kitchenette to the tiny bathroom was soaked. As it turned out, one of the pipes underneath the sink broke earlier.

"What the fuck?" Words just came out of my mouth. I cleaned up all the mess and I couldn't help but to compare all this to what was going on inside of me. I was overflowing with emotions that I could no longer withstand. I could not stand living in the ugly trailer that was parked near a huge pile of garbage and some old, rusty automobiles. I hated that Rex had to be on the leash all day. Virginia's criticism towards me, which she was using as her weapon in her attempt to control me, was getting really old. I called my friend Jared, my classmate, and he came to rescue me.

"Why didn't you call me sooner? I can't believe you've been living in this dump." Jared was verbalizing his thoughts while helping me to load my stuff in his car. Virginia wasn't happy that I was leaving. She was accusing me of being a coward who run away every time that had to face even the slightest problem. I wasn't even talking to her, happy that I didn't have to deal with her anymore. I stayed with Jared for a month in his guest house that he was renting from his parents. Then one day one of the volunteer firefighters that I used to work with, Stewart, called me on my cell phone. He told me that he would try convincing his son in having me as his roommate. It worked. I moved back to Glen Ellen and I had my pager back. I was working, studying and volunteering again and everything seemed to be in order.

Then Stewart's son told me that he wasn't comfortable with me living in his house unless the two of us had a relationship, so I had to move out. His father came to my rescue and he offered me a room in his house. Stewart was sixty years old and he looked his age but the way he always made me laugh had a very magnetic effect on me. I liked when after sixteen hours of work I'd go home knowing that I'd find Stewart still not sleeping. His waiting for me to make sure that I got home safe was very endearing. I liked the new fence that he built for Rex and Nel so I wouldn't have to worry about my dogs. He made me feel safe and it was something that I hadn't felt in a long time. I don't know what got into me but I had sex with him. It must have had a lot to do with my poor self-image and my nonexistent self-worth. Maybe I did it because I liked living with him so much and I was afraid that he'd ask me to leave.

But soon things started to get worse. I started to demonstrate my insecurities due to my overwhelming fear of rejection. I was in constant need of having a serious conversation with Stewart which was annoying the hell out of him. He finally told me that I had to find a new place to live. I stayed in his house until I was done with my finals. It was right before Christmas, and with chief's permission I was living temporarily in the firehouse. I stayed there for three weeks. Even though chief and his wife invited me to their house for Christmas dinner, I didn't go, since at work I picked up on all the shifts that nobody else wanted to cover. Working through this holiday time was the best way of numbing my feelings so I wouldn't have to feel sorry for myself. My co-workers were sure grateful. I was glad that I had a break from school and even more glad that I got an A on my EMT course.

I passed the National Registry exam on my first attempt and I got my official EMT license after that. Chief of course was very proud of me. Hungry for more I signed up for more classes at the college. I took Anatomy and Physiology, Basic Heart Arrhythmias, which was designed to teach the use of EKG and I took a boxing class as well. In the meantime, chief convinced a local woman name Stacy to rent a room for me in her big house. Stacy wasn't just a "regular" woman and she meant a big deal to the fire department. Her late husband used to work as a battalion chief and all her seven children were firefighters. Her daughter, who was working as a firefighter/paramedic in Napa, was my role model. Stacy's property was in the mountains and the fire department had an extra engine parked right in her yard, next to the house. The six months at her house went by fairly quickly. I finished my classes with straight A's and I also got the badge for successfully finishing my probation period with the fire department. In my dark blue uniform and with my shiny silver badge people were mistaking me for a police officer. It was amazing how much respect I was getting from total strangers. For the first time in my life I walked really straight. I wasn't hiding my neck in my shoulders anymore and I was placing my feet firmly on the ground. My boots connected with the earth making the sound of somebody who's very confident and familiar with the territory.

In a school event in which we sprayed kids with water from the engines, the young girls were telling me that they wanted to be firefighters one day just like I was. I was a totally new person with totally new values. I respected life like I never had before. I was thinking of safety day and night and yet that wasn't either boring or overwhelming. Protecting lives was giving me the desire to live fully and to protect my own life. The thoughts of suicide could not coexist with my new zest for life. I was so much in love with my new role that I even dared to imagine becoming a doctor one day. I would find a way to go to school for the next eight years. It didn't matter to me that I was already thirty-one years old. I was just glad that I found something in life that was making sense. I was so happy to have a goal for a change. My old love for learning and for improving myself returned to me and I didn't want for it to go to waste. I was starting to feel empowered as if I was really in charge of my life and my destiny.

But of course things never went for me the way I planned. I tried to get a job on an ambulance but that wasn't happening. Then chief informed me of his decision of retiring and that wasn't good news for me either. Without him and his open mind I knew that things wouldn't be the same. On top of everything I lost my car since my lease came to an end and I didn't pay my last two payments on it. I was riding up the mountain on my bicycle and that wasn't as much fun as if I did it for recreational reasons only.

I toyed with the idea of going to Hawaii before, so I already had all my quarantine papers for my pets taken care of. All I needed was the guts to actually do it; the guts to leave everything behind, once again, and to start all over. Two days before my scheduled flight to Honolulu, I flew to Los Angeles in the hope of establishing some contact with Teddy. I drove to Orange County in a rental car. Teddy's social worker sounded as cold in person as she did over the phone. She was insisting that there was nothing that she could do for me and so I finally told her that I wanted to talk to her supervisor. The man seemed a lot more sympathetic. As he was listening to my story while looking at pictures of Teddy in a photo album that I brought, I could tell that even the social worker was warming up to me. The supervisor promised me that they would stay in touch with me and that I would be informed in case any changes in this child custody case changed. I left Southern California with only trace of hope.

Ahmed

"Ladies and gentleman, I'm captain McCarthy, and I want to inform you that we're getting ready to land. The temperature in Honolulu is eighty-two degrees as of this moment. I hope you enjoyed the flight and I want to thank you for choosing Hawaiian Airlines."

"OK, we're here. Now we'll need to find some place to stay, even if temporary, and then I'll have to find a job." I was trying to think clearly even though it was very hard considering the fear of the unknown I was facing.

"One thing at the time; let's first pick up Rex, Nel, and Milky Way from the quarantine office." I was giving myself instructions in my mind.

I went to the quarantine office, and an employee told me that my companions would be released to me in about an hour. I walked back to terminal.

I saw a man smoking. I asked him for a cigarette.

"Of course; anything for you my dear, we have everything here. Everything you need. Aloha. Welcome to Honolulu."

I inhaled the cigarette as if the nicotine was going to solve all my problems.

"What brings you to Honolulu?" He asked.

"I wish I knew the answer to that." I said.

I didn't feel like revealing my past to him but I didn't feel like being rude to him either.

"Ten years ago I divorced my wife and I left Egypt. I've been living here ever since. I'm Ahmed by the way. What's your name?"

"Elzbieta," I answered.

"What a beautiful name. But of course, beautiful woman like you must have a beautiful name. How could it be otherwise?"

Ahmed appeared to be in his late forties. His light colored wardrobe accentuated his darker skin. He had short dark hair and around his temples I could spy traces of white hair. The noticeable dip in his chin and his very dark eyes added charisma to his friendly and outgoing personality. Ahmed spoke with a thick accent that was characteristic of people whose first language is Arabic.

He liked to talk a lot. He spoke decent English but his incorrect use of grammar proved he didn't learn English in school. He owned a small transportation business, and they picked up tourists at the airport. After chatting for a while, Ahmed offered to let me and my furry kids stay at his office for few days, until I could find something better. He knew that it wasn't going to be easy to find a housing rental in Honolulu that would allow "pets."

Ahmed's downtown office was dirty, with dead cockroaches in every corner of the old building, which once served as a medical center. Rooms were stuffed with boxes, some old furniture and piles of garbage covered with dust. The only room that looked like an actual office was the one that had an actual desk, phone and computer in it.

The place looked depressing but I didn't have the luxury of being picky. I was just glad that Rex, Nel, and Milky Way were with me. One of the rooms with the most damaged ceiling had an old bed in it and I decided to get some sleep there.

Ahmed seemed very helpful but I really didn't know him or his real intentions towards me, for that matter. I felt suspicious toward him and I didn't trust him much.

Meditations

While staying at the office, Ahmed was letting me to shower in his apartment. The office looked a lot nicer after I spent few days cleaning and decorating it. The drivers coming in and out were getting on my nerves though and I was missing a sense of privacy. Ahmed himself was getting on my nerves more than anybody else. Yes, he was charming and funny and I liked when he brought food and when we'd smoke cigarettes, chatting and laughing for hours sometimes. I liked his company but his obsession with me was giving me uneasy feelings. I tried to be as clear as possible with him so he wouldn't get any idea that I was interested in him. I felt like he was using the uneasy position I was in, to pressure me into being with him. I hated it and sometimes I hated him for doing it to me. I couldn't stand when with that incorrect grammar of his he kept asking me the same questions over and over again.

"Tell me what I am for you? If I help you, I want to know it. I am your friend, or what? I need to know that if you going to stay in my office. I need to know my position with you. You sleep in my office and I help you, no big deal, but I also am man. That's the meaning; we have a membership [relationship] or what?" Ahmed's less than perfect English was almost as irritating to me as it was his persistence in annoying me. I told him numerous times that I wasn't interested in having sex with him, or with any other man for that matter. He kept ignoring the unwanted information on purpose, and so after a while, whenever I'd hear the familiar question, I'd answer him in a distant manner:

"I don't wanna talk about it. Leave me alone." But he wasn't willing to let me be in peace and so my only way to get away from him was to lay down with my eyes closed.

Ahmed hated when I was ignoring him. He didn't like when I wasn't looking at him and when I was remaining silent. I could tell that he

241

was hoping that I would get tired of boredom caused by lying still on a couch that I made out of a car seat.

What Ahmed didn't know was that while my eyes were being closed, I was experiencing some pretty amazing sensations that were far from boring. Forced by the circumstances, I found myself meditating with such devotion like I've never done before. In those moments the world around me was ceasing to exist. I didn't care about the phone ringing, or about the drivers talking among each other, nor did I care about Ahmed's attempts at gaining my attention. I was completely immune to the outside world. I was untouchable. No words or even unfriendly remarks were able to distract me. I was feeling fearless since I didn't think that I had anything else left to lose. For the first time in my life I truly didn't want to desire anything and amazingly, that decision was bringing me a sense of peace and freedom. I've always felt strong energy flowing through my hands, whenever I closed my eyes, but this time I was feeling the current a lot stronger.

This time the strong vibration was taking over my entire body. A sensation of mint-laced air was entering my body and was having a refreshing and reenergizing effect on me. The incredibly intense and clear colors that I was seeing with my eyes closed were bringing me excitement. Those colorful shapes of light appeared to be dancing for me, promising that there was something magical deep within me. From violet, to intense green, then to incredibly intense red and then to most deep turquoise, that colorful light was brightening my inner world. A few times when I opened my eyes, I was able to see a turquoise aura around my hands and my feet. I stared at it in disbelief and deep amusement.

The more I focused on admiring it the more intense in color and visibility the aura was turning. Other times, when I focused on feeling the sensation of the energy flowing through my body, I experienced different effects. My body was feeling heavier and heavier with each moment that I paid full attention to it. The current was getting stronger with each breath that I inhaled. It was giving me the sensation of being plugged into an incredibly powerful outlet, without suffering from electrical shock. After a while my body felt completely rigid. I felt like I couldn't move and I felt like even the task of breathing was done by somebody else. Eventually the current of energy got so strong that I started to hear a buzzing noise. The noise was getting more and more intense and the only way to describe it would be to compare it to a noise of a jet engine ready for take-off. At that point I was somehow instinctively saying the word "Love" in my mind. Each word was causing the energy to vibrate even stronger. I started to feel like some Force was trying to suck me out of my physical body. I couldn't tell exactly what it was but I could feel some magnificent presence of God or something that was waiting for me to let go of my fear. I trusted that Force but at the same time I was petrified of the idea of letting go completely. My fear was comparable to a fear of dying. I knew that my anxiety was slowing down the vibration so I was repeating the word "Love" in order to stay on that level. I also knew that I couldn't do it much longer without being drawn into a different realm.

I gave up then. I was too afraid. Even though in the past I had read about Out of Body Experiences, I wasn't feeling quite ready to be separated from my body while still being alive. I was sad and disappointed but the fear was simply too great and I couldn't overcome it.

"What if I got lost "out there"? What then? What if I couldn't come back to my body, what would I do?" Those doubtful and fearful thoughts worked like a magic in slowing down the vibration and in silencing the buzzing noise. After a while I still wasn't able to move but I was starting to feel my body again. First I felt my head and my face. To my horror I discovered that my mouth was so relaxed and lose that it felt as if all my teeth had fallen out. I was petrified because I still couldn't move my arm to check if that was the case. I was much relieved to discover a few moments later that my teeth were intact and that the only side effect of my deep mediation was saliva drooling from my slightly opened mouth.

Later, when I went to sleep, I had a dream that was different from any other dreams that I've ever had. In my dream I was floating above my own sleeping body like I was somebody or something else. From the above I was looking at that sleeping woman who was so beautiful in my eyes and in the eyes of the souls that were surrounding me. I knew that I was looking at myself. I could not get over the fact of how beautiful this woman was, how much love I had for her and how dear she was to me. She was wearing a beautiful white dress and I was admiring her purity and her innocence. I was watching her concerned look on her face while she was completely immersed in her sleep. I was feeling strong compassion and understanding towards her. I wanted her to know how much love I had for her and that she meant everything to me. I wanted for her to be able to feel about herself the way I was feeling about her. When I woke up in the morning I still could feel that intense love I was feeling in my dream. I felt like with my inner exploration I was finding something priceless, something not of this world. I was thrilled and very eager to discover something amazing about myself but unfortunately my desire for it was stopping me from obtaining it. Every time I closed my eyes and let my expectations inhabit my mind, I was doomed to the disappointment that always resulted in me falling asleep. It was very discouraging. I was yearning to be in that state of peace and clarity at all times. I wanted to be able to get back in that state in a snap of my finger. I did not feel like I was better than anybody else or more awaken or anything like that. I was simply desperate to get away from the suffering and unhappiness that I was feeling.

Still, there were moments when I was able to connect with that magical inner world. Those moments were usually "sponsored" by my feelings of an ultimate desperation. Whenever I felt like I couldn't bare my inner pain any longer, I let myself feel fully the humbleness that resulted by my lack of control. Honest and genuine humbleness appeared to be the key to the inner world that was so promising and so rewarding. Many times, when I was feeling like I couldn't do it by myself I tried to imagine that I was surrounded by helpful Angels who were sending their love towards me. Their presence, whether real or not, was encouraging.

One evening I was lying down on that primitively created couch and I was feeling extremely fed up with everything that was going on in my life. I did not want to be around anybody and I was glad that Ahmed was busy talking to his drivers in the other room. I was tired and I was feeling cold but I didn't feel like I had the energy to get up and to get a blanket. I was toying with the idea of asking Ahmed to bring me one but I soon rejected that thought. I was sick and tired of him making me feel like I owed him something because of his help. I was sick and tired of people in general who do something nice for somebody just to expect who knows what in return. I was feeling deeply disappointed to be living in the world I was living in. I was yearning for a different world and a different life. I was yearning for a place where I could be free from manipulation and free from power struggles. I was yearning not just to be independent but to be totally free.

Then a strange thought crossed my mind;

"*Why can't I ask Angels to bring me a blanket?*" I thought it was a crazy idea and I didn't honestly think that it would result in anything worth the effort. Nevertheless, just for the heck of it, I said a silent prayer in my mind:

"*Dear Angels, I'm cold and I'm tired and I don't like the blankets that this world has to offer. Everything in the world I live in comes with attachment. If somebody offers help to anybody; that person immediately wants something in return for that charity, even if it's just to feel good. People don't want to realize that while helping others and while making a big deal out of it, they're making those less fortunate feel like shit. Not many people like to help somebody and then to immediately forget about their noble deed. We humans, like to use the things that we supposedly need, to control each other. You want my love and my approval? Fine, then behave like I want you to. That's what we do to our own children. I just don't want to be part of this scam any-*

more. I still can't help but to feel like I want my needs to be met and so I find myself subjected to this conditional love.

Can you give me the blanket that I feel like I need? Can you warm me up so I wouldn't have to need some piece of material to do it for me? Could you please cover me with your heavenly blanket?" I finished my prayer without expecting anything wonderful to happen. I did tell myself to keep my mind opened though, just in case. Some short time later I began to experience an incredible feeling of being covered by a blanket that was made out of nothing else but pure love. The feeling of cold that I was experiencing before was evaporating away from me. I was beginning to feel not only warm and comfortable but also safe and cozy like I've never felt before. The feeling of being safe was so intense that I could never find the right words to describe it. The coziness created by the heavenly blanket that I felt around me was also indescribable. My gratitude for it was naturally immense even though I felt like it wasn't expected from me. I slept like a baby and my lifelong battle with poor sleep did not have any effect on me that night.

A Room of My Own

Since I did not want to have serious discussions with Ahmed, he tried to do everything he could to pressure me into conversing with him. He liked to use fear as one of his persuasive tools. He believed that the thought of not having a place to stay would soften me up. I knew that despite my unwillingness to be with him, Ahmed would not want me to leave. Nevertheless his attitude was exhausting to me. There were many things that I liked about Ahmed but his trying to pressure me into being with him was not one of them. The thing I liked the most about him was his sense of humor and how he always knew how to make me laugh. Sometimes I felt flattered to be the center of his attention. Other times his obsession with me was overwhelming and annoying. His admiration towards me that was reflected in his eyes was making me feel good about myself. While staring at me, he looked like a young and excited boy who found a treasure and who wanted to keep it at any cost.

"You perfect. You perfect to anybody. Any man would be lucky to have you. You beautiful, you perfect age, you crazy, funny and dangerous. I'm scare from you. Danger, danger. You are dangerous." While he was showering me with compliments, I was repeating silently in my mind:

"He's just like every other man. He'd do anything to be with somebody that he can't be with. As soon as he'd have sex with me, he'd change completely. He would have no respect for me and he'd probably kick me out." I was convinced that I was right and I didn't intend to have that proven to me. I was looking online for a room to rent but since I hadn't been able to find a place where they'd accept my dogs, I decided that I'd just stay in the office for a while. I was hoping that as soon as I would find a job that Ahmed would give me some space. I went to a nearby hospital to see if they were hiring ED Technicians and I was told to apply online.

Later that evening Ahmed's burst of criticism towards me was stronger than ever. He was accusing me of looking for rich and single guys online. I had no idea where his absurd idea came from and frankly, I didn't care. His burst of jealousy was making him look unattractive and even paranoid. His attempts to control me were extremely tiring but I intended not to pay any attention to it. But Ahmed wasn't giving up. He was orbiting around me like a maniac and he wouldn't shut up. His face was red and he was spitting while shouting. I had to listen to him saying what a horrible person I was, how I only cared about myself, and how I had a hidden agenda. For a moment I let the criticism get to me and I started to doubt myself.

"What if he's right? What if I am a selfish person who only cares about herself? Maybe that's why my life sucks so much?" My low self-esteem was depriving me of energy. I started to feel depressed.

"No! Fuck no! That's exactly what he wants me to do, he wants me to doubt myself. I am not a bad person and I deserve to be respected. I deserve to have a good life and I deserve to be with the type of people that I want to be with. I don't need to have people in my life who try to control my every move. This is ridiculous! I'm out of here!" With a new set of thoughts in my mind, I began to feel relieved. I did not want to tell Ahmed that I was planning on leaving because I knew that he would try to stop me. I knew that he would use his charm to convince me how sorry he was and to promise me that he would never behave this way again. I also knew that he wouldn't be able to keep his promise.

I went to see a guy named Hassan. Hassan was a student at Hawaii Pacific University and he was looking for a roommate. I found his ad on craigslist while I was still in California. He wanted me to move in with him but his cousin, who was living with him, changed his mind about my dogs when I already had my airline ticket to Honolulu. Hassan was very glad to see me and I could tell that he really wanted me to live with them. He came up with a brilliant idea of finding a temporary foster home for my dogs. It was hard at first for me to make such decision but I knew that I had to do what I had to do. I placed an ad on craigslist and the response I got was overwhelming. I was receiving few emails a day with the subject: "Temporary foster home for two German Shepherds". People were sending me practically their resumes to convince me that they would be a perfect fit for my situation. Most of them were stay-at-home moms who were looking for furry companionship. One woman named Heather intrigued me more than anybody else. She was a twenty-five year-old mother of two little boys and a wife of a military guy. They all lived in a two story house that was on a military Base in Kailua. Ahmed didn't suspect that I was planning on moving. I had him convinced that the temporary foster home for Rex and Nel was for their own good. He agreed to drive me to Kailua where I introduced my dogs to Heather and her family. Heather immediately fell in love with Rex and her husband Trey seemed to like Nel a lot. Their two year-old son Kevin and the nine year-old son Patrick were jumping in excitement while petting and hugging my dogs. I knew that I had a temporary home for Rex and Nel.

"Heather, is it OK with you if I take them back with me today and I bring them to you in a couple of days? I just wanna make sure that I can do this. I've never been separated from them for more than few days." I tried not to cry when I was talking to her.

"Sure; no problem. No, I understand. Look, I can come pick them up if you want me to. And you know that you're always welcome here when you want to come and visit them, right?" She seemed very sweet and very understanding. A few days later, as promised, Heather came to Honolulu to pick up my dogs. She didn't get offended when I asked her to sign a paper stating that I was the owner and that she was the temporary caregiver. That same evening I packed all my stuff and I called taxi so I wouldn't have to carry all the luggage and Milky Way, even though Hassan's apartment was just few blocks away. Most importantly I didn't want Ahmed to follow me because I knew that he would.

"Where you going? Don't go. Wait. Let's talk." Ahmed looked sad, guilty, and lost.

"Ahmed, I'm leaving and don't even try to stop me, OK? Please. Don't make things any harder, there is no need for that. I don't hate you but I don't want anything to do with you, OK? You have your issues and I have mine and it's just too much for me." I was talking in a calm yet confident manner.

"You don't understand." He looked like he was about to cry.

"Yeah, you're right, I don't, and you know what? I don't even want to understand anything." I was talking to him while dragging my suitcases down the stairs.

"You don't understand. I'm in love with you," he said and I paused for a moment.

"No, you're not. You're just obsessed with me. Now, I have to go; the taxi's waiting." I looked cold even though I was feeling sorry for him.

"Wait, please wait! At least keep the keys. Please don't go." He was trying to hold on to my hand and the taxi driver was looking at both of us with obvious discomfort.

"Where to?" The cab driver finally asked me when I finally shut the door.

"Just go straight and then make a right. Just get me out of here," I told him while looking behind to make sure that we weren't being followed. Hassan's apartment was small and dirty and infested by cockroaches but at least I didn't have to deal with Ahmed anymore. The first thing I did was to send out several job applications online for different hospitals. I got one positive response and I was asked to take an EKG test. Hassan was very sweet and brought me all kinds of books from the university library so I could refresh my memory. I passed the test but I did not get that job. I still had many other applications that were pending and I was still optimistic about getting the job I was looking for. In the meantime I was planning to get in the best physical shape so I could be ready for my future firefighting career. The written test was still few months away and I was already preparing for it with a special book on how to take a firefighter's exams. I was swimming in the ocean every day and I was running on the beach.

I was drinking plenty of water and feeling pretty good until one day when I sensed somebody running right behind me. I turned around and I saw Ahmed. I knew that he wasn't jogging for the sake of staying in shape.

"Hi. How are you?" He tried to sound as casual as he could but his effort didn't look natural.

"Hi. I'm good, thanks. Have a nice day." I answered with a serious face and I kept running hoping that he'd leave me alone.

"Wait, I wanna talk to you for second. Can we talk?" Ahmed insisted in conversing with me and I began to feel furious.

"Ahmed, I told you; I don't wanna talk to you so leave me alone. Look, you can't just follow me like this and you can't pretend like you're…"

"I don't follow you. I want to…" He tried to interrupt me.

"Yes, you are following me and you know that I am not that stupid to believe your crap. You have to leave me alone or I will call the cops. I mean it Ahmed. If you won't leave me alone I will call the police. Don't make me do that. Just stay away from me."

"But…"

"Stay away from me or I'll go to that store, I'll ask for the phone and I'll call the cops." I was looking him straight in his eyes and I was making gestures with my hands to make myself very clear. Ahmed looked hurt and I tried not to let myself be affected by the sorrow written on his face. I was reminding myself in my mind that I had to be very clear and very firm with him or he would never leave me alone. A few days later, Ahmed was waiting for me near Hassan's apartment. I was very upset to know that he had discovered where I was living. I couldn't even say anything and I just tried to show him with my body language and my hand gestures that he was crossing the line. From across the street Ahmed was pointing at an envelope that he was holding and he was making a gesture as to reassure me that he wouldn't talk. I let him approach me and I let him hand me the envelope. I thought that it was a goodbye letter and for a moment I felt relieved. I was feeling bad for being so mean to him but I didn't feel like I had other choice. His obsession with me was suffocating me by taking my sense of freedom and my sense of privacy away. In the apartment I opened the envelope and I saw two one-hundred dollars bills in it. I felt very tempted to keep the money since I didn't have any left. Then I thought that by keeping his money I would keep allowing Ahmed into my life and I didn't want that. I ran out, wanting to give him his money back, but he was already gone.

My new roommates Hassan and his cousin were very nice to me but I wasn't comfortable with my new living arrangement. Hassan was even cooking for me but his constant need for my company was taking too much energy out of me. I didn't feel very social and as stressed out as I was, I really wanted to be left alone. I didn't like to talk about myself and there was limit to how much I could sit and listen to Hassan's stories. He was a cool guy and very funny too but I really, more than ever, needed my space. I didn't feel like I was in a position to disregard him by not paying any attention to him. I knew that he enjoyed my company and I enjoyed talking to him too, but that sense of obligation I couldn't help but feel was overwhelming for me.

I wanted to be alone even if that meant for me to live on the street. I wanted to talk when I felt like talking and I wanted to be quiet when I felt like being quiet. More than anything I didn't want to feel like I had to explain anything to anybody. I felt extremely powerless and incapable of taking good care of myself. I felt like on some deep subconscious level I was convinced that I did not deserve a good life. I felt like I had no right to exist and that there was not a place in this world for me to live in. In my mind I wasn't worthy of being alive, much less of having a home and a normal life. I was a bad person who had bad habits, who didn't deserve anything good. I was simply a loser and a quitter. I was a lazy, untalented, incapable, fucked up, thirty-one year old, selfish woman. This woman obviously needed to take some drastic measures if she ever wanted to get rid of her enormous ego. This woman would have to go through the humility of living in a shelter if she ever wanted to be worthy of anything. She would have to start all over from the bottom and build her strength and character before she could be respected.

Shelter

I called Heather and I told her of my intentions of staying in a shelter. She was quite shocked and she even asked me if I wanted to stay with her but I told her how I honestly felt about all this. I told Hassan that I was moving in with Heather so he wouldn't feel bad about me leaving. I didn't want for him to feel guilty. Heather agreed to take Milky Way and most of my luggage with her as well so I wouldn't have to carry it around with me. I went to a charitable organization that was nearby, to ask about shelters. The man who gave me the directions looked more than astonished. He spoke slowly to me like he wasn't sure what was going on. The shelter he suggested to me was right by the piers.

The security guard first thought that I was a volunteer. When I told him that I was looking for a place to stay, he told me that the shelter didn't open until 5:30 p.m. I waited at the gate among other homeless people who looked very exhausted. There were people from different age groups and different ethnicities. Many of them were there with their entire families. Some children were sleeping in their mothers' laps; others were having discussions with their peers. Some men and women were forming a line while sitting in their old cars. Everybody was waiting for the security guy to announce that it was time to come in. Occasionally I heard somebody asking what time it was.

"Almost five thirty. They should be opening at any moment now." It was a phrase that seemed to be repeated a lot. Those who had watches kept glancing at them as if such gesture was going to speed up the time. Lack of shade from the intense tropical sun was disturbing, but nobody seemed eager to complain about it. Everybody seemed humbled by their situation and some people looked insecure.

When the guard finally made a gesture to let us know that we could approach the building, everybody rushed in, in a hurry. The building looked like an old warehouse; it had tall ceiling and no windows. One of the employees explained to me that I could not stay there unless I was approved and then recommended by some people in an office located on King Street which was quite far away. She gave me the address and she suggested that I should go there first thing in the morning. Apparently the shelter had a screening process that took a few business days in which it was determined if particular homeless person could live in this particular homeless shelter. It was already after business hours, and I didn't know where else to go. I was advised to go Downtown, to an emergency shelter for women, so I took my small backpack and I headed in that direction. The emergency shelter people demanded from me some proof of being homeless.

"What? You're telling me that I need a certificate of being homeless so I can stay here tonight?" I was staring in disbelieve at the woman that was talking to me through the microphone that was installed in the window.

"Come back tomorrow with a certificate of being homeless and we'll be able to accommodate you. Without some proof I cannot let you stay here." She was looking at me like I was some kind of con artist. I did not feel like knocking at Hassan's door and lying to him that I missed the buss to Kailua and the idea of spending the night at the beach, all alone, wasn't that appealing to me. I still had fifty dollars that was left from the two hundred dollars that Ahmed gave me, so I decided to spend the night at a hostel. I took the city bus all the way to Waikiki and for twenty five bucks I slept among several female tourists. The next morning I went to King Street. After being interview by several people, I was told that I could live in the shelter, but not before my TB test was pronounced negative. One of the social workers advised me to stay at the emergency women's shelter until then. He wrote me a letter stating that I was officially homeless.

"I can't believe those people turned you down like that. I've never heard of a homeless person who needed some proof of being homeless. Can you believe that, Carla?" The social worker was talking out loud while signing the letter. Some employees were rolling their eyes.

"What will they come up with next?" A woman who was holding the phone like she was on hold was expressing disapproval in her face.

"I'm gonna have a talk with them. They better not be doing it again to somebody else." The social worker's protective attitude felt very refreshing. That evening the emergency shelter people had no choice but to take me in. They made a copy of my driver's license and they asked me to sign some registration papers. After that I was given one-day-pass to the shelter.

"You must register every day in that window and each day you'll be given similar pass. The shelter closes at 10:00 p.m. so you must be here before that. We do not admit people that come late. You are expected to follow shelter's rules at all times. We serve three meals a day. Now that you are in our records, you are allowed to stay here for three months rent free. This is an emergency shelter and anybody who stays longer than that is expected to pay rent in the amount of ninety dollars a month. Also, should you find another place to live in, and after three days should you decide to come back here, you'd be expected to pay the ninety dollars rent fee. All this is written here and I need you to sing your name here below. I will give you copy of this so you can keep it as well as the copy of the shelter's regulations. Do you have any questions?" The woman handed me her pen.

"No, I don't think so. I think I'm good, thank you," I answered while signing my name.

"OK, you're all set then. Just give me a second and I'll be back with your copies." She got up and she left the small, dark room we were in. While waiting for her, I tried not to let the sense of humility get to me. I tried to remind myself that this was my first step towards my true independence. When the woman finally came back with the papers, I was relieved that I could go outside. I was also relieved to know that I had a place to sleep, no matter how inconvenient it might have looked. It felt very refreshing to know that I didn't have to be nice to anybody if I didn't feel like being nice. The idea of being able to say what was on my mind, without fearing unpleasant consequences, gave me a sense of freedom. No matter how awful and humiliating my situation might have looked to somebody else, I was actually starting to enjoy my sense of being in touch with my own self. I was me and not the person who felt obligated to please others in order to survive. I was homeless but I felt that I had more dignity and self-respect that I've ever had before. I was actually proud of myself. I didn't try to numb my feelings and the reality didn't seem absurd to me. If anything I was actually feeling fully present in the moment. I was still there and nothing seemed big or bad enough to threaten my existence. I was alive, at the bottom, but still alive.

Feeling humble was not the same to me as feeling insecure. The humbleness seemed actually to have created a sense of confidence and even a sense of peace in me. The need for judgment, whether towards others or towards my own self appeared to be diminishing on its own. It felt incredibly freeing to look at the people around me without being tempted to criticize anybody. Observing other homeless women without condemning them for their lack of life-skills was giving me a deep sense of tranquility. Watching their faces and seeing my own self in them was definitely a good feeling. The next day I took my small backpack and I headed towards the office on King Street. On the way I stopped by one of the hospitals that I applied for a job. The lady from human recourses confirmed that she has received my application. She asked me briefly about my experience as an EMT and firefighter and then she informed me that she'd be in touch with me. The people on King Street appeared to be glad to see me.

"Did they give you a hard time this time at that shelter?" The social worker asked me.

"No, everything went smoothly. Thanks for that letter," I answered.

"Well, looks like you won't need them anymore anyway. You've been approved and you are all set to move in to our shelter today." He was smiling.

"Really? Oh, that's great." I was smiling too.

"They have all your papers and they know that you're coming tonight. They're gonna take a picture of you there and they're gonna give you a pass. Good luck." He shook my hand.

"Thanks."

At 5:00 p.m. I was sitting at the gate among some people who remembered me from the other day.

"So, they're gonna let you stay." Some of them were stating the fact out loud.

"Yep. Looks like we're gonna be roomies." I was feeling almost uplifted. The shelter at the pier was a transitional shelter, meaning that all its residents had a written plan on how to transform their lives. Many of them had full time jobs. One young girl, whose bed was right next to mine, was enrolled in an EMT course. Some families were on the waiting list for housing. My goal was to land a job at the Emergency Department as an ED Technician and in the more distant future, to pass all the entry exams for the Honolulu Fire Department. The transitional shelter didn't seem as depressing as the one in Downtown. I could feel the sense of community in this place. Everybody seemed very friendly towards me and not just the group of young, single men who tried to get to know me. People were asking me if I needed anything and I could tell that they were very curious to know what kind of circumstances brought me to this place. Some older women immediately started to treat me like their daughter. Their affection towards me and their protective attitude was sweet, tender and sometimes even funny.

"These boys are looking at you like they wanna eat you alive. They all want to help you, but don't let them fool you, they're all animals." They made it sound like I was in danger. I was nodding and smiling while realizing that I was causing quite a commotion.

"Beat it! Keep walking that way. What are you looking here for? Did you lose anything in here?" I thought it was hilarious how those women were trying to scare away those men who liked to walk in the proximity of my bed. In this warehouse structure everybody was living and sleeping in one big opened space. There were numerous cubicles, literally the size of cubicles that some office would have, that were assigned to each individual. In my cubicle I had a single mattress that took all the space. A white sheet that was nailed on top was there to give me some privacy.

This shelter provided only one meal a day. At 6:30 p.m. some people from different churches would bring some food that they would feed us with. The food tasted more than awful. It was always based on meat and since I was vegetarian again there was very little that I could eat. My fellow homeless people were very understanding and there was always somebody who shared with me their piece of bread or even desert, if there was any. They made me feel as if they liked that I was one of them. It was almost as if my presence was helping them to accept themselves and their situation. I understood where all this was coming from. Most people who were either working there or who came to feed us were looking at us with pity written on their faces. Their feeling sorry for us wasn't making us feel any better. I couldn't help but to feel that some people were seeing us as the ultimate losers.

Perhaps we were thinking very little of ourselves, which was reflecting in our attitude and our body language. The thing that annoyed me the most was to see those volunteer church people who looked so proud of themselves for charitable deed they were doing. Their excitement caused by their "selfish" action was incredibly irritating. It was very obvious that it was all about them and not about us. We were merely there to fulfill their desire of expressing themselves as compassionate individuals. They did not seem to notice what their glory was doing to us. They seemed completely taken by the satisfaction derived from being in a better position. They were giving us food but they were taking a lot more in return. They were taking our pride of being human beings and children of God. They were taking our energy and our spirit.

After waiting in a line for food, I liked to take my share and go outside where I could eat my food in peace. I liked to sit directly on the pavement because it made me feel more grounded and more in touch with myself. After dinner there was always somebody who didn't mind sharing a cigarette with me. There was a cool security guy who liked to tell me his stories and there was a homeless fellow in his thirties who kept asking me on a date. It was endearing how persistent he was even though I kept rejecting his offer.

The place we were living in wouldn't be as bad as it was if it wasn't for the hours of its operations. I hated that we all had to leave the shelter before 9:00 a.m. and that nobody was allowed to come back until 5:30 p.m. It was very tiring and unflattering to have to wait at that gate every single day. At least the shelter allowed its residents to be absent for two nights a week so on the weekends I was able to take a bus all the way to Kailua to see my fur-babies. Rex and Nel were very afraid that I would leave them and so they were guarding me the whole time I was there. Milky Way was meowing as if he was trying to ask me:

"Where the hell have you been all this time?" It was hard to have to go back to Honolulu but I believed that I was doing the right thing.

I was getting emails informing me that my potential employers, after careful evaluation, had decided to hire somebody else. I still had plenty of applications pending so I wasn't losing my hope yet. I was trying to keep my mind as well as my body in good shape and running on the beach was an affordable way of doing so.

Hurt

When I saw Ahmed approaching me with that big smile on his, I paused for a moment to catch my breath and then I started to run in opposite direction. Feelings of fury and powerlessness, created by being stalked, were taking over me. Ahmed kept following me, demanding to have a talk with me.

"Ahmed, leave me alone or I swear, this won't end up good for you. You're pushing me to do something that I don't wanna do. You're forcing me to go to that police station. Why do you want me to do such a thing?"

"I don't follow you. I was running and I saw you, I swear." He was trying to make me believe in his innocence.

"So what? Even if you were running, I told you not to bother me. Do you have any idea how upset this makes me? What do I have to say to you to make you understand that I don't want to be bothered? What will it take to keep you away from me? If you don't believe me that I am dead serious and if I can't stop you, then you give me no choice but to go to police. Maybe they'll stop you, if I can't." I must have looked very mad because he left me alone.

"*For how long though? When will he appear in front of me again? When will he stop making me feel like I'm being followed?*" I could not honestly answer any of these questions that were piling up in my mind. I was afraid to face the truth that he wasn't in control of his obsessive behavior because that would mean that I would have to do something drastic. His lack of respect for my decision was very disturbing, just as disturbing as it was to have a sense of freedom taken away from me. The feeling of freedom that we take for granted when we walk around without worrying of being spied on.

I knew that if I wanted for this to end, I had no choice but to use help from authorities. I hated myself for just thinking of such a thing and a sense of guilt was stealing my sense of peace. I also knew that my peace was being stolen from me by his stalking me; and by not being able to do anything about it. I walked for about half an hour until I reached a police station. The officer took my complaint very seriously. After filing a report he told me that he had enough evidence to make an arrest. He asked me if I wanted to press charges.

"I feel so bad knowing that he'd be in jail because of me. Is there a way of giving him a warning or something? I just want him to stop following me." I asked the officer.

"Well, if we go to see him right now, we'll have to put him in jail for harassment. What you can do, you can go to court and you can get a restraining order against him. That could make him realize that you mean business and he could leave you alone. In a worst case scenario, once you'll have a restraining order against him and he'd decide to still follow you, you'll call 911 and he'll be in jail in no time." I was surprised to see how seriously the officer was taking my case. I followed his advice and I went to the courthouse. The judge waved the small petition fee due to my financial situation and I was informed that a notice to appear in court was going to be delivered to Ahmed. I still felt awfully guilty but I kept telling myself that I had to do what had to be done. I was on my way back to shelter even though it was still before 5:30 p.m., when Ahmed "appeared" in front of me again.

"Oh my God! What are you doing here?" I was obviously mad to see him but I was also mad to know that he found out that I was staying in the shelter.

"Just give me five minutes, OK? Five minutes. I promise I will stop bothering you."

"Yes you will and you wanna know how I know that? I just came back from court. I filled a restraining order against you. I feel horrible but you gave me no choice." I didn't know what else to say when I noticed big tears in Ahmed's eyes. I felt like the most evil person in the whole world.

"Oh God, Ahmed. Why do you have to do this to me? Why? Why are you so obsessed with me? You didn't even seem to care about my feelings when I stayed in your office."

"I know. I know. I'm sorry. I treated you like shit. It's my fault that you left. I made you do that. I'm sorry. I feel very guilty." Ahmed's tears were rolling down his face and it was breaking my heart.

"Do you wanna smoke a cigarette together?" He asked more with his eyes than with his voice.

"Sure. Just one, but then I really have to go." As hard as it was I tried to remain distant.

"I brought you this. I think you like it." He handled me a bag.

"No thanks. I really don't want anything from you. I told you that."

"I know but I bought new towels for you. And some clothes. See? All white, just like you like it." He tried to convince me in accepting the gift.

"Just stop it, OK? I told you; I cannot take anything anymore from you, OK?" I placed the bag in front of him. He looked hurt, confused and generally lost.

"I know you hate me," he said with profound sadness in his eyes and his entire face.

"I don't hate you Ahmed. But I do think that it's for the best for both of us not to be involved with each other at all. I think you just need to move on and I just have to do what I have to do to get my life to work for once." It made me feel very sad to see him hurting so much.

"I know. And that's what I want. I just want to help you. I feel guilty. I found a house, it's for you. It has four bedrooms and its white, like you like it. I paid deposit and I will pay for first few months rent. You can do whatever you want, I will not bother you. It's your house and I will leave you alone. Just let me do this because I feel too guilty. Just take this house and I promise you will not see me again. You came to Honolulu to start new life and I didn't help you. Please, just let me help you." He was talking fast maybe because he saw me rolling my eyes. I was extremely tempted to accept his offer but I was also afraid that such decision, if not now then in the future, would cost me my independence. I was very angry at him for tempting me like this. I knew that I could take the house and then tell him to leave me alone but I also knew that it would be extremely hard, if possible at all, to get rid of him. I did not want to have to go through this ever again.

"I don't want the house. And I really have to go now. You know you can't keep following me anymore, right? You know that once the judge issues the restraining order and you bother me, I'll call 911, and they'll put you in jail. You know that, right?" I was looking at his face moistened with tears.

"I'm sorry Ahmed, but things got out of control and I have to do what I have to do to protect myself," I continued.

"Protect yourself from who? Me? I'm the best thing that happened to you on this Island." He was crying like a boy now and people passing by were staring at us. My homeless fellows who were heading towards the gate were also glancing at us even though I could tell that they were trying to be discrete.

"I've got to go now. Bye Ahmed." I took my small backpack and I headed towards the gate. Ahmed kept standing there as if he was paralyzed. I was hurting from feeling guilty of causing so much pain to him and that hurt was making me feel even madder at him.

Restless

Sleeping at the shelter presented me with many challenges but one particular issue was the hardest to deal with. Every night, around 3:00 a.m., I was awakened by the loudest, the most vibrating and the most annoying snoring coming from another cubicle. For two weeks I dealt with it by listening to loud music from my radio. My ears were hurting me from the ear-piece I wore while sleeping and my head felt like it was ready to explode every morning. One day when the battery finally died and the snoring woke me up at 3:00 a.m., I knew that I could not take it anymore. I got up and I wandered around shelter until 5:00 a.m. Then I took a shower and I headed towards the long table that was used as a check-in point. I handed my shelter pass to a woman covering the shift.

"I won't need this anymore. I'm not coming back." I said to her. She looked at me like she wanted some explanation but I didn't feel like saying anything else other than bye. I had some quarters left so I called Heather and I took a bus to Kailua. Heather didn't know that I left the shelter for good. Later that evening she told me that she enjoyed my company and that her kids really liked having me around. She said that I could stay at her house as long as I needed and I took her offer this time.

"Look, I'm serious, when you're here; things seem a lot less chaotic and more fun. We like having you here. I know I do." Heather really made me feel welcome at her house. I had my own room upstairs and I was with my furry babies again. Heather was not only warm and sensitive but she was also very open minded person.

She offered to drive me to Honolulu on the day I had to appear in court. Seeing Ahmed sitting on the other site of the court room wasn't easy. He looked humbled, sad, and insecure, and seeing him this way wasn't making me feel any good. My eyes were burning me as if they were responding on their own to my pain and guilt. We sat there watching other people presenting the judge with similar issues. Finally, when it was our turn, we approached the bench. Ahmed didn't fight any of the allegations against him and the judge issued the restraining order for three years. I still felt very bad but I also finally felt relieved. It was finally over. Ahmed had no choice but to leave me alone.

Heather and I liked to chat sometimes, particularly when everybody else was asleep and when we could actually hear what was being said. In a house dominated by boys there was hardly ever a quiet moment. Additional children from the neighborhood were coming in and out unannounced, slamming doors back and forth. The atmosphere was lively but very chaotic. Heather's boys immediately bonded with me, probably because they could tell how much I liked them. Her husband Trey was nice to me too, even though I knew that he was uncomfortable with my disapproval of corporal punishment. I knew that I wasn't in a position of telling him how to raise his boys, so instead I always found a way to turn things around so nobody would get spanked.

"Oh you know what? I asked them to do that for me. I didn't know they weren't supposed to. I'm sorry, it's my fault." Trey knew that it was all baloney but he was playing along. This whole family was extremely dysfunctional but at the same time its members were extremely loving and giving individuals. Heather was the first person ever that told me that I should write a book. She kept insisting on it even though I was telling her that I had nothing to write about.

"You should really think about it. I don't know why, but every time we have a talk, I have this strange urge to tell you that you should write a book." She wasn't teasing me, she was being serious.

"Heather, it's very sweet that you have so much faith in me, but what on earth would I write about?"

"I don't know. I guess you could write about the issues you've been struggling with. I mean, don't get me wrong, but looking at you I would think that you are this most beautiful, happy person who can have anything she wants. I'm sorry for being so honest but if I didn't know you I'd be like, I hate this bitch. Don't look at me like this, I'm being totally honest!" She paused when she saw my eyes getting wide.

"Well, let me finish, OK?" She was having a good time at my expense.

"Yeah, yeah, go ahead. Tell me what a bitch I am." I was laughing with her.

"That's not the point and you know it. I don't really know how to explain this but when you talk about how insecure you feel, how unhappy you are, it makes me feel like there is some justice in this world. Wait, wait, wait, that didn't come out right, did it? What I meant is that it makes me feel better knowing that somebody so gorgeous like you still feels what I feel and still has to go through things that I have to go through. And when you talk, you really have these deep insights about life in general. I don't know, I just think that I would like to read a book if you wrote one. Does it make any sense?"

"Yeah, I guess it does. You think it's great that I'm miserable," I was teasing her.

"You know what I meant." She couldn't tell for sure if I was joking or if I was being serious.

"I know Heather. I'm just giving you a hard time. No, but seriously, I really wish that I could see myself the way you see me and I wish that I could make myself to write that book. I just don't see it happening. I wouldn't even know where to start. I hate my life and I don't even wanna think about it, I just wanna forget everything that ever happened in my life. I move from place to place, hoping that I could get away from whatever it is that's been chasing me. And it's not like I've been successful at this, I mean, you can see how I'm living my life. I just don't know what the heck it will take for me to face whatever it is that I need to face and to make a difference in my own life? I'm lost. I realize by now that I can't outrun what's within me but at the same time I have no clue what else I should be doing. So OK, so you look within yourself and you face your fears and your pain, and then what? What happens then? You tell yourself that you are not the little girl anymore that you once were and that you are a strong woman now. You tell yourself that you deserve a good life but you still keep reliving your past. I just don't know what it will take for me to break free from this prison I've been living in. Running away seems like the only option I have. And I don't just mean moving physically from place to place. I mean running away by constantly eating, smoking, watching TV, sleeping, basically doing anything that would numb my feelings, even if just for a moment. And you know that I tried all this meditation crap and everything, and still, I can't figure out what it will take to change my life once and for all. What will it take for me to stop attracting those same circumstances that make me feel the exact way I was feeling when I was little? I don't know, I really don't know how all this works and I don't know how could I write a book about something that I don't understand."

I was grateful to Heather for listening to me and for encouraging me to write a book but I still thought that I didn't have what it would take to make it happen. She seemed disappointed to see how much I doubted my capabilities and how little faith I had in myself. Every time she got a chance, she didn't hesitate to bring the topic back and every time she did, she heard the same thing from me.

"I am not writing anything."

After two months of staying at Heather's house, I began to feel very anxious. Taking little Kevin on walks to the beach was my only way to get away from everything and that wasn't enough. Not having a car and depending on Heather's military pass to cross the gate was also contributing to my deep sense of lack of independence. I was dreaming of having even just a tiny shed where I could live alone with my animals. I thought that I could feel peaceful only if I'd live alone. Besides I felt embarrassed that being thirty-one years old, I still wasn't on my own. No matter how many times Heather told me that she was happy to have me there, she couldn't convince me that I wasn't an intruder. I finally told her that I called Ahmed, asking him if he would help me find a small place and that he agreed to do so. Heather didn't hide her disappointment but she also tried to be understanding.

"I think I'd do the same if I were in your situation. I mean, really, I think I understand. I'm sad that you're leaving but I also hope that you'll find what you're looking for," she sounded very sincere.

"Thanks Heather. Thanks for everything you've done for me. Promise we'll stay in touch." I hugged my girlfriend.

"Of course," she said.

"Do you think I'm crazy for asking Ahmed for help after all we've been through?" I asked her afraid that she would judge me.

"No, of course not. He always told you to call him if you needed anything, right?"

"That's right. Oh well, even if I am crazy, so what?" I tried not to judge myself.

Ahmed wasn't trying to hide how happy he was to see me again. He did look like he was in shock and like he couldn't believe that I was back in his office again. I could tell that he was trying very hard not to upset me this time. He was extra nice to Rex and Nel as well as if he was trying to bribe my German shepherds so they would bond with him.

He drove me in his tour van to a place where I was scheduled to take the written test for the Honolulu Fire Department. A couple of weeks later I found out that I did not pass that test. I was very angry and very disappointed with myself. The good thing was that I was invited to an interview in one of the emergency rooms. I spoke to a hiring manager for at least an hour and I really felt like I was going to get that job. But then few days later I received an email that proved to me otherwise. That's when I decided that Heather was right; I had to write that book. I was sick and tired of everything that was and wasn't going on in my life and I knew that the book could potentially change all that for me. Unfortunately it seemed impossible for me to make myself write anything at all. I did not want to talk about myself or my life and I had nothing else to talk about. I did not want anybody to know anything about me and the idea of bringing my painful memories back and sharing them with anybody who knows how to read, was simply unbearable.

"Heather, I can't freaking do this." I was crying to my girlfriend on the phone. In pure desperation I forced myself to write few pages, knowing that it was far away from being any good. After reading the material Heather told me what I already knew.

"I don't know Elzbieta. I mean it's not that bad but I can't help but to notice that you're not going deep enough with this. It's like, I don't know, I can feel that you don't wanna talk about it and you just wanna skip everything and you just wanna be over with it." She was being very perceptive and very honest.

"I know, and yes, you're right. I just don't know if I can do this. I'm trying to force myself as if my life depended on it. Who knows, maybe it does but at the same time, this is like the hardest thing that I've ever had to do. I mean, just to even think about all this and then having to write about it, oh God. I hate this so much. You have no idea." I wasn't even able to express exactly how I was feeling. It was as if my entire body and not just my mind, was resisting the whole idea of writing this book. Doubtful thoughts were stealing any motivation that I could still have left in me.

"Who the hell would want to read all this and what's the point of a book if there is no happy ending?" Thoughts of a similar nature inhabited my mind and were depriving me of any energy that I could have left. My negativity was bringing me down and I didn't feel like I could stop it. I was angry at myself for the kind of life I was living and I wanted to do something that I could have actual control over.

Unknown Number

I surprised Ahmed, four months after the day we met, with an offer that he couldn't refuse. I wanted to have a baby. I wanted to have something in my life that I could love and cherish and I was hoping that having a baby would force me to do things differently. I knew it was a crazy idea but I was already at the verge of losing my mind. Of course Ahmed was more than happy to have sex with me even thought he wasn't thrilled with the idea of being simply a sperm donor. The sex was awful, but the thought of the possibility of having created somebody special, was giving me euphoric feeling. I was aware that it wasn't responsible of me to do such thing and I knew that I wasn't thinking clearly. I stopped having sex with Ahmed as soon as I thought that I was late. I thought I was pregnant even though the home pregnancies tests that I kept taking were showing negative results. My period wasn't coming and Ahmed was also convinced that I was pregnant. We had some relatively good times. There were moments when Ahmed was sweet to me. He was bringing me fresh fruit every day and he was making fresh salads for me and the baby.

He was very clingy though, as if he was completely addicted to me. His need of being constantly around me was overwhelming to me. It became even more overwhelming when his issues with jealousy began to surface once again. His insecurities that I guess were causing his paranoia were absolutely driving me crazy. His accusations were like a flash back from my childhood when I had to witness my father accusing my mother of cheating on him.

"You're fucking my drivers behind my back! Motherfucker bitch!" I knew that Ahmed knew that it wasn't true and yet I couldn't figure out why he was doing this to me. I couldn't figure out if he was taking drugs, or whether he just enjoyed creating these scenes as way of venting his frustration. Nothing was making any sense since one moment he was nice and the next one his face was turning red and I could tell that the storm was coming. Many times I lost my temper and I threw things at him. I screamed while kicking and punching him as hard as I could. Strangely Ahmed seemed to calm down then but even more strangely I was feeling that he was really enjoying all this.

I began to realize that his outbursts of jealousy were rehearsed acts and that he was getting something from it. He had the strangest, the most manipulative mind that I've ever seen. He looked completely psychotic in those moments and I would lie if I said that I wasn't afraid of my life sometimes. His mind was completely twisted and I didn't know what to expect from him. He was following me even if I just went to buy some cigarettes. He was hiding in different rooms trying to spy on me. I don't know how but he got a hold of my password and he was checking my emails. He liked to admit that he knew what I was writing in my emails, like that was giving him a sense of control over me. He loved to play with my mind and that was really creating doubts in me concerning my safety. I still felt like he had a good heart but I knew for a fact that he didn't have a good mind.

"Whose unknown number?" That meant, who's the person that's been calling your cell phone with an unknown number? Ahmed gave me the cell phone and he used that as yet another way of controlling me and driving me crazy. He was checking the outgoing and incoming calls like he was hoping to find something suspicious. I found out eventually that it was him who was calling me with that unknown number. It was incredibly disturbing every time when I answered the phone and I couldn't hear anything.

"Ahmed, stop this fucking bullshit! I know it's been you that has been calling me." I yelled sometimes knowing that he was behind all these calls. Surely enough, he'd walk in the office shortly after that and he'd demand to know:

"Whose unknown number?" The anger that I was feeling towards him and his mind games, was boiling inside of me to the point where I was afraid sometimes of losing control. I was afraid that I would snap one day if that didn't stop.

Alone

Spending a few days at Heather's house was never a permanent solution. Ahmed would always come to get me promising me what a different person he would be and that he'd never do stupid things again. I always believed him because I wanted to believe him. With him I had some kind of sense of security even though it was costing me my nerves and my mental health. But now that there was a possibility at least that I could be pregnant, I knew that I couldn't allow for this to happen to my baby. I had to get away from him and I had to get away far enough so he wouldn't want to come to get me back.

On craigslist I found a place for rent on the Big Island for three hundred dollars a month. It wasn't a real house; it was more like a shed without utilities or even water. Still, this thing had a roof and it was standing in the middle of acres of land filled with fruit trees. The owner said that picking the fruit for consumption was included in the rent. He also said that he always needed some part time workers on his tree farm. All I had to do was to force Ahmed into buying airline tickets for me and my dogs and into covering my first month rent.

It wasn't easy but after my screaming and breaking things that were breakable, followed by complete silence and refusal to talk to him, he finally caved in. I was scared of the idea of sleeping alone in a cabin without windows or doors, in the middle of jungle, but I was even more scared of the idea of continuing to live with Ahmed.

At least I had Rex and Nel to protect me. Milky Way couldn't come with us because he had run away from the office. My assumption was that he jumped off the window. Ahmed felt bad about it and he posted some flyers with Milky Way's picture and the promise of reward of two hundred dollars for anybody who'd bring the kitty back. Nobody called, and even though we did spot my cat hiding underneath the neighboring school, we weren't able to bring him back. Milky Way was completely deaf and he was petrified of strangers. I knew that as scared as he was he would not come to me even if I called him. One day I tried to surprise him from the back, knowing that he couldn't hear me coming, and I tried to grab him. I kept holding onto him even though in some survival reaction he was biting me as hard as he could. I wanted for him to see that it was me but I don't think it was possible. After seeing red blood all over my hand and some on Milky Way's white fur, I finally let go of him.

It was only then when I started to feel sharp pain. My hand was swelling right in front of my eyes. It looked like it was bitten by numerous snakes. I went back to the office realizing that I would never be able to get my cat back. When Ahmed saw my hand he wanted me to go to the Emergency Room but I refused. He got get some disinfecting medicine and pain killers from the pharmacy for me. He took care of my wounds. He liked taking care of me and he loved when I needed him. He knew how to be sweet when he wanted to be sweet.

The trip to the Big Island turned out to be a real nightmare. Ahmed bought the airline tickets for me and my dogs but he also acted like a real jerk the whole time. I was trying to understand that his disrespectful attitude was his way of protecting his feelings but still, he was making it impossible for me not to hate him. After checking in Rex and Nel, he left me at the terminal and he drove off in his van. He knew that apart for my first month rent, I had no money whatsoever. He knew that there was nobody to pick me up and to drive me for an hour to my secluded destination. It was already dark and I wasn't even aware that Hilo on the Big Island was having its raining season. I was sitting in the terminal, waiting for the boarding to start, and I was trying to imagine which stranger I would have to ask to give us a lift in his pick-up truck. I was overwhelmed and scared and I wasn't even trying to stop my tears from rolling down my face.

"Did you really think that I would leave you alone?" I turned around and I saw Ahmed.

"I'm going with you. I take you to that place. You can't do it all alone." He was smiling and even though I still hated him immensely, I was grateful that he was there. I was so emotionally exhausted that I wasn't even saying anything to him. Throughout the whole flight my head was shaking uncontrollably. Ahmed was being sweet again. Whatever anger he felt before was now replaced with deep sense of guilt. That was his personality; he did that a lot; one moment he'd be a controlling jerk and the next one he'd try to prove otherwise. In Hilo, Ahmed rented a minivan and while following directions I scratched on a piece of paper, we headed towards my new place. An hour later we found the gate that we were looking for and we entered private land that looked like a jungle. It was completely dark and all we could see were big branches of some exotic trees smashing against the windshield. The dirt road was very uneven and we all kept sliding from side to side in that minivan, hoping that we wouldn't get stuck.

"Oh God, I cannot let you live here all by yourself." Ahmed's concerned face was making me laugh.

"Just keep driving, OK? There! You see that road? You have to make a left there." I was giving him directions hoping that they were right.

"That's a road? Are you sure?" He looked like he didn't believe me.

"Yeah I'm sure. Go, go that way. I don't know, I think....I'm sure. Oh God, I think we're lost." I looked at him and we both laughed.

"OK, this is not funny. Just keep going straight, OK? Just drive straight. This shed or this primitive cabin or whatever it is it must be somewhere here. We'll find it. Just go. Keep going this way." I was pointing at the road that looked like it hadn't seen a human foot for ages. Finally, after a while, we saw a tall roof in the middle of a small glade.

"That's it! That's it! That's the freaking place! We found it!" I shouted and my dogs began to pant in response to my excitement. Since we didn't bring any flashlights with us, we had to use the mini van's lights to let ourselves inside the cabin. The sleeping area was upstairs and Ahmed had to help my dogs in climbing what looked more like a ladder than stairs. There was no mattress and we all had to sleep on the floor. Mosquitoes were finding their way through old net that served as a wall for this upstairs bedroom. It was a cold and rainy night and the surroundings looked dark and scary. Good thing I wasn't alone.

"How on earth will I sleep here all by myself?" I was asking myself while trying to fall asleep. The next morning we all drove to a small town to have breakfast. After that we went shopping for portable mattresses, pillows, covers, flashlights, knives, and some groceries. In the afternoon Ahmed said goodbye to me and he left in his rented minivan. While watching him driving away, I felt extremely lonely, but I was also extremely determined to be on my own. I found some paint that my landlord left for me knowing that I wanted to paint my new place all white. I spent the rest of the afternoon painting the primitive looking walls of my primitive looking house. The biggest part of the cabin was its roof that was shaped into a capital letter A. It was made of metal and that amplified the sound of the rain. The thin wooden sheets used for the walls had square holes where windows were supposed to be. There was a door but it wasn't attached to the frame yet.

Surprisingly, this tiny place had an actual toilet in the corner. The previous tenant had brought this beat up piece of commodity. He installed some pipes that allowed the waste to drain a few feet away from the cabin. The only water supply that this place had was provided by rain, which was captured from the roof into a large plastic bucket. The bucket was standing on four wooden poles and it had a hose that could be turned on and off and served as a modest shower. Right behind this was a medium-sized banana tree forest. Black wild pigs were frequent guests to this piece of land which resembled Africa. The aroma of passion fruit was spreading in the air. Guava, mango, avocado and coconuts could be found around as well. Huge jackfruits were hanging from branches, adding that much more of an exotic texture to this naturally rich environment. The ocean could be seen from my place, although reaching it through that jungle and tall grass didn't seem very realistic. In order to go to the beach I'd have to drive or walk for an hour, following the main road.

When it wasn't raining hard in a way that it made me think of a tsunami that was about to envelope the island, I could see the smoke coming from the not so distant volcano. When the sun went down, the loudest frogs in the world would start to sing all at once. Before I was properly informed by some local people, I mistook this sound thinking that some nocturnal birds were responsible. It was not only very loud but it also resembled the noise of hundreds of sea gulls fighting over a piece of food. I liked listening to it. This unusual sound was giving me that much more of a feeling of being in a jungle.

The not so good part was that at night, the sole idea of being all alone there was giving me uneasy feeling in my stomach. With no lights nor windows or a door that could be locked, I was very aware of my vulnerability. I could not be more grateful for the companionship of my two German shepherds. Rex and Nel were sleeping with me in my bed and beneath my pillow I had a big kitchen knife and a flash light. I knew that I would have used my weapon if I had to. I was hoping though that this wouldn't be necessary. I was very aware that in places like that, the word of some single girl living all alone could spread very quickly. I was trying to keep a low profile and when I walked for more than an hour to a nearest town, I wore a baseball hat and I ignored the curious drivers of passing cars.

The Ring

I knew that it would take some time to adjust to my new living arrangements but what I didn't know was that Ahmed wouldn't let me get too used to my new place. In those approximately two weeks that I stayed there he flew to Big Island four times to see me. Eventually people from the rental car company put his name on a black list, after realizing that wherever he'd been driving was causing a lot of damage to the car's surface. Ahmed kept insisting on me going back to Oahu and I kept rejecting his offer. I wasn't very happy where I was at but I also couldn't forget what it was like for me in Honolulu.

I enjoyed Ahmed's visits though, especially since that meant that I didn't have to sleep alone at night. He was very sweet and charming again since he knew that he didn't have another choice this time. He was funny again and he was making me laugh very hard. We would drive around the Island exploring its beauty and the time was passing in a relaxing atmosphere. Ahmed was contemplating on renting or even buying a little house there. His obsession with me seemed a lot less overwhelming this time. His dedication to do anything just to be with me was a lot more sweet this time, perhaps since it seemed a lot less controlling. He was starting to look attractive again in my eyes. I knew that if I did decide to keep my place that he would spend a lot of his money in improvements. I knew that eventually I would have a generator, a small fridge and even perhaps some old pick-up truck to drive around.

I'm not sure exactly why but when he said that he would not fly back to Honolulu without me I agreed to fly back with him. I was tired of the constant rain and I knew that whatever sense of happiness and sense of peace I was looking for, wasn't really there with me.

I felt relieved to be back in Honolulu even though I've never liked living in the city. Ahmed was trying to be nice to me again and things didn't seem as bad anymore. At some point my period arrived, confirming that I wasn't pregnant. I felt sad and I cried a lot but I also felt relieved. I was very touched to see how disappointed Ahmed seemed. He said that he wanted for us to get married and at some point I actually told him that I wouldn't mind that. I even got excited about the idea of having a big Egyptian wedding and I even told my family of the possibility. I knew that I wasn't in love with him and I wasn't even trying to lie about it but at the same time it felt good to be desired so much. Ahmed's face lightened up and his eyes moistened when I sat on his lap and I told him that I decided that it wouldn't be so bad if we did get married. He still looked like he wasn't sure if I was for real but I could tell that he really wanted to believe that I was. It was almost Christmas time and I knew that Ahmed was planning on giving me a surprise gift. Still I was very surprised when one day he sat on the edge of my office bed and he slide a diamond ring on my finger. Nobody ever has done it before and I was incredibly touched by his gesture. I was enjoying every moment of it even though I knew that I couldn't marry him.

"Ahmed, I'm sorry. I don't think I can do this." I said to him knowing that I told the truth.

"Just wear the ring." I tried to take the ring off. He pushed it back.

"Alright, fine, but you know that…" I felt guilty for enjoying the attention on his expense.

"Just wear the ring for now." He insisted without letting me say anything else. Even though I knew that I wasn't planning on ever saying "I do" to him, I did like wearing that ring. It was saying to me and to the world that somebody wanted me bad enough to go through trouble of planning a life together. The ring was promising me that I would not only be desired but that I'd also be loved and that I wouldn't have to be alone anymore, if I didn't want to be. The ring was giving me a strange and false sense of security. It was embracing my finger and my heart with warmth and sense of tenderness.

Determination

In January I received an acceptance letter from Hawaii Pacific University. I was thrilled by the idea of going back to school, and Ahmed told me that he would help me financially in reaching my goal of continuing my education. I picked my major in premedical studies and I registered for five different classes. Ahmed bought all the textbooks for me and he promised that he'd help me with my tuition fees at the end of the semester. Knowing that it would cost him almost seven thousand dollars per semester and that he was still willing to make it happen for me was making me feel very grateful towards him.

That's when I went to court and I filed a petition for an annulment of the restraining order that I had against him. We both had to appear in court and I had to explain to the judge my decision. I could tell by people's faces that they weren't very used to this type of hearing. Ahmed was very happy to have his record cleared. He kissed me and hugged me while saying to me that he now knew that I cared about him.

School was filling up my time completely as I was determined to get straight A's. In each class I sat in the first row and I was always fully prepared. I could tell that teachers liked my full participation and my excitement towards learning. I always dressed in simple sweat pants and t-shirts, with my hair always in a pony tail, to avoid any kind of unnecessary distraction.

I was never late, and I wasn't interested in forming an acquaintance with anybody. On average, I was at least ten years older than the rest of the students. The thought of working towards a Bachelor's Degree in Pre-Medical Studies was exhilarating. Sitting in classes, reading books at home and writing papers was time consuming but it also felt very rewarding. I was tired but I was also happy with the sense of fulfillment I was getting. Ahmed seemed very proud of me and that wasn't making me feel bad either. A month later however, he started to resent my not paying any attention to him. I tried to resists his old ways of manipulation by ignoring him that much more.

"I think I'm going to Egypt. Yeah, I'm going to Egypt." He liked to say that whenever he wanted me to feel insecure about my living situation.

"Ahmed, my paper is due tomorrow and there is no way that I will let you sabotage my grades for me. Do whatever you want; go to Egypt if that's what you want, but please leave me alone so I can finish writing this thing. OK?" I knew that he wasn't really planning on going anywhere but still, his way of demanding my attention was very distracting.

"You can't stay in the office if I'm gone. I don't trust you. I know you. You bring my drivers to fuck them here if I'm not here. But I'm not gonna leave you like this. I'm a good person and I can help you with renting a room for you and your dogs. I give you some money but you can't stay in the office when I'm in Egypt." He continued to play his mind games with me. This went on for days. To make it look like he meant what he was saying, Ahmed began to pack his suitcases. He was living in the office with me since I refused to live in his apartment with him. His place didn't allow dogs and I didn't want to be separated from Rex and Nel.

I knew that his trip to Egypt was his way of forcing me into being more interactive with him. I hated when he was doing that to me. I hated it especially when he was being this moody because I didn't feel like having sex with him. I couldn't take it anymore and after a big fight, in which he threatened me to put me out on the street, I went to school and I withdrew from all my classes. I was sad and disappointed but I was also much relieved to know that he couldn't use school to manipulate me anymore. When Ahmed saw that I wasn't attending classes, he panicked, realizing that he pushed me too far this time. He felt very guilty and he tried to convince me to go back to school. He even wanted to pay my tuition fee right away. I saw his mood changing a million times before and I could not make myself trust him anymore. I realized by then that the less I wanted or needed from him, the better things were between us. Ahmed was using the oldest trick in the world; he wanted me to have what I desired so he could manipulate me by threatening to take it away, if he didn't get from me what he wanted. He wasn't happy when he understood that I wasn't going to change my mind about school.

"You were happy in school. What are you going to do now?" He was trying to be nice again.

"I'm going to write that damn book!" I said it more to myself than to him.

"I have to do this. I have no choice. I must force myself to write that stupid book. I don't care how hard it's going to be and I don't care whether people will like it or not. I really need to do this. This is the only way that I can somehow change my life. This is my only hope. That's it. I will write this freaking book now!" I was making myself feel upset so I would have that much more determination to sit and write. My laptop was staring at me with its blank page and it was extremely hard to even think about what I would write. I had to fight my negative, doubtful thoughts. I was using my anger and dissatisfaction with my current situation to fight the battle for me.

Arrival

During the first few days I was able to write barely one page a day, but at least I was writing something. I wasn't thrilled with my work but I knew that I couldn't let my doubts stop me and I knew that I had to continue writing. Maybe because Ahmed was still feeling guilty about the school thing, he was actually being supportive of my new project. He was bringing me food and he was teasing me how rich and famous I will be one day because of my book. I was reading to him every day the pages that I wrote and he was giving me his feedback. On some days, things were going smooth and we were laughing and joking about the book and on other days we were at each other's throats. In days or nights when he was kicking me out from the office, Heather was coming with her kids to pick me up. Every time this happened, a few days later Ahmed would show up at Heather's house trying to convince me things would be different. I didn't believe him, but I didn't want to stay in Kailua. I was really focused now on writing and Heather's noisy and chaotic house wasn't really an ideal place to do so. To deal with Ahmed's constant accusations and criticism I learned to be very aggressive. Many times getting physical with him was the only way to stop the verbal fights that he loved to engage me in.

"Shut up! Shut the fuck up!" I got up from the couch after waking up from the noise that Ahmed was making. He was pacing around while saying some ridiculous things about me. I headed towards him and my serious face must have told him that it wasn't wise of him to be waking me up like this, because he ran into the small office room. He shut the door behind him and he blocked it with his foot.

"Open that fucking door right now!" I was shouting at him in a fury. The door had a window made of a thick glass in its upper part. Luckily for me this window had a decorative plastic like material glued to it from my side. Without even thinking I punched the door with both of my hands and I saw Ahmed's terrified expression on his face. The noise of shattering glass made him let go of the door. I stood there in disbelief myself while checking my hands for cuts. The whole window was gone and the only reason my cuts were small was because of that decorative material that protected my hands. Ahmed was quiet again.

"Why do you love so much to have drama in life? Why are you so addicted to it? Don't you ever get tired of it?" I asked him without expecting a truthful answer.

In April I was going to turn thirty two years old. Ahmed wanted to do something really special for my birthday.

"You could buy an airline ticket for my mom so she could visit me." I suggested without too much hope. Ahmed did buy the ticket for my mom. He rented a two bedroom, pet-friendly apartment in Waikiki to impress my mother. On the day of my birthday, the two of us went to the airport to pick up our guest. I was still in disbelief that this was actually happening. I hadn't seen my mom, not even once, in ten years and it was hard to even imagine that she was about to stand in front of me. While nervously waiting at the gate, we were asking all the passengers if there were still more people coming from that plane. Impatient and anxious I told Ahmed to check with airlines to see if they had my mother's name on their boarding list.

"She's here! She's coming! Ahmed, she's coming!" I was waving at him and at my mother simultaneously. My mother was smiling and waving at me from a distance. Seeing her for the first time in ten years was having a shock-like effect on me. I felt like as if I was stoned or as if I was sleep-walking. I wasn't able to talk and my mother understood that very well. After we hugged, the nervousness diminished a little bit.

"We thought you got lost in Chicago or something. I thought I was going to have to fly there to pick you up." I said to my mom and she explained to me how lucky she was to have met a Polish lady that helped her in switching planes. My mother did not speak any English and I was afraid that she would get lost at Chicago's airport. I introduced Ahmed to her and he gave her Hawaiian lei made of fresh flowers.

"Welcome to Honolulu." He said with that charming smile of his. On the way back to the apartment I spoke half the time in English and half the time in Polish. I was translating back and forth what was being said.

We let my mom take a nap as she'd been traveling for two days. I still couldn't quite believe that she was with us and I kept checking the master bedroom where she was resting.

"How is this even possible? Thank you. Thank you for bringing my mom here." I whispered to Ahmed. He looked very happy and pleased by his actions.

That afternoon Heather came to celebrate my birthday. She brought her boys with her and her neighbor who I also invited. Kevin and Patrick were busy playing with the balloons and the rest of us were getting tables ready outside on the balcony. Everybody immediately liked my mom and her spirit. I was so happy to see her having such good time. After dinner we had two cakes; Ahmed bought one for me and one for my mom. Then Heather's friend played the ukulele and we all sang with her. Everybody was having so much fun so I suggested that they all spend the night in our place and they all agreed. The next day we all went to the beach, continuing to have a good time. My mom was speechless from admiring the exotic beauty of Hawaii. She kept pointing at all the flowers which she'd always been a big fan of. She was amazed at how all the landscaping was well-maintained and carefully taken care of.

"This place is so clean. Not just the beach but entire city is so litter free." Her amusement was very entertaining to all of us. The next few days the three of us drove around the Island to show my mom what Oahu is about. We rented three bicycles and we rode them along the beach. Rex, Nel and even the new kitty-cat Lily were with us, enjoying the trip. I was laughing and watching my mom riding her bicycle way ahead of us.

"I told you that she was better at riding bicycles than you and I. You didn't believe me." I couldn't stop laughing from watching Ahmed having a hard time on the dirt road which was full of rocks. The dogs were way ahead of us too, following my mother. Lily was bouncing in a basket at the front of my bicycle. I was so happy. I could do this every single day. Seeing my mom so happy and relaxed, watching my pets having so much fun, all this was giving me a sense of peace and harmony. My mom loved sitting in the water and I loved watching her enjoying it so much.

"Mom, how do you like Hawaii so far?" I asked her even though I knew the answer.

"It sure looks like a paradise on Earth." She said not without a trace of melancholy in her voice. I knew that my dreams were same as my mother's dreams. I knew that she put a lot of hope in me and my book. I would hate to disappoint her. I kept writing as many pages a day as I could. She kept preparing food, cleaning the apartment, washing our laundry and walking my dogs. It was incredible to wake up in the morning knowing that there was somebody who cared about me more than anything else.

Ahmed liked my mother's company and the two were getting along. Unfortunately though he didn't always make her feel comfortable. He didn't seem to understand that by giving me a hard time he was really giving a hard time to my mother. With his frequent mood swings and his outbursts of paranoid jealousy he actually made her fear for my life.

"He doesn't look normal when he's like this. Are you sure he's not taking any drugs? One moment he's OK and then the next moment he's acting all crazy. He's eyes get red and his face doesn't look good when he gets violent like this. I'm honestly worrying about your safety. I think the best thing would be if you just came back to Poland with me. I know I can't stay here like this. I don't feel like I can take this. I wanna go back home. I think that this would be the best thing to do. And in the future, when you'll have your own place and your own money, I'll come back then." I had to agree with my mother even thought it was so hard to let go of her. I told myself that I had to be grateful for the three months that she spent with us. Ahmed of course felt very bad when she was leaving and of course he wanted her to stay. He tried to convince her not to leave like he always did with me but my mom, as sweet and as forgiving as she is, she can also be very determined.

Eight Dollars

Before we drove her to the airport, I promised my mom that I would do everything in my power to make this book a reality. I also promised her that if in a reasonable time this wasn't going to happen, that I would come back to Poland. She seemed reassured by my promise. A month later I was on the phone with my mother when I suddenly realized that I was late. I hadn't been very intimate with Ahmed but there was that one time when he was being nice and attentive and when I allowed for the two of us to have intercourse.

"OK, whatever you do, just don't come inside me. I could have those days, you know?" I said to him without realizing how naïve I sounded. Of course Ahmed came inside me. The following weeks I hadn't paid that much attention to my frequent headaches thinking that it was the stress that was causing them. The nausea wasn't alarming me either since I felt that way many times before whenever I hated my situation. The loss of appetite was something that I was actually glad about, hoping that I could lose a few pounds. I went to a drug store to get a home pregnancy test just to make sure that I was OK. I got the cheapest single test and a pack of cigarettes thinking that wasting eight dollars for a test was worth the peace of mind.

I was fighting with Ahmed again so I was staying at the office. I was waiting for my old friend Fiona who still lived in LA, to rescue me. She promised me that she would get me a ticket and that I could stay with her for a while. We were supposed to find some temporary solution for my pets too. I wanted to leave Hawaii, hoping that if Ahmed wasn't anywhere near me, I wouldn't go back to him. His need for controlling me was suffocating. It came to the point when he would even take all the food away to punish me for my alleged cheating on him. When I went to a restaurant to inquire about a job, his outburst reached a maximum. He didn't want me to work so according to him I wouldn't have more opportunities to fuck around. He stopped taking food away though, after that episode.

Now, I was peeing on a stick and I was dreading the results. The two pink lines started to appear in front of my eyes like they didn't care about anything. My eyes bulged and I covered my mouth afraid that somebody could hear me screaming.

"Oh my God! Oh my God!" I kept saying it like there was nothing else to say.

"What do I do now?" I finally asked myself. I promised myself that I would never have another abortion. And no, I haven't regretted the decision that I have made ten years ago, but this time I was thirty-two years old. This time I should be more mature and brave enough to raise a child even on my own.

"I'll just be a single mother then." I said to myself while hiding the test and the package that it came with.

"What if I did marry him?" I asked my mother on the phone after I told her about the baby.

"Maybe you should. Maybe it wouldn't be so bad. I don't know what to tell you. You can always come back to Poland and raise the baby here." She tried to be very supportive even though I knew that she was very concerned.

"I'm afraid that he would use the baby to manipulate me even more. I know that he could use the baby to control me that much harder." I was telling my mom knowing that she knew exactly what I was talking about. I finally decided to tell Ahmed about the pregnancy.

"How you know for sure it's mine?" What other response could I have expected from him? When it finally sunk in his brain that I was pregnant with him, his attitude changed one hundred and eighty degrees. I could tell that he was hoping that the baby would bring us closer together. He bought a new engagement ring and he wanted me to wear it.

"Ahmed, this ring is super ugly," I said to him.

"But you're keeping the baby, right?" He'd been asking about it for days, even though we already scheduled a day for abortion.

"I told you, I can't do this. I can't have this baby, not like this." I've been saying the same thing over and over again to him.

"You change your mind every five minutes. You said you would keep it." He was being very persistent.

"Yes, that was for a moment that I felt that way. And then the reality sinks in and I can't even breathe. Ahmed, I cannot and I will not bring a child to this world knowing that she or he will have to go through things that I had to go through. That is not something that I can live with. I don't care if that makes me selfish and I don't care if others would condemn me for this or not. All I know is that if God will let me I will have my child only when I'll be ready to receive it. I will not bring a child to this world only so she could experience the misery that I've been experiencing all my life. No way. I will not do that. This is my right to make such a choice. As for the future, I will renew my old belief in not having sex at all until I'll get married. That is the only way that I can prevent these painful experiences from happening ever again." I was expressing my feelings even though I knew that Ahmed wasn't truly listening to me. He was hoping that I would change mind before the procedure but I didn't.

The Betrayal

Despite not having a happy ending or at least anything conclusive I had finished writing my book up to this point. I was lucky enough to have it edited by a woman who offered her service for free after familiarizing herself with the content. I titled the book "You Can't Outrun What's Within You" and I self-published the memoir with no money down after getting tired of opening emails from publishers and literary agents that sounded all the same:

"Thank you for submitting your book proposal to us. Unfortunately, your story is not exactly what we are looking for at the moment. Best wishes and good luck with your adventure of becoming a published author."

"I don't need your wishes or good luck; I'm in charge of shaping my own destiny! I'd rather do it my own way, anyway. Self-publishing may be relatively new, and it may still have some bad stigma about it, like everything new does, but it sure does have its advantages that your stupid publishing house could never offer me!"

I repeated that to myself, over and over, in order not to lose my spirit. The truth is though that I wasn't convinced about my book either. I had sold some copies through my website, and my editor kept reassuring me that my story was interesting — I even managed to appear on local TV news. Still, I knew something was missing. I just had no clue what that would be.

Ahmed was still angry with me for the abortion but I was strangely relaxed. Our lives went on for a while in the same old pattern; days filled with sweetness and having fun together, interlaced with days when we despised each other. In the peaceful moments with my Egyptian companion, I regretted that I didn't keep our baby.

"Why are you looking at me like that?" he'd ask me while massaging my feet.

"Like what?" I didn't want to reveal my thoughts to him. I was trying to imagine whether it would make a difference if I'd try to accept him the way he was.

"What if I just learn how to live with his jealously and his controlling behavior? Maybe if I am more emotionally available to him, these symptoms of insecurity would diminish if not disappear completely?"

I was picturing us walking down the beach while holding our little Safaa (the Egyptian name we both picked for our unborn baby), and watching Rex and Nel running playfully along the wet sand. I loved that image in my mind and I was tired of it being just that; an image, nothing more. Ahmed was far from being my perfect match, but in addition to his love/obsession towards me he possessed many qualities that I found charming and intriguing. We also had a very strong, what I would call; spiritual connection.

The truth was, though, that I was deeply disappointed with my life, and I felt completely incapable of changing it. Accepting Ahmed and the idea of becoming his wife was the only thing that seemed to be in my control. I decided to marry him and to start a family. Surprisingly, my decision brought me into a state of contentment. I began to look at him in a more tender way and I started to allow myself to care for him. While taking our usual walks on the beach, I planned in my head our simple wedding day. I still had some doubts, but I forced myself to push them away hoping that once I said "I do," those uncomfortable feelings would disappear completely.

"I'm going to Egypt for two weeks." Ahmed's announcement was a surprise to me, and not a good one. I missed him terribly. I was so relieved when he finally came back from the trip. We were still engaging in our fights even though I was trying my best not to get mad but when Ahmed suggested that I get a job, I began to feel suspicious. Until then he never wanted me to work; he liked having control over me. When he started coming home very late, I didn't believe that it was because he fell asleep at the office.

A few times I drove to his work-place at three in the morning. He of course wasn't there. I couldn't take it anymore. I could tolerate nearly everything, but rejection was one thing that I could not accept. I started to slip into a deep depression. I was lying on the couch day and night and I was hardly talking to him. He seemed almost happy with the arrangement even though I could sense the guilt in his eyes and in his posture.

In the morning he tried to sneak into the apartment unnoticed by me. He was gladly buying me bottles of wine which I started to ask for. This is how I spent Christmas; alone with a glass of red wine wondering where he was and with whom. When New Year's Eve came I couldn't take the empty walls of the apartment which were starting to suffocate me.

I got dressed and I went for a walk in Waikiki just to be among people. The loudness of happy tourists that gathered everywhere to celebrate the New Year and the fireworks gave me a deep sense of sadness. I kept walking alongside the famous beach with all its restaurants that hired live music for this special occasion. Some of the guests were staring at me with curious looks. A few men found the courage to strike up a conversation with me, but I wasn't in the mood to socialize with anybody. I felt so alone. I sat on the beach and I finally cried few tears. A boy in his twenties asked politely if he could join me. Beaten up internally, I felt flattered by his interest. We spent some time chatting but when he invited me to have a drink at a bar, I refused. I headed back home. It was past two o'clock, and shortly after I lied down on the couch Ahmed decided to see if I was home. He sat on a chair with a look on his face that was meant to express the disgust that he felt for me. He began to express his feelings:

"I hurt you the way you hurt me. You will see. You will c-r-y-y-y . You don't know anything. You don't know shit." He tried to gain my attention.

"Ahmed, I know you're fucking someone so spare me this speech alright? Do whatever you want. I'm going back to Poland anyway." I had been thinking of doing so ever since his absences began, which became an every night ritual.

"Ha ha ha ha ha! Not just someone. If you saw her you would cry. I promise you!" He smiled. His facial expressions were making him look unattractive again while he continued with his threats:

"I promised myself that I will hurt you and I will. All my life I make it so you will suffer, even if I lose my business I don't care. I will do what you did to me. You fuck around everywhere with everyone. I know that. You think I don't know anything. Just wait and see; you will cry."

There was no point in having a discussion with him. Just as in those moments of intense paranoia he was making no sense and I was simply giving up.

Online I convinced Dean, the guy from South Africa to get me the money I needed for a ticket. Even though I was free to go at any moment I kept postponing the trip. I did not want to leave Hawaii and no, I did not want to leave Ahmed. In some way I loved him. As sick as it might have sounded and as self-destructive as it was, I had strong feelings for this man who turned paradise into a living hell.

Hard Decisions

Prior to making this incredibly difficult decision, I was having a reoccurring dream in which I fought physically with my father, attempting to kill him. It was very unpleasant and tiring and it was leaving a bitter taste every time I woke up. That same night in which I made the decision of not getting mad, and not hating Ahmed, the dream with my father returned only to surprise me that I was having an actual and assertive conversation with him in it instead! As days went by and as I kept insisting with my "inner" practice, those dreams kept showing up each time revealing a small but sweet progress in my relationship with my father. This was very encouraging; to say at least. It made me not want to go back to my old ways but it was also somewhat confusing because in the process of it I could not help but to develop loving feelings towards a man that was not good for me.

There seemed to be no end to my confusion since in fact the day I started all this was the day when Ahmed started to leave me alone more and more. His constant absence was giving me some space that I was longing for but not without having to pay a high price of feeling intensely hurt by the rejection. At the moment I didn't realize that my subconscious choice of ignoring him on the outside was responsible for us growing apart and eventually for him going away from my life for good. Apparently part of me wanted it to be this way. What I call "Higher Me" was leading me through this and I was following it by listening to my feelings no matter how difficult it was. Still the part of me that I call "My Persona" or "My Ego" was trying to resist the reality, desperate to keep things the way they were. This part was trying to improve things in my relationship by taking it to the next level and it was totally unwilling to let go. This inner battle was extremely difficult even though I knew that if it wasn't for my low self-esteem and my lack of sense of security I wouldn't be going through all this. I knew that if I truly loved myself and that if I believed in myself Ahmed would never be part of my reality. Nonetheless it seemed a lot easier to withstand everything and to do whatever would take so that someone else would love me rather than trying to appreciate my own self. To cherish and to admire myself seemed beyond my capacity.

Throughout the time I spent with Ahmed for the first time in my life I barely learned how to accept myself the way I was. This acceptance started early on. While he would say awful things to me about me, I would remain quiet and I would repeat to myself in my mind:

"I am what I am. Who gives a shit if I'm lazy, incapable, or if I smell good or bad? I am what I am and all those negative and undesirable qualities are part of me. Cause I am everything. I am One." Each time I had this inner conversation I felt more and more in peace with myself and that reflected in my growing confidence that could not be taken away by anything external. My certainty that was originating from within me was amusing my partner. He would often change his tone and with pure admiration written on his face and in his eyes, he would confess to me:

"I don't know how you do this I swear. I try to drive you crazy but you're the one who ends up driving me crazy. How you do that? You're so unpredictable. You're something else I swear. You're different. You're danger. I've never seen anyone like you. Dangerous girl. You're like the snake you have tattooed on your arm. You attack and then you pour the poison to whoever tries to harm you. You're not a bad person; you just protect yourself." Ahmed's eyes were expressing then nothing else but pure admiration and deep desire in understanding me so he could own me. I loved those moments. I felt so alive, so in control and so stable! I felt so grateful for him for I knew that he was being my teacher. Without even being aware of it he was forcing me into all this. In this rather strange way he was teaching me how to once and for all stop hating myself. Once I would finish with this lesson I would move on into the next level of appreciating myself. I knew somehow though that the teacher would be replaced. I didn't want for this to happen and yet I was allowing the change. It was all part of "The Plan" that God; The Higher Me, had for me and I had to be OK with it. I had to surrender to it without expecting that anyone would understand me or the things that I did or didn't do. Including myself. This inability of foreseeing things and this lack of understanding were wearing me out though.

In this strangely depressing yet very liberating time I've been giving a lot of thought to the meaning of my existence. Life tasted very bitter to me. The constant need to struggle just to stay alive had worn me out completely at this point. There was no sense of fulfillment, excitement or joy present in my life. I did not want to continue living this way, but I also didn't want to die. There had to be something that I could do to change the course of my destiny.

Since that time when little Teddy came into my life, I did not just believe — I knew — that everything was connected and we were all one. I knew that the best way to guarantee positive change in life was to bless others by helping them accomplish the things they may have been unable to do themselves.

Children proved to be a perfect example. Helping Teddy was out of the question since his mother made it perfectly clear to the social worker that she didn't wish to have anything to do with me. My hands were tied and all I could do was to try not to think about the impact my unexplained absence had to have on him. I felt very discouraged by the limitations the system imposed on me. Hence, my frequent thoughts about going to a place like Africa, and extending my help there. I wanted to get a permanent home, not an orphanage but a real home, for at least a few little ones. I didn't have a specific plan on how I would achieve that, but my desire for it was the starting line.

I knew I would have to raise or make my own money to implement my plan. I shared my ideas with Ahmed but he didn't seem to understand my perception. He did agree, however, to take care of Rex and Nel in my absence. I had the money for the ticket and I could travel at any time, but I was hesitating. The trip looked scary and even scarier was the thought of leaving my fur-babies for an unknown period of time. In the seven years we had been together, the longest time we were ever apart was when I stayed at that shelter, which was only two weeks! Even then I visited them on the weekend.

I felt confident that Rex and Nel were going to be alright with Ahmed, but I wasn't sure whether I was going to be OK without them. That's when Ahmed reassured me that in case my trip needed to be extended, for whatever reasons, he would ship them both to me. This would of course be our last resort since I was planning on coming back to Hawaii and I knew exactly how challenging bringing pets to the Islands was. It took me almost six months to take care of the mandatory animal quarantine so my fur-babies didn't have to stay locked up in quarantine for four months. Instead, they could be released immediately to me at the airport. The whole thing cost a couple of thousands of dollars.

That wasn't even the most challenging part, though. The hardest thing was the trip itself. Rex, Nel, Milky Way and I, we spent four days and nights at the San Francisco Airport before we were finally allowed to embark the plane. First the airline wanted an additional seven hundred dollars for Rex because of his "extra" weight. I argued with the managers about it and they finally allowed Rex to travel with his regular ticket. Then the numerous managers I called upon insisted that my kennels were not airline approved and when I corrected that they didn't like Rex's size.

"I know you've got the maximum in size kennel but he still doesn't look too comfortable in it. He has to be able to move around it freely without any discomfort." The airline people kept repeating each morning while taking the measurements. The time spent at that airport was a real nightmare but I was not willing to give up on Rex. He was coming with us to Hawaii. I prayed a lot those days and nights like I've never prayed before. Finally some supervisor felt sorry for me and to make everyone happy she asked the cargo people if they could give me one of their huge wooden crates that looked like was made almost for a horse transport.

Now I wasn't going to put my fur-kids and myself through all this again unless it was absolutely necessary. The only reason I'd make them fly a long distance like this again would be if I'd be absolutely sure about not coming back to Hawaii. That wasn't the case, though, and so for them having to remain on the Island made a lot more sense.

Goodbye

When Ahmed did not come home for two nights, I started to pack. I couldn't sleep. The pain I was feeling was unbearable and the idea of going away was supposed to keep me at least somewhat sane.

I knew my mission in Africa would help with my healing process. But since I was going to Europe first, the unresolved emotions from my childhood were tearing me apart.

While I dreaded the thought of being back in Poland, there was not enough oxygen for me in Hawaii. I was thrilled with the idea of seeing my family for the first time in a very long time, but I was also scared.

It was 7:00 a.m. when Ahmed entered the apartment and saw I was ready to go. The surprise on his face was replaced by a sense of relief. It hurt like hell.

"Will you take me to the airport, please?"

"What time is your flight?"

"We've got to go now. I still have to buy the ticket at the airport."

"So where did you decide to go?"

"First I'm going to Poland and then I'll be traveling to Kenya. But before I get there I have to stop in New Jersey for few days. I'll stay at my cousin's so I can do my passport in New York City. I can't fly on a passport that has expired."

"Please make sure that Rex and Nel get their anti-flea treatment each month, OK? You know they're predisposed to that flea-allergy and I don't want them to get dermatitis. Please promise me you'll do that," I said with tears in my eyes.

"Don't worry; they'll be fine. I've got all their documents you gave me. See? I put them right above these books. Don't worry. Nothing is gonna happen to your kids. Stop worrying. Come here Rex. Come here Nel. Tell your mamma that she worries way too much for no reason." He was trying to calm me down while petting my dogs. I was crying like a small child.

"I've written you an authorization letter in case you need one. Please make sure you don't lose this folder. These are all the documents that Rex and Nel have. All their quarantine papers, all their microchip certificates and all that are here. Don't lose it! You'll need all this in case of any emergency. All right?" I was talking to Ahmed like he was a pre-schooler. My eyes were red from crying and it was making him feel guilty. Rex and Nel were whining the same way they normally did whenever we'd take them for a ride or for a walk.

"Mamma's gonna be back. It's just gonna be a little while, that's all, OK? Daddy's gonna take care of you, OK?" I petted them as always, both at the same time. My heart was breaking. Rex and Nel were standing on the balcony wondering why on earth they weren't the ones jumping in the van as usual. Nel was barking out loud which was something she didn't do often.

"Oh God, it's like she's telling me not to go." I said to Ahmed.

"They'll be fine." He replied.

Leaving Rex and Nel was excruciatingly painful. It felt as if my heart was torn apart. I felt angry with myself and God. It didn't seem fair that in order to help myself, by helping homeless children in Africa, it was necessary for me to temporarily separate from my own fur-kids. I was angry at the state for its mandatory, time-consuming, and expensive animal quarantine process that was making the option of traveling with my companions, to say at least, unreasonable.

Nevertheless, I believed that not just me, but also my beloved fur-kids would benefit from the transformation I'd undergo while helping helpless children. I knew that Rex and Nel were going to wait for me. I knew that in their own ways, they were going to be proud of their momma for making a sacrifice such as this one. Their sacrifice was not going to be wasted, either. All three of us were not only going to be together again, but we were also going to be rewarded with an even deeper sense of connection.

Oh God, Not This Again!

In New Jersey my cousin came with her two year old son to pick me up from the airport. She lived with her husband and her father in a nice home. They all insisted that I stay with them for at least a week or so. I had not seen my cousin or my uncle since I was maybe ten years old so I thought it wasn't such a bad idea to catch up with them. No, I'm not talking about uncle Mietek who expedited us to the orphanage when we were little. This was a different one. Uncle Mietek was also living in the States with his family as he had managed to win a green card on some lottery. I've never visited him.

I felt welcome at their place and I opened up a little bit about my recent troubles with Ahmed. My cousin discouraged me from going back to Poland an offered me to live with them for a while until I was able to get back on my feet.

In the morning I took a pregnancy the test.

"They're pink, both of them, aren't they?" I said to her while showing the results.

"It looks that way. Well, congratulations! You're gonna have a baby; that's a wonderful thing. Maybe you guys will work this thing out. Who knows? Guys sometimes do freak out at first but then…look at my husband. Remember I told you about his first reaction when I told him I was pregnant? And look now; see how happy he is to be a father? Everything will work out, you'll see. We'll be coming to visit you and your new baby in Hawaii." Iwona's optimistic attitude calmed me down a little. Still anxious, I called Ahmed:

"I'm pregnant." I told him firmly. He turned on me with an anger that resembled pure hatred.

"Listen to me; you can't come back here. I will hate you, you and the baby. In fact if you come here I will hide. I won't be at home. You won't find me." His words hurt more than I could take. I knew I could go back there and that sooner or later he would eventually accept the reality but the pain he was causing me was not allowing me to do so. I could not imagine myself being in that state and having to deal with his coldness towards me.

I'd already made up my mind that abortion was not an option and I was going to keep this baby even if it meant I'd be a single parent. I didn't know what to think anymore or what to do for that matter and I shifted my focus toward loving my yet unborn baby that was growing in my womb.

"I promise you; we are going to be all right. This time we will make it. You have me and I will somehow take care of you. I will do my best to make sure that every moment in your life you will feel loved. I promise you will not be longing for that the way I've been doing. It will be different for you. You are my baby and I will protect you. I will care for you and always, I mean always, I will show you how much you mean to me. We may be poor and we may have some challenges along the way but one thing you will not lack; and that is love. Your mommy loves you already and that is one thing that you may always count on. There will be no yelling; no anger, and no chaos in your life. I'll make sure of it. I will always talk to you in a way filled with love and I will always explain things to you in a patient way. You are MY BABY and that's all it matters. You are mine. You are my half Polish half Egyptian princess and you will always be more than beautiful in my eyes."

While saying this to my baby I was feeling intense love that was bringing me joy even though the fear in me hasn't subsided. The thought of being a single parent was petrifying and not so much because of the money. It was painful to imagine the baby's father not being there to watch me getting bigger and bigger. It was painful to think that he would never be teaching our child to speak Arabic. Or that he wouldn't be spoiling our little Safaa behind my back.

"Don't tell mommy that I gave you this or we'll both be in trouble." I couldn't help but to imagine how he would treat her or him. I was really hoping it was a girl.

Now we could really have our Safaa. She was already here, for the second time and this time I wasn't so scared of having her. This time I wasn't going to reject her.

I fell asleep knowing that I was going to be a mother and not knowing whether Ahmed would eventually decide to be a father or not. I was very happy. I was expecting to face some initial difficulties of course, but that was something that wasn't new for me.

Then at 5 a.m. a sudden and intense pain woke me up. Terrified that I could be losing the baby, I went to the bathroom to make sure that I wasn't bleeding, but I was. Not heavily, but there was enough blood to know that something wasn't right.

"Oh God, please no! Do not take this baby away from me, please. Please!" My cousin drove me to the emergency room.

"You're gonna be all right, don't worry. There're plenty cases when women bleed during pregnancy and they still give birth to normal and healthy children." She was trying to cheer me up the best way she knew how.

I was so disappointed with myself. I looked at my cousin who was younger than I and who was somehow able to have everything that I've been dreaming about. She had a husband, a two-year-old son, at least one of her parents was living with her, and she was getting along with everybody. She was about to buy her first house. Everything I dreamed of.

Why wasn't I able to do the same thing with my life? Why was I screwing everything up? Why did I have to constantly sabotage myself? How come I've never succeeded at anything? I felt deep embarrassment and humiliation, which was making me feel even more insecure.

At the hospital the doctor confirmed that I was pregnant. She informed me about it in a way a clerk in the store would inform you that they run out of something you were looking for. It was only when she saw tears in my eyes, when she made an effort to show some concern.

"Look, it's not a hundred percent sure that you will miscarry, OK? You need to be seen by a doctor on a regular basis to see if this pregnancy has a chance of survival. If you want you can come back here in forty-eight hours and we'll run the blood tests again to see if the hormone level is rising."

I still couldn't decide where to go. I felt like I was suspended in nowhere and I hated that I was obligated to drag my body someplace so it could survive.

To Make Dreams Come True

I was at the airport dreading the thought of embarking the plane. This wasn't because I was afraid of flying. Terrorists' attacks have never intimidated me either. The real terror I've been trying to avoid for so long was in finding myself back home. Facing my family after all these years, completely broke and after all still pregnant, could not be easy. I didn't want to go there and yet I was headed that direction. Nobody was really forcing me and yet I chose to go there. I wasn't expecting for anyone to welcome me with understanding since I wasn't even understanding myself or my actions. Total defeat and total surrender was the state I was in. Embarrassment interlaced with highest insecurity was governing my mood. At the same time I was excited about the thought of seeing my family for the first time in ten years. Some new family members I had to yet meet. Being in such a vulnerable state I was hoping I would find some moral support.

My youngest sisters came with my brother in law to pick me up from the airport. Magdalena and Monika weren't the two little girls I remembered. They were all dressed sexy and they kept giggling at the sight of my amusement with them.

"So; you thought we'd stay little forever?" They were teasing me on our long drive back home. The road was covered with snow and my brother in law; Marta's husband had to drive real slow. While chatting with my family I observed my mother land. The cold weather so characteristic to this part of the world was taking me into my past. Everything else was different; the new beautiful homes everywhere, the new businesses, new cars on the road and even people were less gray than I used to remember. The new population armed with their cell phones was giving me an impression of more uplifted country, more in a hurry of gaining what had been lost in the past under the Russian regime. There was no sight left of the Communism from the old days and it looked like the nation was doing everything possible to make sure that the history would not repeat itself. Also traveling had been made so easy since Poland became part of European Union. You could almost smell a sense of freedom in the air, a freedom that was denied for so long and for which "my" people had to fight for. The fear that used to dominate the atmosphere and the people in the old days was nowhere to be found. It felt good to see all this change. For the first time in my life I didn't mind at all to be Polish. I was no longer embarrassed of my roots and that felt well too. I was actually appreciating my origins and this was new to me. I was feeling little bit guilty for not having faith in my country and for judging it so harshly before. I was feeling very humble.

My family welcomed me the best way they knew how. It felt like they were shocked and concerned with my new situation. It felt as if they weren't allowing themselves to be too affectionate with me. I didn't feel understood, and if it wasn't for my youngest siblings, I would have felt completely lost. In the eyes of my older siblings I was messing up my life and I needed tough love for a wake-up-call. Everybody had their lives put together somehow and according to my family it was my turn to do the same. I was different, I was making them worry and my selfish way of living life was bringing me misery. Being seen this way was like visiting my childhood, like reliving my worst nightmares. I loved my family and I hated how I was never able to feel part of it for real. In attempt not to hurt anybody's feelings so I wouldn't have to regret that later I decided to keep my disappointment inside me. I was afraid to say anything just like I was afraid not to say anything. The level of discomfort kept rising until two weeks later I bought a one way ticket to Athens to visit the rest of my family and to see if things would be different there but they weren't. Still pregnant, knowing that slowly, but surely my baby was leaving my body, I was at the edge of losing my mind. The accumulation of emotional pains I was feeling was more than I felt I could handle. I kept calling Ahmed on regular basis. It felt humiliating how desperate I was. He would always limit himself to reassuring me that Rex and Nel were doing fine. He'd make them whine by talking to them in baby voice so I could hear it for myself that they were fine. He seemed to enjoy the empowerment he felt due to total sense of control he now had over me. He had my precious dogs and now my heart too in his hands. There was nothing good about being in such vulnerable position and not knowing how to get out of it. Hearing from everyone around that I was the one responsible and the one to be blamed for everything was not giving me wings either. I wanted so bad not to exist but not bad enough to pollute my mind with harmful thoughts.

I needed some trace of hope. Going to Africa was the only thing that made any sense to me. To help even if only few small children and to change their lives forever were going to be my medicine and solution for my broken life and my broken heart. I found nothing noble in my decision; it was simply a matter of business. In my understanding the Law of the Universe said that whenever we want something we can get it the fastest way if we provide such thing to someone else that needs the same thing. So, if we want to be happy we need to make someone else happy. If we want more money we need to give some to those who need money as well. I tried this approach in the past few times with Teddy and almost immediately it brought me quite astonishing results. I was now so determined to create a better life that I made myself believe that this was the only way for me to go about things. What exactly did I want now the most? I wanted not to have to struggle anymore. I wanted desperately for my life to change for better and for good this time. I needed to have a sense of security. By now I seemed to have embraced the fact that true happiness did not depended on anything or anybody that was outside of me. At the same time I didn't believe that renouncing everything and living in a cave on a mountain would bring me closer to such state of Self-Realization that I've been longing for. It was a confusing matter to me; no doubt. Could I do everything that was in my power to make my dreams come true and at the same time could I remain detached from the expectations of the outcome that I desired? And what exactly was in my power? Certainly the numerous attempts of changing my own life, no matter what approach I assumed, had failed, right? So what was the point of keeping on going in that direction? Why would I keep on slamming my head against the wall and keep expecting different results? I sure didn't like the thought of waking up one day old and all wrinkly and having no other choice but to accept the fact that my methods did not produce the results I had in mind. So what exactly could I do differently this time? What was it that I haven't done yet? If I've failed at changing my own life in a definite way, did I have what it takes to change someone else's life in such way? Could I make somebody else's dreams come true? Somebody's who needs it real bad and who's not in a position of obtaining it on its own. Could I give up and reject completely the so popular, and so much believed in conviction, that in order to be able to help others we MUST help ourselves FIRST? I could... Maybe it was time to change. Maybe it was time to say fuck the fear caused by the lack of conformity from around. Maybe it was time for me to go to Africa; find some children that were living on the street and buy them that damn house. It could be a group of children, perhaps siblings, where the oldest of them being a teenager, would be able to take care of the new household.

Now What?

Now how on earth was I going to do that? I had no money whatsoever and I was living in Athens off of my younger brother Rafal. I did not speak Greek and my attempts of getting a job at some bars turned out fruitless because of that. Dean; my "internet friend" from Africa who had sent me the money so I could go back to Poland kept refusing to help me this time:

"I will not buy you a ticket to Kenya, no way. You can get killed there, I'm not kidding. And why do you need to be in Kenya to help children? You can do all that in Greece or in Poland; you don't need to be in Africa to do all that." Dean was looking at me through the camera on my laptop with that same firm and unbreakable look on his face each time I mentioned my new intentions to him.

"Whatever Dean; you know me and you know that I will get there somehow sooner or later; with or without your help." I was getting very frustrated with him. I had explained to him that I wasn't going to be there completely alone. I had a friend named Elisha who was from Kenya and whom I had a chance to get to know while staying at Ahmed's office. Elisha came to Hawaii on a government program to expand Kenyan culture in the USA. He had a master's degree in business and marketing and he was a guest speaker in Hawaii Pacific University. He has appeared on local TV discussing the cultural issues with the mayor of Honolulu. He wasn't a crook but most importantly; he had a big heart and even bigger desire to help those less fortunate even though, or maybe I should say: BECAUSE like me he was struggling financially all his life. I've spent hours talking to him in that office over a period of few months and I became very fond of him. He always reminded me that if I'd ever decided to visit Kenya I was more than welcome to stay in his small apartment which he shared with his wife and their three children. I took his offer and I informed him via email that I was coming to Nairobi as soon as I succeed in raising the money for the mission.

My family was totally against my new idea and so any kind of support from them was out of question too.

"I know you have a big heart and you want to help the whole world but that is not the way to do things. You must help yourself first in order to be able to do so for someone else. There is no other way and you know that, Elzbieta." I had to hear that from my siblings each time I attempted to convince them to put their forces together and sponsor my adventure. Even if lack of money would not have been an issue here, I knew that no one wanted to have to deal with that sense of responsibility of sending me to a land where safety was at the very best questionable. I couldn't really blame my family for their attitude towards my new "mission" but at the same time I couldn't help but to feel anger and resentment because of it. I was no longer pregnant which was confirmed by the doctor to whom my very concerned Greek brother in law took me to. Again, I was experiencing paradoxical emotions within me; the feelings of pain and anger caused by the loss interlaced with strange yet understandable sense of relief. Now I really had nothing that would stop me from going where I had to go and from doing what needed to be done. Lack of financial freedom created countless obstacles in my way before, but it never rendered things impossible in my agenda. This time it wasn't going to be any different. First thing I knew I had to do in order to accomplish my new goal was to decide that anything else other than me being in Africa and transforming someone else's life in a definite way, was simply more important than the air needed by my lungs. Done! That desire in me was now bigger than anything else. The trip and its purpose were now my priority number one and nothing else mattered nearly as much. The next step was to convince my subconscious that all this was obtainable and that it was obtainable NOW; not in the near future, not later on when things would improve but simply now, at the present moment despite of the fact that all odds were against me. In order to trick my subconscious, which I knew would be controlling the actions that I would eventually take or fail to take; I kept repeating most of the time at loud to myself:

"Look Elzbieta, when you want something in life and you want it R-E-A-L B-A-D, you always, and I mean always manage to make that your reality. Look back and examine all those times when nothing stopped you from being exactly where you wanted to be. You wanted to live in the US for example; you got that. Nothing had enough influence to overwrite that for you, not even the fact that you had to make a decision of over-staying your work visa and lying on your job applications in order to keep on pursuing the so called "American Dream". Yes; you may have had to live in discomfort of constantly watching your back and making sure that no individual with low principles could ever find out about your legal status, but still; you were where you wanted to be and the Universe did nothing else but to provide you with such opportunity. Just look at the amazing way that God/Universe allowed you to leave the country without anyone noticing anything and without you getting a red stamp in your new temporary passport that would say "No Re-entry Allowed". Wasn't that amazing? Wasn't it incredible that after September Eleventh' national security issues, before embarking on that plane destined towards Europe; that man looked at your passport and all he said to you was:

"Nice picture. Have a safe flight." Remember how calm you tried to remain despite the fear caused by the possibility of uncovering of the fact by the officials that your past 7 years in this country was considered unlawful? How awful did it feel to risk the possibility of ever returning to what you've been considering your home? And yet despite everything, despite taking an enormous risk while deciding to live the US borders, some incredible force was watching over you, wasn't it? This time you can count on the Universe to back you up with your newest plan just as you did, even though mostly subconsciously, on numerous occasions in the course of your life." I was making short and firm jabs with my hands in front of my face like I was fighting away any doubt, as I was saying these words in a very slow and determined manner.

"You are going to do this and you are going to do this now. You are going to find the way to be in Africa and you are going to succeed with your plan of getting a house for some small children that are right now going through some trash in attempt to fill up their overgrown stomachs in order to survive. Nothing it's going to stop you from this mission and you know that so please don't waste my time anymore and please direct my thoughts and my actions the way that will create the circumstances necessary to accomplish all this and to accomplish all this as soon as possible." After having such motivational self-talk and after the initial high from it being gone, I started to feel depressed. However, I knew that this temporary depression state that I found myself in was the result of me feeling even if just temporarily but still very limited; a feeling which I hated with all my heart. I also could sense though that it was in my power to make that negative mood work for me rather than against me. So; there was no point in fighting or resisting it. This not so new companion was going to be there with me for a while and I had to make a room for it no matter how reluctant I was feeling about the idea of "her" and I spending time together. I tried very hard not to hate Miss Depression who had stolen my life away in my past so many times before.

"OK fine, you're here again. God only knows why. And why exactly do I need you in my life? Here is our bed and there are the cigarettes since its all you really care about, so go ahead and make yourself comfortable. Just do me a favor and try to hide when my brother comes home since I don't want to feel guilty for making him worried. Deal? Now knock yourself out and do what you know how to do best which is sleeping. Go ahead and sleep my life away for now." I knew that "she" didn't like my tone but at the same time there was very little "she" could do about it.

"It's really hard for me not to hate you for messing up my life the way you've had done so far, but God is my witness I will try to tolerate you for now at least." That was my way of accepting the fact that no matter how hard I'd try, I could NEVER outrun the monster called Depression that was living rent free deep within me and which could not be evicted despite the endless efforts on my part. As a result of my trying to make peace with my inner undesirable tenant, I started to withdraw from my family, which I knew was affecting them a lot. I felt guilty about it but I couldn't stop myself from following my inner instinct which was telling me to stay away from anyone who wasn't supportive, even if just emotionally, of my mission. I pretty much had to stay away from the whole world…

The Video

With the very noticeable dark circles under my tired looking eyes, I stared for a moment at the video camera that was set up to capture my monologue.

"Hi everybody. My name is Elzbieta and I need your help." I paused for a moment to gain the courage in opening up in front of the whole population that was gathering on internet sites these days. I had to remind myself that it didn't matter what people were going to think of me as the result of this video being posted on youtube. I was determined to have my plan carried out successfully and the way I saw it was that if the humiliation was the price I had to pay for it in order to do so; so be it. I tensed my jaws and after inhaling and exhaling forcefully the air I looked back in the direction of the camera lens while scratching my head at the same time:

"OK, well…here is the thing…" I knew I didn't look confident at all. I knew I look confused, lost and miserable more than anything else. I looked the way I felt. I did feel and look honest and very straight forward though. I proceeded explaining to the viewers why I needed the money and I gave them a short glimpse to my recent past in order to explain my action. I wasn't really convinced about the effectiveness of my new marketing tool provided by the latest technology but I wasn't losing my hopes yet either. One week later though, after collecting through my website a single donation in the amount of ten dollars, my spirit felt really being crushed by the reality of indifference that appeared to be spread wide around the globe. I had to constantly remind myself about remaining faithful to my vision despite the lack of obvious results and despite the fact that depression was taking the best out of me. Sometimes around 3 o'clock at night, while trying to avoid making any noise, I'd leave my brother's tiny bachelor's apartment and I'd go for a walk. The incredibly ancient city of Athens had a lot to be admired for. I'd stare at the Mediterranean Sea that was spreading its glorious depth in front of me and I'd imagine that I was standing on the beach in Kenya instead. To make sure that the realization of my request to Universe was being expedited and granted, I'd allow myself to feel, with full intensity, the burning sensation of my desire. It wasn't pleasant to do so, considering that my impatience was trying to steal my self-imposed positive attitude away.

"You are already there. You... *(pause)* are already *(pause)*... in Kenya." I'd have to say that out loud to myself repeatedly. At this point in my life I really didn't bother to think in silence anymore. It became my habit by now to talk to myself as if I was talking to someone else. This way I could assure the quality of thoughts I was harboring towards my own self and if there was ever a need; I could easily correct my inner dialogue. The simple worries like:

"What will people think of this crazy woman that talks to herself?" were replaced with thoughts like:

"First of all who gives a shit what people think, second of all; with today's ear-piece cell phones being so popular; I'm not the only one who looks that way."

Now, I knew that using such vocabulary as "shit" wasn't entirely fitting in the program of maintaining a POSITIVE attitude. I also knew though that Rome wasn't build over a night. Hence I believed that assuming a realistic approach that would allow me to use such words in order to emphasize the importance of the message was highly beneficial.

I had no intention whatsoever of becoming one of those annoying individuals who to the outside world appear constantly cheerful and optimistic. As far as I could understand things these people were in denial and that's why they'd always appear to attract that kind of almost involuntary reaction from others that was designed to put them down. I wasn't going to make that mistake happen. Not again...So; my new approach was going to be less black and white and more adaptable to fluctuate according the needs. At this point of my life I understood and somehow even learned to manage my inherited tendency of being an extremist. Being an Aries; a zodiacal sign known for such characteristics, made such transformation more than difficult. Eventually though, mostly due to the painful consequences (life's lessons) I had to embrace the fact that life without extremes was a lot less bumpy. And so I've taught myself for example things like how to feel powerful and limitless without sacrificing the indispensable quality of remaining humble and grounded at the same time. Each and practically every single time I'd forget to do so, I'd find myself in a humiliating position that would open my eyes to harsh reality. I did not wish to live in denial any longer and so I wouldn't waste my time and I'd swallow my pride and I'd make the necessary correction in order to prevent the same mistake from happening again. It wasn't easy. Whenever

I'd feel good about myself and which would result in increased level of my confidence, I'd have to make sure not to invite the arrogance in. Sometimes it was really hard not to take advantage of the momentum and not to try "blow somebody's head off" with my reaction. The submissive part of me that was starved for any kind of attention for all those years was now acting out in ways that often would prevent me from acting rational. It was demanding for me to be stand up for it and it wasn't yielding to anything and to any one until I made sure that its needs of being acknowledged and respected were being met. I had a hard time with it since being assertive wasn't something that I had practiced a lot before. Now I was attempting to master the quality of communicating my feelings to the world, while still attempting to remain firm, understanding and compassionate at the same time. I had a lonnnngggg way ahead of me...By the reactions on my relatives' faces I could tell that I was quite often losing my battle. Nevertheless I was very determined to succeed with my "transformation from within". No one really knew what on earth was going on inside me. My family worried a lot about me these days and that wasn't easy for anyone but I somehow felt that for the time being I had to be secretive about all this. I could not divulge to anyone my new understanding because if I did, this could have potentially slow the process for me. I chose the safer yet the more uncomfortable approach of leaving everybody uniformed about the inner changes I was going through. Again; that was presenting me with many challenges considering the fact that nervous and excessive talking was one of the methods I had developed in order to dispense my anxieties. My need to please others and to make sure that no one else other than me got hurt as well as my urge to explain myself to everyone, ended up on my "Issues to be Eliminated List". For the very first time in my life, despite of being accused of selfishness before, whether that was the case or not, I was now putting myself and my needs first. I was still scared and hesitant about it but that was the start. Going to Africa WAS for ME. Helping others WAS for ME. I didn't need anyone's approval in following my heart. I was finally beginning to take that kind of power back to where it belonged; I was handling it to Elzbieta. My new way of thinking was bringing me some pleasure despite of the fact that my mind was still inhabited by fear. I could tell that this transformation was not going to be painless. Yet I knew that if I didn't follow up with my new direction; life would throw at me so much more pain and that I was not sure if I'd be able to bare that anymore. So, the way I saw things; it was entirely up to me; meaning the choice was still mine yet; I really had no other choice. And that was my choice; that I had none. I had to wake up and shake myself off from the brain fog I've been living in until now. I had to have the courage to be more than what the combination of a circumstances/society/upbringing and whatever other bullshit we tend to believe in, has molted me into. I had to become the Real Me. The true version of who I **REALLY** was.

The Good Samaritan

Around day twelve from the date I had posted my video I received notification of payment in my inbox. Some guy name Marek has sent twenty dollars to support my mission. His comment though was worth a lot more than that. He was expressing to me how impressed he was with me and more specifically with the courage I've shown through my action. In his note he was wishing me the best and I could tell that he did not expect to hear back from me. His way of expressing himself appeared very humble, almost insecure. I sent him an email in which I was expressing my gratitude not just for the money but for the encouraging words especially. He immediately replied to my message. I felt so flattered by the way he made it sound like he was corresponding with a famous author. He offered to rebuild my website free from any charge and he did an excellent job. Looking at my new site I couldn't help but to wonder how on earth I was able to sell whatever number of copies of my book so far. Marek was originally from Poland so we communicated in my native language. He lived in Holland with his Dutch wife and their son. He immediately gave me that sensation of being trustworthy. He was funny, witty, respectful and very down to earth. The sense of humor in the emails that went back and forth between us caused so much laughter that I started to feel less and less depressed. This guy, whom I've never met in person, was the first Soul on this planet that made me feel like I wasn't completely out of my mind for wanting to go to Africa.

"If I had the money I would pay for that ticket to Kenya for you, you know?" Yes, I knew he would. In the mean time I managed to get two job interviews at bar-restaurants hoping to make and save enough money for the trip. Didn't get any of those jobs and my ignorance of even basic Greek language was presented to me as the reason for it. Knowing

English wasn't enough. I was pissed off and disappointed but I wasn't giving up my hope that was powered by my determination.

"If I want something and I want it bad enough; I shall have it! And so I will! I will now get to that damn Kenya somehow!!!" I don't even remember how many times a day I would repeat those words to myself. Just like I don't remember exactly whether Marek purchased the copy of my book before or after that glorious day in which he informed me that he was going to wire five hundred euros to my bank account! That was like around seven hundred dollars then. The cheapest, one way airline ticket to Nairobi was for that amount. I purchased it online without wasting any time. I had less than a week to start packing and organizing things. There was no money to get any anti-malaria shots etc, so I didn't. I knew though that I had to have twenty five dollars for the tourist visa that I would get at the Nairobi's airport and that I would need some food money. I convinced Dean in sending me four hundred dollars. I lied to him saying that I borrowed some money for food from my sisters and that I needed to give it back to them. He would never send me that money if he knew where I was going with it... I knew that he didn't think it was possible for me to go to Kenya with only four hundred dollars. Intentionally I kept Dean unaware of Marek's generous act. I wasn't proud of myself for being deceitful but I figured it was a small price that I had to pay. I was finally flying to Kenya! Exactly two weeks after I posted that video on youtube.

My Brother

"Rafal, I am not going to Kenya to live there. I will do what I have to do and then I'll be back. You'll see. I'll be back in a couple of months." I was trying to convince my younger brother who had tears in his loving eyes.

"Yeah, yeah. That's what you said last time. And then you were gone for more than ten years." He had a good point there. I didn't know how to take the pain and hurt written all over his face away from him.

"I promise." My words seemed cheap. The same sense of guilt I had when leaving my siblings behind in that awful orphanage was now stealing my faith and my confidence about my newest project.

"I really, really have to do this. I WILL be back this time." I knew that no matter what and how I said it; nothing would stop my brother from experiencing the excruciating pain of losing his sister once again. That was hard, extremely hard. Rafal was a lot like me in that aspect that he wanted more than anything for everybody to be together and happy. Also like me he had lots of anger piling inside him. He was longing for that sense of belonging the way I did. He's been trying his best to make my stay in Athens as pleasant and as comfortable as possible. He was making meals for me, making sure I had cigarettes and all that even though he was struggling financially. He was sleeping on the floor so I could have the tiny bed for myself. I could have stayed with my other two sisters who had their own big apartments but I knew how much it meant to my brother that I chose to stay with him instead. Plus I really felt like he wasn't judging me and the life I was living. He made me feel like he was very proud of having a sister like myself. It was very funny and sweet how he would introduce me to his guy-friends and how he would tease them about me being completely out of their league.

"She is a walking perfection. You mortals don't deserve to even look at her, mother-fuckers." He'd say very convincingly in his broken Greek and they would translate it to me in their broken English. We'd laugh, smoke cigarettes and sip on the wine.

"Your brother is a mother-fucker but when he's right about something he's right." The compliments were pouring from left and right.

"You piss off my sis and you're dead meat." Rafal's threats were revealing his protective side.

"Dude, why would anybody try to piss off the most beautiful woman on this planet? Did you lose your mind or something? Did you hit hard that head of yours?" Such dialogs went on and on for hours sometimes. Some of his friends were born in Poland and so they helped with the translations that went back and forth between Greek, Polish and English.

"She's not only beautiful but she's also going to save the world. Starting with Kenya." The guys' exaggeration was making me laugh. My brother would get tense every time someone would mention my now confirmed trip. I could still notice though that those comments were making him feel proud. He's sister wasn't seen as a beautiful but empty vase. He's sister was seen as a hero...

"I could never do what she's doing. Not in a million years. I'm telling you bro; you've got a saint here. She's not just your sister; she's everyone's sister." The guys were trying to show me their deepest respect but I couldn't help but to laugh. I was glad to see that these gatherings were helping Rafal with overcoming his resistance to the reality of me having to leave again.

The day of my departure was pretty challenging as well. My mom gave me her blessing by making a cross gesture on my forehead. The fear, concern and anger where the emotions that she was trying to hide from everyone. I started to cry and she immediately scolded me in an attempt of stopping her own tears.

"That's what you wanted so go and do what you've got to do." Her tone was cold on purpose even though she tried real hard to sound supportive. My mother was angry at me. I had to bear the uncomfortable sense of guilt. It wasn't the first time that my selfish need to follow my heart wasn't giving her any other option but to have faith that I would be safe. I was escorted to the airport by my two sisters; Bozena and Danuta and my three nieces. I thought it was sweet how the little girls were all dressed up for this occasion. At the checking point my family watched me yelling in English at the woman that was refusing to complete the boarding process. I called for the manager:

"Why on earth do you need my return ticket? What for? I don't know how long I'll stay in Kenya. I'll buy my return ticket when I'm ready. Maybe I'll go from Nairobi to a different country. Maybe I'll decide that I want to see more of Africa, then what? Why would I waste my money to pay extra for two-way ticket if I found a good deal for one-way ticket?"

"Ma'am, we just need to make sure that Nairobi's officials will let you into their country with your one-way ticket, and that you will not be stuck at that airport, that's all we are trying to do." The manager wasn't helping; it was making me feel like those times when Poland was under the Communism.

"What is this really about? I think this is simply discrimination! I won't put up with this! You see my Polish passport so what; you automatically assume that I cannot afford to travel? This is discrimination! I am a citizen of European Union, whether you like it or not and I will not put up with this kind of bullshit." The people from neighboring check points were now staring at me in silence.

"Tell me what right do you have to discriminate me like this? If I had a Greek passport or let's say US passport, would we be still standing here and wasting time like we are doing right now? I don't think so." I continued.

"Ma'am calm down. We are just following the procedures."

"I know the procedures. I've been flying all over the world since I was eighteen so don't try to make me look like I don't know what I'm talking about, OK? Here is my ticket and here is my passport and I need to be on that plane right now. I don't want to have to later run through the security check because of all this." The man looked at my family standing behind me and then he exchanged few words with the checking in woman.

"Do you have a sufficient amount on you Ma'am that will allow you to purchase the return ticket while in Kenya?" She asked with a forced politeness.

"Yes I do." I replied with firmness.

"OK, here is your boarding pass. That's your gate number. Have a safe flight."

"Thank you." I said without meaning it.

"Jeee-sus Christ!" I turned towards my family.

"What was all that about?" Danuta asked.

"Oh nothing, that same old issue when people think they're better than you because of their origins." I didn't feel like going into details. I didn't want for them to worry more than they were already doing due to this trip.

Africa

Elisha was late. I asked a stranger to use his cell phone.

"Yes, I'm already here. I've been waiting for you for like half an hour now." I tried not to sound too irritated or too bossy.

"I apologize. We are on our way. We'll be there shortly." My friend's Kenyan accent was forcing me to listen carefully; something I had a hard time with in general. In my eyes I still viewed myself as a self-centered person. However my self-importance was really, and I mean really, bugging me at this point of my existence. I didn't know exactly what to do with it. I was tired of swimming from one extreme to another in an attempt of sorting things out internally. It felt like I had to choose either to be arrogant or to be passive and submissive. None of those extreme states felt good. Finding the middle ground and sticking to it appeared virtually impossible. Generally speaking; I continued with hating myself and my life. Irritability, anger and even inner rage inhabited my heart full time. Love was nothing but a four-letter word; nothing else. Compassion? Yeah; I still had some of that, maybe even not that little, but love? Hmmm...Love felt strange to me. Love felt unknown. Love felt... absent or at least dormant. I still felt "not good enough" and I still didn't believe that I deserved to be loved. Not an easy burden to carry around...

I quit my contemplations when I saw a taxi pulling in front of me. Elisha got out and he gave me a hug. He helped me with putting my luggage into the trunk.

"How was your flight?" He asked.

"It was alright. Actually wasn't that bad." I replied. I was very self-conscious in trying not to sound like a "spoiled, white woman".

315

"Elzbieta, this is Fan. She's a very dear friend of mine and she'll be with you the whole time. This way I can be comfortable knowing that you're safe. Nairobi can be a really dangerous place, especially for a single woman who's from a different country." He explained.

"Hi Fan, nice to meet you." I shook her hand. The native Kenyan woman appeared to me as a very strong person who had endured many challenges in life. Her strong body structure as well as her dark, tense looking face made her look older. She was my age. Fan's short coarse hair appeared to be unevenly cut. It was unwillingly, almost forcefully rapping around her sympathetic, but very sad face. Her dark eyes were unveiling melancholic-like emotions. I was under a strange impression of looking at somebody who, like myself, was trying to suffocate her deepest desires and passions. I was also looking at someone very smart, very courageous, someone of giving nature and someone very capable. She seemed to be wearing an aura of energy that felt like determination/focus, fearlessness and willingness to sacrifice. She was gaining my trust/sympathy every minute that passed by even though she wasn't talking very much. She seemed present and absent at the same time. She was definitely unlike most people that I had met.

"So, what do you think of Kenya so far?" Elisha asked.

"From the outside of this taxi window it looks a lot like Hawaii, actually. In many ways it reminds me of Big Island. Seriously, the nature and the temperature are very similar."

The city of Nairobi looked extremely busy. The colorful busses that were always full beyond safe capacity were loaded with all kinds of luggage on their roofs. The driver's assistants/conductors were shouting the names of the destinations they were headed to. People were jumping on board in a hurry as if there was something extraordinary happening at the end of that journey. The conductors, half way hanging from those lively vehicles were pounding loudly on the metal roofs as to announce to the drivers that it was safe to take off. To me it looked as if those buses never really made a full stop. In this bumper to bumper traffic small beat up cars were trying to pass one another at any cost and by all means. Drivers appeared to be continually expressing their discontentment with their gestures while trying to maneuver their worn out vehicles. The hot air was filled with a sensation that a domino effect collision was about to happen at any moment. Parts of this capital city looked very modern with its western looking high-rise buildings, hotels and all that. Other parts made you realize that the citizens of this part of the world were facing some very serious economical challenges. Foot-traffic, although just as crowded as the motorized version; appeared a lot less chaotic and a lot more orchestrated. The numerous pedestrians that were crossing streets back and forth were very respectful of the traffic laws. Nobody seemed to dare to cross the street unless it was permitted and safe enough. This noticeable contrast was giving me an impression that those who were motorized felt superior to those who were traveling on their feet. I was very surprised and pleased to see quite frequently numerous silhouettes of tall young women wearing a fashion updated business suits. In their smooth movements they looked very respectful and very classy.

An hour after being picked up from the airport I found myself in front of a very cheap looking motel. It cost me a thousand Kenyan shillings, which was more or less ten US dollars, to reach my destination. Fan and I were going to stay in a room together until we'd figured out what to do next. The room was rented to us for a thousand shillings a day and the amenities included a very modest breakfast. Besides metal bars in the window, old curtains, a table, and two single size beds. There was nothing else in our new residence. We were lucky though to have our own miniature-size bathroom that had a shower hanging over the toilet seat. I locked the room and the three of us went downstairs. The dining area looked just as "cozy" as the rest of this place. It was basically formed with few tables, few non-matching chairs and an old version of TV that was broadcasting News in English. The walls looked old and dirty. The lack of roof was permitting some of the day-light to this depressing surrounding. The guests were staring at me with an obvious interest of trying to figure out who was I and what was I doing there. I was drinking my tea while listening to my friend when I realized that I was scared. Petrified actually.

"Gosh; these people must think that I have some super natural powers or something!" My realization deliberately kept in secret was giving me uneasy feeling. My Kenyan companions kept expressing their joy and their gratitude for my presence. In their eyes I was the solution to their long desired changes that their country needed. The pressure was too much. I've never hidden from them my financial slash social slash whatever position I was in at the time and I couldn't understand how come they were so willing to put so much faith in me! I started to feel very nervous.

"OK Elisha, we'll see you tomorrow then. I'm gonna take a quick shower and I'm just gonna rest for now. And tomorrow we'll all go to those slums as planned." I shook his hand.

Back in the room, Fan started to notice my nervousness. She turned on the hot water switch for me and then she went outside to buy the kind of fruits that would make me happier. Later we sat on our beds facing each other. The woman was a good listener.

"We're gonna do this, I just don't know how the hell we're gonna do this yet. All we really have is the three hundred dollars and my video camera and we're gonna need to take some videos hoping that we will get some response from some people. Which reminds me; first thing tomorrow morning we'll need to purchase that portable wireless internet access." I kept talking nervously.

"I managed to come all the way here; I am not backing up now." I continued. When my anxiety level dropped I finally allowed Fan to express her ideas. She was telling me how she would like to see more help directed towards the forgotten rural areas spread further away from the cities.

"Do you know what I really would like to do?" I asked without expecting an answer.

"I really would like to just rent a house or something, bring few homeless children in, keep shooting and posting videos of our everyday life and then just take it from there. How much would we need to make this happen?" This time I wanted to know.

"A hundred dollars. Yeah you can get a place for about eight thousand shillings a month." She informed me.

"Are you serious? Then let's just do that!" My level of excitement was now helping to erase previously experienced insecurities on both of our sides.

Kibera

Elisha and I bought a large box of cookies and a big bottle of concentrated fruit juice. The two of us took a bus to Kibera; the largest slum located at the peripheries of Nairobi. My friend informed me that approximately 1.5 million people lived there. Fan didn't come with us. She had few things to take care of in the city. The weather was sunny and the air was hot. White and fluffy clouds that resembled cotton were floating effortlessly throughout the azure sky. As I sat in the crowded bus that was swinging from side to side due to the neglected roads, I couldn't help but to think how surreal this whole thing was. I was in Africa; a place on Earth which I had been fascinated with ever since I could remember. I recalled one of my favorite books that I read as young girl and which action took place on this amazing continent. I still felt the enormous, burning desire of exploring this part of the world. I've never forgot how in geography classes I stared at the map, attempting to memorize the position and shape of each country that was part of this nature-wise rich land. Now, as a thirty three years old woman, I wondered:

"How come this home of such highly spiritual beings had been invaded and taken advantage of by the rest of the world and when would this abuse/neglect finally end?"

"OK, this is our stop. Here is where we get off. This is Kibera." My friend informed me. Elisha and I headed towards an area that looked like a one big collection of crowded roofs made of rusted metal. The orangey-brownish color of it almost matched everything else around. The slops on the narrow dirt roads and the grit-based walls were interlaced in some places with the green banana trees. The colorful laundry carefully stretched on ropes indicated that actual human beings were residing here.

The hilly landscape accentuated this dramatic view that much more. Some pigs were digging in more distant piles of trash. Children were walking around in small groups. The youngest ones would stick their thumbs in their mouths, while stiffening their tiny bodies at the view of a white woman. The whiteness of their eyeballs, pronounced by their serious dark faces, was very piercing. Their dirty, shoeless feet, and pregnant-looking stomachs were making me sad. Gratefulness I was feeling for the existence of these brave Souls was warming my heart. I could feel their pain, their sorrows, their fears/anxieties and their sense of powerlessness. I could still remember those emotions very vividly. Those unwanted feelings never really left me. I've never outrun them.

"Oh boy." I would sigh from time to time while touching the walls in order not to lose my balance.

"OK, we're almost there." Elisha must have had felt the need of giving me encouragement because he'd repeat those words quite often. It was how this man was; very considerate and sensitive to everybody. We were going to a small orphanage that was run by local women that resided in the slum. Elisha was video-taping our visit so I could post this short movie on my website in hopes of raising money that was needed for our mission. At this point the internet was our only hope in achieving our goal. The orphanage was a one small window-less dark room that was similar to the neighboring households. It had a small yard in front that was surrounded by those walls made of that orangey-brownish in color dirt. There was no grass whatsoever, and apart from a few "incarcerated" chickens, the corner was vacant. Inside the room I saw small children in company of few women. Some were sitting directly on the dirt-based floor and others made themselves more comfortable on few wooden sofas that were there. Besides that the room did have one table that was in the center and some white sheets that were hanging on the walls. You could hear the chickens roaring and grumbling from the outside.

"Hello. Hi." I greeted everybody insecurely. The women were expecting me since Elisha arranged this visit in advance. None of them spoke English so my friend had to serve as a translator. As soon as a sat on the ground few children surrounded me. A small, maybe two year old girl crawled into my laps in a hurry. I hugged her with shyness. The women laughed loudly and kids immediately started to giggle. Another girl, who seemed more reserved, decided to sit on my laps as well. She hesitated for a moment but when I extended my hand towards her she jumped into my lap while observing others for their reaction. They all laughed again and she now smiled for the first time since I've arrived. The women helped in dispensing the cookies and juice Elisha and I brought. Children kept waiting patiently for the not so frequent snack they were about to have. They kept giggling at the comments of their caregivers that were trying to inform me about their cultural habits. There was no complaining, no nagging nor any other negativity in their demeanors. After eating and drinking everybody seemed to feel completely at ease. The little girl that was in my lap fell asleep. Others started to teach me some words in Swahili. Occasionally we'd get interrupted by crying of a child that felt that it wasn't given enough of attention. The talking and laughing continued until the end of the visit.

"Thanks for taking me there Elisha. I've never seen anything like this before." I said to my friend on the way back to the motel.

"Yeah, I wanted you to see this. Poverty is our big issue here in Kenya. They need help, they really need help." He said.

"I understand that and I wish there was more that I could do for them. I do need to be very realistic though. At the moment the most we can do is to try to secure the lives of few, perhaps three or four small children. And I want those children to be the ones that have absolutely nothing and no one to take care of them. I want to get to those that are actually living on the street. So; Fan and I will do all that around the area she grew up in. Nairobi is way too expensive anyway for us to continue to stay here." I explained.

"I understand. That sounds like a good plan."

"You see, I don't want just do some charity work here. I don't care for that. I want to transform completely even if a single life. I want to give a house; a home, a new life to a child that has none of the above." I clarified to him my intentions.

African Hospitality

The next day Fan and I said our goodbyes to Elisha as he was helping us with embarking the mini-bus that was headed to Kapsabet. We all agreed that without much money we were better off in a small town/village where Fan's family resided. We needed all help we could get.

"So, you're saying that there are homeless children where you grew up as well?" I wanted to make sure.

"Yes, and there is no such thing as an orphanage in that area." Fan explained.

"So they're living on the street? Where are those kids sleeping?" I continued to investigate unable to comprehend the reality of some few year old sleeping in some piles of garbage outside the town.

"What do they eat every day?" I wanted to know.

"Whatever people may give them. Whatever they find." Fan kept answering my questions.

"How are we going to find them? How will we know that they don't have any family that will look for them if they come to live with us?" My thoughts were rushing one right after another impatient to get an answer.

"Those children usually hang out in the same areas and pretty much everybody knows who they are. You'll see." My new best friend was smiling afraid to say: *Just be patient…*

"And they're not gonna be afraid to live with us?" I couldn't stop with the questioning.

"Of course not, why would they? They'll be very happy, wouldn't you?" She answered.

"And you're gonna do all the cooking and all that, right? Cause I can't do any of that. Not with no money and in these conditions. Not that I know how to cook anyway. I'll do my part in raising the money and you'll be the mommy. Deal?" I looked at her in a serious way and she laughed:

"Of course. We'll do just fine. Don't worry."

The mini-bus traveled for five hours until we finally reached our destination. The journey was excruciating. The limited space was giving me claustrophobia. The pears that I just ate were tormenting my stomach. Knowing that there would be only one quick stop for a bathroom brake was creating a sense of panic in me.

"Ooooh, why do I have to go through all this?" I was talking to myself while hanging my head outside the window. The blowing air was supposed to distract me and therefore help me with calming down my nerves and my pains. A couple of zebras and some monkeys I spotted "reminded" me to remain more grateful and less demanding. I was where I wanted to be, after all. Impatient about achieving the final goal but still; I was on my way…

I was very glad when we finally reached our destination. The bus stopped in front of a noisy and busy flea-market. The bus-stop itself was a small wooden structure containing a small office, a tiny convenience store and a single wooden bench in front. The ground/dirt had that famous orangey look to it. Loud speakers announcing the hottest deals were competing for their share with noisy and rhythmic local music.

"Oh my goodness." I kept exhaling slowly. These words I'd say quite often while pursuing my latest project/adventure. In a way, I loved what my eyes were seeing, and yet, I was glad that what was in front of me, wasn't part of my everyday life. I couldn't help but to feel grateful that my struggles weren't as difficult as the struggles of people I found myself among. I was feeling grateful for the opportunities and advantages that life had provided me with. Boy was I feeling grateful indeed…I had so many more options, I had so many more ways, so many more tools at my hands. So many more choices. Perhaps few of these people, if any, had the chance to see so much of the world the way I did. Still; I was once where they were now. This overwhelming sense of poverty that seemed to be ruling their lives was reminding me of my own upbringing in extreme scarcity. How much did I hate going to bed with an empty stomach. How awful it was not to have warm clothes. I mean; not just some designer clothes but simply essential wardrobe necessary to prevent digits from having to be defrosted in a hot water. How depressing the house was when not heated in the winter time. How anxiety producing were those fearful thoughts of losing and not having a place to call home any longer. What about the teeth, they were never inspected and were often causing so much pain? What about the lack of freedom to do things you'd love to do that comes with the lack of money whatsoever? Or about that embarrassment that you feel when you try to hide how poor you are. Or that awful feeling that God must hate you pretty intensely for punishing you so severely and for not letting you have more than what you deserve...

"Are you feeling any better?" Fan asked me.

"Yeah, little bit." I replied. I kept walking half way bent forward while massaging my stomach with my hand. Fan was caring my bags while holding the video camera that was on. We left my big suitcase at the bus stop office for now. Later on, Fan's family members were going to pick it up for me, so I wouldn't have to drag that gargantuan thing. We were headed to a different market place where one of Fan's sisters had a small store.

"Mzungu! Mzungu! Mzungu!" Kids and adults were trying to get my attention. Apparently it means "white woman" or "white person" in Swahili language. I didn't like the feeling of drawing so much attention. I didn't like to be called "white woman". I kept ignoring everybody around me.

"Mzungu! Mzungu! Madame! You need taxi? Madame!" The locals were being very persistent with trying to render their services to "a loaded with money tourist." I wasn't even answering to them. Seeing how annoyed I was, in her native language, my friend was telling people to leave me alone. It was working.

The farmers market was a very colorful and lively place. The primitive structures designed to hold the produce looked more exotic than poor. I liked the simplicity that was surrounding me. I liked to watch women dressed in their colorful outfits taking care with such a proud manner of products they were selling. Piles of bananas for sale that were hanging above pretty much everywhere were adding to this tropical atmosphere. I was feeling in my heart very strongly the Spirit of the place I was in. It was strong and proud and much, much alive!

"Elzbieta, this is my sister Juliana and that's her husband. We'll be staying at their house until we find a place." Fan introduced her family. The couple was in our age range. They owned a small booth from which they were selling different household materials. They immediately gave me the impression of a very kind, respectful, hard-working and loving people.

324

Juliana's smile seemed as pure and as innocent as a smile of a child. Her perfect white teeth were constantly exposed by the very welcoming expressions on her face. I felt safer just by standing next to her. Juliana's full figure could cost her few points in the "acceptance scale" of our western society but I couldn't help but to feel admiration for the inner and the external beauty I was seeing. This hard working mother of five would help tremendously, later on, with our mission. Being in the late pregnancy stage she never looked tired nor did she ever complain about anything. She always insisted with helping to carry things. She didn't talk much and when she said something her voice sounded as soft and as sweet as she looked. Her eyes were always smiling. Her presence was giving me the encouragement which I needed so much.

Later that evening we took a taxi to Juliana's place. Nobody had warned me that as cute and as cozy the house would look; it had no electricity, no running water nor a bathroom. I panicked at first but I was able to relax eventually. I realized that this home had something more essential; it was filled with love and mutual respect. The half a mile walk towards the house caused by the lack of road on which the automobile could travel was real fun. Nieces, nephews and neighbors were all helping us to carry the luggage. They were all smiling, laughing and exchanging some comments in their native language. The toothless yet extremely energetic and expressive grandmother ran out of her house to welcome me and to give me her blessing. It felt good. It felt real good to feel that sense of belonging. These people made me feel like they were really honored to have me there. Their shyness, modesty and their authenticity was very refreshing at least, for lack of a better term. I started to feel less insignificant and more aware of the depth of the influence I was having on others. My self-value was rising rapidly and unstoppably. My inner transformation that was beginning to take place could not be reversed. I had finally taken full control over my life! I was finally doing what was very difficult to do but what was very right to do. I was being true to myself.

Juliana's house was built out of dirt like most of the neighboring houses. Detached toilette shed, or outhouse, was her husband's newest project. The clay was still fresh and very orangey in color. The big hole inside didn't have any wooden support on it yet. This commodity was something the family was very proud of. They all giggled and laughed at my complex look on my face while approaching it with a roll of toilet paper in my hand.

The house had four, very small rooms in total; each one having its entrance leading directly outside. The windows were super small and the ceiling was low. The room considered as kitchen was the smallest of all. Only two people at once could fit in it and not without having to bend or sit down on the floor. The floor itself, just like the stove, was made out of that beaten up dirt. The small round hole in the stove was designed to support the metal pan in which the meal could be cooked. It was also the only entrance for the wood to go in. As simple and as modest looking; the house and its surroundings were kept in an immaculate order. This was very characteristic of all the neighboring homes. There was no trash, no collected old items, nothing like that. Whatever these people had was utilized in a very creative manner. It gave you that feeling that they appreciated and cherished every single thing they had.

Down the mild hill on which Juliana's house was standing there was a river; a "Laundromat" and a drinking water source for all the locals. Everything looked exotic to me, but harsh, very harsh. It was one thing to look at it but totally different thing to live it.

In the evening which like in Hawaii starts here around 6 p.m. due to earth equator's proximity, we all gathered in one of the small rooms. The darkness dispersed by oil lamps was replaced with a silence only an uncivilized world could allow. No noises coming from TV, radio, computer, kitchen appliances or any other commodity which I had been already craving enormously. The simplicity of everything though had its beauty if only it wasn't interlaced with such enormous sensation of ongoing struggle.

Juliana with the help of Fan and her oldest daughter prepared the dinner. I watched in silence this teenage girl cutting the green leafs into the bowl. Her tall and slim figure as well as her bold head gave her a tomboyish looks. Everything else about her was more than feminine though. The graciousness in her moves and the soft look in her eyes were dominating her already friendly personality. A little bit shy but extremely curious she seemed very pleased with my compliments about her loyal assistance in household chores. She spoke English since she was attending school but she was more interested in finding out about me than talking about herself. I wasn't inclined to broadcast any of my life's adventures so I was just watching her which was giving me a sense of peace.

The meal wasn't as bad as I was afraid it was going to be. The family had sacrificed one of their chickens to honor my presence with a luxurious dinner. The tomatoes Fan and I bought at the market were adding to the juiciness to this modest version of stew. The only thing I couldn't really eat was the mash made of local produce called ugali. That thing was colorless and tasteless and yet somehow it was able to trigger my gag reflex. Sitting on two beds and some other creative supports we all ate the meal in a very relaxing atmosphere.

"Come My School!"

The next day Juliana, her husband, Fan and I headed towards the town in a search of a place for rent. It was late March and the raining season was starting slowly but surely. The hot tropical sun continued to disappear behind the clouds that were getting darker with each passing moment. Occasional drops of warm rain were reminding me of how much I missed taking a real shower. My mind kept processing the thoughts and worries about finding the right place and bringing those few children to their new place. The next step was going to involve raising somehow around ten thousand dollars. With that money I had already decided to purchase a land and a house for Fan and those homeless children she already agreed to take care of. I kept reminding her to keep it a secret what we were doing. I did not want to draw any attention. I did not want to give an impression that some woman came to buy homes for people in exchange of taking care of neglected children. Considering the fact that I was the only white person in the whole area; rendering myself invisible wasn't really an option but I was not going to add to it. The news of a taxi driver delivering a "mzungu" to Juliana's house was already spreading across the market place. I wasn't thrilled about being the latest talk of the town. I tried keeping the low profile as much as possible. When passing by a school I tried ignoring the kids that were calling me.

"Mzungu! Mzungu! Mzungu!" The children all dressed in the same two-colored uniforms were sticking to the poorly supportive fence to have a better look at me. I waved at them as to say: "I see you but I have to keep going."

"Come my school!" I heard a single voice followed by group laughter. Seeing my shy smile more children found the courage in expressing their desire of my visit to their place of learning.

"We are very busy today." I tried to explain.

"Come to our school! Come! Come!" Their persistence was melting my need of remaining unseen.

"Oh what the heck! I'll just go shake their hands through that fence," I said to Fan and she followed me with the camera rolling. The children thrilled with my approach started to push hard against the barrier. As I was shaking their hands the giggling and excitement was rising just like the number of students who wanted to see closely what was happening. Some more athletic boys were climbing the trees to have a better view. The joyful reaction at my touch and the fights for it was simply overwhelming. The fence started to collapse under the weight which wasn't designed to carry.

"Oh my goodness!" I was trying to hold it but the force against me was greater than I could withhold.

"Go back! Go back! The fence is coming down!" I yelled few times.

"Go back! Go back!" Few children started to repeat my words while pushing others away.

"OK, OK, I go." I heard compliance in their voices. I decided to keep moving in order not to create too much of a commotion. As I was walking the children kept running parallel to me from behind the fence. The noise of excitement resembled the noise created by sport fans on a stadium.

"Come to school!" The students weren't giving up.

"OK, OK, I'll come to your school." I said unaware of squeaky wave my response would create.

"Oh boy…" I covered both of my cheeks with my hands. I reached the gate and I was immediately surrounded by children to which shaking my hands appeared to be the most entertaining thing in the world. I could not help but to smile in amusement. The children's energy was overpowering my fear of being a burden to the teachers who were in the classrooms performing their jobs. I did not intend to enter the school property. However, grabbed by some of the more courageous young girls I followed their lead.

"Oh my…" I heard Fan laughing while watching me disappear in the cloud of dark red and blue uniforms. We approached the school building in a bustle that sounded as if the Messiah was there. A female teacher with a menacing look came outside.

"Quiet! Quiet!" she commanded. Some words in Swahili were exchanged to explain the circumstances. The woman told me to sign in the guest book with the principle while she continued to settle everybody down. The principle came outside his office as well. He addressed some introductory words to the gathered students. At least a hundred children if not more stood in silence listening to him while staring at me. I was so not comfortable but I did give a short speech as asked.

"So, let's see if you boys and girls were paying attention," said the principle.

"Where is Ezzybata from?" He asked.

"From Poland!" The kids replied unanimously.

"How many days she's been in Kenya?" He continued with the quiz.

"Six!" They replied. The excitement in children's eyes continued to sparkle until they reached that gate again while escorting me back. Fan was laughing and smiling the whole time.

"Oh boy. Was this an experience or what?" I said to her and we all went back to marching.

The Children

After walking for hours I was simply exhausted. That's when we decided that I would rest in Juliana's store while everybody else would keep on searching for the place to rent.

"OK, just find whatever you can. We really need to move in like tomorrow the latest." I said to Fan. In the evening we all went to see a house that Fan thought was the best fit. The place wasn't far away from town and it was fenced all around. The landlord was living next door and his wife offered the usage of their well since there was no water on the property that was for rent. The house did have electricity though and that was definitely a bonus! Tired of spending the night in the darkness I couldn't wait to move our stuff to our new place. I sat on the ground while purposely ignoring the eager to make money face of the landlord. He agreed to rent us the house for eight thousand shillings (around one hundred dollars) a month without the security deposit. He handed us the keys and promised to come back later to replace the missing light bulbs. We had the place. Now we just needed to go buy some mattresses, few blankets, some plastic dishes, towels, cooking pans, some groceries, and we were ready to bring the children in! I looked around. With excitement Fan was finishing mopping the floor made of cement pavement. Juliana was sitting and resting for the first time since I met her. Our new metal-clad environment was feeling quite safe. The tall wooden gate and the metal-based fence were giving a sense of privacy. The side of the house across from the court-yard was covered with metal sheets that were painted dark green. This house that was once a commercial store had four rooms that had doors leading directly outside. In the middle of the yard there was a small metal shed that had two rooms which were occupied by two local athletes. The boys were supposed to leave the premises within thirty days but that never happened. One of them in particular sort of became part of our mission. He helped around a lot and there was always an extra plate of that scarce food we'd have to eat waiting for him. The yard itself was covered halfway with tall, unattended grass and half with pavement that was broken into pieces in several areas. In the right corner there was a large water tank that unfortunately was empty and out of service. In the left corner there was a small shed divided into two single door-size rooms. One of those rooms was our toilette.

"Oh, this is gonna be fun..." I was thinking skeptically while in order to do my business, I was trying to bend without touching anything.

The following day our small group headed towards town again. Buying the mattresses and few other things was exhausting; the main reason was the restricted amount of money we had at our disposal. The vendors were expressing lost looks in their faces each time I practically yelled in discontentment:

"That's waaayyy too much! This is crazy. I can get a mattress like this for this much in the US. Let's go to another place." Everybody looked tired but the thought of being taken advantage of wouldn't allow me to just give in.

"No, no, no, no, no, no." I was shaking my head while talking to the merchant.

"There is no way I'll give you that much for these mattresses. You want a thousand shillings for each? No way! Look; I'll give you five hundred for each and I'll take six of 'em. OK, start putting those aside." I pointed the ones I liked the most.

"No, Madame! That's crazy. Madame; give me four thousand for these four and I'll throw one for free! Alright?"

"Alright. That's fine." I said with relief. As much as I trusted Fan and her family, in every occasion I had, I kept making a point of the need of managing the money wisely. I could tell that my strict attitude was causing some tension and was taking the fun away. Nevertheless I was the most directly responsible for the success of our project and I wasn't going to risk it with carelessness.

In the afternoon Fan and I went back to town again to buy some groceries. Juliana with the help of few local women that were informed about our intentions went to search for the kids. Those children were pretty much known to everyone as they would hang out around the market place in hopes of "catching" something to eat. On the way back it was raining pretty hard when the two of us had finally reached the gate. We opened it and we saw that we had some guests. The door to the boy's shed was open. Juliana among few local women was smiling at us.

"They found them." Fan translated to me.

"What do you mean? They found the kids? Where are they?" I asked. I leaned towards the door and I saw four small children. The two girls and the two boys looked scared and insecure. They stared at me with their mouths open. The clothes they were wearing were better suited for rags. All four of them were barefooted. Their small bodies were as dirty and as neglected as their wardrobe. Their coarse hair was way pass due for hair cut, something which was very much so extinguishing them from the rest of the population. Their dark skin was very dried and overall they looked exhausted and dehydrated. The women tried to express their gratitude while I was unlocking the door of the room predestinated as our kitchen. I was still pretty much in shock.

"Oh my goodness." My famous phrase was the only thing I could really say. I was in disbelief how happy I was feeling. I had in my hands the lives of four precious and innocent children. I had the power to shape their destiny. I had the power to take their struggle away. I had what was needed to make a difference. In that moment I felt enormous gratitude towards Elisha and Fan particularly.

The women dispensed the candies we bought. Fan made some modest sandwiches and everybody ate in a hurry. Without wasting time we started to prepare the children for their baths. Fan kept boiling the water in a single pan. There was no stove so she had to do it on a borrowed from our neighbor coal operated kettle. The eagerness in which the children formed the line to take the bath in the small plastic mixing bowl surprised me. The women were laughing out loud at my amusement. Children's street-learned confidence was now erasing the fear from their faces. They looked fully engaged and a little bit still in disbelief. Watching them you could see what full appreciation meant. I had never seen children whose desire to be scrubbed was so vividly written on their faces! Their heart touching way of checking if all the dirty spots were gone was amazing to me. The athlete-boy from the shed kept videotaping all this so I could post it online. It was quite a commotion taking place in our barrack. Later in the evening when everybody else left things calmed down a little bit but the excitement stayed present. The children dressed in my old clothes were jumping and bouncing of their new mattresses that were still wrapped around with the plastic packaging. They were trying to stand on their heads while kicking their feet in the air.

"What are they saying?" I kept asking Fan to translate.

"Denis is saying that this is his mattress and they are not allowed to come near his area." She informed me and we laughed. Denis and Joan were siblings and they looked the part. Denis was a strong and loud boy and you could immediately tell that he served as pack leader until now. He was what we estimated about nine years old but because of lack of nutrients all these children's heights didn't exceed the height of a five year old. While picking my clothes Denis made sure that he got the jacket that had "Fire Department" written on the back. He practically ripped it out if my hand when I pointed it at him. His sister Joan was more reserved. She had incredibly piercing look in her eyes. Even though I was going to treat all children equally I could sense that this girl was going to have a special place in my heart. It wasn't because of her left hand being deprived of few fingers. It was how smart she appeared to be and how serious she was about the role she assumed of protecting her "street" family. She was about eight years old. The other two kids were also a couple of siblings. Elizabeth was Joan's age and Laban might have been six years old. The boy smiled a lot and he liked acting silly. At the time I still didn't know that blood-sucking parasites were responsible for the round shape of his pronounced stomach. Elizabeth looked like she was afraid to fully trust anyone and she acted as if her job description was to be on a constant look out for the bad things. She was constantly alert. I could not describe the emotions I felt while observing those children finally falling asleep from exhaustion. Joan's eye-lids were only half way closed even though she was sound asleep! It was as if she wasn't convinced quite yet that they were all completely safe. Or perhaps her mind was resisting the idea of going to sleep, too afraid of discovering that all this was nothing but a dream.

"Oh my God. That's how they've learned how to sleep on the street, isn't it?" I whispered to Fan

"Must be. Can you imagine?" She was as touched as I was.

Furniture-wise our bedroom was empty except for the mattresses that we placed directly on the pavement. The mattresses itself were single size and they were very thin. The thicker mattresses cost twice as much and that was something I didn't feel like we could afford. Each of us had one new blanket that wasn't generating enough heat in this raining season that began to cool the air at night. We had the lights though. What a treat that was!

"What do you think their life looked like until now?" I asked my friend. We were lying down while enjoying the view of the children sound asleep. Despite the chilly rain pounding against the roof loudly there was warmth and coziness inside the bedroom. Fan had left the kettle that still had reddish coals in it. Sensitive to cold I was still wearing my jacket in bed.

"They had a rough life. That's for sure." She stated.

"I mean I had no home and I had to face some harsh reality of being on my own but I was like fifteen then, not nine or six years old. How on earth were these kids able to take care of themselves?" I tried to imagine being in their position.

"Not just that. I wouldn't be surprised if Joan and Elizabeth had to protect themselves from the advances some older homeless boys were probably making on them. It's unfortunate but these kind of things happen." She said.

"Gee. I don't even wanna think about it." I looked around the room. The kids were sleeping on their stomachs completely immersed under the blankets. Through them I was feeling the deepest appreciation a human being can experience. By imagining being one of them I could sense the relief that comes from knowing that you are safe. The knowing that you are loved and that you are not forgotten, that your life matters, that YOU matter.

"They're really happy Elzbieta. They're really happy." Fan smiled. She looked just as content and just as peaceful. This woman's dedication and her big heart were very inspiring. She had mastered her own ways of handling everyday tasks with very little resources. She was very strong minded yet she knew how to remain flexible and diplomatic. She was a born leader. She had a clear vision of how she wanted to make changes and boy was she faithful that that vision. She wasn't showing any discouragement caused by her position as she was convinced that I was the answer to her prayers. She was prepared to do anything it took, including soothing my sometimes neurotic character and she wasn't afraid of taking the load of pressure onto her shoulders. Her strong belief that anything could be accomplished if desired bad enough and her expectations for success were responsible for her driven attitude. In her mind there were no limiting boundaries or challenges big enough that couldn't be overcome. In many ways the two of us had a similar way of thinking. We both were extremely motivated with our new project and we both kept motivating each other. It was nice for a change to work with someone who had similar goals/intentions and similar attitude. Honest care from the heart, readiness to go extra mile, willingness to sacrifice, willingness to do whatever it takes as well as "never give up" attitude were the pillars of the foundation we were forming.

The Forgotten One

The following day started almost as regular as any day would start in a regular home. Children woke up excited. Their faces had that cute expression that said: "What is today going to be all about?" They kept jumping on their mattresses while Fan was preparing breakfast.

"What are they arguing about?" I inquired.

"Oh, the girls are getting mad at boys for messing up their new clothes." Fan laughed. I watched Joan and Elizabeth folding the few skirts and shirts that I once wore.

"You better be niiiiiiicccce!" I shook my index finger towards the boys. The kids giggled and then went back to their new routine of jumping, giggling and arguing. I went back to editing our new videos. The portable internet we purchased wasn't fast enough to upload the movies to youtube so I decided to put them all on disc and mailed it to Marek. He agreed that he would handle that for me from Holland. While working with my laptop I'd paused from time to time in order to feed children's curiosity. They'd form a circle around me to see the images of themselves in movies we shot.

They continued to laugh while commenting out loud. From the pointing of fingers followed by giggles and soft punching I could tell they were making fun amongst themselves. Based on the direction of those index fingers and the looks I could tell that I was not safe from the comments either. I kept smiling while enjoying their reactions. Later on Elizabeth started to pull softly on my long hair. Seeing no objection coming from me Joan joined her immediately in their new play. Denis and Laban giggled shyly from the safe distance as though not sure if their sisters weren't crossing some boundary line. The soft touch of girls' small fingers was having a soothing effect on me. Even though I didn't speak Swahili I could tell that they were talking about my hair. They had a dreamy look in their eyes while feeling the soft texture of it. They argued about the length of it while pressing the ends towards my back. Elizabeth playfully placed the pony tail she made over her own head. Everybody laughed at her new look. The kids kept investigating my head with Columbus-like curiosity. They were pressing hard on my skull to see better the dark roots of my bleached hair. I wished I could understand the explanations for my multi-colored look that they were giving to each other. The girls were doing the talking and the boys sat there with open mouths while playing with their toes. Filled with affection; Joan's and Elizabeth's caresses felt like sincere expressions of deepest gratitude. I could also tell that I was being an im-portant role-model in their eyes. While still remaining very respectful the children were feeling comfortable around me. I was enjoying their pres-ence and the ongoing discoveries of their personalities. They were making me smile, rarely without laughing.

In the afternoon Fan and I headed towards town again. Between Juliana, her oldest daughter and our athlete-boy we didn't have to worry about children being left alone. On the way back home we noticed that there was a commotion going on. Our new kids were rushing to show us their new shoes that were sponsored by Juliana and few other locals. The kids were stepping in funny ways as to present their dexterity in them.

"Oh my goodness. This is wonderful. Thanks Juliana, that's very sweet of you guys." I felt so glad that these people were not expecting for me to solve all the problems. As we entered the kitchen we saw among few other woman a small, maybe five year old girl. She stood there with that same insecure and lost look on her face the way the pair of siblings did the day before. She looked like she was about to cry. Fan immediately started to translate:

"This is Winnie. She was at the market all alone and crying. She was part of the group. All five of them used to hang together. She sepa-rated from them for a moment yesterday and then she couldn't find them anymore since we brought them here." I was listening carefully. I felt bad for Winnie but at the same time I wanted to make sure that we weren't being scammed. Fan warned me that if people were under the impression that we were some major charity; led by desperation many women would literally drop their offspring at our door. She explained to me that Juliana confirmed Winnie's belonging to the "pack".

"OK well; now we have five of them." I said causing obvious sense of relief in everybody. I was being very strict as for the number of children in our household and everybody knew the reason for it. It wasn't because of the money only and the costs related to raising high number of children. I simply didn't believe in creating an orphanage. This wasn't my goal. The idea was more of helping to shape a close family, even if only circumstances-related, by providing the essentials for living, not just surviving. The competitiveness, obeying the rules, cold institution feel was not something I was looking for.

Winnie fully relaxed once she joined the rest of the kids. They engaged in explaining to her what she missed and what was happening in general. She had envious and sad look on her face until she understood that she was being included. Her eyes started to sparkle and she begun to boss around the kids. It was hilarious to see how she was getting away with it. She looked like a boy even in the dress she was wearing. She had an aura of a trouble-maker. Being the youngest and the smallest would explain how that forced her to learn to be pushy and demanding. Winnie was funny as hell, the way that she was prancing around with those puffy expressions designed to control every one. The rolling of her eyes from disapproval or her expressive face and the arms crossed on her tiny chest were a frequent view. She had to be the first one to do everything. She was eager and fearless. She was definitely adding liveliness with that tiny posture and huge personality of hers.

The Officials

Longing for sense of space while working on videos I moved my stuff to one of the rooms that was at the end of the house. This room became my office, my bedroom and my bathroom. Fan was taking care of the house while I was looking for ways to raise some money online. The videos were still in route via snail mail to Marek and obviously were not uploaded yet. The speed that things were going was getting on my nerves. I knew that unless some people saw what we were doing there was no point in asking for anything.

Not knowing what else to do I updated my status on facebook:

"Thanks to your generosity and believing in me I have made it safely to Kenya! Thank you guys. You know who you are. Look out for videos that are coming soon." I got few replies from same friends that were strongly disapproving of my trip before. Their attitude was different this time. Particularly one guy seemed excited about my rewarded perseverance. I knew this guy for some time now. We dated briefly while I was in Northern California until he dumped me for his ex through an online message. Six months later he emailed me how sorry he was, saying what a huge mistake he had made. I slept with him for the first time then and…he dumped me again using the same method of communication. He had been emailing me from time to time while I was living in Hawaii asking me if I'd meet with him if he took few days off to fly to Oahu.

I wasn't interested. Now he was messaging me on facebook again, describing how amazed he was by me and all that. I was replying with straightforwardness:

"Words are cheap. We need food. Can you send us some money?" He did finally send the first hundred dollars. He got tired of me leaving comments such as:

"Nice picture. Who cooked the dinner? Are there any leftovers for us?" We sure were glad to receive the donation since there was practically no money left. I could have had at the most five dollars worth of money and despite of what might be a common belief that is not much even in Africa these days. Due to democracy and capitalism times when there was a huge difference in living expenses were over. It was nothing like I thought that with twenty bucks you could feed, dress and even provide a medical care to a child for a whole month! Kenya being one of the most developed African countries was a quite expensive place to be. In fact many things were more expensive even compared to the US. Anything considered a luxury was at its peak price hence for example my internet access cost me fifty bucks a month. The five hour trip to capital in that crowded mini-bus was ten bucks each way. Food-wise prices were not even close to as low as I would hope and therefore we were all eating very little. Our meals were nowhere near what could be considered basic food. Fan was doing the best she could with what she had but the meals still turned out lousy. For breakfast we all normally had a cup of tea. On better days the tea was sweetened and milk-flavored which was making this hot drink a lot more tolerable. Lunch; often identical to dinner was made of some boiled green leafs, cabbage, and ugali. The last one served as a substitution to rice which was a lot more expensive. It sort of looked like a mixture of cooked but dried rice and mashed potatoes but unfortunately tasted nothing like it. I could not eat that thing no matter how hungry I was. Since I was losing so much weight and started to look anorexic, Fan started to buy the more expensive potatoes just for me. I felt bad at first but she rationalized with me:

"We are all used to ugali. You are not. You need to eat something before you start fainting." Once Fan discovered that cooked bananas reminded me of potatoes she replaced our diet with it. Avocados were relatively cheap but I was getting sick and tired of eating them every day. Tomatoes were a treat. To ease the discomfort Fan and I would often sit and laugh about our life style.

"You know what? Lots of people are obsessed with losing weight these days. Dieting is a big industry. You know what we should do? We should start a business where we invite people here and make them live with us for like a month. They'd sure go home in a better shape and more appreciative of things in general." The two of us were talking and laughing a lot together. With each day I was becoming fonder of her. As my self-protecting guards were lowering and as my trust started to grow I asked her to be completely in charge of the household.

She liked that I wasn't as bossy and as controlling anymore. The more I stepped down the more she amazed me with the creative ways of dealing with things. Besides she was really good with the children. She had raised her own son that was now eighteen years old, all by herself. Her tall and very respectful boy visited us few times just like her other sisters and her mother did. They'd stayed with us for few days. Her family always brought us some bananas and whatever they were growing in their neighboring villages. The children loved the company we always seemed to have.

I placed my laptop on the mattress and I went outside sensing that there was something going on. I saw Fan sitting on the pavement and two men standing in front of her with their arms crossed and their legs spread. One of them was our landlord. I didn't like what I was seeing. The men's postures transmitted the energy of superiority and Fan's face looked insecure. Whatever all this was about, I decided to approach them with an attitude that meant:

"Who the hell do you think you are to come here uninvited? You are on my property now. How dare you cause this disturbance?"

"What is going on?" I asked while supporting both of my hands on my hips. I spread my legs to show that they were not the only ones who knew how to stand in an overly confident way. The unknown man was wearing business-like attire. He was holding some documents in his hands.

"Good afternoon. Are you running this place?" He asked.

"I'm renting this place if that's what's you're asking. Is there a problem?"

"Well, we got a word that somebody had opened an orphanage for children here. We were ordered to examine it to make sure that everything is up to code. See Madame; I'm afraid this broken pavement for example is not safe for children, things like that." He explained.

"Also, you will need a special permit to continue your charity which can be issued to you once the proper papers are filled and the fees are paid. I can assist you with all that." He continued.

"Weh weh wait a minute." I interpreted him once I heard the word fees.

"With all the respect; I came here to help the children. Not to feed the government's budget. We are struggling as it is. I don't have the money to spare. Maybe in the future we'll do that. Right now the papers of the nonprofit I have from the US will have to be sufficient." I said.

"You mean you already have papers of an NGO?" He asked looking surprised.

"What's NGO?" I asked in reply.

"A nongovernmental organization. In other words; a registered charity." He explained.

"Yeah; we call that a non-profit. It's a tax exempt organization that has charitable purpose. Give me one second; I'll just show you the papers I have." I went inside to retrieve my files. The official looked less sure of himself and more friendly once he examined all the documents of my nonprofit registered in the state of California.

"This should work for now. I don't see why not. I'll let the office know that everything is as it should be." He stated. He exchanged some words in Swahili with our landlord and they left. The next morning after barely waking up I headed straight to the kitchen to satisfy my thirst with a cup of tea. I didn't even have the usual cigarette yet so the mood I was in couldn't be good. In my colorful Christmas pajamas, with my hair blowing in all different directions, I opened the door and I saw another male "guest". He was sitting on the chair by the table. Fan was busy making the tea and the children were sitting in the corner in silence.

"Hi." I mumbled. I looked at the man and immediately I could tell that he wasn't the part of the family/friends or neighbors.

"Elzbieta, this is a police officer. He was sent by that same office that the other guy came from." Fan started to inform me and I started to boil inside.

"Are you kidding me? Now when is this gonna stop?" I was ready to explode.

"No, no, Elzbieta! He's very nice. He's very supportive of our project. We've been drinking tea and talking." Fan rushed in seeing how upset I was getting. The police officer that wasn't wearing a uniform turned out to be nice. He expressed how much respect he had for what we were doing and he wished us good luck. After he left I said to Fan:

"OK, we've got to stop those visits from becoming a habit. This is just too stressful. I'm sick and tired of people that sit on their asses doing nothing to help and the moment someone else dares to do something they immediately try to get involved and to try to control things. I hate the idea of paying the government fees for something that the government should be grateful for."

"I know. I don't like how the government handles things either, especially here in Kenya. They're all corrupted up there. Money, money; everybody's just hungry for money Elzbieta. I'll talk to our landlord's wife later. She told me that her husband used to hold some important position in the local politics back in the days. Apparently he knows everybody in this town." Fan shared her concerns with our landlord's wife. She told her about me feeling uncomfortable with the living arrangements due to the lack of privacy, and the official visits/inspections stopped once and for all.

Beliefs

Marek finally had received the CD and he posted the videos on youtube for me. In the email he expressed how impressed and inspired he was. He also informed me that he was going to try to raise some money for us and that he was going to send us a package of clothes that he collected with a help of his wife and a friend. The time was passing but the videos were getting few views and even fewer responses. Between receiving occasional small donation now and then paying for the rent, the internet, the coal, the food; we were pretty much starving again.

The children never complained. Together with Juliana's oldest daughter they carried buckets of water from the landlord/neighbor. They loved engaging in household activities from washing the dishes to sweeping the floor. They never had to be asked to do anything; they pretty much initiated everything on their own. Respect for things and deep appreciation was constantly present in their attitudes. It was very joyful to watch them taking their baths outside. They were taking them all together every day. With those naked dark bodies they looked so adorable while washing their clothes and shoes in that after-bath water. They knew how to preserve things almost instinctively. They helped each other to dispense the Vaseline on their heads and lips to prevent from drying out too much. Unlike me they seemed practically untouched by the fact that we were forced to eat very little. At meal times they always remained very serious and silent. They followed with their eyes every move Fan made while preparing the food. When it was finally ready, Denis, who was sitting in the nearest proximity to the kettle, would take the plate from Fan's hands and he'd pass it to Winnie who was the farthest away. He'd keep passing the plates until it would reach his turn. After the brief prayer said with eyes closed, everybody would engage in eating their food. Nobody seemed to have any energy or time to engage in conversations. Nobody was interested in chatting. The mouths were busy with performing mastication and the hands were busy with scooping any possible leftovers the plates could carry. The silent thankfulness for whatever was on those plates could be felt in the air. The collective focus was on food and food only. The only sound heard was the humming noise of the rain that became every single evening's event by now. Every day I could see the appreciation in Fan's eyes for my being there. For eating the inedible, for sleeping practically on the ground, for bathing in a small plastic bowl, for craving like crazy the TV, for missing my old life style, and for not complaining too much or too often about it. To suppress the unwanted desires Fan and I would often engage in motivational talks:

"We will get that damn house for you and the kids somehow. You're gonna have your own piece of land and a home soon enough. I promise I will not stop my efforts until this is achieved. The worst case scenario if nobody out there helps us with those fundraisers; I will go back to Europe or US and I'll get a job. It may take a while to save ten thousand dollars but I will do whatever it takes." I didn't like the idea of leaving but I had to consider such possibility. Dean was chatting with me online again and he was ready to buy me a return ticket at any time. He also kept refusing to support my mission saying that I was doing it all wrong:

"You're not in a position to help anyone Elzbieta. You're not even able to help yourself. You look horrible. I've never seen you so skinny. You look sick with those dark circles underneath your eyes. I'm telling you; you need to go back home. Go and take care of yourself first and then you can go back and help them." I hated the fact that he sounded right and I appeared to be wrong.

"Yeah, whatever. Thirty two years on this planet didn't teach me how to do that so what makes you think I'll suddenly know how to do it now? I'm not gonna waste anymore of my time on trying to figure out how to end my struggle. I'm gonna do what I set my mind on doing. I'm gonna end someone else's struggle first!" Dean knew how stubborn I was and how upset I'd get when anybody tried to persuade me from following my instinct.

"Damn it! If you're not gonna help us then stop trying to make me doubt myself. I hate when people do that. I've got to go now. I'll talk to you later.." I would disconnect the skype-call with sadness wondering why as human beings we had to be so self-preserving. Why couldn't we be so more unified and so more considerate of each other? Why did we have to be so "me, me, me and me" all the time? What made us so freaking selfish and indifferent? What made us so insensitive? How could we change? How could we evolve into something better? Something a lot more dignifying and less empty and superficial. To me it was clear by now that it was our core beliefs that were behind all that misery that seemed to be spread all over the world. The belief of being disconnected/separated from each other was responsible for all the suffering in the world and in everybody's lives. If sufficient number of people had the guts to change that perspective we could live in a different world. Remaining faithful to the idea that we are all one inseparable entity, is the key to permanent and desired change. This is the first and the most important step and without it all the efforts remain fruitless. At this point of my life I was determined to live my life according to my new sets of beliefs:

"I am one with everyone and everything. I am connected and loved. I am powerful. I am a child of God and I DESREVE to be happy."

I wasn't going to waste any more time and energy on trying so hard to manipulate things outside of me. Externally what had to be done; had to be done but continuing on doing it without making sure that the beliefs/thoughts matched the desired outcome was simply insane. It was hard to work on my thoughts all the time. It wasn't easy to constantly observe them and replace them each time they were not aligned with the outcome I was looking for. It was difficult to remain patient and faithful to this process of transformation. I knew the change wasn't going to happen overnight. I also knew that I've had it with the way I was living my life until now and that I'd do anything, no matter how hard it would be, to change that once and for all. I was too determined not to waste time and so I would not allow myself to think in my old, unexamined ways anymore. On days when it was particularly hard to remain optimistic I'd say to myself:

"Keep doing what you're doing. Do not give up. You know the Universe will give you back what you are sewing right now. Soon. Soon enough."

Prayers

Unable to purchase any more food Fan and I decided to ask local women that supported our project for assistance. Juliana spread the word among them that we were struggling. They not only agreed to bring whatever little food they had but they all came to our place dressed up in "Sunday dresses" to show their respect.

"Oh my goodness!" I looked at the gate and I saw a line of women carrying bags on their heads. Some of them I've met before at the market place.

"Oh my goodness! Hi! It's so good to see you." We kissed on cheeks and shook each other's hands with affection.

"Hi Elzbieta!" The women were really excited to be part of our project. Earlier, Juliana and few of them stopped by to bring some clothes for the children so they were all dressed up as well.

"Ooooh! They look so good! Look at them!" The women seemed really glad to see the changes.

"Ooooh wow! I can't even recognize them. They look so healthy! Look." They were touching the kids' shaved and moistened heads.

"Their skin feels soft. Look." Some women were speaking in English some in Swahili. The atmosphere was feeling positive, loving and fun. I kept running around like a chicken with its head cut off. My voice was high from excitement and I couldn't stop from sighing:

"Oooh gosh… Aaah…" I was touching the shapes of bottled sodas that Juliana's husband brought a whole case earlier. The athlete-boy was busy videotaping the event. The women one by one handed me the produce they had brought. They seemed so happy that they were able to contribute. Their pride felt different from the pride that those volunteers at the Honolulu shelter exhibited. There were no feelings of superiority, pity or any of that in those African women's attitudes. There was humbleness around. There was pure and cheerful shared joy in the air.

"Oh this smells ssso good! " I rubbed my face in chives enjoying its aroma and they all laughed.

"Thank you sooo much! Thank you." I placed each produce in the bowl that Fan was holding.

"And this is? Aah, cooking fat. This is a cooking fat, not butter. I thought it was butter but it's not." I pointed the yellow cube towards the camera and then I gave it to Fan.

"Tomatoes! Oh my goodness I loooove tomatoes! And this is? Oooh this is ugali. But thank you, thank you for bringing this too. Potatoes! Yeaaah! We have potatoes! I've missed them ssss-ooo much." I hugged the bag like I would hug a small baby. Kids giggled and women laughed. After settling everything in the kitchen we took all the mattresses outside and we all sat in a circle. The sun felt warm and the traces of depression I was feeling earlier were gone. The prayers of women made me feel like it was Sunday afternoon. They were asking God to support our mission and to give encouragement to all those involved in it.

Everything that was said in those prayers was pretty much an expressed gratitude. It felt good, especially when the women started to sing. We were all clapping our hands and moving in the rhythm of the songs. My fears and insecurities were evaporating. I was surrounded by people that may have had very little materialistically speaking but whose hearts and spirit were greater than anything in the world. I sure felt glad I was there among them. I admired their voices and their commitment to the songs. They were singing from the depths of their hearts and the powerful uplifting energy could be felt in the air. From time to time Fan translated to me the lyrics which were often created on the spur of the moment. I heard my name and the names of people who had donated so far in the songs that were all directed to our Heavenly Father. The singing and dancing seemed to be instinctively orchestrated. In uninterrupted rhythm and with impressing gracefulness the women were taking their turns in performing in the middle of the circle. They were hugging the remaining participants. They were extending their arms in a gesture of allowing the blessings to flow onto us. This lasted several hours and no one seemed to be hungry, thirsty or tired. Almost as if with our spirits being nurtured our bodies felt completely satisfied.

The Package and the Soccer Game

"It has arrived Elzbieta! It's here. The package's here." Fan exclaimed while entering my room. Juliana and a group of people that assisted her with bringing the medium sized box marked with all kinds of post marks entered the room. The kids were trying to make their way through the suddenly crowded doorway. The athlete was holding the camera ready to roll. He had it with him in his room most of the time since he became our camera-man. The young boy was really eager to help and to participate in whatever we were doing. He was respectful and much liked by the kids. They played with him frequently but they also listened to his instructions. They looked up to him.

"Yeaaaay! Finally!" I was just as excited as everybody else was. Marek had emailed me that the package was on its way and it took only one week from the day he said he had sent it 'till we got it. Together with his wife and a friend that had a small store they collected some really nice clothes for the kids. I was so glad that they included several jackets as well since evenings in Kenya remained chilly due to intensely pouring rain. Marek also bought a brand new soccer ball and a popcorn maker for us. Retrieving the items from the box was fun. Everybody was engaged with the process but not without the discipline. The kids were standing patiently while the clothes were being divided among them. Some older boys that were our guests were busy with pumping the new white and blue soccer ball. The air was filled with anticipation. After the division all five of the children went to their bedroom to put on their new clothes. Their small mouths seemed unable to remain closed this time. It seemed as if they were shooting words with the same speed an M16 shoots the bullets. It was so pleasant to see them dressed in those colorful and well fitting out-

348

fits. There was no more need in folding the excessive material and tying it around their hips with some ropes. The children looked real good in their new shorts and t-shirts designed with different logos.

"Ah. That's what I'm talking about. Is everybody ready to go to play soccer?" I asked while bouncing the ball in my hands. The colorful cluster headed towards the gate with excitement.

"Where is the ball?" I yelled distracted.

"The ball? Denis has the ball." The athlete regained control of the group. I watched the children rushing towards the big soccer field that was not very distant from our place. Their bright silhouettes stand out against the orangey, almost reddish in color dirt road we were marching on.

"Where're you going?" An elder local man paused to shake my hand expecting to engage in a chat.

"To play soccer." With a smile on my face, I continued to follow my rambunctious flock. At the field, which spread on at least two acres, there were many other local children that were chasing their beaten up form of a ball. They all stopped what they were doing driven by the curiosity at the sight of us and our shiny toy. They gathered around us quickly expressing their desire to participate with us. We separated into two teams and the game began. The running, the cheering, the scoring of goals; all this was causing shortness of my breath. I wished I were in better shape, still the kids looked thrilled with my efforts of being part of the game. After a while I withdrew from the game and I sat on the grass to observe the activity. The green grass and the rolling across children that seemed to be the happiest children in the world, were creating mosaic of what life should look and feel like. It was so touching to see some of the kids helping each other to adjust their clothes. There was immense sense of care in their gestures.

Every Day Issues

I loved these children. They were so easy to manage, so eager to please, so hungry for affection, yet without being too needy. I had yet to witness vulgarity, brat-like behaviors or any serious misconduct for that matter. These children had self-discipline which I imagined they acquired on the street. Their gratefulness expressed so vividly in their expressions on daily basis made me want to provide the whole world to them.

I loved watching them being just children. Every morning I would sit on the ground and while smoking my cigarette I'd observe the interactions between them. It was amazing to see how in such a short time these kids learned to be care-free. They seemed always fully present in the moment, always together, always engaged in doing something. They did not need to be entertained and they never looked like they were bored. I'd usually wake up when they were already up and running. Their singing was often my alarm clock. They liked to sing a lot especially when Fan and I were watching them. They liked even more when we were teasing them. I don't doubt that they felt loved and that they knew that their difficult past was just where it should be; in the past.

Since we built a play house together, it became a focal point of their social gathering. The wall of our house and the L-shaped fence already created the majority of the structure. We added roof by hanging two large sheets that we bought used at the market. Some pieces of wood found in the small shed and the large stones served perfectly as furniture. Some old plastic and glass bottles were neatly set on the fence-originated shelves. Filling them up with water and dirt was one of kids' favorite things to do. They looked like tiny adults while bustling around their tiny house. When Fan started to use their place to make a campfire since coal wasn't always purchased due to our money deficit; the small house looked and felt even more real to all of us. The cloudy smoke escaping openings as well as the orange flames on top of the burning pieces of wood were adding warmth and coziness to our environment.

I liked the livelihood of our place. I liked how we always seemed to have guests but not the intrusive kind. I liked how everybody felt comfortable and I liked the sense of unity that could be felt. I felt very protective of everybody and everything. I felt responsible for everyone. Safety was always on my mind:

"Fan, please tell those two boys that I don't want the other guys visiting them in their sheds anymore. We need to keep track of everything that's going on here and I don't want to constantly watch if the gate is closed."

"I agree with you. It's nice of you that you let them stay here. They don't need to take advantage of that. I will talk to them this evening." Fan always had my back. She dealt with every issue serving as a communication channel between myself and everybody else. She always did exactly what she said she would do and I liked that about her. Like myself she liked to speak what was on her mind without sugar-coating too much. She was less angry than I was and more soft-spoken, but she still remained adamant most of the time. While listening to my reasoning I could tell that she tried to learn to imitate my confidence. The truth was the two of us were learning constantly from each other. We had plenty of not so good sparks between us as well but they were always short lived. Most of those times it was Fan who had to withdraw her attitude first knowing that my position was stronger and I wasn't going to let go of it unless I wanted to.

"Elzbieta, we really need to put the kids in school. We shouldn't wait any longer." She tried bringing this subject up every day which annoyed me quite a bit. I didn't like how pushy she was being with me on this.

"Yeah Fan, I understand that but we don't have that kind of money right now to place them in one of those small private schools you want them to attend. Go ahead and take them to the public school for now. I told you what my number one goal is. My biggest concern is to get you guys that house and that piece of land so you'll be safe and comfortable. Anything else; if I do help with it; it will have to wait. I promised you one thing and I intend to make that happen. Now anything else is not in my agenda right now." I could be generous but I could also be very shrewd when it came to money.

I did not like the pressure of anyone expecting anything from me and I made sure that this was very clear. I could tell that Fan felt offended many times with my asking to keep track of the receipts but I felt I had to remain strict. Each dollar collected from the few people that supported us didn't come effortlessly. Hours of editing videos, sending messages to people I knew, without creating nuisance, wasn't as easy as it looked. In fact I hated doing it. I hated the super slow internet connection that was measuring limits of my patience. I hated the fact that in order to survive the guy which liked dumping me so much had to be back in my life. I felt stupid when while flirting with me he was giving me false impression of caring about me. It irritated me like hell to watch his status update full of pictures from skiing etc while the promised fundraiser for us seemed always postponed by something. The occasional hundred dollars sent by him always came with the not required explanations of how things were tough for everyone these days. I knew that no one was going to step outside their comfort zone to make our goal a reality. I knew I'd have to go back and do all that myself. Impatient from not seeing the results I was mentally getting ready to leave even though I didn't like the idea of it.

The Birthdays

Fan and I returned from town where we went to buy some corn so we could make popcorn with our latest kitchen appliance sent by Marek. That morning there was quite some excitement in our kitchen. The flying white puffs of popcorn were occasionally spattering from the regular stream which they were supposed to follow. The unpredictable directions they were taking as well as the missile-popping noise they were creating were responsible for the animated atmosphere. The kids were laughing at loud while sitting in the corner. Juliana and Fan tried to help the naughty heated corn in entering the bowl accordingly. Nothing was going to change their destiny of fulfilling our empty stomachs, not even their clever way of jumping to the dirty ground!

The noise of the electrical popcorn maker was bringing in me the nostalgia for all the wonderful inventions of civilization to the point where it hurt. The popcorn itself, as little as I found it of interest before; was creating heavenly sensations in my mouth now. The kids surrounded the bowl placed on the ground with same enthusiasm starved birds throw themselves at a handful of rye seeds. They ate it with that same kind of speed. Our few guest enjoyed the delectable treats as well. It was pretty amazing to watch the branches of effects a thoughtful gesture of sending home equipment could have. I tried sharing this moment with Marek by capturing it on video. We all appreciated the "movie evenings" we were able to experience. It was so nice for all of us to sit around my laptop to watch the movies that a son of the local woman let us borrow. The noise of popcorn being eaten created a sense of being in the movie-theater for me. Marek also had sent the CDs of "Everybody Loves Raymond". Fan in particularly liked to watch that show with me.

"Oh look at the kitchen how nice it looks." She'd interrupt from time to time with a sad look on her face.

"Look what they're eating! Ooooooh God!" I'd join her in this sadistic pleasure of inflicting pain on ourselves. The show that made me laugh so much before was now generating the pre-shot audience's laughter only.

Towards the end of April, Marek sent a donation so we could have a cake for my thirty-third birthday. Since we didn't know on what day or even what year exactly the children were born we decided to integrate this occasion by celebrating six birthdays instead of one. We invited Fan's family, the local women that prayed with us and our landlord's wife. We bought a case of bottled sodas and cookies. It was cheaper this way and we could accommodate larger number of guests by choosing cookies over the cake.

The night before the big day children delayed with going to bed. There was just too much elation to handle. We all sat in the kitchen immersed in drawing and cutting birthday's decorations. The athlete was helping me with writing on papers all six of our names with the markers. The kids were busy with drawing and cutting shapes of hearts, stars and sun shines. They had never celebrated anything before and the excitement was almost turning into tension. In the morning the anticipation's level reached its peak. The kids were groomed and dressed up by the time I got up. Fan was busy with preparing hot water so I could wash my hair as well. Later Juliana's oldest daughter and I went for a walk to pick up some wild flowers.

We were able to find some plants that had small azure flakes. Together we decorated one of the usually empty rooms. We placed three mattresses on the floor against the walls on which we taped the previously made decorations. In the window we attached some wild green vines. On the small table covered with sheet we placed the flowers and the cookies. To preserve the space, the case of sodas was conveniently slipped under that table. We didn't have balloons so we hung transparent plastic bags filled with air on a rope that spread across the room. The music coming from the portable radio borrowed from the athlete was adding to the buzz.

"Happy birthday to you! Happy birthday to you! Happy birthday dear Elzbieta, Joan, Elizabeth, Denis, Laban, Winnie, happy birthday to you!" The kids kept practicing the song that they learned the night before. They loved giggling and clapping their hands hard each time they finished to sing. Finally the guests arrived. This time there were some children as well as some men present. They all brought some bananas and hard candies for us. Suddenly the room got dark from the number of people that was trying to fit in it. I did not expect that we would end up having three dozens of guests otherwise we would have prepared everything outside.

The locals didn't seem to mind sitting on the mattresses one next to another. Few chairs from the kitchen were added; however few individuals still had to stand in the doorway. Customary to the local tradition the guests engaged in a prayer and then singing. I noticed few new faces and the curiosity written in their eyes.

"OK, now it's time for the cake." I announced while lighting the dry straws that Fan pulled out of the broom. Nicely cleaned they were now stuck into a few cookies serving as candles.

After singing happy birthday we all indulged in eating and drinking. The treats were gone in a hurry. Injected with sugar boost children kept themselves busy with bouncing the balloon-imitations among each other. The few men disappeared and all the women engaged in a chat. One of the guests showed the sign of discomfort and when I asked for the reason some woman explained:

"Her husband doesn't want her to go any places. She's afraid he's going to beat her up when she gets home."

"He beats me anyway; even when I don't go anywhere so let him be angry." The young mother of two who came to support us on that "prayer day" explained. The conversation took the direction of domestic abuse. The women were expressing how fed up they were with men and their sense of superiority over the weaker sex. They were pretty surprised to learn from me that such phenomenon is very common in Europe and the United States as well. In my short time in Kenya I became big fan of Kenyan women and a lot less fan of Kenyan men. Generally speaking I did not like the sense of superiority and arrogant attitudes men were exhibiting. What was infuriating me even more was the fact that women seemed to work much harder, less flattering jobs and it was quite rare to see a man helping with children or house-chores. Fan's family and few others seemed to be exception to the rule. That is why when invited as a guests to a local wedding I refused sitting in a row where all the proud men/priests/counselors of the parish etc were seated. I did not like their self-important looks on their faces. I enjoyed my time sitting and eating among women even though the row was much farther away from the bride and groom's table.

The atmosphere in the room lightened up once we all put a joke spin on the situation. We laughed as we discussed the possible ways of empowering the female population. Later we all went outside to sing and dance. A few latecomers joined us without interrupting the ritual. It was getting dark when the guests headed to their homes, rushing in attempt of beating the inevitable rain.

Leaving

As time passed, I realized the fundraisers for our mission were not going to happen. I got tired of pushing through emails people that weren't really going to spend their time on it. I did not like the feeling of asking for too much.

"Fan, looks like I'm gonna have to leave Kenya and do all that by myself. We don't have another choice." I said to my friend after coming back from a trip to Nairobi. I went to the capital in hope of meeting some wealthy people that Elisha arranged appointments with. Our goal was to convince them in sponsoring our project. The secretaries of all three CEO's of major companies cancelled informing of the need to reschedule the meetings. Sitting in a cheap motel, unable to even connect to the internet because of constant black outs, I decided not to waste any more money.

Physically I had been feeling very lousy lately and only later when I went back to Greece I discovered the real reason for it. I got infected with stomach parasites that were sucking all the energy out of me. I was reliving my childhood nightmare all over again. I was spending most of the time in my room on the mattress. The pounding headaches were keeping me up every night all night long. The intense nausea would not allow me to stand on my feet for very long. I lost my appetite completely and Fan started to get concerned at the sight of untouched meals I was leaving in my room. My mood; just like my weight; kept dropping lower and lower with each passing day. I felt guilty for not raising any more money not even for food. For the last time I asked the same guy who wrote to me once again how sorry he was for misleading me and how he "unexpectedly" found someone real special, to send us two hundred dollars. With that money I paid for the government fees needed to register the organization as a NGO. I wanted Fan to be in full control and so the papers were filed in her name, not mine. Dean booked my airline ticket to Athens. He was glad that I finally "came to my senses" and he was excited about the idea of finally meeting me in person somewhere in Europe. I was sad that I had to leave, even heart-broken. The children had started attending school already, something that was sponsored by Fan's family. They looked so cute in those blue uniforms. In the evenings, narration after narration, Fan and I would discover what was being taught in each class.

"A B C D E F G..." The kids were showing of how they had learned to sing the whole alphabet in one day. Apart from having one Swahili class schools in Kenya were conducted primarily in English. I was feeling disappointed that I wasn't going to be there to witness the joy of moving in to their own house. I knew I would have to do everything from a distance.

"Fan, just so you know it's gonna take a little bit of time. At the beginning I'll be sending you just enough to cover the rent. You're gonna have to manage everything else on your own. I don't know exactly how long it's gonna take me to come up with the ten thousand dollars but I can tell you one thing; I will do everything in my power to make sure that you guys have your own place as soon as possible." Fan seemed as convinced as I was. She knew I was going to keep my word.

Noticeable Changes

"Oh my god! You look like a walking cadaver! It's a good thing mom is flying back to Poland soon so she doesn't have to look at you like this." My siblings were concerned with the shape I was in. Mom was just glad that I was back. My family did express how proud they were of my accomplishments though. They were still critical of me but a lot less invasively. They were more willing to give me some credit for my unconventional reasoning this time.

"My crazy sister." Danuta liked bragging about me to her friends.

"I'm telling you; these are some lucky kids. Your sister's a brave person." The friends' comments erased the last remnants of disapproval. After getting medicated and properly nourished by my family that felt guilty just by looking at me I was finally back to my regular size. Since I didn't speak Greek, but I did know Italian, I decided to go to Sardegna to get a job. Dean paid for the ticket unable to win the logical argument of me having better chances to be employed there. Giuseppe and his family were glad to see me again. After a couple of weeks spent on eating and revisiting everybody my Italian papa with his son in law drove me to the East Coast of Costa Smeralda. I got the job at a small bar/ice cream place that was maybe three hundred feet away from the old bar I once worked and which was now out of business. My new job stunk and I was tired of waiting for the season to bring new costumers. Boredom and monetary dissatisfaction as well as the controlling ways of the boss and his unofficial girlfriend that worked with us led to my decision of leaving the Island. I told my boss naively about wanting to just earn enough for the ticket he fired me knowing that I'd be on his mercy.

"Well; you can have Giuseppe pay for your ticket or you can sleep with me once and I'll take care of it for you." As obnoxious as he was I decided to take that alternative. I numbed myself with a bottle of wine and I did what had not been bringing me much satisfaction in more "normal" circumstances for some while now.

Back in Athens I stayed with my sister Danuta again. My mother and my younger brother had already left for Poland. I decided I'd wait until Danuta and her family would drive there in their car. Each year they'd spend August there. My older sister Bozena and her husband justified not leaving Athens with the fact that their daughter Afrodyty was too little to travel. In Poland the whole atmosphere was marked with the upcoming preparations for the wedding of our sister Barbara. The old wooden house, augmented by a brick built extension was always full of people. My sisters and their own families were visiting frequently. The life style in general looked improved a lot since my growing up. All my siblings had their own place. They all had at least one car per household. There was no luxury or anything like that but things appeared to be at least somewhat manageable. It wasn't like the old days when more than frequently there was no food on the table. My father had also calmed down a lot. He was still drinking but not nearly as much as he used to. From time to time he still engaged in verbal fights with whoever came across but those arguments were nothing compare to the ones that took place in my childhood. There was no more intimidation in his posture or his attitude. This time it was my mom, my younger brother or even grandma who was more aggressive with our once big time rageaholic alcoholic. These days my father seemed actually more agreeable than anybody else. He liked spending most of his time in a tiny room that he built for himself in the barn.

The "kitchenette"; name by which this place was referred, couldn't be any bigger than nine by twelve feet. It was located right between two stables which were occupied one by horse and the other by a cow. Inside the room my father had everything that he needed. There was a wood-combustible stove, a single bed, our old china closet, small TV set, a radio, and even sink with running water. Right by the stove there was an old-fashion looking door that led to dark chamber where potatoes were stored. The relatively big window next to the front door was allowing some day-light to brighten my father's abode. My mother was frequently visiting this new residence. Apart from helping with cleaning and cooking she seemed to enjoy watching TV in the company of her husband. Both of my parents had developed quite strange relationship with each other.

Nevertheless their marriage seemed functioning more than it ever had in the past. There was a lot less drama created by anger and blaming from both sides. My mother and my father appeared to be more autonomous and this freedom for the personal space was allowing the inevitable tension to be released in less destructive ways. For years now both of them were spending six months every now and then in Greece helping with raising their grandchildren. I was surprised and pleased to see how comfortable my nieces were with their grandpa who never raised his voice at them. It was so sweet to watch them being such untouchable little princesses.

I was surprised with many things indeed. I actually had a daily conversation with my grandmother; the mother of my dad. She really seemed this time like she appreciated our family. Actually my younger sisters and especially my brother were unmistakably her favorite ones. I liked to see how in her own ways she was exhibiting affection that was addressed towards people I cared about the most. It was a nice change.

The once so negative disharmony/hatred and mutual aversion, were now replaced with solidarity that said:

We are all in it together so let's respect one another the best we can. This was no longer the grandma who tried to resist my younger siblings from being permanently registered at her residence. As a matter of fact; my entire family, including myself, my mother, my nieces and nephews, even my brothers-in-law were now permanently registered at the property surrounded by pine-forest. The other grandmother had passed away years ago. It felt good to know that nobody was holding grudges against what happened in the past. Nobody was using it to win verbal confrontations. The discussions like:

"Your family's so evil that they don't even care if they remove the roof from over children's heads," were not part of daily routine anymore. The thing that was so pleasing was that mutual blaming seemed to have been removed from the overall dynamics that our family had assumed. We were even keeping in touch via internet with uncle Mietek, well; more with his children who seemed very eager in getting to know their cousins. Years of struggles and uncountable numbers of challenges seemed to have finally helped with unifying this big and awesome family.

This time it was more possible to relax and to enjoy the colorful diversities each family member brought to the table. The every weekend barbequing that was summer's ritual was gluing the sense of togetherness this family needed once so badly. Yeah, nothing was perfect like it is in a picture, the occasional arguments among us were inevitable but they were handled generally with more assertiveness. The old, more manipulative, ways of the power struggles seemed to have lost its attractiveness to all of us. A strong desire to face the truth, no matter how inconvenient, affected everyone. The straightforwardness and more flexible attitudes were more common. On some level, everybody finally comprehended the damage a judgmental attitude can produce, and nobody seemed eager to inflict pain on another by such approach. This family of mine, that was far from being perfect, had something new that was priceless. It had the improved self-value of each member and the overall new valuing of the family.

After Barbara's wedding things at home cooled off a bit and there wasn't as much excitement in the air anymore. For a whole decade I had missed these kinds of ceremonies, as well as new comings to this world of my nieces and nephews. It was nice to be able to be part of it this time. I enjoyed watching my gorgeous newest family-additions jumping playfully on the dancing floor. I admired the poise and charm my teenage nephews were conveying in their gentlemen-like behaviors. It was nice to see my mother less stressed out and more willing to put her own needs first for a change.

Bad News

The summer was practically over. Danuta and her family went back to Greece. With school starting the crowd at the country home became smaller and less frequent. Most of the time it was just the five of us: grandma, mom, dad, my brother and I. Rafal kept busy helping grandma with collecting hay from the pastures and bringing trunks of trees from the forest that belonged to our family.

"Woahw! Woahw! Woahw!" My brother's dominating tone of voice directed to gain control over the rebelling young horse had become an every day event. Dad was cutting the trunks into small blocks and stacking them together into a growing pile. Mom and I were neatly stacking the wooden blocks in a small shed. The reserve for the quickly approaching freezing winter was bringing a sense of abundance I so missed as a child. I could tell that my mom was glad to see the new way my dad and I interacted with each other. She compelled me to pick the grapes for him which was predestined to turn into a home-made wine.

"She cleared that damn thing better than those sparrows would. I don't see a single grape left on these vines." My mother smiled at dad's proudly announced observations.

"Elzbieta, put some shoes on and go with your dad to pick up a carboy." Mom and the rest of family had learned to call me by my full name as per my persistent request. Ridding in the wooden cart, harnessed to our mare, through those deeply dense Polish forests felt quite like a scene from a movie. The young foal was performing all kinds of tricks on this traffic-free dirt road. He'd amuse me each time with the intentional dragging of his feet, remaining far away from us on purpose just to engage in a full sprint towards us moments later. To hear the loud, rhythmic stamping of his hooves; p-poo-poom, p-poo-poom, to see the fully extended main, the working muscles and that hilarious look on this foal's still oversized head was simply exhilarating. My father could not hide the joy my child-like amusement was giving him.

"Yep, that's our Cooboosh; the trouble-maker." He'd light cigarette after cigarette throughout the trip and I'd smoke with him. My father and I had a new arrangement when it came to satisfying the nicotine cravings. He'd give me money and his bicycle and I'd ride that old thing to the nearest village to purchase them. He'd give me a pack from time to time when my mom or my siblings came up short with money.

"Did you buy yourself a soda with the rest like you're supposed to?" He'd ask me when I handled him the shopping bags filled with some beers and other food items that were on my mom's list. My previously felt embarrassment of not having anything in my life was now replaced with a more pleasant feeling of being loved despite everything and of being taken care of. Unlike in my childhood I was feeling safe this time.

"Elzbieta, why don't you go to kitchenette and finish selecting the grapes for me." Mom tried everything she could to get me out of the room in which I was hiding from the cold weather that was inevitably taking over and from my depression that was doing the same thing. Cleaning up the fruits while listening to the radio turned out to be quite relaxing activity. I was interrupted from time to time by my father who kept checking on the status of the boiling sugar-enhanced water that was being used to fill numerous carboys placed on the floor. I felt sad at the idea that I'd be leaving soon again. I knew that my mother in particularly wanted me to remain home and build my life there in Poland. My sisters were encouraging me to do the same. My family didn't hide the fact that my urge to return to Hawaii was hurtful to them. It made them feel as if I didn't wish to live among them. Of course that wasn't the case. I cherished my family and I was dreading the idea of being all alone again. However my mission in life, whatever that was, wasn't completed yet. More importantly I missed my dogs and I was sick and tired of having to worry about them. Back when I was still in Kenya in one of the phone conversations I had with Ahmed, to piss me off I guess, he told me that he got rid of my dogs. Later I found out he was just toying with me but before things got cleared out I sent bulk emails to everyone I knew urging people to call my ex-boyfriend. The intervention of my friends worked out and Ahmed let me hear Rex's whining voice the next time I called. In that period of time, one of my friends; a recipient of the bulk email, suggested to me that I put his name and his phone number as an alternative emergency contact with the microchip company. Since it was hard for me to do so all the way from Africa, he managed to contact the microchip company on my behalf. They could not change the records without me contacting them, but after he explained where I was they agreed to make a note of giving him a call in case of emergency.

Through the emails and messages my friend tried insisting on me changing the emergency contact permanently through forms that could be submitted online. He wanted me to remove Ahmed who was on that list as a primary emergency contact.

I never made those changes. I thought that it was much safer to have two contacts, instead of just one in case anything bad happened. Sure enough some four months later the friend emailed me that Rex was at the shelter. There was no time to figure out how the hell he got there. There was only time for swift action. I called Ahmed immediately and he promised he'd go to the shelter to retrieve Rex. At the same time my friend was going back and forth with messages telling me how he was taking care of everything. According to him he was able to convince shelter in finding a temporary foster home for Rex. Then few weeks later I was reading how since the foster family couldn't keep him any longer, that he took Rex to his house. Everything appeared to be under control. I was more than anxious to fly to Hawaii but I still had few challenges to overcome before I could do that. I still had to get approved for a visa and then get the money for the ticket.

Around the time when I was finally ready to fly back to Honolulu I received a very troubling message from the friend who was keeping Rex at his house for me:

"Bad news. I came home from Halloween late last night. Both dogs, my Buddy and your Rex are gone. The window screen was knocked out like maybe they jumped out the window. The gate was closed but they weren't in the yard. I think the fireworks scared them. I have looked all around and cannot find them anywhere. I put a call into the shelter and with chips they will call or if a vet gets them they will call too. Hopefully soon. All my neighbors know, so if they see them they will tell me. Sorry. Looking everywhere." The messages that went back and forth calmed me down a little bit knowing that Rex had someone to look for him.

Awkward

"Where to?" The taxi driver asked me.

"Downtown Honolulu please". I replied. I had nowhere else to go so Ahmed's office was my destination. I was exhausted from the long flight. It was sad not to have anyone greet me, not even a simple "welcome back". It was painful not to have my dogs jumping up and down at the sight of me. I still had to figure out where I would stay and how I would bring Rex and Nel home. Ahmed wasn't at the office so I took the bus to Waikiki intending to wait for him by the apartment building. I hadn't seen him in approximately nine months and from the conversations we had over the phone I could tell that he was serious about that same girl with whom he cheated on me with. Ahmed sounded like he still hated me and blamed me in some ways for dissolution of our relationship. He's purposely lowered voice; his slowly spoken words always appeared full of resentment towards me.

"Well; I thought you liked Kenya. I thought you decided to live there permanently. "He'd say to me in a way that sounded sad and like he was trying to hide disappointment."

"I think of moving back to Egypt myself. I'm thinking about starting a business there. Ahmed's hesitancy about us possibly getting back together was showing me that he wasn't completely clear about the decision of letting me go. From the tone of his voice I could tell that he was enjoying hearing me say that I was missing him. The fact that he had to hold on to my dogs for so many months showed me that he had to at least contemplated about the idea of us getting back together. I knew they were creating inconvenience to him and there couldn't be any other explanation for his selfless act.

Exhausted from flying across the globe I sat on the ground by the front door. An hour later the neighbor greeted me with a very surprised and judgmental look on her face.

"Do you mind holding the door for me?" I asked her.

"Um, you know? I don't feel very comfortable doing that. You guys had this rocky relationship and I wouldn't want to interfere with anyone by letting you in." She answered slowly.

"If you want me to I'll knock at the door upstairs and if anyone's there I'll tell them you're waiting here, OK?" She added while scanning my *"What the fuck is wrong with you woman?"* look. Few minutes later I heard the elevator's door opening. Ahmed's nephew leaned forward to see through the glass door.

"Ah, it's you. Come, come inside." He smiled while holding the door for me.

"Do you want some tea? There is nothing really else in this apartment." He poured the water into a pan. I sat on the couch on which I spent hours and hours sleeping before. The place didn't look any different, I was hoping that this was a sign that my ex was living with his nephew only.

"Now what exactly happened with my dogs? Do you know anything?" I asked.

"Oh, the big ones, yeah, the German shepherds. Those were your dogs, right?" He replied.

"Yeah, Ahmed was taking care of them for me. I don't know exactly what happened, but I just recently found out that Rex ended up at the local shelter. One of my friends said that he recovered him for me, but supposedly just recently, Rex ran away from his house. I don't know exactly where Nel is, either. Ahmed told me on the phone that she's with a foster family waiting for me at their home. He said he still has these people's phone number. I hope it's true," I explained. I was feeling very anxious for many reasons.

"Hello." Ahmed greeted me in a carefully chosen formal tone. He looked older, little bit overweight, and his thinner hair had more gray in it. He didn't look like he was happy to see me. The general atmosphere was commanded by the general awkwardness. Ahmed's cold attitude was hurting me.

He promised to get a hold of people who had Nel.

Eduardo

A friend named Linda introduced me to Eduardo, who had a restaurant in the city. She wanted to convince him in giving me a job. I was feeling humble and grounded. I was taking control over my life again. I knew I was going to be OK. Now that concerns with meeting my immediate survival needs didn't have to be my first priority, I could devote myself to getting my dogs back and to getting that piece of land and a house for Fan and the kids.

I wasn't planning on asking Eduardo with assistance with the Kenya project, and I didn't really expect any help from him with it. I thought he'd reject my idea the way most people did. When Eduardo asked what I was looking for in life, I answered very truthfully:

"My number one goal is to get a house for my friend and five children that she's taking care of that live in Kenya." I was prepared to hear how ridiculous I was and how I wasn't in a position to think of anyone other than myself. Eduardo was a very straightforward person and the thing that he liked even less than wasting time on choosing words carefully was to be bull-shitted by anybody. He had zero tolerance towards people that were not straight shooters like himself. His loud voice and his "F-ing this, F-ing that" way of expressing himself served as a warning for anyone who'd try to even think of fooling this man. He had a big heart but he also had even bigger ego which he wasn't in denial about. He didn't like wasting his energy on feeling small or on questioning his life. He liked being who he was and he was comfortable about it. He loved his big family as much as he loved creating new things in life.

"Show me those videos from that Africa." Eduardo commanded in his usually bossy tone. His very positive reaction to my short movies was encouraging. He liked how things were naturally portrayed and how "nobody was crying or begging for money".

"This is some good shit you have here. This is good; this is life as it is. This is not that bullshit that you see on TV. I like this. I really do. It's simple and honest. It's done naturally. This is not that organized and edited crap they play on TV to make people feel guilty so they would donate." He was complementing my work while clicking on different videos. Happy because Eduardo seemed impressed with my work, I opened up and told him how important finishing this mission was to me. I wasn't thinking about sounding right or wrong. I wasn't interested in throwing a good pitch. I simply spoke from my heart. I allowed myself to feel excited about it without worrying about being judged.

"I don't care what anybody says; I will get them that house somehow. I just know I need to do this. Not so much for them, but for myself." I kept talking while looking at Eduardo who was leaning backward on a chair with arms crossed on his chest.

"Well this is easy," he said, interrupting me.

"Find the place first, talk to the people selling it and tell them you'll make payments on it," he said. I told him I already had a property in mind.

"It's a small house on a half-acre, Fan found it when I asked her to look around," I informed him.

Eduardo and I went to Wal-Mart to send the first thousand dollars to Kenya. He reassured me that we'd be sending the remaining of the down payment within a couple of weeks or so.

The two of us "clicked" quite well and everyone around thought that there was something going on. Friends and family all assumed that I was his latest girlfriend, although that wasn't the case.

Eduardo and I made an arrangement that for helping him around the house he'd send eleven hundred dollars each month to Kenya for me. I gladly took that deal.

Where the Hell is Rex?

I told Eduardo about my missing dogs. I asked if I could keep them at the house once I found them. I was afraid that he would say no. Rex and Nel have been on my mind every single day since the last time I hugged them. It was excruciating not to have them with me and not knowing exactly how they were doing without me. I wanted to make sure, though, that Eduardo would value having me around enough to consider adding two big dogs to his household.

"I don't see why not. We already have chickens, cats, my son's dogs. I don't think it should be a problem," he answered after a short pause.

"K! Great! You mind if we drive to that area where my friend lives to see if Rex is wandering around? I'll go knock at neighbors' doors, every single one of them if I have to. I'm pretty sure someone just took him home. Or he may just be hanging out at the beach with the homeless people. He's the type of dog that everyone loves; smart, friendly and affectionate. Not to mention beautiful. After we find Rex I'll call my ex and I'll bring Nel home, too." I got all excited like a little girl. He liked my company and with each day I felt safer in his presence.

"Let's stop at the animal shelter first. Maybe someone brought Rex there," said Eduardo.

At the shelter I gave the receptionist Rex's microchip number. She took her time to look into the files on the computer. She could not find anything.

"Well, that's strange. My friend told me he called you to alert you that Rex could be lost. Could you check under my friend's name?" I persisted. I slowly spelled his last name for her.

"OK, I found it. This is your dog, right?" She twisted the computer screen so I could see the picture.

"Oh my god! Yes! That's Rex! So you did find him! Oh my god. Thank goodness we stopped here." I was feeling ecstatic.

"Oh, he's been adopted." The receptionist's words crushed my euphoria.

"Yeah, he was here in August and he was adopted shortly after he got here," she continued while staring at the computer screen.

"What the fuck?" I yelled without self-control, when I heard her saying words that made absolutely no sense to me. Emotions of anger, resistance to the reality, sadness, and hurt were squeezing the unwanted tears from my eyes.

"We only have to keep the animals for ten days here at the shelter. After that if no one claims them we have the right to put them up for adoption." The receptionist talked to me in a flat, matter-of-fact way.

"All this just makes no sense to me. My friend told me he picked him up and Rex was at his house. If you want me to, I can bring you all the emails so you can see, I still have those. Then he told me my dog ran away on the Halloween night, that he got scared by the fireworks. So how can you tell me that Rex was adopted out back in August? That just makes no sense," I argued.

"Your friend never picked him up. That's what it says here."

"What do you mean he never picked him up?" I couldn't believe her.

"The notes that I'm reading here say he called us, he did say that he was going to take the dog home but then he never showed up."

I couldn't even catch my breath. I couldn't understand how anyone could do such a horrible thing to a person. If she was telling the truth about my friend, then why wouldn't anyone try to reach me and let me know what was going on? What kind of sick world we lived in?

"Why didn't anybody made an effort to let me know what was going on? Why wasn't I informed?" In response, I received a blank stare from the young receptionist. She looked lost and eager to go back to whatever she was doing prior to my arrival.

"Look, I've had my dog with me for eight years, since he was seven months old. I brought him here from California. He's not just my dog; he's my child. I think if you just call these people who adopted him and explain to them the situation and the whole mix up, I'm sure they'll understand. It's only been a couple of months since he was adopted out, and I'm pretty sure they'll understand once they know what happened. Please, just help me get my dog back."

Eduardo stepped in insisting about the call being made to those people who had Rex. The girl behind the counter finally agreed that after getting permission from the manager she'd call them on my behalf. The next day she informed me that the military wife who got Rex for her husband needed more time to discuss the issue with him, but he had been deployed to Iraq.

Hope inhabited my heart. I could not imagine anyone not doing the right thing and not returning Rex to me. Things seemed to be turning out surprisingly well when I got the message that my other dog, Nel, was at the shelter. Apparently she ran away from the foster home my ex found for her and someone brought her in, the same way they did with Rex.

"Let's go already. Let's pick up your dog." Eduardo got impatient with me saying:

"Ooooh my god, I can't believe this! I can't believe this. I can't believe I just found Nel."

At the shelter, after paying some fees and filling out some papers, they finally brought Nel to me. She looked confused at first but when I sat down on the floor she jumped joyfully and she started to lick my face. I kept petting my dog while silently apologizing to her for having to leave her for so long. I promised I'd never ever do that again.

"I've never seen a dog so happy," said Eduardo, touched as well. I was overwhelmed with joy. I could hardly contain the happiness that I was feeling. I felt loved by some Mysterious Power that allowed me to have at least one of my dogs back.

"She must have run away sensing I was back. She probably went to look for me. What a smart doggie."

The three of us were in the car ready to go home when Eduardo noticed through the glass door a black Doberman pincher.

"That's a nice dog," he said while putting the car in reverse.

"That is a nice dog. These people are dropping him there. I overheard them saying that the husband is being relocated by the military to the Mainland," I said, and I realized that it was now too little too late to change the course of history.

Eduardo jumped out of the car. After few short minutes the nine months old Doberman pincher was sharing the back seat with Nel.

The Letters

Having not heard back from the woman who was in possession of Rex, Eduardo and I drove every day to the animal shelter. From supervisor to general manager we heard the same thing over and over again. Eduardo was losing his patience:

"Look, she wrote a nice letter to this lady explaining to her the circumstances and asking politely to have a heart and to give her dog back. We even offer this woman to pay for her inconvenience. Read the letter yourself and tell me if there is any harassment in it. Here, the letter is opened, see? Since we don't have her name or address we're asking you guys to mail this letter to her."

"It's against our policy. We're not allowed to do this." Different people with differently employed positions were repeating themselves. Finally Eduardo got a hold of some general manager/director of operations, who told him that he'd look into this matter more closely and that he'd get back to us. The next day he left a short voice mail on Eduardo's cell phone saying that there was nothing that could be done.

"Don't worry, I'll get a hold of this guy later. He's gonna send this fucking letter and he's gonna send it today. Makes me wanna sue those mother fuckers! Fucking bullshit people like this shouldn't fucking live let alone run a nonprofit for animals. Where are their fucking hearts? Fucking idiots!" This time Eduardo's usage of strong adjectives did not bother me at all. In the evening a boy that worked for Eduardo said to me:

"Boy you should hear him talking on the phone with that shelter people when we were at the restaurant. He was maaad. He was yelling like

373

crazy. He was saying some shit like: this poor woman goes to Africa to save some homeless kids, she has the guts to do this all by herself when she herself has nothing, and when she comes back to Hawaii she finds out shit like her dog was given to someone else."

"Really? He was that upset?" I asked.

"Telling you; everybody stopped doing what they were doing. He just went on like crazy. He was yelling shit like: I'll sue you and I'll sue that woman who has Rex. And I'll bring media's attention to all this. See you in court!" The boy imitated his boss with excitement. Later Eduardo handled me his phone and he told me to listen to the new message that the director of operations left. He was saying this time to bring the letter in and that they would be mailing it to that woman on our behalf. At the shelter the director himself took the letter from us. My hopes, that this person was going to assist me in getting my Rex back, vanished almost immediately when I saw his superior-like attitude. The man was being very short with us. He sounded as if he was trying to appear very official. He seemed uncomfortable and he was giving me very bad vibes. Through his unfriendly attitude I could sense I was being judged and condemned in his mind. He was looking down at me the entire time. The man was attempting to explain to us that he was going to send this letter as a favor and how he was acting against the shelter's "regular" policies by doing so.

Back at Eduardo's place I was reading over and over again the letter addressed to that woman. I was pretending I was being her reading it to see what effect it could have and how would I possibly react if I was the recipient of it:

"My name is Elzbieta and as you know by now I am the original owner of the German shepherd that you have adopted. I apologize for the inconvenience caused by this whole situation that resulted from one big misunderstanding. I do not wish to blame anyone for what happened; I simply feel the unstoppable urge of getting reunited with Rex.

I am sure that you have already become attached to him; there could be no other way. I've had my dog since he was a puppy and I know how smart and how sweet he is. He is also a very loyal dog. Well, the truth is that he's more than a dog to me; he's like a child to me. In eight years he brightened my life and the life of my other German shepherd; Nel whom I just got reunited with and who misses Rex just as much as I do.

I understand that you may blame me for not assuring better my dog's safety while traveling aboard. Please know that I did everything that I thought needed to be done and that what has happened was simply out of my control. I had to travel to Europe and then to Africa to raise money for homeless children in Kenya. If you wish you can visit my website to

374

see for yourself that what I'm saying to you is the truth. While I was away, my ex-boyfriend unexpectedly dropped Rex at the shelter. As I panicked I asked my friend to get my dog out of there. At the same time I called my ex and I begged him to take Rex back from there. My ex did go back to that shelter and tried to retrieve him but they would not release Rex back to him since my friend was already appointed by me as the guardian. Now this "friend" of mine has told me that he did pick up Rex and that he had him at his house waiting for me. That was not true according to the shelter which I found out about when I went there to ask if they have found Rex. (The day before I came back to Honolulu my friend said that he ran away from his house.) So that is how I've learned that you have adopted Rex.

I'd really appreciate if you'd let me have my dog back. I'd be more than happy to reimburse you for whatever you've spent on Rex until now. I know it's a lot to ask, especially since you don't even know me but please understand that I don't see any other possibility as an option here. I want my Rex back. I hope that you will understand that I cannot imagine spending the coming Christmas without my baby."

Not hearing back anything from anyone Eduardo and I kept driving back and forth to the shelter. The workers and the volunteers where giving me dirty looks clearly blaming me for the commotions I was causing. On one of those days I discovered that it wasn't Ahmed who dropped Rex there. The supervisor uncovered one of the many missing puzzles for me:

"Yes, I remember very well having a conversation with you ex-boyfriend. He's that middle-eastern looking guy, right?" The supervisor seemed friendlier than anyone else did at the shelter.

"Yes, that's my ex. So you confirm that he did indeed show up here to take Rex home."

"Yes, he came here a couple of times. He was not the one who dropped your dog here by the way. Someone else did." She informed me.

"Who was it then?" I asked feeling guilty for how little faith I had in Ahmed and I how I rushed with my assuming that it was him who dropped my dog at that awful place.

"That I cannot disclose. But all I can tell you is that it wasn't your ex who brought Rex in." She answered.

"So wait a minute here. Let's say that it's true that my friend screwed me over and he never picked up Rex like he said he did. You guys did have Rex's microchip number though and so you knew that he had two emergency contacts on that list, one of them being my ex. You also knew that I was out of country. Now my question is this; if this guy never showed up to pick up Rex, but my ex did come to the shelter, like you just told me, then why did you not give Rex to my ex-boyfriend?"

"Well, we thought that the other guy was going to pick him up."

"Well I know, but he didn't. So then why didn't you call back my ex and tell him to come back and get my dog for me once you realized that the other guy wasn't coming for him?" I was as persistent as a flea on a dog's tale.

"Honestly I don't know. I don't think we had his phone number on file." She hesitated.

"Then all you had to do was to call the microchip company and they would give it to you. Ahmed's name and his phone number are registered as a primary emergency contact."

The supervisor did not have clear answers to my questions. Even though she was trying to show most empathy than anyone else did at that place, she still expressed to me how little there was that could be done to resolve this issue.

Not willing to give up on my fur-baby, I sat down to write the second letter to the woman who had him. I didn't have much faith left in her at that point but I didn't know what else to do either. I worried that my Rex ended up in such shrew's hands. Sometimes I wondered whether the shelter had sent my letter to her at all. In the second letter I decided to be even more direct:

"Hello,

The New Year just begun and I hope that this can mean a fresh start for all of us and so without wasting precious time I wish to be very direct with you.

I want to buy Rex; the German shepherd you have adopted from the shelter. Would you be willing to sell him back to me? If so, would you please let me know the amount that would make this happen?

Please know that I cannot continue to communicate through the shelter as there is a limit to which the shelter can interfere in this matter. If you wish to remain anonymous while negotiating the price, you can still do so by communicating with me through emails for example. I'm sure you know that if you don't have it already, you can get a free email account that will allow you to send emails without revealing your identity.

I'm doing my best to prove to you that I am solely interested in buying Rex. I don't have any doubts as for how much you are already attached to him but I also believe that you understand how much he means to me.

Again, please let me know the amount that would make you comfortable and that would allow me to have my dog back.

If this situation is a question of morality to you, then please understand that I take full responsibility for losing my dog. Yes; Rex deserves the best care and if I could change the past I would never travel aboard and I would never leave him in anyone's care other than my own. Believe me; I have learned my lesson the hard way and I just hope it's not too late to correct my mistake. We all do make mistakes in life, especially with the loved ones, don't we? I am not even asking anymore; I am begging for a second chance."

The truth was I wanted to write to her what an awful person she was and how I wished that she'd rot in hell for what she was putting me through but I could not afford such gesture. At the shelter the same director of operations made very clear to Eduardo and I that this was the absolutely last time that he was going to send the letter on our behalf.

Not Giving Up

The woman who was holding onto Rex never replied to any of my letters. I was more than devastated. Beating myself up over what may or may have not happened if I had never left for that trip to "save the world", wasn't helping at all. Finally I had decided to get together with Ahmed and the guy that said that he had picked up Rex. The meet up turned out not as fruitful as I was hoping. I learned that my ex-boyfriend had placed both Rex and Nel in the same foster home shortly before the whole ordeal with the shelter. The people that were caring for my dogs were close friends with his housekeeper whom I knew from when I used to live with him. Ahmed explained to me how uncooperative the shelter was with him when he went there to retrieve Rex.

"The first time I went there they didn't even wanna let me see him. I made a scene and finally the supervisor let me see Rex." Ahmed recalled.

"You mean you got to see him while he was there?" I asked.

"Yeah, he was there! He was all whining and made me freaking wanna cry. I petted him and I told him: daddy's gonna be back to pick you up. I had to go back home because the shelter asked me to bring all his papers with me. So I went to the apartment, took that folder you left with me and I went back there thinking Rex was coming home with me. And then when I got there they told me Rex wasn't there anymore. They said that your friend had just picked him up."

"I did pick him up. He was at my house. He ran away on the Halloween like I told you he did. If they are mistaking is probably because Rex was there the second time." The guy stepped in to defend his honor.

"Well then let's just go to the shelter, all three of us and let's see what they have to say to all of this. If they're freaking lying like this to me then they better do something to correct this situation."

"No problem. Let's go then," said Ahmed. The other guy though wasn't as willing to participate. He tried to argue how he did not see what good his presence at the shelter would do. He did not even agree to talk to them over the phone. Later he sent me a message asking me not to ever contact him again. The reason behind his decision was that I was just creating too much drama in his life.

Days after days, and weeks after weeks, I kept bugging the shelter employees hoping that they would take at least part of the responsibility for the whole mix up and that they would assist me with getting my dog back. I could not understand why they would not even try to put some pressure on that woman who obviously wasn't going to give me my dog back willingly. I kept demanding explanations regarding of what exactly happened and why wasn't anything being done to correct the mistake. In the attempt of trying to get rid of me the shelter people informed me that "the official internal investigation" performed by their officer was closed. In their view the officer that worked for that shelter found absolutely no evidence proving that the shelter was at fault. I was of course not allowed to see any paper work; not even the stray animal admission forms or any documents for that matter. Everything was excused by the confidentiality policy.

"Yes ma'am, I was the one who personally delivered her that second letter you brought to us and to be honest with you, I don't believe she's gonna give you the dog back." The same animal officer who was supposedly in charge of the investigation told me when I went to see him at the shelter. Whenever I'd bring the subject of a law suit the shelter people would try to make me feel like I didn't have a case against them.

"All you can really try to do was to take the adopter to court. Not the shelter. Even then I don't think honestly that you'd win. But you could subpoena her information and all that through the court. We cannot give you her name. We have to obey our privacy policy." The director of operations always seemed overly confident and even cocky as if on purpose. I despised all those people that worked there and the institution itself. I could not understand how, what normally may be viewed as a noble organization, could be run in such heartless, corrupted manner.

Christmas Time

I was very discouraged after the conversation Eduardo had with an attorney that he knew regarding Rex and his situation. He was on the phone with him while I was sitting on pins and needles on the couch. The lawyer didn't sound convincing or sympathetic. All he seemed to be interested in was the three thousand dollars for the retainer fee he was asking for plus the FIFTY THOUSAND dollars that according to him would take to win the battle in court.

"The shelter's attorneys will play a game with you guys and they'll keep asking for extensions trying to postpone things. They can afford that and they know it. Does she have that kind of money to keep going with this? Basically what they'll try to accomplish is to make her run out of the funds for the legal representation. So unless she has that kind of money sitting in the bank, I don't see how she could be successful at getting her dog back." I did not like what I was hearing. I knew I had to find a better, more realistic way to get my baby back just like I knew I could not give up on Rex. I felt defeated. In the following days thoughts like trying to make peace with the idea of never seeing Rex again were crossing my mind. For some brief period of time I forced myself to accept the harsh reality. The pain was always tormenting me though, refusing to leave me alone. I was tired of approaching strangers at the parks and on the sidewalks. Any German shepherd I saw, I had to make sure it wasn't Rex.

"It's a small Island. I'll find him."

As promised Eduardo and I went few more times to Walmart to send the money to Kenya. Three thousand dollars later, right before Christmas my friend and the kids moved in to their new home. Fan told me over the phone how including Juliana and her family, how they all cried that day from joy. I tried to imagine the emotions kids and Fan must have felt while looking around and realizing that the land and the house was theirs. There were only four remaining payments in the amount of eleven hundred dollars each to be made and after that the title deed was going to have Fan's name on it. For hours sometimes I stared at the picture of the house that was sent to me. It was small and it was made out of that reddish clay most homes were build with in that area. It had metal roof and two windows in front that had actual glass in it. The front door made out of thick wooden boards was between those two considerably big windows. A small wooden bench was buried in the ground in front of one of them. The electrical box on the side was revealing that the house had once electricity in it. The red land was almost entirely covered with green grass. As modest as it was the place looked cute and cozy. In my mind I tried adding a wooden porch covered with colorful flowers, a well taken care of vegetable garden on the side and numerous banana trees on the property.

"Wow, I did it! I really made it happen." Thoughts like these were generating lots of positive and loving energy inside me. I'd sit by the outdoor bar at five o'clock in the morning while sipping on my hot coffee and while puffing on my cigarettes I'd tried to imagine the feeling of joy that only owning a house could bring.

"Wow, what a feeling that must be. What is it like to walk around and know that you can do whatever you wish with your place? What does it feel like going to sleep without worrying about the rent that is due again? What is it like knowing you don't depend on anyone? How does it feel knowing that nobody can kick you out? How safe it must feel to know that there is a place in this world reserved just for you?" Occasionally I couldn't help but to feel little bit envious and jealous towards Fan. I wished someone had done this for me but those emotions were not long lived. I knew it was only a matter of time, some efforts on my part on keeping strong beliefs and that I'd also have what I've always dreamed of. I was relieved knowing that what not long ago seemed extremely difficult to do was now very closed to be accomplished. In my mind meeting Eduardo was not a coincidence. To me it was karma doing its job. In many ways I could see the resemblance in how he was treating me with how I treated Fan. Exactly the same way I was with her he was questioning sometimes my motives. Through Eduardo I was able to see how bossy, demanding and unreasonably expecting I was with her sometimes. I also could see how the same way in which Fan had been indispensable to me, I now felt indispensable to him. His pushing me to be in charge of the big house occupied by numerous habitants was not different from my throwing such responsibility on Fan's shoulders. His admiration for my domestic abilities seemed equal to how impressed I was with her ways of handling things. My protectiveness over my Kenyan friend was now being

mirrored in Eduardo's protectiveness of me. Same way I tried letting go of control with her I was now slowly being allowed to do things without being micromanaged. Just like I cared about Fan I didn't doubt I was now cared for by Eduardo. He and I both had some general trust issues that were resulting in occasional verbal disagreements but things were never left unspoken. We handled those rare situations in ways typical to Italians; loud voice, theatrical gestures, you're this, you're that, F-you, F-you too, OK; we're good, let's have a cigarette. Eduardo never made me feel like my staying there was in jeopardy because of my occasionally sharp tongue. He always seemed to come to peace with my opinions knowing that I did care for him and that I had no interest in "kissing anyone's butts".

"There is that look. Don't start doing that thing you do with that jaw again. There it comes. You look like a man when you do this." He'd often make me laugh when he'd allow himself to look scared by my nervous habit of masticating my teeth with my mouth closed when stressed out. Eduardo was definitely not the easiest person to handle, something that all his family and friends were well aware of. Just like me he had some serious issues with anger but unlike me he didn't like holding his emotions back. He didn't mean any harm with his explosions directed towards anyone who'd "step on his sore toe". He just wasn't too close friends with assertiveness. Loud and commanding voice was his favorite tool in ruling the world. We'd all tease him what a mafia boss he was while drinking wine and enjoying good food on parties/gatherings he liked to throw. The thing that everybody seemed to like the most about this man was that he was authentic. He didn't pretend to be anyone else other than what he was and that was exactly what he wanted from everyone else in return. That is why despite his temper people were very comfortable around him. Well most of the times. What was impressing to me was Eduardo's fast and ninety nine percent of time correct judgment whether of a person or of a situation.

"Now tell me, what do you think of that person?" He liked quizzing my wittiness after such parties.

"OK, you want me to be completely honest with you?" I liked to proceed expressing my opinion which such sentence just in case he'd get offended by it. Then without sugar coating I'd tell him my exact first impression.

"Ha ha ha ha ha!" He'd laugh at loud while leaning back on his favorite chair.

"See? You don't get this from schools. You only get this kind of perceptiveness from living a full life. It's obvious you've been all over. You know almost instantly who you're dealing with. You are NOT naïve.

You are street-smart. You see things that most people wouldn't even notice. You could be an excellent spy. You don't ask questions, you just have natural way of making people comfortable. You gain people's trust easily." Eduardo flattered me sometimes with compliments but what I enjoyed even more was to see genuine intrigue in his eyes. His face would then have that expression that said:

"Who the hell is this girl for real? And what exactly is she doing at my house?" Sometimes I'd tease him with sayings like:

"Yep, I'm working for the CIA. We're investigating one of your friends. Come on, do you really think someone like me would want to clean someone else's house for a living? You didn't fell for that, did ya? I know you didn't." I'd wrinkled my forehead while playfully exhaling smoke from the long, skinny cigarettes that Eduardo bought for me. He'd looked at me with a trace of reservation in his eyes.

"You're full of it." He'd say expecting me to start laughing which I did. Eduardo and I had some good times sitting and talking nonsense mostly. For Christmas time we went to Walmart one more time to send twelve hundred dollars that I owed my sisters for my ticket back to Honolulu. Eduardo actually offered that by himself.

"I want you to relax and not worry about anything." He justified his generosity. While cleaning the house I found five humongous teddy bears and I asked Eduardo if we could send them to Kenya which he agreed to do so.

"You and this freaking Africa thing." He complained while watching me stamping on stuffed animals that were resisting fitting into cardboard boxes that he brought from the post office.

"K, let's go, let's go! Hurry up! I don't wanna be stocked in line for hours there. Ken and the kids will be here tomorrow and we still didn't get the Christmas tree. Hurry up with this. We need to go do that shopping. Come on Elzbieta!" Eduardo's never patient nature was intensified by the widespread holiday fever.

"Why don't you get three of them? It will look nice. It'll be like a forest on the deck." I said while examining different shapes of Christmas trees.

"You're right. Why not? Why didn't I think of it before? Let's just do that. Come on. Let's start putting this one in the car." Eduardo's level of energy seemed to be reaching its peak.

"K, let's move! Let's go!" He'd yell more to himself and he'd get curious looks from bystanders.

"Opaaaah!" His favorite phrase was showing his contentment with accomplishing a task.

"Oh boy" was the phrase that more often was coming out of my mouth like in that moment of fighting for the space in the car with those coniferous branches.

Cleaning and Organizing

Christmas had always been my favorite, most important holiday and I was grateful that I wasn't all alone like the year before. With party after party though, with having to deal with different family members who always seemed to need some assistance from the "housekeeper", I simply couldn't wait for everybody to just leave. My not so favorite guest, something which I wasn't secretive about with Eduardo, was his first wife. The pretty but snobby woman was convinced that by befriending me she was going to figure out what exactly was going on between me and her ex husband. I didn't like how she looked at me with that sense of pity that said:

"What went so wrong in your life that you ended up cleaning a house for a living and having a relationship with someone so much older than you?" Again, I wasn't justifying myself to anybody and so I wasn't correcting anyone who thought that I was romantically involved with Eduardo. I tolerated the woman's curiosity until one day when she made a mistake by thinking that I was interested in her giving me advice.

"I was in your position when I was your age. I know how it is. I see myself in you. I think you should go to live some place like New York. You could do so much better there." She kept talking while lying on the couch and I tried ignoring her while washing the dishes.

"What is it that your sisters do for a living?" She asked.

"You know? I don't really like to talk too much about myself. No offense. It's just how I am." I answered tired of being scrutinized.

"Ooh, I understand." She paused with a look that said:

"I just found the missing puzzle!" She then went on with saying things like:

"I know how it is. I know why you don't feel comfortable sharing things. I know how a man can control a woman when she doesn't have anything. I had been through that when I had no money and I understand how you feel that you need to put up with things you normally would find unacceptable."

"OK, you know what? This stops right here." I threw the cloth that I used to dry my hands. I passed the kitchen's counter and I stood right in front of the couch that she was spread on.

"Listen; you don't know me and you don't know anything about me. Money or no money I always do what I want in life. I am HERE because I CHOSE to be here. Let's not have any of these conversations anymore." I said firmly deriving pleasure from the stoned look on her face. Unaffected by the awkwardness in the air I went back to cleaning.

"I'm telling you man; this girl is no bullshit. She'll tell you straight to your face what she thinks. Ha ha! Got to give her credit for that." Eduardo could not wait to brag over the phone to his friends about my altercation with his ex. He always observed me carefully trying to make sure that I was happy. He knew that when true movies channel was on and when I was buried between pillows on the enormous sofa that I had completely tuned out everybody who may happen to be there. I could tell that he tried being less aggressive in general knowing that I was not comfortable with yelling. Feeling anxious I would usually go back quietly to my room if he got frustrated with anyone.

"Elzbieta! Where did she go? Where is she?" Eduardo didn't like when I disappeared. I never wanted to interfere but I felt bad seeing how his well intended way of handling things was causing sometimes chaotic atmosphere and frustration. Sometimes I'd try to calm his nerves:

"Eduardo, you're gonna give yourself a heart attack for no reason. Come on, it's not the end of the world. I know they're grown up but they're still young. They're still kids. They'll learn, don't worry. Just be more patient with them. They're good kids."

"Well I don't want them to think that they can just do whatever they want, leave mess everywhere 'cause their daddy pays you to clean up after them. They need to learn how to appreciate things, like you appreciate things. You need to start telling them to keep that door shut on their side." Eduardo knew that just like he did I hated when someone just expected from me anything or took my efforts for granted.

"I'm not going to raise your grown up kids. That's not my job." I kept telling him that each time he brought up the subject of me disciplining his three children that lived on the other side of the house. The remaining apartment units were occupied additionally by six different tenants that were friends with Eduardo. The house and the fenced deck area looked pretty much like a small European plaza; doors leading upstairs and downstairs, people constantly going in and out, dogs, cats and even some chickens roaming around. The place looked always busy and Eduardo had finally someone who would wear the sheriff's hat for him, and that was me.

"OK, those garbage bins outside the house; I'm not going to keep organizing them if people don't learn how to properly dispose their trash." I threatened.

"Good point. I'm sick and tired of all this bull shit. I'm the only one here who pulls out those bins when it's day to be picked up. If I don't do it nobody else will. Nobody takes care of this place. That's gonna have to change." Eduardo responded. Later we taped a notice letter to each door. The letter informed everyone about new monetary consequences for not segregating properly and for leaving disposable materials anywhere else other than inside the bins. Everybody knew I was behind those new rules. They all got accustomed to the view of me wearing my dirty clothes, swiping the floors etc. Nobody however was going to question the fact that even thought Eduardo may had let some things slack before that now this wasn't going to be the case if I complained. Eduardo liked the newly organized surroundings so much that he started to engage the boy that worked for him in helping with getting rid of those old broken appliances left in the drive way.

"We don't need this old couch here, do we? Why don't we throw away this thing too and put some flowers here instead? It'd be nice. This looks just too trashy. I hate this couch in front of the house like this." I'd share my thoughts while we'd take a break for a cigarette. The next thing Eduardo and I would drive back and forth to Home Depot dragging all kinds of flower plants back home with us. I enjoyed digging in the soil. I enjoyed even more looking around and seeing the positive changes. Eduardo loved when guests were complimenting him:

"This place finally starts looking like it should. Nice. It looks real nice Eduardo."

"Oh man, I'm telling you; she's the best. I'm telling you; no one knows how to clean better than Elzbieta. I mean it. She's like me; when she does something; she means business. None of that bullshit crap of cleaning on the surface only. She'll go and strip everything apart and she'll get to the corners. Best thing I don't even have to tell her anything. She does everything on her own. Look, look here in the kitchen. Have you seen anything more organized than this? Eh? What did I tell you? Now look at her watching her movies and ignoring us like she's not even here. You want some wine honey? Get something to eat." He'd yell while passing with guests by the entertainment center.

"No thanks. I already ate." I'd respond as usual without turning my look away from the huge TV screen.

"Don't disturb her. She looks way too comfortable over there." Someone would always say to him.

"Telling you; she'd be a perfect wife. When she works, she works and when she rests; stay the hell out of her way. She's perfect. She doesn't bother anyone and she doesn't wanna be bothered. She's very easy to live with." Eduardo would go on with praising me knowing that I could hear everything despite the loud volume of the TV. Often he'd go on with explaining the big changes he was going to make to the house.

The following days indeed we'd drive to Home Depot a lot. Cutting long boards, drilling, holding screws and painting became my newest activity. Since my days consisted more than often of ten hours of work he didn't mind paying me hourly. When the ten bucks per hour compensation reached the balance of eleven hundred dollars we'd drive then to Walmart and he'd sent the money to Kenya for me. All the money I earned went towards paying off the house for Fan and the kids and I wouldn't even see a penny of it. I wanted my goal to be reached as soon as possible.

"You should be proud of yourself. You've been working hard and you're almost done with that Africa dream of yours. What you gonna do with all that money when the house is paid off?" Eduardo liked questioning me when we were having coffee in the morning.

"I don't know yet. I'm doing one thing at the time."

"Don't be stupid and don't keep throwing all your money to that Africa. I know you. I know you promised them that house but when it's paid off you need to start saving it for yourself. You need to start thinking about you and what you need to do to have a normal life." Eduardo liked coaching me as well.

"What I'm gonna do after this is done; I am finally gonna get married. That's right; don't look at me like I'm crazy or something. I'm telling you; I WILL find that perfect husband. You'll see."

"Good luck with that. You're too picky; you're not gonna find the kind of man you're looking for. He doesn't exist. He only exists in your mind. But hey; who am I to tell you this? Who knows; you could find what you're looking for after all. At least you'll be legal in this country which would be a good thing. I don't doubt for a moment that you can find someone who'll want to marry you like right away. Just like that. I could marry you like this. But you will always run into that same problem; you will always be controlled by that man until you'll get US citizenship. Don't even try telling me it's not gonna be like this." Eduardo always insisted on his point of view on this matter.

"Nope, the man I'm gonna marry it's gonna be different. I have my own ways of finding out what kind of man I'm dealing with. I will know immediately if he's the right one for me." I always responded in self assuring tone.

"Oh yeah? And how you're gonna do that?" He never seemed tired of asking me about the same thing over and over just like he never seemed to like my answer:

"Simple. The moment I'll find that man that has similar values and principles to mine, I'm gonna ask him if he will marry me just for my papers. If he agrees to do so knowing in advance that I will not sleep with him, I'll know for a fact that he cares about me. And that is the kind of man I'm gonna marry. Someone who's not selfish and someone who sees things the way I do. AND; he's gonna be close to my age; thirty five to forty five years old."

"Ha ha! Good luck. Hey, you want me to hook you up with some rich doctors and lawyers that I know?" Eduardo liked offering his assistance on that without really meaning it.

"No thanks. I'll find him on my own. I don't care so much if he's rich or not. I do love money but that we can make together." The more I heard my own words the more impatient I was getting with fulfilling one of my life's biggest dream. I kept rejecting the piling thoughts like:

"You haven't met him until now, what makes you think that you're gonna find him now, just like that? What exactly do you believe could make things different for you this time? Why out of a sudden you're luck should change?" While taking Nel for walks I'd keep repeating at loud to myself:

"You know what? I'm gonna find him now because I say so, simple as that. That's right. Not only am I going to meet the man of my dreams and get married, have that freaking US citizenship once and for all so nobody can fucking intimidate me because of my freaking status, but I will also finish my damn book with a happy ending the way I wanted this to be. And I'm gonna get Rex back. And all this is going to happen now simply because I say so. And the only reason all this didn't happen yet is simply because I didn't want it BAD enough. Well now I do. Now I want this bad enough that even imagining any other possibility is not an option. If I have to visualize it every freaking day, if I have to pray on my knees, if I have to get rid of all my negative thoughts, keep imagining Angels sending me love and helping me with all this; I will do WHATEVER it takes. After all, I AM loved by whoever/whatever created me. And if that's the case; nothing stays in my way! That's right Nellie. Momma is gonna get married now and you're gonna have a daddy! And Rexie-Chexie is gonna be back with us like the old days." Hearing excitement in my voice my dog would start jumping trying to nibble on my hands.

"Yeah that's right. If God loves me so much that he brought you back to me after all that freaking ordeal then I don't see why God wouldn't give us the kind of life we deserve after all we've been through, right?" I'd pet her and she'd show me how much she agreed with me by swinging her tail and sticking her tongue out. Each time I looked at my dog, grateful beyond the words for having her back, I was reminded of how protected by some Force we seemed to be.

"Don't worry Nel; Rex will be back with us too. Sooner or later; he will. I know you miss him. I do too. Yeah I know."

I'd Rather Die

Working directly with Eduardo on rebuilding things around the house was more challenging than cleaning and organizing everything all by myself. I generally never liked people telling me what to do and I was more than capable of having an attitude if I felt too restricted.

"Oh my god Eduardo give me a break! I'm doing exactly what you've asked me to do. Stop freaking yelling. I can't hold this board much longer. I'm keeping it the way you asked me to. Can you just hurry up?" Verbal altercations became more frequent these days.

"Don't start with this bullshit now. How hard can it be to do this?" Eduardo's usual argument had irritating effect on me.

"Can I just do this myself? It'll be much faster. Come on, I can put these screws in all by myself." I could be just as stubborn as he was and that was the problem. I knew he liked my company but I didn't like being just an assistant. I was getting bored and irritated with watching him do all the work while I'd have to just stand there ready to take the orders:

"Gimme those screws. No, not these! The three inch ones! Come on Elzbieta! I don't have all day for this bullshit! Forget it. I'll get them myself. You and your freaking attitude." He didn't like when people weren't fast enough with reading his mind. Eventually in order not to kill each other we had to come up with a new agreement. Eduardo did the main job with the boy that worked for him and I painted the walls and whatever the two of them had just built. I was at safe distance from less frequent now yelling and screaming accompanied by the noise of saws and drills.

I was almost finished with demolishing the old deck on the other side of the house. Eduardo loved how I came up with the idea of building sort of a shed for the old wood to be recycled in into mulch.

"Can you believe this girl? Look what she did? We don't even have to worry about getting rid of all that old wood anymore. I'm telling you she handles that saw better than most man I know. This girl works better than not just one, but ten men put together. I'm not kidding. She can be moody as hell but she's the best worker I've ever seen. I'll always give her credit for that. She just needs her space which I don't have a problem with 'cause I know things will get done. Look how nice all this looks." Eduardo was showing proudly the yard to his business partner who visited him frequently. Jerry was my most favorite visitor. He was funny and I could always sense appreciation and respect coming from him. I always felt as if he thought very highly of me. He used to like telling me what a positive effect I had on Eduardo and how things became a lot less chaotic since my arrival.

"He needs you. And THIS IS your home. Don't you get it?" He'd say to me if I'd mention the idea of renting a room someplace else when things got "heated" and when I craved a sense of privacy. I liked Eduardo and I was grateful for all his help but there were days when I just wished I could disappear. Physically and emotionally exhausted, I resented Fan sometimes. I was angry that all my money, every single penny of it, was going towards paying off her house. Of course no one was forcing me to do so, but since I gave her my word, to me it meant I had no choice. I couldn't wait to be done with it and so I was pushing myself hard working ten, and sometimes even twelve hours a day. Beside work I had no life whatsoever. No friends, no hobbies nor doing anything just for fun. Drinking coffee at four thirty in the morning was my only leisure time besides falling asleep with a TV on in the late evening. I was feeling better about myself in general though for being so determined. I was proud of myself and my efforts. I liked how I didn't have to ask anyone for money and how completion of my project was in my hands. I loved working hard and I hated it at the same time. I loved myself yet I felt embarrassed of myself as well. Mostly I had a hard time with accepting the fact that I wasn't living the kind of life I wanted to have yet. Trying to constantly come up with some new plan for getting Rex back that would work was constantly on my mind as well.

"I am a beautiful person and if I were a man I'd marry me in a second." I'd tell that to Eduardo but what I was really doing I was telling it to myself. He'd have that complex look on his face as to say:

"She really likes herself. Ha. And she's not shy about it either." He seemed amused with the level of my confidence sometimes. What he didn't know was that my mind was busy with segregating my thoughts such as:

"No, you're not stupid and you're not selfish. You are most definitely not ugly. You are a loving and caring woman that's beautiful inside out. I WOULD marry someone like you in a second. I WOULD want to have someone like you as a friend. I would LOVE to be around you if I were someone else. That's right. I would never want to let go of you. You deserve the best in life. You deserve to be treated with utmost respect. Always. You are sweet and your life needs to be filled with sweetness." I was getting so good at those new inner conversations that sometimes I'd verbalize them at loud.

"I love my own company. I like being around me." I'd say to Eduardo when asked why I wasn't more social with everybody. Nobody beside me knew that I was busy with examining my self-image and with getting to know the woman I was. Slowly and not without making series of mistakes I was becoming my own best friend. The need to stand up for myself was growing inside of me with each day. I felt like in my life I needed to get up and shout:

"Listen everybody; it's my fucking turn to talk! It's my fucking turn to be noticed and to be properly acknowledged. It's my turn to shine. I am not unimportant, insignificant or powerless the way I may have seemed to be. Nobody is going to make me feel like I'm worthless anymore. I'm taking my power back whether you like it or not." I realized that associating with Eduardo was teaching me how not to be afraid of being completely honest and the importance of not keeping everything boiling inside me. I was still trying to learn expressing myself in the most assertive way possible but that wasn't always as easy as it may sound. So the evening when Eduardo asked me to assist him with building the deck I tried telling him that I was tired and that I was done for the day. He was not in a good mood and so he allowed his anger to take control over his emotions. After being screamed and yelled at I told him that I was gonna go to my room anyway.

"Well go fuck yourself then! I don't need your help." He yelled frustrated.

"You know what? I'm just gonna do exactly what you just told me. I'm just gonna go and fuck myself." I answered with a resigning tone. Back in my room I started to browse through Craigslist's rooms/shared ads. I was talking to myself in order not to be scared:

"Nobody's gonna talk to me like this. I don't deserve this. If I continue allowing people treating me disrespectfully things will never change for me. I'll always find myself in situations where I'll feel like there is nothing that I can do to stop people from walking all over me. I know he means no harm with this yelling and screaming but I'm too tired of exposing myself to all this. If it was someone else that I saw being treated this way, especially if it was a child, I would NEVER accept that and I'd never be just OK with that. So why am I OK with this when it comes to me? Why? Why is it OK for anybody to raise their voice at me? How do I give people that permission? If I do that because I'm depending on them then I will make sure that I will never depend on anybody again then. I will rent a room, I will get a better job and I will make sure that no one will even have a chance to disrespect me." I wanted so badly to establish a more healthy sense of boundaries with people that were in my life. I've had improved a lot on letting others know not to cross the line but I still had some learning and work to do when it came to my high tolerance of unacceptable behaviors. The good thing was that the older I was getting, the more sick and tired I was becoming of everything and therefore more determined to make changes. Any kind of fear like being rejected, not approved, being all alone, it had no more power over me. I've been everywhere and I've done everything. I've been on the street and I knew that as uncomfortable as it may have been it did not make me cease to exist. I've been through heartaches and I knew that my heart was still beating for me. Whenever fear would sneak on me causing me to have shortness of breath I learned to make myself stop all the negative thoughts and I'd repeat out loud to myself phrases such as:

"I'd rather die than continue to live in constant fear. I'd rather die than continue to be treated without respect. I do not have to put up with anything I don't want to put up with. I make choices in my life and I choose to be good to myself. I choose to love myself the way I've always wanted to be loved. Life in constant misery it's not suitable to me anymore and so miserable suffering has to end now. It has to go. There is no room for it. Not in here there isn't. Go someplace else. Find someone else to smother. In here there is only space for love and positive energy. If you're not making me happy, whatever you are, you need to stay away from me and you need to exist in different dimension only. It's my life so I make the rules here and in this space and time I create what I like the most and that is a sense of beauty and a sense of harmony."

My Ex's Girlfriend

Eduardo did not like when I told him that I was searching for a new place to live and that I was going to move real soon. He was mad at me for "making issues out of nothing." I was very determined thought and when I noticed that he had cancelled my cell phone line so I couldn't contact potential roommates anymore, I became infuriated. I felt the way I did in the past; trapped.

"I'd rather sleep on the street or on the beach than having to feel imprisoned." I was thinking while realizing that the walls of the small room I was in were "collapsing" on me. I could not bear the feeling of having no other choice but to make peace with Eduardo. I was not going to accept certain things like being yelled at and I knew that he wasn't going to give in either.

"K, let's get the fuck out of here! Right now." It was completely dark outside when I finished with packing my stuff. Eduardo looked surprised and even madder when I handled him the keys. I knew his hostility was his way of protecting his feelings and I didn't really believe when he said that he wasn't going to pay me the seven hundred dollars I've earned. He wasn't that kind of person and I figured he'd give me the money later once he'd cool off. I took my bags and Nel and I headed towards Waikiki. I wasn't sure if Ahmed was still living in "our" place since he had been planning on moving into a one-bedroom apartment.

"God, I hope he's still there." I dragged my small suitcase hoping he wouldn't drive by and see me. I was afraid he'd figure where I was headed and he'd leave the apartment for the whole night on purpose so he wouldn't have to deal with me. At the building I followed some neighbor

to the elevator. I pressed the number seven button not knowing exactly what the rest of the night was going to look like. After reaching the seventh floor I placed the luggage in front of the familiar door. I didn't see Ahmed's van parked downstairs so I knew he wasn't home yet but I knocked few times just in case. The same girl that once said to me: "He's my boyfriend", the one that Ahmed cheated on me with, opened the door.

"Hi, is Ahmed home?" I asked. I knew I looked exhausted and stressed out.

"No, he's not." She answered looking perplexed.

"I'll just wait for him here." I said to her and I sat down on the floor next to my dog and my bags.

"Oh you don't have to wait here. You can wait inside. Come in." She opened the door wide for me. I was surprised by her gesture and I wasn't sure of her intentions. I wasn't going to let her feel pity for me and so I was looking down on her. I sat down on the couch like I owned the place. I lighted my cigarette with a sense of superiority over her expressed in my posture. My mind was generating thoughts like:

"You may have him but you're still nobody. I may be in a tough situation right now but I will overcome this soon like I always do. You instead will never be not even half of the person and woman I am."

"Can I say something to you?" She interrupted my thoughts with a question that was formed in a shy manner.

"Sure, go ahead." I answered still feeling superior on purpose.

"I just wanted you to know that I am really sorry for what happened. I mean it. I really did not know at first that you guys were still together. When I first met Ahmed he told me that you guys were not together anymore and that you were just living in his apartment as a roommate. And then when I saw you that day downstairs and how hurt you looked I felt so bad. And then I felt so stupid for believing everything he told me. I just really wanted you to know that I still cannot forgive myself for what you went through because of me." I sat there listening to her words more in disbelief than when she told me to come in earlier. She looked insecure and her body language assumed apologetic tinge. She continued to amaze me with her warm and welcoming response to me and my situation:

"Oh no, you won't have to stay at the office. You'll stay here with us. Don't worry, I'll talk to him. He may think and act like he's in charge but he knows that in reality he can get away only as much as we're willing to put up with it. You know him, you've been with him. You know what

I'm talking about." The next couple of hours we sat on the couch, smoking cigarettes and laughing about ourselves and our common denominator; Ahmed. It was pretty amazing how fast we dropped our guards and how we weren't withholding anything.

"You know, I freaking hated you and I wished that you would rot in hell. And that day I really wanted to punch you in your face." I said to her.

"I don't blame you. I'd probably feel the same way if I were you." She answered.

"You know Elzbieta? One thing you should know is that the way I feel is that Ahmed never loved me or anyone else the way he loved you. He really, really loved you. He was like freaking obsessed with you or something. He never really got over you and on some level I don't think he ever will. And I'm OK with that. I mean look at you! How could I compete with someone who's so freaking gorgeous, so fun to be around and so smart? I may be many things but I'm not delusional." She continued.

"You're way too sweet." I said to her trying not to show too much how content her words were making me feel.

"No, I mean it. He would never stop talking about you. Even when I first met him and when he lied to me that you guys had broken up, he'd never shut up and he'd always wanted to talk about you. Elzbieta this, Elzbieta that, Elzbieta's writing a book, blah blah blah. I was sick and tired of it. I remember when he showed me your website I just went like: oh yeah, she's pretty. And then he was like; she's gonna sell her book and it's gonna be big and I told him: it's not like its Harry Potter or anything. Honestly, I was just freaking so jealous of you. I mean come on; you're beautiful, you want to help the world and you're writing a freaking book that I know if you really want to, you'll make it a bestseller. You're so freaking determined. You don't give up. You're so inspiring. You give me hope just by being here. You really have this kind of impact on people and you don't even seem to realize that."

"Wow! You really know how to make people feel good about themselves. I can see how Ahmed would not want to let go of you. I remember he used to tell me repeatedly how he was gonna go to Egypt and how he was gonna find himself a nice Muslim girl. So how is it that man like him finds what he's been looking for without even leaving the city? Just like that. I thought you were just some trashy girl but you're not at all what I thought you were. Not even close. You're kind, you're hilariously funny, you seem to truly care about him AND you are Muslim exactly like he wanted you to be. Honestly he's stupid for not having married you yet.

I'd marry you in a second if I were him. You know what I'm gonna do? I'm gonna do exactly the same thing he did; I'm gonna obsess about the kind of man I want in my life, I'll may even talk about it like he used to talk about his freaking " nice Muslim girl" until I'll finally meet that guy. If someone like him can go out there and get exactly what he's looking for then I don't see why it should be different for me." I was getting all excited by how enlightened I was feeling thanks to my ex and his girlfriend. It still hurt to know that I had been rejected but now I had medicine for my pain. Now I knew exactly how to go about it and I wasn't feeling hopeless anymore.

Ahmed was very uncomfortable with me staying there and thank goodness he kept busy working long hours. I enjoyed his girlfriend's company a lot more when he wasn't around. We had fun trying her outfits for my new job interview at one of the designer boutiques. She seemed real excited when I came home announcing:

"I got that job!"

"I told you, you would! What did I tell you? You walk in there with this kind of confidence, looking like this and they'll hire you in a spot. Now you won't have to work for ten bucks an hour anymore. You'll make good money there, I'm telling you. I used to make so much commission when I used to work in the boutique that's not even funny. In good season I used to bring like five thousand dollars a month. And you're gonna meet tons of nice guys there, you'll see. You'll find your dream husband in no time." Her excitement was very contagious. I didn't mind anymore than the main reason she was so happy for me was that I wasn't going to be a threat to her once I'd find someone. I was beginning to feel not only relieved but very optimistic. I was proud of myself that out of numerous applicants, after passing several tests that the company used in screening their potential employees, I was one of the selected ones for the new job. I had collected my money from Eduardo after he had emailed me about it asking when I was coming over. When I went there he was being nice to me again even though he was trying to make a point that it was all my fault:

"What pissed me off was when you said that you were working and that you were on the clock when we went for a ride with the dogs. I mean, I treat you with a nice meal at that restaurant and you got the guts to tell me that you were on the clock and you think I should pay you for that? No way in hell will I do that." I let him vent at me knowing that getting into debate would make no sense.

"Look, whatever happened, happened. You still have your job here so why don't you just pack your things and tell your ex and his girlfriend that you don't need to stay there anymore." He said.

"No, I don't wanna find myself in that situation ever again. And you and I know that we'd be fighting again if I'd move back here." I answered.

"People fight, so what? It's normal. Don't make a big deal out of it. Well, whatever you decide just know that you'll always have a job here and that room will always be yours."

"K, thanks Eduardo. I'm gonna get a new cell phone and I'm gonna email you my new number. Please call me when you get my new driver's license in the mail, OK?" I said goodbye and I went back to my new life.

It was my first day at my new job and I was super excited. I recognized few faces of the other applicants that were hired as well. In my mind I tried finding the reasons for which many others were not chosen. Apparently everybody felt similar way because phrases like "Oh so they picked you too" were circulating the conference room we were gathered in. After receiving the welcoming booklets and after listening to a lecture of what to expect, each of us was called separately to an office to fill out the papers.

"OK, I'm not sure if this temporary driver's license extension will work to be honest with you. I'm gonna check with the supervisor but honestly I think that most likely you'll just gonna have to wait 'till the actual driver's license arrives in the mail. You're gonna have to come back with the actual driver license. Then we'll be able to file all those papers. I can't really let you work until then. Sorry." The young manager talked real fast without realizing that with each his world my whole world was shrinking again.

The atmosphere at the apartment was also getting heavy since Ahmed started disliking how much time his girlfriend and I were spending together. He started to demand from her to follow him everywhere. When we were alone, she told me that he was convinced that the reason I was there, was that I was still interested in being with him. I felt annoyed and irritated in his presence. The more he was trying to control his girlfriend the more relieved I was that I wasn't with him anymore. For the first time in a long time I started to feel that comfortable feeling that comes with knowing that the rejection you had to endure for so long was over since you didn't give a damn anymore about the person that had rejected you. It was a good feeling and it was growing in its intensity with each passing day. I was finally healing. I could finally see clearly the end of my agony. I knew I owed that to this "nice Muslim girl" and I felt grateful towards her more than she realized. Whatever her real intentions may have been, she had helped me with building up my torn self-esteem in such a short time. But then, the awkward evenings when I started to hear her crying, begun:

"Oh my god! You're still in love with her! You hear that Elzbieta? You hear what's going on? My boyfriend still has feelings for you! Tell her! Tell her that! Tell'er in front of me! Tell'er that you're still in love with her and that really you'd rather be with her! Come on, go ahead! You two have this powerful history and you're better together anyway." Ahmed was real good at making things to appear in a certain way and I knew that the creation of the latest drama was his way of making sure that I'd leave before I'd even start my new job and before I'd even have a chance on saving some money for rent.

THE *One*

I moved temporarily back to Eduardo's house. I started to work again there but I was not hiding the fact that my search for a room was not over. Now that I had my own cell phone I felt in control the way I wanted to be. My sister Monika lent me some money again so I could get back on my feet as soon as possible. I found a tiny room in a crowded house for six hundred dollars a month that allowed dogs. I moved in the same day I found it. The room was big just enough to contain a single size bed, a dresser with a small TV on it and even smaller refrigerator. The remaining walking space between the bed and the wall was literally two feet wide. My new numerous roommates were all pretty much in their late twenties so the atmosphere in the back yard was always energetic. One of them had decided that I had lots in common with her bartender coworker and since I wanted to do more than just thinking and talking about meeting my ideal man, I agreed to go with her to that bar.

"How old is he?" I asked my roommate to make sure I wasn't wasting my time.

"Thirty something. I think he may be thirty two or thirty three." She answered.

"A little bit young but I can give a try." I said.

"Oh I'm telling you, he's just what you said you're looking for. He's serious, considerate, he's a one woman man, he wants to start a family like you do and he's real cute too. You'll see. You guys will really fit well together. He's sweet, he's been looking for a woman like you who knows exactly what she wants. He knows martial arts the way you like, telling you I feel that you two may even end up getting married. I wouldn't be too surprised if you did." She got me all excited with how strong she believed in being a perfect matchmaker. I took a shower and scrubbed all the spotted paint that was on my body from working at Eduardo's house all day long. I styled my hair and I put some make up on. I chose a black top and a pair of blue jeans to wear. I wanted to look sexy but casual. I didn't want to look like I was trying too hard to impress anyone. I was feeling nervous though. I was thinking:

"Oh god, what if I'm just about to meet the man that could turn out to be THE ONE?"

"Daaaamn you look hot girl!" Accustomed to see me with my hair up, always wearing some old clothes covered in paint and muddy dirt, my roommate looked very surprised when I stood in front of her and asked her:

"Ready?"

"K, let's go! Oh this is gonna be fun. I can already see the looks on my colleagues' faces when we get there. Ha ha! Can't wait." She sounded almost mischievous in how much fun she was having. At the bar heads turned into our direction the way they usually did when I walked into similar establishments. I refrained myself on purpose from looking too eagerly to find out who was behind the bar serving the drinks. My roommate and I sat on the tall chairs and we waited for the bartender to finish serving some girls that looked like they were in their early twenties. They seemed totally taken by his charming personality. I knew that he had already noticed me because just like I did, he looked as if he was trying to keep it cool. Discrete smile on his face, and not as secretive as intended looks exchanged between the workers, told me that he did not expect me to be that attractive. He finally approached us in a nonchalant way. My roommate introduced us and for a moment we just kept staring at each other, both smiling uncontrollably. My mouth opened and questions like: "Sooo, how did YOU ended up in Hawaii? Where were you before?" quickly evolved into "What are your dreams? What kind of life would you like, where and how exactly would you like to live your life if money wasn't an issue?"

"Ha ha! You don't waste your time, do you?" He smiled.

"Nope. I'm almost thirty four years old and I decided to be more direct than I used to be to save myself some time with all this. You have a problem with that?" I asked.

"Nope. Not at all. I actually find it amusing." He flirted back with me. From the way he filled my glass with wine up to its edges I could tell he did not want me to leave.

"Sooo, what do you think of him?" My roommate could not wait to hear my opinion.

"Oh yeah he's cute, I like him. He really seems like he's a real nice guy. If he wasn't hiding behind that stupid baseball hat he'd actually look very handsome. He kind of reminds me of Richard Geer. Doesn't he look a little bit like him with that dip in his chin?" I said to her while he was busy serving other clients and she agreed.

The next day my roommate asked me if she could give to the guy my phone number. Apparently he wanted to get to know me better. He called me later asking if I'd go out with him.

"Look, I work ten hours a day without taking days off and so I'm usually super tired when I get home. On top of everything I stepped on a nail at work and my foot hurts so I'd honestly prefer to just stay home. If you want you can just come over here and we can just hang out in the back yard." I said to him. It was dark outside when he showed up. He brought a bottle of wine with him. I was still in my work clothes and my foot was wrapped in some old cloth. I figured if he was going to last he had to like me for who I was and not just for what I looked like. He was good looking and fun to be around but my biggest concern was to find out if he was also a deep person. The evening passed in a relaxing atmosphere. I liked the guy a lot actually and I could see him fitting into my "big picture".

In many ways we seemed to have similar way of thinking, which was a good thing. I was having good time with him and I agreed to take a taxi to go to his place. He was a gentleman and eating pizza while watching TV was the only thing we did. We both looked comfortable lying on the couch. Not too much talking this time, no cross examining, just being there in the moment and laughing at loud at the TV show's characters. This went on for another week. I'd look at him in silence and I'd wonder if I indeed met THAT guy. I needed to be a hundred percent sure of it before I could allow myself not only to have sex with him but also to open up emotionally towards him. The only way I could think of measuring this guy's inner depth in a short time like this was for me to find out if he'd be willing to sacrifice his freedom and if he'd be willing to marry someone who needed a green card. I needed to know that such man would be able to do that for me. It was my way of making sure that whenever we'd get in a fight I'd never have to hear him saying to me: "You only married me for papers." This guy was pretty much everything I wanted a guy to be but was he also an old soul like me and would he do the right thing even if that would present him with inconvenience? I didn't doubt that if I dated him long enough that I had what it took to make him go down on his one knee and ask me if I'd marry him. Somehow I felt that if I just told him straight forward about my legal status and my need to take care of it pretty much right away that he wouldn't be there for me. Having that impression didn't make me feel good and so one day I did tell him what kind of situation I was in. I took the taxi back home while trying to guess:

"Do you think he'll call tomorrow? Hmmm.....I vote he won't." I was right but I sure wasn't going to cry about it. I knew he could not have been The One.

The days were passing as usual and other than seeing the progress in making smaller the amount owed on Fan's house in Kenya with each payment, the life just seemed dull.

"Hey girl, you wanna go to a land blessing ceremony with me on Sunday? There's gonna be lots of interesting people there." Linda asked me over the phone.

"Well, I'd have to take a day off but I guess it wouldn't hurt me to get out of the house for fun for a change I guess." I answered.

"What have you been up to? Are you still working for Eduardo? You never call me. What's wrong with you? " She inquired.

"Nothing, I've just been feeling super tired. Just working every day and not doing anything else. There is no time or money to do anything else." I answered.

"What do you do with all the money you make?" She always insisted in knowing everything.

"What money? There is rent to be paid and don't even get me started on how ridiculously expensive the food here in Hawaii is." I complained. I wasn't going to explain to her that in order to save everything I could for Africa I was making some huge sacrifices.

Putting a picture of some good looking guy as my wallpaper on my desktop was not enough to let the Universe know that I was ready to receive what was righteously mine. So I took the day off and I got all ready to meet Linda who was coming to pick me up. I styled my hair and I put some make up on the same way I did when I went out to meet that bartender. I wore the same outfit but this time I got more braved and I put my high heels on. Since the evenings in March were still not as hot as I'd prefer, I decided to take my black leather jacket with me as well.

"K, he better be there! God, I mean it. This man I've been looking for better be at this event we're going to. I'm sick and tired of waiting for that day. I'm sick and tired of turning my head when I see a tall guy to see if he's not the one by any chance, OK God? Come on Angels, do whatever you've got to do and whisper into his ears that he has to go to that land blessing event." I was talking to myself while waiting for Linda who wasn't showing up or picking up her phone.

"Great. I took a day off and I got all dressed up for nothing! No, you know what? I am meeting this man and I am meeting him today! Come on Nel, let's go to Waikiki!" With Nel running next to me I was ridding the bike towards the ocean. I was still pissed with Linda for standing me up when I heard a loud honking. It was her driving towards my place. I stopped and she pulled over turning to the next street.

"Where're you going? I'm coming to pick you up." She yelled.

"Yeah you were supposed to pick me up like two hours ago. You weren't coming so I wasn't gonna waste my day." I answered still irritated.

"Come on, let's go. We're late for the ceremony. Sorry I got held with my girlfriend." She apologized and I threw the bike in the back of her truck.

"You look good today." She noticed.

"Thanks. I'm ready to meet that husband of mine." I smiled.

"You and your man hunt. K, you wanna drop your bike off first?" She asked me.

"Yes please." I answered getting excited that my day wasn't going to get wasted after all.

"Listen, after we drop your bike I just have to stop in Waikiki to pick up my friend." She informed me.

"Sure no problem." I said.

"My friend Patrick, I'm telling you this guy's such a nice guy. He's not good looking or anything but he's a real sweetheart. He's one of the nicest people I've ever known. He's been helping me so much and he never wants anything in return. And he's good, like with everything. He knows how to fix cars, he's been helping me with computer stuff, there's just nothing he doesn't know how to do. And he's a real gentleman." Linda kept talking as usual and I kept quietly smoking my cigarettes. I tried not to think too much what the moment was going to feel like when we'd finally arrive at the event and when a tall muscular man would approach me with that look on his face; "Where the hell have you been hiding all my life?"

"He's been staying at a friend's boat." Linda kept interrupting my thinking.

"What? Who you're talking about?" I did not like being brought back to the reality.

"Patrick. My friend. The guy we're going to pick up. Get out of your dream land." She scolded me with her disapproving look.

"Don't worry, I'll find you a rich guy to marry. That's not hard at all, that's easy. You just need to get out of the house more. There are millions of good looking wealthy guys that would marry you in a second. You have no problems girl. You're freaking gorgeous, you still look like a model for god's sake. Did you look at yourself in the mirror this morning? You know I don't get you. You act sometimes like a fish out of water when there is really nothing you should worry about. When I was your age and I was still pretty I had the world at my feet. You need to learn more how to use your beauty girl." Linda kept preaching me the way she always liked doing. We finally reached the pier. She used her cell phone to let her friend know that we were there. Immediately after that a dark silhouette emerged from one of the numerous boats that were in front of us. A guy that could be in his late thirties approached our vehicle. He had dark hair that were thinned on top and a goatee that partially covered his serious looking face. He was wearing a pair of blue jeans and a black long sleeve shirt that had slim white stripes on it. His shoulders were wide and a bit hunched forward. His pace was fast and decisive.

"Oh wow. He's not THAT bad looking." The thought that immediately popped in my mind surprised me. I could not understand why I would be intrigued so much by this man. He looked like he wasn't more than six foot tall and I specifically asked God for a man that was at least six foot four inches in height. I've always wanted my man to be much taller than me. I wanted him to have to lean towards me in order to kiss me.

Patrick did have that darkness about him which I liked a lot. The lines on his face seemed to be aligning in such way that was revealing a strong character. He looked like someone who was quiet but who could be real stubborn if he had good reasons for it. He's full red lips had a visible scar that was extending towards the goatee. Noticeably missing third tooth had to be the reason for which his smile seemed restrained. What I was taken the most by was how he seemed to smile more with his eyes than anything else. The prominent lines in the corner of his eyes and the warmth coming from that direction were giving this man a complex look. His overall appearance could be best described as someone who could be real dangerous if he wanted to but at the same time you could tell that unless you were a bad guy you had nothing to worry about.

The Deal

Patrick did not behave like most men when they met with me. He did not look surprised to see how pretty I was nor did he seem taken by me which I found extremely irritating. He did not look like some guys that tried hiding their impression on purpose either. Nor did he look like those who were not even daring to think that I'd be interested in them. He looked "neutral" and I did not like that. He was igniting curiosity in me making me feel like I almost disliked him for that. I felt annoyed by him not knowing exactly why. He didn't seem intimidated by me so what was his problem? I knew I did not look or act superficial so why was this guy acting like he didn't care if I was there or not?

"Patrick, why don't you show Elzbieta how the boat looks inside?" Linda suggested.

"K." That's' all he had to say; K!

"Whatever. I don't give a damn about the boat." I thought to myself.

"Come on Elzbieta, go see how it looks inside." Linda insisted.

"Fine." Was all what I had to say. I waited for Patrick to open the gate. I followed him to the boat and then I went inside. The place looked messy and disorganized.

"This is where you live?" I realized I sounded snobby.

"Yes ma'am." He answered.

"OK, well, let's go." I rushed him impatient to meet the man of my dreams that could be on his way to that land blessing ceremony. In the truck the three of us were talking small talks. Patrick wasn't saying a lot. I could not understand why I wanted so much for him to like me. In general I grew out of the need to be approved by everyone. Being in my thirties I had no problem with being disliked and I had even less issue with showing others how I felt if I wasn't a big fan of somebody either.

I knew very well how to ignore somebody and unlike in my early twenties I did not feel bad about it. So why did I keep having the feeling that this man should like me? Why did I care so much what he thought of me? Usually if a man didn't seem to be particularly paying attention to me, even if I did find him intriguing, I'd just automatically disregard him completely. I had always been against women chasing after men. In my opinion it was men's job to proceed with courtship and not vice versa. As opened minded as I perceived myself to be I still cherished some values that could be considered more conservative or even old fashion.

"Can we stop at McDonald real quick? I'm so freaking hungry that by the time we get there I'm gonna pass out." I asked. When we parked the car Patrick jumped out of it in a hurry. Before I even got the chance to do it myself he opened the door for me. He stood there with his arm extended towards me and his eyes focused entirely on me. I felt very pleasantly surprised. I got out of the car and that same "kundulini" feeling I had earlier when the thought "He's not THAT bad looking" popped into my mind, was now making me experience the "goose bumps" again. The impression that came more from within than anything else was telling me:

"If I were with this man, I'd be treated like a princess." His gesture felt nothing similar to the ones made by players. There was an aura of trust that Patrick's eyes and his body language were exhibiting. The respect he conducted himself with appeared to have more to do with than just being raised right. It was emanating from deep inside of him. He was no doubt a real gentleman. I stood in line waiting for my cheeseburger enjoying the fact that a strong man was standing right next to me.

"Hmm…Naah. There's definitely something about Patrick that draws me towards him but I don't think he's the one. Nah. He's not as tall and he lives on a boat for god's sake. Well that does make him kind of mysterious. Yeah but no, I don't think so. But why do I feel like I want him in my life? Maybe because he seems to be such a good person? That could be it. I think I just want to have a good friend like him in my life. Yeah I think that's what it is. Definitely." I was thinking to myself while trying to be discrete with scrutinizing my "new friend". I paid for my order and I waited for Patrick to complete his. Back in the car after eating while driving everybody seemed to had satisfied their hunger except for me.

"Here, have my apple pie. I'm not gonna eat it." Patrick handled the sweet to me and again that same warmth descended on my body.

"Hmm. I think he does like me." I thought while eating the desert.

"Finally, we're almost there. Listen guys I need to stop at my friend's house to feed my dogs." Linda announced in her usual "got to do this, got to do that", "I'm over the place" manner.

"Patrick you won't mind doing that for me while I'm taking care of some stuff inside the house, right?" She asked with that expecting attitude of hers.

"No ma'am I won't mind at all." He answered. I liked how when Linda disappeared inside the house that there were just the two of us; him and I.

"Oh god they're so cute! Are all these dogs Linda's? Does she live here?" I asked Patrick.

"Yeah, she's staying with her friend 'cause her old place got flooded recently." He explained to me.

"So, what do you do here besides working for this guy that likes to scream from time to time?" He asked jokingly.

"What do I do here? Nothing. Just live here like everybody else." I answered still feeling the need to remain reserved.

"I mean; how did you end up here in the US?" He continued with a look of an interrogator who was questioning an international spy.

"I used to work for CIA." Irritated with his "I know better than that..." attitude I remained all serious. I did not feel like telling him about modeling, visas or anything about my past for that matter.

"So what exactly did you do in Iraq and Afghanistan?" I changed the subject.

"You mean when I was in the Navy? Well, I was on submarine and I did different things but most recently I was there mostly as a sniper." He answered.

"You mean you were shooting at people from the distance?" I asked curious.

"Yeap. Well, only at the bad guys." He explained.

"That sounds kind of cool. Why did you get out of the Navy?"

"Got tired of killing people."

"Did you kill lots of them?"

"Plenty enough." He sighed.

"Still have nightmares at night. I don't sleep well." He added.

"Why? Cause you feel bad about it? You shouldn't. Sometimes you got to do what you got to do. Who knows, maybe because of your courage and your sacrifice I'm still here. You shouldn't focus on negative. I know I feel sometimes like I wish I had license to kill. I have an anger issue in case you didn't noticed." I laughed. He smiled all the way with his eyes.

"Well, I'm actually over my anger by now. Nothing really gets me anymore. I've seen and I've done enough." I didn't like how mysterious he sounded. I thought it was his way of trying to impress me.

"Nobody's ever anger free. Not completely at least. I don't think so. Nel, tell 'em that; he's full of it." I answered annoyed. Nel started to punt with excitement as she did every time I gave her my attention. Linda had finally finished whatever she was doing and we drove to the event. She was going to take some pictures for the guy that organized this ceremony and she asked Patrick to take some shots of the whole land from the nearby mountain.

"It's like you'll be doing your old job except you'll be shooting with camera." She teased him. The ceremony was interesting with all different Hawaiian priests dressed in colorful togas and wearing different in size and colors leis. Some natives were performing exotic dance, some guests were giving some speeches, and other people were busy preparing the food stand. None of all this was getting my full attention thought. My eyes were scanning left to right for that dream man of mine. Could he be among the guests or could he be one of those half naked natives that were flexing their muscles in the rhythm of music? I was getting more and more frustrated realizing that I wasn't finding him.

"I'm gonna go get something to eat. Did you want anything?" I asked Patrick. Linda was lost among people attempting to take interesting pictures.

"No thank you. I'm not hungry. I'll keep an eye on Nel for you." He offered.

"Are you sure?"

"Yeap. I'm positive." He replied.

"OK, fine. I'll be back." I walked towards the tables and I stood in line that started to form rapidly. I picked two plastic plates, instead of just one, thinking:

"I don't believe his not hungry." The food looked delicious and the verity of it was quite impressing. Fresh and grilled vegetables, different kinds of salads, coleslaw, fresh mozzarella, pastas, mashed potatoes with gravy, meat, fresh fruit and cakes, all this sure looked appetizing. I was

410

headed with two full plates towards where Patrick was sitting when Linda showed up in front of me.

"Oh thanks." She grabbed one of the plates without even asking assuming it was for her.

"What the hell? Oh well I'll share mine with him." I didn't want to verbalize my thoughts at loud.

"Come on, eat some. I brought it for all of us." I insisted and Patrick gave in my persuasiveness. Linda took some pictures of us while we were eating and laughing. I was very comfortable in the presence of this former soldier. I liked his sense of humor and I definitely liked how safe he made me feel. I started noticing that he was enjoying my company just as much.

"I'm gonna get some more food." I went back to the line. Some ladies in their sixties started to show their curiosity:

"Are you a model?"

"Nooo." I didn't like people asking me this question.

"You look like you could be. You look like those girls from magazines. Tall and skinny, nice hair, beautiful face." Their compliments were making me uncomfortable.

"I'm too old to be a model." I said hoping they would drop the subject. A tall, African-American woman pointed her index towards me:

"Listen to me my dear. Don't ever think or say to anyone that you are too old or too anything. You are a creature of God that made you perfect the way you are. Embrace the beauty he gave you. Don't be shy about it! He made you gorgeous for a reason. If you're saying you're too old to be considered pretty then where the heck the rest of us fit in?" The women nodded their heads. We stood their talking and joking while waiting for the line to move forward. Later I was sitting and eating with Patrick when that same woman who pointed her finger at me called me:

"Hey, there you are. I wanted to talk to you for a moment, if you don't mind. Let's go somewhere more quiet, shall we?" I agreed and I told Patrick I'd be right back. We walked away from the crowd and we sat down on the ground by some old and rusty trailer. The woman lighted her cigarette and I did light mine too. She looked very sympathetic and almost comical with her full of energy; "I don't care what others may have think of me", "I'll tell you what's been bugging me," kind of personality.

"So, ever since you said that you were too old to be a model I had this strange urge to talk to you. I've been having this strange feeling that I have some message for you even thought I don't know what that would be." She started talking while clearly enjoying the sensation that the nicotine was giving to her.

"What is it that you want in life? What is it that you've been looking for and you feel like you can't get it no matter how hard you try?" She asked.

"Right now?" I paused to buy some time.

"Of course right now. Not when you dead. What is it that's missing in your life?" She insisted impatiently.

"A husband. I seem unable to attract the kind of man I want." I answered.

"My dear, you need to stop wasting your time with wrong people. There is nothing that God and Universe won't give you if you take your time to ask for it. I did that; I asked God when I was already in my late forties. Sick and tired of wasting my youth with some morons, one day I finally sat down and I wrote a letter to God/Universe, whatever you wanna call it. I wrote in that letter everything I wanted in my husband. I wrote everything that mattered to me the most. What kind of relationship I wanted to have with him. How I wanted both of us to be able to grow spiritually together and to push ourselves to have the most amazing life that we were meant to have together. Someone compatible with me and someone who'd be on the same page with me, you know what I mean? Shortly after I wrote that letter I met my husband and it's been everything I wanted it to be. And you my dear need to do the same thing. When you go home you need to sit down and you need to write that letter. I'm gonna give you my address and you're gonna mail it to me. In six months I'm gonna mail it back to you. You'll be married by then to that man you've been looking for, take my word for it." She sounded really convincing. I agreed to do what she told me to. Patrick and I left the party in Linda's truck. We went to the place where she was staying and we waited for her there. She was coming later with some friend. It was dark outside and sitting in the car felt actually quite romantic.

"So, what's your legal status here in US?" Just like that, the way nobody did before, Patrick asked me about my papers situation. I looked at him surprised.

"*Should I tell him the truth just like that or should I change the subject? Did Linda opened her big mouth and started telling everyone that I needed a green card?*" Different thoughts were creating different feelings inside of me. Anger and frustration were one of them. I trusted Patrick by now and I knew he wasn't the kind of person that would ever use such information against me. Nevertheless anger was boiling within me because of my inability of changing the compromising position I found myself in for so many years. Eduardo's and Linda's yakking about it every time they got a chance wasn't making me feel any better. I didn't like how others seemed to like talking about it as if they liked comparing themselves to me glad that they didn't have to be in my shoes. I was fed up with making others feel better with that.

"Did Linda say something to you?" I asked in reply. I was ready to start cursing.

"No, why?" His answer calmed me down a little bit.

"Ah." I looked at him like I wanted to figure everything that was there to figure about this man.

"Why, are you offering?" Even thought I was smiling I still looked like I meant business.

"Ah…That wasn't why I asked."

"Oh." I was ready to give up there.

"But I wouldn't be totally opposed to that. As a matter of fact I may be able to help you with that." He answered smiling back at me. I leaned back towards the window to have a better vision and to make sure that what I was hearing wasn't just some guy's clever way of getting to my pants.

"Well, you know if we got married I wouldn't have sex with you right?" I wanted to make sure he knew where I was standing.

"You don't need to tell me that, I know that already." He answered still smiling.

"Then why would you wanna go through such inconvenience?" I insisted in knowing his real motives.

"Is it that hard to believe that I just feel like helping you?" He answered my question with a question. His eyes were sparkling from the amusement he seemed to be experiencing on my expense.

"Well, you know what? I could pay you like a thousand bucks a month for this favor until we'd get divorced." I said while watching his face that was getting serious and almost mean looking.

"Look, I'd never do that. I'd never take advantage of you like that. If I'd marry you I'd do that because I know you need help with staying legally in this country. I'd never ask you for anything in return. That is not who I am." I listened to his words and I wondered:

"Wow, is it possible that I am looking at the man that I have been longing for all this time? Could it be that I had finally found him? Could it be that my desire for it as well as the urging circumstances had finally led me to this moment? Like in movies, could I end up marring him just for papers and then madly fell in love with this man that was willing to do the right thing just to make things easier for me? My intuition is telling me that he is going to be in my life one way or the other. Is it possible that my heart is trying to tell me something that is completely against what my mind has been conspiring? But he's not as tall...I know I could get over that but how will I know if I'd fell in love with him for real? How will I know if I did fell in love with him, that my feelings weren't just the result of gratitude? And what if that even was the case? Who's there to say what really love is? Who's there to dictate me how, when and in what manner should I or should I not love somebody? I've had already given up the idea that I would get married only when I'd have my house, my money and all that. Why could I not give up the thought that the way I fall in love has to be in a certain way? And what way would that be? Does it have to be a rich man that smashes his Mercedes into my beaten up automobile like it happened many times in those Harlequin books I loved reading so much when I was fifteen? Would he have to take me to his mansion and make all my troubles go away once and for all? Would that be considered real love then? Because he's successful, capable and all that, would this prove that my love for him cannot be anything else but genuine?

"Let's do it then. Let's get married." I said to Patrick knowing that he wasn't going to back up with his "proposal".

Chatting

Linda finally showed up with some old woman and she told us to have patience with her while she still had some business to discus.

"You two look too comfortable." She said looking surprised at my feet resting on Patrick's lap. He was massaging them gently and I was feeling relaxed. Both of us didn't feel like there was anything to be explained. She went inside the house with her friend and Patrick and I continued having fun with our "deal making".

"So, you know INS will ask us all kinds of questions to see if we are married in a legitimate way, if we have sex and all that. We're gonna have to not only live together but we're gonna have to know everything that we need to know about each other. We're gonna have to look like a real couple." I said and he agreed.

"How long have you been living on that boat?" I asked.

"For a month." He replied.

"Where were you before that?"

"In prison."

"You've been to prison?"

"I spent a year in jail." He tried reading my facial expressions.

"For what?" I asked.

"Sexual assault." He hesitated.

"I'm on probation for having sex with a fifteen year old girl." He added slowly as if he was completely afraid to see my reaction.

"Gee. That's some serious situation you're in. And I thought my life sucked. Well, this is gonna be more interesting than I thought." I smiled and I saw relief in his eyes. I didn't feel like cross-examining him for anything. I didn't feel like he owed me any explanations.

"You know what, I'll just give you copy of my book to read so I won't have to tell you all my life story. And we'll just take one day at the time." I added. We continued talking and laughing without even thinking about Linda's making us wait for her to give us a ride back to Honolulu. I found out that he'd been married three times and he had two biological children and one that he raised as own that lived in mainland. He was only two years older than I, and I wasn't hiding from him that some choices he made in his life weren't always the best in my opinion. But who was I to judge? My life was full of poor choices I made. Blaming my circumstances for it was no longer in my style. I had learn that seeing things exactly for what they were and not making big fuss about it (fully accepting it in other words) was the best thing I could do for myself. And if I was able to embrace my own mistakes I sure could do the same when it came to Patrick. He was kind and thoughtful the way few people I had pleasure meeting with and that was more important to me than anything else. Even though I knew him for few hours only I felt safe with him more than I felt safe with anybody else before. He gave me that feeling that consciously or subconsciously he would do nothing to harm me nor would he try to get "even" with me if things didn't work out between us. I've been craving such feeling for as long as I could remember. My trust in people and faith in their goodness had been compromised more than once and to be able to have such emotion again was more than just refreshing. To make things very clear; I'm not referring to a niceness of people who remain civil with you for as long as you comply with them and for as long as you keep fulfilling their expectations. I'm talking about real kindness that remains such no matter what. In my eyes Patrick had that quality and I knew that I would not be willing to let go of him because of it even if things got difficult. I could somewhat see how not much different from mine his life was one big mess. It didn't take me long to figure out that his big heart and as Linda had put it; "his sweetheart personality" had made him vulnerable and predisposed to being taken advantage of by others. I decided I'd be there for him no matter what just like he was willing to be there for me. I didn't know exactly how challenging things would turn out and that I'd be put through series of tests. It started with him saying to me:

"I will do what I said I would to help you but it may take a little bit of time. My last wife and I had been separated for two years now and she's been back in mainland but I still have to check if our divorce was ever finalized." He informed me and I sensed troubles.

"Don't worry, I'll take care of it. Worst case scenario I'll file for a divorce again. I don't think she's gonna come all the way here to contest it and I think I should be able to get it by default." Maybe he didn't know or he didn't want to believe that there would be numerous things she'd try to do in attempt to turn his life into a living hell like it wasn't already where he was. I had a feeling that we'd go through some headaches before we could get married. The way I tried looking at it was: what better way could there be to get to know each other and to perhaps even measure our feelings in case those did develop in the curse of all this? I still was going to send that letter addressed to the Power of The Universe but now I was hoping than this would just assure me that Patrick was indeed the right man for me and that I wasn't making a big mistake by marring him in such a hurry. I was hoping that all this would turn out into a romantic tale. I wanted God/Universe/Angles to guide me through all this and I promised that in return I'd follow my heart/feelings more than my mind and its ideas of how things should or shouldn't be.

"Tell me, what makes you think that I deserve to be helped?" I asked Patrick to see what he thought of me.

"Really? You're gonna sit here and try telling me that you don't know how great you are. I saw you in the car with Linda and I thought you were a pretty girl. Yeah I did notice that. Not exactly the type I'd normally go for but that didn't change the fact that I knew you were good looking. The more you started talking and the more I watched you I realized that your beauty is transcending from within you. You are more beautiful inside that you even are outside. To watch you being the way you are; very simple and natural and so comfortable with yourself it's a very pleasant thing. I have no doubt in my mind that you're physical beauty could never be compared to the beauty that you have inside. It shows. It gives you that glow that you don't see that often in people." While trying not to enjoy too much what he was saying in order not to have my judgment obscured I was looking closely into his eyes to see whether he meant everything and whether he wasn't just exaggerating on purpose. I was looking for what I've always looked for in people; sincerity. I've had been manipulated endless amount of times just like I've had used this primitive tool more than once in getting what I wanted. By now, even though mostly instinctively, I wasn't as bad at discovering real motives behind someone's act. I wasn't as eager to blindly believe people as I used to.

On the Boat

The next day I agreed to meet Patrick at the boat that he was staying. On my bike with Nel running next to me I headed towards Waikiki's pear. It was after 6 p.m. and I was still wearing my work clothes. I never went home to take a shower. I was excited and curious to see whether I'd still be intrigued by this man once I'd get to know him closer. I was feeling like a little girl riding her bike towards the newest adventure. Nel seemed just as excited as I was. I was trying to foresee whether Patrick inspired by my visit would have cleaned up his mess. I was passing by impatiently the numerous tourist/pedestrians who were giving me curious looks, some commenting on how cute my dog looked. I was full of energy despite of having woken up at 4 a.m. and having worked since 7 a.m. I was having something new going on in my life. In the past five months it's been nothing but work and saving/sending money to Africa. Now this was about me! Now it was my turn to have fun. Patrick looked and acted almost as casual as the day before right when we just met. The boat looked still the same; he never took time to take care of the mess. I was disappointed and irritated by his passiveness. I watched how slowly he moved while pouring the water for Nel. I was annoyed to see how little energy he seemed to have. Everything he was doing in his life at this point seemed to have been only to avoid prison while staying at some friend's boat in exchange of making some repairs to it. He had no money, no real income and no desire to improve his life whatsoever.

"Money means nothing to me. I had everything I wanted and I wasn't a happy person. I could care less about money." He said to me as if he wanted to annoy me even more.

"Whatever. I hate when people say that. Money IS important. If it wasn't for the money those five kids in Kenya would still live on the street. So don't even tell me money means nothing, OK? I hate when people do that." I was already arguing with him like we were a real couple. The more he tried convincing me in seeing his point of view the shorter I was getting with him:

"I don't buy any of this stuff you're telling me so don't even try. I know what I know. Now let's talk about this divorce thing. What is it exactly that we need to do first?" I was getting impatient afraid that I was going to change my mind about marring Patrick before he was legally considered single again.

"Tomorrow I'll call the court to find out more." He said and I couldn't help but to feel disappointed once again with him for having wasted a whole day.

"Why didn't you do that this morning? I thought we had agreed on that?" I asked.

"I was working on the boat. And we agreed to farther discuss the details and that's what we're doing, aren't we?" He answered and I thought:

"Oh boy, is he gonna be like this the whole time; full of excuses? I hope he doesn't think he's just gonna keep alluring me to this boat while he's buying himself some time. He better not or I'll freaking get that out of his mind right away." I was not enjoying my visit as much as I've had planned. I was trying to figure him out as much and as fast as I could. I was having a hard time with it. He was still that considerate and sweet guy but he also seemed ineffective in living his life to his fullest potential. Not that I was everything I've ever wanted to be but at least I was doing everything I could think of to change that. I noticed there was a sense of victimization in his attitude.

"Look Patrick, I don't really wanna hear about the war and what you went through over there. I'm sure it was horrible but I don't see why you should feel guilty about it. You did what you had to do so get over it. Nobody put the gun to your head and nobody told you to go to Iraq or Afghanistan. You did it because you wanted to. I personally love that you did what you did and I'm very grateful for it. But when you speak with that melancholic and nasal voice of what a horrible guilt you feel and how you have nightmares at night it really annoys the hell out of me. So I don't wanna hear any of that stuff, k?" I was trying to cut him short before giving him a chance to, what it felt like, get away with manipulation. I didn't think he was doing it on purpose, as a matter of fact I didn't believe he was even completely aware of it himself. He clearly had some Post Traumatic Stress Disorder there going on but in my mind a man like him COULD and HAD TO handle it better. If I was able to see him as a real hero that he was then why on earth wasn't he able to see himself that way? His "poor me" attitude was a huge turn off for me and I wasn't going to tolerate it.

"Snap out of it Patrick, just get over it." I rubbed my two fingers quickly to make a sound effect.

"Stop freaking dwelling on it. I don't wanna listen to that and I'm not going to." At moments I wondered why he didn't just told me that he was tired and that I should go home.

"What would you like to do in your life?" I asked him to change the atmosphere.

"What I would like to do? I'd like to cook. I'd like to be a chef." His answer made me wonder whether a part from being two genuinely caring people we had anything else in common.

"Do you have any other interests other than cooking?" I asked again.

"Yes, as a matter of fact I do." He smiled understanding where I was going with it. He pulled out piles of papers from the drawer that was conveniently built above the narrow bed that we were sitting on. I looked at his face exhibiting traces of shy almost like new born hope. One by one he showed me different drawings of tattoos he had made, designs and business plans for jewelry store, menus for his restaurant etc. I was impressed with seeing how much thought and energy he had put into all his future plans.

"What's that?" I asked while pointing at numerous pages of what it looked like hand written manuscript. They all had a red stamp on top that said: Censured/ Oahu Community Correctional Center.

"That's my book." He answered.

"You're writing a book too?" I asked starting to feel excited.

"I have been. I don't think about ever publishing it though. I'm writing it for myself." He replied.

"We'll see about that." I answered while scanning through the pages enthusiastically. From the little I read in a hurry I knew I loved his writing style and I knew that the story was going to be more than interesting.

420

"This is freaking great! I'm gonna read all this. I love your writing style. It's similar to mine in many ways actually. Well, except yours is a lot better. But that's only because I had to struggle with my language barrier while writing my book. Yours is written in a little bit more sophisticated way and that's because you're writing in your native language. You write a little bit more eloquently than I do. This is how my book would read like if I was writing it in Polish. Actually; I'm freaking jealous of your writing, because it's a lot better than mine to be honest. I'm gonna read all this." With sparks in my eyes I started telling my possibly future husband how much I liked his work. He seemed more pleased than really surprised by my reaction as if he knew that he had a God given talent.

"Actually I wanna start reading it right now. Could you please make me something to eat?" I commanded more than I asked. I lay down more comfortably on the narrow bed.

"What would you like?" He smiled, clearly enjoying seeing me being captivated with part of his hand written book.

"Anything. Just throw whatever you can. Whatever you have over there it's good." I answered in a way that wasn't hiding that I didn't wished to be distracted from the story my eyes were uncovering. I followed eagerly the lines of words that were printed with a pencil in a clear, military style. I found it amusing how a tough looking guy on the surface, suffering from a PTSD, could find such descriptive words and make them flow so effortlessly. Through his writing he was unveiling his sensitive side and I loved him for that. Through his story he was making himself sound honest with himself and straightforward. Even more amazingly there was not a trace of victim like attitude in the author of the memoir I was reading. I was amazed by his writing and without even being aware of it; I was starting to fell in love with him.

"What's so funny? Why're you laughing?" Patrick would ask me from time to time while stirring on noodles he was making for dinner.

"Nothing. Your writing makes me laugh; the way you put things. I like your sense of humor. I like how you describe things. I wish my book was written more in this way." I answered drying my eyes from tears created by my laughter. The more I was reading the more I was realizing that if I had never met Patrick and if I was reading his book I would want to not only know him personally but I would also want to make sure that I'd treat him differently that most people had in his life. I would want to show him what a wonderful person he was in my eyes. How much I admired his strength and his courage. How impressed I was with his perseverance with always trying to do the right thing and how taken I was by him. Patrick's manuscript, even thought containing still only small part of his story, was making me feel connected to him. Everything was starting to make more sense to me. I could finally understand more as to why I was so intrigued by him and why I was so drawn to him. I didn't have to look anymore for characteristics that we had in common. In many ways we were practically identical. More or less our outlook at life was the same. The feeling that I had met the right man, just a little bit "rough on the edges", was growing in my heart. I did not want to idealize him, as I was afraid that he was already doing it with me, but I did tell myself to try at least not to be so harsh on him. He seemed already beaten up enough by his life. His spirit and his faith both seemed to had been broken and it gave me an impression of barely hanging there, not even on a real rope, but a thin hair. I had in front of me a man whose sensitivity was greater than my own. A man that would take all the blame in the world before even considering hurting anyone. A man that was very hard on himself and a one that wanted to please everyone. A man that was more a giver than a taker. I felt that way about him the moment I laid my eyes on him. I knew that if anything, in many ways he was better than me.

Proposition

"How are we gonna deal with this sexual frustration?" I asked Patrick.

"It's gonna be hard but we'll manage." He replied.

"You know if we're gonna live together and we're gonna be so close we may end up falling in love with each other, right?" My own words broke the peaceful silence that was filling the softly rocking boat. He just smiled.

"Yeaah." More than saying it I moaned with my face half buried in the pillow. I didn't want him to stop massaging me. I enjoyed his firm touch and I enjoyed the sexual tension that was building up between the two of us. I felt safe and comfortable knowing that he wasn't going to do anything I wouldn't want him to do.

"As a matter of fact I think it's too late for that. I think, no, I know; I already love you." He said and I raised my head. His word made me feel pleased and uncomfortable at the same time.

"Patrick, you know we have to stick to our plan. Please don't start saying things like that. I don't wanna hear that." I laid my head back on the pillow trying to ignore the admiration in his sweet, and of an unusual shade of brown eyes. It was hurting me to see so much pain in them and I didn't like that feeling. As usual I was using anger to cope with the uncomfortable feelings. Love and intimacy were sure on the top of that list. I knew that if I wasn't already, I could easily fell in love with Patrick but I needed that safe cushion called time. I needed to be able to be mean and nasty to him sometimes. I needed to put him through different trials which he would have to pass with flying colors to see whether he would last through the stormy weather of my "borderline personality disorder" before I could allow myself to start opening up to him.

"I'm going to sleep." I informed Patrick abruptly stopping the movements of my body that was enjoying too much his touch. From the corners of my eyes I could see the sadness on his face and all I could think was:

"He's just gonna have to toughen up." Ignoring him completely I turned my back towards the wall. I fell asleep.

"Elzbieta. Elzbieta." Patrick was pocking me gently forcing me to wake up.

"What? What? What is it?" Completely disoriented I opened my eyes.

"Nothing, I just wanna talk to you about something. I may have a solution for our problem." He said like it was OK to wake me up at two in the morning. I stroked my eyes with both of my hands.

"Patrick, don't ever do this to me. Don't ever wake me up in the middle of the night. I don't care if you can't sleep, I don't care if you have PTSD, I don't care about anything! You do not freaking wake me up in the middle of night like this, do you understand that?" Towards the end of those sentences I wasn't talking to him anymore. I was yelling at him. The anger and frustration that only a person who had a life time problem with being able to fully relax and rest while sleeping, was now trying to suffocate me. I sat down while covering myself with the blanket.

"What is wrong with you?" I asked Patrick trying to use a more calm tone with him this time. He looked guilty and embarrassed. I exhaled the air forcefully:

"Look, I have a problem with sleeping just like you do, except I don't cry about it, OK? I don't sleep well. I never had. So the moment you wake me up from the little rest I'm trying to get; it won't look pretty." I lightened the cigarette to calm myself even more and to help myself with coping with the sense of guilt I was feeling for snapping at him. Patrick was trying to apologize but I was already feeling too awaken to go back to sleep.

"What is that solution that you thought about that couldn't wait until the morning?" I asked in a friendlier manner.

"Well, I found the way in which you won't have to go through the hassle of answering intrusive questions from the immigration about our sex life and you'll be able to obtain your US citizenship like in six months instead of two to three years." He answered.

"What on earth are you talking about?" My voice still contained traces of spitefulness even though I was talking now a lot slower as opposed to earlier when I was shooting words uncontrollably like a gun machine.

"It's gonna be easy, for you at least. I'm just gonna go back doing what I know how to do best. I'm gonna go back to Afghanistan. Don't worry; they'll help me with speeding up the divorce papers. I won't leave before marrying you. Trust me, I've seen guys going through this before with their wives; INS will not have the ability to question you whether you sleep or not with your husband that's oversees fighting in the war." He explained.

"But you're not with the Navy anymore so how would you now go back there? I don't understand this. This makes no sense."

"I know. And I wouldn't be going with them. I'll be going with a private agency that hires people with experience like myself for specific missions to work with the military guys. Actually I've already texted my friend that I'm going to accept their offer. They've been trying to make me join their team since I got out of the jail. Well, they've been wanting me to be the team leader 'cause that's what I used to do when I was oversees. And honestly I've been seriously considering going back there anyway."

"What about your resent criminal record? Wouldn't that stay in your way?" I looked for the ways to undermine everything he was telling me. I didn't like what I was hearing not because it didn't sound true but because I was afraid that it could. I've only known him for two days and I already couldn't bear the thought of being apart from him.

"You don't understand how this works. The government doesn't give a shit about the court's records and they can tell them pretty much to shove it if they want badly someone to go out there and do their dirty job for them. The government has the power to make things disappear. They need people like me with experience and no criminal background is going to get in their way of getting what they want if you know what I mean. They don't give a shit about me either. They just want their job done. And they've seen me in action. They know I'm exactly what they need. I cannot tell you what it entails exactly. I cannot even really tell you what I did or didn't do there 'cause it's all considered classified but trust me; if I go there, you're gonna be well taken care of. " As I was listening to his words I was trying to see whether he was attempting to glorify himself in order to feel less inadequate and less powerless or something. What I was seeing was a man that seemed to be still deeply affected by the hatred towards the job that he had performed for twelve years, pretty much his all adult life. Could he have been so good at it if he didn't believe in it? Well, I despised cleaning more than anything in this world and according to others I did it better than most people did.

"Are all these scars on your chin and on your scalp from the war?" I asked while gently following their uneven shapes with my fingers.

"Yes ma'am." He answered softly. He didn't seem eager to brag about it.

"How did you get the one on your lip?" I asked.

"Explosion." He answered again without getting into details.

"You were close to where a bomb exploded?" I insisted with questioning but this time I did it with less suspiciousness. Like most people I had some vague ideas about the war happening in the Middle East. In my mind most soldiers were just there to make sure that nothing bad would happen and from time to time some of the less lucky ones would get killed more by an accident than anything else. He smiled like he was looking at an innocent little girl, as if he knew exactly what was going through my mind.

"Where I was bombs exploded every day. This one got me when we were riding in a humvee," he answered.

"What's a humvee?"

"It's a type of a military version of the Hummer," he explained.

"Where was the bomb?"

"On the road we were driving through. Terrorists put hidden bombs all the time to combat US soldiers. They won't stop at anything. They'll use their own children to wrap them with explosive materials. I've seen it and sometimes I had to make that call; take the innocent life away or risk for everybody else to be blown away." The sense of being lost I was seeing in Patrick's eyes was melting my heart. I felt bad for being so rude to him only because I knew I could get away with it. I felt bad for judging him so harshly even though I knew I had no real right to do that. For telling him that he had to be stronger than he was and for telling him to stop acting like a victim. I began to understand that my disappointment with him had nothing to do with the reality and everything to do with my exaggerated expectations of how he could and therefore should be. He had to be a super man in order to fit the description of the man I wanted him to be. In my mind he had to not only survive the war while going through the worst possible scenarios but he also had to be able to come out of it with nothing but few scars on his flesh. He had to be emotionally strong and self-sufficient while still managing to remain perfectly emo-

426

tionally available to me. He had to be sensitive while remaining tough looking to the outside world. He could have spent some time in jail for whatever he did or didn't do, I didn't really care about that but I did care whether he was in denial about things or not.

"Patrick, you're not telling me all this stuff about going back to Afghanistan to try to manipulate me, are you? Cause I'm telling you right now; that stuff's not gonna work with me. Besides even if it was true you know I wouldn't let you do that. It's not like I have nothing to say here. I'm telling you; I would not even marry you. So all those things you're talking about doing for me wouldn't even matter." I said to him.

"Well you're not gonna have much choice. I'm gonna go there whether you like it or not since I was going to do that anyway. And you're gonna marry me because you do need those papers to have a better life here. I promise you that you won't have to clean houses for the rest of your life. All the money I'll be making while there will be yours to keep. You'll have that dream house of yours in no time. And if anything bad would happen to me while I'm there, you're gonna be well taken care of so don't worry." He answered like he meant every word he said. The seriousness of his tone and the "a man got to do what a man got to do" look on his face scared me.

"You can't be serious." I said to him sounding not as confident anymore. He wasn't saying anything anymore and now I was getting real mad at him. The tears were rolling down my face from frustration. I was upset with myself for even just feeling tempted with his offer. He had made some good points there. I could not stop hating myself for even considering such possibility of him risking his life to make mine better.

"I don't give a damn about the papers or the house. Do you have any idea what would I go through if one those guys in uniforms knocked at my door to inform me that my husband was killed while fighting for his country? Do you think I'd be like; oh great this man really loved me. He sacrificed he's own life so mine could be a lot better, how noble of him? Do you really think I could just go on with my life knowing that something bad happened to you and that I was directly responsible for it? Are you out of your mind? What's wrong with you? You just made me talk to your mom over the phone like few hours ago. What do you suppose I'd tell this poor old lady; oh yeah, I encouraged your son to go to Afghanistan cause my life sucked and I needed money real bad, sorry your son's dead, please don't blame me for that? Please don't even make me think about it not even for a moment. It just makes me sick to my stomach." I was talking to him in an angry way. I was very mad at him. I was mad that his proposition sounded actually very tempting. The idea that he thought so little of me that he actually believed I'd considered such deal was upsetting me. Or did he know otherwise and this was just his way of impressing me? Whatever it was it was working. The sexual tension I was experiencing before was now growing in me to the might of a thousand at least. Patrick's not perfect but very manly features were now more attractive in my eyes than any other man I've met or seen in my life. His full red lips clasped a bit while bringing lower one a bit forward were now screaming to be kissed, bitten and sucked on without taking any intervals to catch some air. The serious and stubborn look in his eyes was having the same effect on me the way gasoline does to a lighted match that comes into contact with it. Picturing him in my mind all camouflaged while making his way through dangerous sceneries was like watching porn for a man I guess. Imagining that he was doing all that for me was priceless. The powerful emotions I was experiencing made me realize that I wanted him to do this just so I could keep feeling this way. I was going to be the wife of nobody less than a real hero! How could I possibly resist such idea? How could I possibly want to stop feeling so elevated by the thought of being with a man who's literally willing to die for me? How could I not enjoy the power of effect I had on him? If there was such a thing as measurement of love this would break such scale. I was used to having men in my life that weren't willing to stick around because of the million reasons that proved something was wrong with me. Now I had a man in front of me which thought of me to be not less than a Goddess and who was willing to prove his point to me and to the whole world. How did I come to this big change which even though was still making me uncomfortable, was directly responsible for making me feel like I was bigger than life itself? I was being loved and this was no longer just a statement repeated in my newly positive mind. My "outside" world was reflecting exactly what I've always wanted it to reflect. How magical all this felt and how empowering effect it had on me.

"Kiss me." I commanded in a demanding tone.

"No." He replied as firmly.

"Don't play with me. I'm not into games. Just kiss me." I began to feel irritated again.

"No. This wouldn't be the right..."

"Damn it! Stop with this bull shit and fucking kiss me already!" I grabbed his face with both of my hands. Our lips finally met. I was kissing a man who wasn't expecting that this had to necessarily lead somewhere else. A man that for a change wouldn't just do anything to have me but who would instead stop at nothing to make sure that I was happy! A kind of man of which I fantasized about since the time when hormones begun to do crazy things to my mind and to my body. I was kissing my ideal man. His teeth were slipping off my swollen lips and his tongue was examining my mouth while playing hide and seek with my tongue. His hands couldn't decide between holding my face, pulling on my hair or ravishing the rest of my excited and fully awakened body.

"Take me." I whispered after a while noticing he wasn't going to cross that line by himself. The anticipation of feeling him inside me was wearing me off. I wanted now what I knew was going to happen sooner or later. I didn't want to wait. I've waited long enough.

"Are you sure about it?" He paused while looking at me seriously.

"Yes I am." I answered thanking him in my mind for being such a gentleman.

"Wait. I can't do this, not like this. I can't go through another pregnancy and all that." I pushed him away and I sat down.

"I promised myself I wouldn't take any more risks. I could not go through yet another abortion or another miscarriage like I did. No, I will not do this." I explained while attempting to straighten up my hair. I looked serious and upset.

"It's alright. Don't worry. We don't have to do this." He tried to calm me down. We sat there and talked a little bit about my previous painful experiences.

"Do you want to know something that could make you laugh?" He asked hesitantly.

"What is it?"

"Aaah." He exhaled the air forcefully as if he wanted to get rid of some burden.

"As in this moment, even if I wanted to, I wouldn't be able to get you pregnant." He was saying it slowly. His words were reaching my brain not fast enough.

"I had a vasectomy."

"Are you serious?" I looked at him afraid knowing that because of that one sentence all my dreams could end up vanished in the air.

"Don't worry, in most cases its reversible. I'd just have to go under the knife again." He added quickly as if he was able to read my mind. I was feeling angry at him for not waiting to have children the way I did and for having the procedure that could potentially stand in the way of us living a fulfilling life together. To give up the sweet thought of being able to go through all stages of pregnancy and of having my own baby was not an option. Perfectly loving husband, our baby girl (preferably), big piece of land with a country style white house on it, exotic fruits and plants, horses roaming around and my family as neighbors all that was on my vision board which I put together while still staying at Ahmed's office. Could it be that I was mistaking Patrick for that dream man of mine? What if I was just simply giving into the fear of never meeting that right guy? What if all this was nothing more than my own projection of what I wanted it to be? Was I attempting to do God's/Universe's job as opposed to remaining just opened and receptive of its Will and Way like I thought I was doing? How the heck was I supposed to know exactly what was right and what was wrong? My heart was battling with my mind to the point that I couldn't even distinguish which was which. Has it been my heart telling me that Patrick could be the one or has it been my mind hiding behind all this? I needed to know the answer and simple "time will show" could not be it. We're talking about possibly being in the presence of my Soul mate! The same Soul I've been separated with right before my birth could potentially be reunited with me now! It could bring me the ecstasy and exhilaration not even my wild mind could embrace. It could mean that my lonely days or days in the company of wrong people were over. That the search was not unfruitful and that all the efforts were worthwhile. This was big! No, this was HUGE! I needed to know for sure whether I was inventing all this in my mind or whether this was happening to me for real.

"Make love to me." I commanded again.

Life's Lessons

I woke up feeling relaxed and peaceful. The man that was lying next to me was not quite the man he was portraying to be. The man that made love to me all night long on that rocking boat was not insecure or passive. He was decisive, confident and full of control which I loved. His sexuality and his passion were fitting perfectly into the missing puzzle I've been trying to put together. Patrick's almost barbarian look on his face that he had while squeezing the life out of me during the love making was intoxicating. His dark features were getting even darker and even more dangerous looking, with each moment that his hard "manhood" filled me up, making me feel complete again. His broad shoulders and his hairy chest were taking my breath away while making me feel like a tiny woman that's powerless and completely left on mercy of this primitive Tarzan. His lower jaw brought forward and the visible veins busy pumping the blood were giving him a look of a soldier who's not afraid of conquering the enemy's territory. I loved feeling owned by him. I loved the sensation of being in the paws of a carnival animals that was enjoying teasing its prey almost to death. I loved the wild, almost scary look in his eyes. The grip he was holding me with was translating the unspoken words: "You are mine and mine only!" The energy flowing from Patrick's eyes and his movements was shouting at me in the most promising manner: "I will ravish you, I will torture you, I will make you forget your name!" Patrick's surprisingly intense sexuality was illustrating the scenes from all the Harlequin books I read when I was in my teen years. Now I was finally that thirty something old woman that was being conquered in a way and by the kind of man that in the past made my underwear wet just by reading about it. Now I was finally actually living it. I didn't have to imagine or pretend anymore. Nor did I have to think. All that was asked of me was to follow the lead and to allow being pleased like I've never been pleased before.

"*Oh this is gonna be goood.*" The more than optimistic thought would cross my mind while I'd pull away in order to catch a breath. I'd look Patrick into his eyes and without saying anything his face would tell me:" You didn't expect that, did you?" He seemed able to read my face that had an expression that was saying: "Who the hell are you exactly and why the hell it took you so long to find me?"

The next few weeks were a rollercoaster.

"No, I can't do this. We can only be friends that are helping each other. We're gonna stick to our original plan. That's the best thing we can do." I'd tell Patrick every day whether on the phone or in person.

"Sure. No problem." His reply was always pretty much the same. Just as predictable as his response was my reaction to it and so pretty much we always ended up naked in bed together. My hot one moment and cold the next day attitude was driving him crazy but not enough to push him away which was very important to me. He was passing one of the biggest tests that my subconscious was laying out for him. He was proving to me that he was going to last and that he was going to be there even when things got difficult and frustrating. He was also showing me that in our relationship there were things way more important than just being physically with me. I needed that proof that I was being loved for the kind of woman/person I was and not just for my looks/body. Still every day I was filled with doubts whether marring Patrick in such a short time was the right thing to do. I was happy around him and he continued making me laugh but he also continued driving me nuts. It seemed as if every time he wasn't able to tolerate my coldness versus him, he came up with that idea of "making my life easier by leaving for Afghanistan."

"Patrick, stop fucking trying to manipulate me with that bull shit. You wanna go? Just fucking go! OK? Do whatever you wanna do but if you expect our relationship to last, you need to cut this crap. I will not put up with bull shit. I know you're using this whole thing as a confirmation to see how much I love you and I know it feels good to you to see how upset I get at the sole idea of being apart from you but you need to find a different form of validation. Do you understand that? You need to stop depending on feeling good only when I'm nice to you and when you feel loved by me. You need to be emotionally strong at all times. You need to be emotionally independent. That's what I need in a man. In that letter to the Universe I didn't ask for a needy boy, I asked for a strong man. Don't make me feel like I made a mistake. Don't make me feel like rushing things between us was a wrong move. I'm telling you; this Afghanistan crap has to end and has to end now. Do not mention that to me ever again. Do you hear me?" In expressing myself I was using the anger that I was experiencing from feeling so tempted with this "easiest" solution to all our problems.

"Oh god, I'm telling you Patrick I'm sick and tired of all this. I've had decided that in my life I've had enough of everything and I don't want no more drama. This right here is a no drama zone. I don't want no manipulations, no games, no lies, or any of that crap that my life was built of until now. If you're with me on that then we can continue growing together but if you can't make that same decision about your life, for whatever reason that may be, then it means that we are not for each other. Perhaps we can remain as friends but that is all. I will not settle for less than what I've asked for, you understand? I've asked for a husband that will love and cherish me and who will continue to grow with me spiritually. Not someone with whom I'll have to be entangled in those primitive manipulative power struggles that never end. I specifically asked for a man who will always do his best to remain his highest potential and who will help me do the same and vice versa. When I saw you and I got to know you more I thought for sure you were that man. But every time you bring this subject you make me doubt my own judgment about you. So stop doing it. Stop making me wanna change my mind about you." I was pretty harsh on him and I knew that but I felt like he needed it. I felt like he needed a wakeup call. I didn't like saying those things to him just like I didn't enjoy having those thoughts. Many times in order not to give up on Patrick I'd tell myself:

"Just think of yourself when you were like this and when you were acting like he does now sometimes. How much did you wish that someone would look past all those imperfections and that someone would have faith in you and love you just the way you were? How much did you long for that kind of person who would stick with you no matter what even if you were full of issues? And if YOU were capable to address and change most of those annoying traits then have a little bit of faith in him as well. He has that which matters. He has the will to do whatever it takes. Give him some time. He really is trying his best and you can see that, so be patient with him. He'll come along, don't worry too much." I would never reveal those thoughts to him afraid that he wouldn't work as hard on himself if he knew how forgiving I could be.

"Guess what? We need to go to the mall and I have to get a new outfit. That other designer boutique I went to apply for a job, they just called me for a second interview! The big boss just came from California and he wants to see me! I know I'm gonna get this job, I know that. I can feel it. I won't have to work for Eduardo anymore. And I'm gonna make there up to like five grand a month! Oh god, hurry up and come and get me!" I was talking to Patrick on the phone with excitement of a teenager that had discovered the latest and the hottest gossip. These days Patrick was driving a car temporarily borrowed from a person he knew. He was doing that a lot; fixing things like cars and anything that needed repair for very little in return other than just small favors that mostly came as an automatic result of it. It was very frustrating for me seeing him working hard all day long, getting all dirty and greasy without getting an actual compensation.

"Patrick, this is gonna have to change. I know you like helping people and I know you like feeling needed and I understand that but if you are serious about starting a family with me then you're gonna have to change the way you do things. I will not be starving while others are getting a free ride, no way in hell I will do that. You're gonna have to start working only for those people that are actually paying you. And I'm gonna make sure that they pay you the amount you deserve to be paid for the work you're doing. Same thing with this nonsense of doing all these things for Linda for nothing; that's gonna have to stop. She keeps promising she's gonna pay you and we both know that's not gonna happen. I understand you feel grateful to her because she introduced us to each other but that doesn't mean you're gonna be cleaning up her mess for free for the rest of your life because of that." I was talking to Patrick on the way to the mall. He was listening patiently like he did most of the times when I was nagging. I have been learning more and more how talented in many areas Patrick was. There seemed to be not such a thing that he could not fix. He knew cars like he knew the back of his hand. Engines, transmissions, electrical wires all that seemed to be just big toys to him which seemed to effortlessly obey to his will. People were calling him from the ads on Craigslist desperate when other mechanics couldn't figure out the exact reason for their automobiles lack of performance. I'd hear him asking them over the phone about the "symptoms" and him telling them the "diagnosis" just few minutes later. Ten out of nine times he was "right on the money". The other one he was close enough and he was able to resolve the issue once he crawled underneath the car. He was charging his clients for his services less than half of what other mechanics were doing. I had a huge issue with that and I wasn't hiding that from him.

"How do you intent to pay your divorce attorney if you continue to let others take advantage of you like this? This guy is telling you: "Oh yeah yeah I have another big job that I can use you for", but really what he's doing he's just promising you something that he knows it's not gonna even happen, just so he convinces you that you're not losing any money by cutting him such a big slack." Nine of ten times I was right about it. I learned quickly how more than often people were more than willing to use Patrick's good nature.

"When people are complaining to you that they're strapped with money is 'cause they know that they can use you and get away with it. Do not allow anyone to do that to you, because if they do that to you; automatically they're doing that to me and that just offends my intelligence. I bet you anything that most of these peoples enjoy doing things that you and I cannot even afford. When these guys take their wives or their girlfriends to a restaurant for example to enjoy their time and then the waiter comes to present them with their bill, do you think that they start telling the waiter: "Oh you know what? I just had to pay this bill and that bill and I don't have much money left until the next pay day but I promise you that I will tell all my friends and all my neighbors to dine at your restaurant"? Baby I'm just telling you all this because I want you to start asserting yourself. You have a talent and you are better at building and fixing things more than most people out there and you need to start valuing yourself more, OK? It does not make you a bad person when you get paid accordingly for the job you're doing. Actually, the opposite is true. It means that not only you are confident as a person but also that you love yourself like you should and that you respect yourself." I kept nagging. I felt very protective of Patrick and I felt like it was my job to make him aware of the self-destructive beliefs about himself he had assumed in the course of his life. None of these beliefs were new to me and I felt as if the Universe was showing me the "old me" through this man that I was madly falling in love with. I was more than impressed with his abilities that seemed to be spread in every direction. He knew how to fix cars, boats, computers; he knew how to install solar panels, door alarms, how to build swimming pools or anything else for that matter. I've learned that when he was in submarine he was the trouble shooter for the radar and all those electrical things that would make my head spin even if I just attempted to comprehend how they worked. I liked that about him a lot that he was "such a guy." I loved that he had such a big heart. In fact that was one of the "a must" on that list of mine that I made about my ideal guy. I just didn't want that quality to be on the expense of his self-esteem and his self-confidence. I was afraid that my lecturing and my preaching wasn't necessarily the right method that I should use in restoring his self-image but I didn't really know what else to do. I wanted to shake him up somehow in order to show him how great he was. I wanted him to be able to see himself through my eyes. I was somewhat aware that I needed the exact same thing. Observing Patrick closely helped me understand how having doubts about myself and not trusting myself made living my life to my fullest potential practically impossible.

More than Disappointed…

The job interview went more than great. After conversing for more than an hour, answering numerous questions and making my own inquiries I pretty much knew I was going to get that call in a day or two that would confirm that I got the job. Supposedly there were some other applicants interested in the opening but I knew they had no chance against me even though I had no experience in clothing sales per se. I had my looks, my brain, my determination and my charismatic personality. I was more than ready to make good money and to start living more than just on a minimum wage lifestyle. I had no doubt that if I'd put my mind to it, in few months only, my commissions rates could be the highest among all the employees.

The next day, while I was about to leave Eduardo's house I noticed I had a voice mail from the manager that I spoke with on the first interview. His voice sounded all excited while in all that theatrical way he was informing me about the decision his big boss has made:

"Welll…I got good neeews for you. Girl, I'll tell you this much; you really impressed the general manager. Yep, the job is yours. Well, I'll be here tomorrow assisting you with all the paper work and just so you know I already have the new gorgeous two thousand dollars suit for you and all that. We gonna have to do the fitting for you tomorrow as well to make sure everything will look just perfect. It's gonna be fun. I'll see you tomorrow. Bye."

"Oh my God! YES! I knew it! I knew I was gonna get this job! Aaaah, YES!" I said to myself while robbing my face in relief. My renewed driver's license had already arrived in the mail from California by now so I didn't have to worry about the same situation that happened with the other boutique happening all over again.

"Yes, I'm finally getting a new start. I'll be working in a nice place, I'll be dealing with people that have not just money but that have class as well and I'll be making good money. Oh god, it's gonna be so much better. I won't have to wear dirty clothes to clean someone else's mess. I'll be wearing expensive suits. My hair will always be nicely done. Oh god, I can't wait. Thank you God, thank you so much for this." I was thinking while walking back home with Nel. I was too excited to risk losing the balance while pedaling the bicycle so I was hauling it instead. Patrick was the only person I shared my news with. He sounded happy and excited for me as well:

"Congratulations babe. I had no doubt you were gonna get that job 'cause you deserve it. And you looked really sharp and professional in that new suit we picked. K baby I'm finishing up here, I'm almost done so I'll see you later this evening. That's if you want me to."

"Yeah yeah whatever. Of course I want you to. I'll see you later. OK. Bye." I hung up the phone smiling.

"Nellie, Nellie, Nellie. The dark days are finally behind us. Tha-a-at's right." I said at loud to my dog like I usually did and she wiggled her tale in excitement like she usually did when I spoke to her.

The next day I showed up at the boutique at least twenty minutes early. I had parked my bicycle in the designated area by the side walk and I used the chain with lock to secure my transportation method. Once inside this expensive and modern looking two story building I was introduced to some colleagues by the same manager that had left that sweet message on my voicemail. Some costumers were busy with paying for their expensive merchandise.

"Miss, is that you on that big screen? That's you isn't it?" A well dressed man asked me in a noticeable foreign accent. The two ladies that were holding numerous bags with the store name on them were shaking their heads. They were looking back and forth between me and the big screen TV that was showing models on a run way in a fashion show.

"Oh my God, it is her!" One of them exclaimed with excitement. I smiled:

"No, it's not me. But I'll take your mistake as a compliment. Thank you. Now if you'll excuse me I got to take care of something. See you later. Bye." I smiled again this time more because of the amusement on the manager's face that was similar to someone who was thinking: "Oh this is gonna be real fun". The two of us went to the back of the store where there was less commotion.

"K, great. I'm gonna need your green card so I can make a copy of it real quick." He started talking fast as if he wanted to have the boring paper bureaucracy pass behind him.

"Aah. Sure. Well, I do have my driver's license with me and my social security card." I started to pull out from my purse the legally acceptable forms of identification. I handled him my ID's.

"Ahmmm, hmm.." He paused while looking at my driver's license and my social security card.

"Well, this is OK but I'm gonna also need to see the actual green card as well." He added.

"*What the hell?*" The unfriendly thought crossed my mind while realizing that my faith was at stake again. I tried arguing with him that the two forms of ID I had with me were on the governmentally issued list of the acceptable documents for the hiring process. I wasn't sure if it was because this guy himself came to live in US from a different country if that was the reason why he was giving me such a hard time with it. I was looking at him talking to me about the importance of me bringing the ACTUAL green card and I couldn't help but to feel anger and even hatred towards him. Suddenly in my eyes he was no more than just a stuck up manager who must have been enjoying the fact that his legal status wasn't jeopardizing his life style. I realized that his attitude wasn't going to change no matter what I would or wouldn't say to him. Feeling embarrassed, defeated and frustrated beyond the words I lied saying that I'd be back with my work permit knowing that this wasn't going to happen. I left the building while trying to suppress the painful emotions inside me. I didn't feel like going back home nor did I feel like going back to work for Eduardo. I've been mentioning to him that I'd like to start working fewer hours and as far as he was concerned I was just having my day off. I unlocked my bicycle. I started ridding it on Waikiki's sidewalks without knowing where I was going. I was crying. I heard my cell phone ringing in my purse. I stopped the bicycle hoping that it was the manager calling me to tell me that my driver's license and my social security card were enough and telling me to come back to work.

"Hello?" I answered the phone feeling anxious but still hopeful.

"Hey babe, it's me. I was just calling you to find out how's your first day at work." Hearing Patrick's happily unaware voice caused me to feel hopeless and irritated. The anger that was building inside of me wanted to be released at any cost even if it meant hurting someone I cared about. I wanted to at least partially blame Patrick for something that I was tired of blaming myself for all the time. I felt like because of him not taking care of his divorce fast enough I had to pay the price of losing the job I put so much effort in getting.

"You know what? You are just like all those Americans that don't give a shit about the rest of the world and the worst part of it is that you can't even fucking appreciate the opportunities that you have simply because you were born in this part of the world and not the other! You all just take things for granted! You are all arrogant spoiled brats! Just like Sean; my fucking ex from California. He wanted to marry me when he was SUPPOSDLY in love with me but if he loved me so much like he claimed he did then why didn't he just marry me when I was ready for it? He knew my legal status from the beginning. He knew how difficult that made things for me. And still at the beginning of our relationship when he did wanted to marry me I had the guts to tell him that I would rather wait until I was sure that I was in love with him as well. I didn't want him to ever have to wonder if I married him just because it was convenient. That's how fucking naïve and stupid I was then! Two and half years later of living together he decides I'm not a marring material anymore and here I am now, wasted my fucking time just trying to prove to someone that I loved them for real and not because of some ulterior motives. People get married all the time because they need a sense of financial security or because they get pregnant and all that is socially and legally acceptable. But marring somebody so you have the right to stay in this freaking country? N-o-o-o-o, that is below the line of decency! Why do I even give a shit about all this? Why do I lower myself to the level of people that are judgmental and that really don't know shit about life? You know what? I will never do that fucking thing again. I will NEVER try to prove anyone whether I love them for real or not. So IF we do get married, don't EVER try questioning me, whether I married you because I had to, or because I wanted to. You understand that? That is why from the beginning I told you that I wanted to get married for papers only so I would never have to answer any of those stupid accusations! You all…"

"Babe? What happened today?" Patrick finally found the courage to interrupt my outburst that was emphasized with my crying at loud.

"What do you think happened? I went to my new job all happy and all excited and then the whole fucking sky collapsed on me when I heard that fucking stuck up manager telling me that I had to bring in the ACTUAL freaking green card! That same bullshit situation that happened with that other boutique when they told me to bring the ACTUAL driver's license because my temporary extension from DMV wasn't good enough. You know what? I'm sick and tired of all this. I'm not having a good day so… you know what? Don't even bother coming to see me. At least not until you get those divorce papers finalized. Until you'll have those papers in your hands and until you'll show them to me I don't wanna see you at all. It's been two months that you've been sending her that divorce petition and all I hear is that she doesn't wanna sign it and that she doesn't wanna communicate with you. Well get a fucking private detective that lives in Texas, or whatever the fucking state she lives in, that can find her and have him deliver those damn papers to her. I'm not gonna just wait forever for that witch to let you have your divorce! You have been letting people using you your whole life and you've allowed your stupid exes to suck the life out of you. I don't know how you can still be OK with all this but I DO know that they're not gonna do that to me! No fucking way!" I pressed the red button on my cell phone to hang up the call. Almost immediately the phone rang again. I didn't answer it. After looking at the display showing two missed calls I finally answered Patrick's third attempt to communicate with me. He was now pissed at me trying to tell me that my anger reminded him of his wife that's he's been separated with and trying to divorce for two years now. This comparing me to her made me even angrier:

"Don't even try for a moment comparing me to any of your exes! Don't even go there! OK? My crying about my stupid papers and mentioning Sean has nothing to do with me comparing you to anyone. If anything I've always told you that your willingness to marry me just for papers proved to me that you were different than anybody else I've ever met. Whatever issues you've had in the past, leave them there. I am who I am. I am not like your first, not like your second and as sure as hell I am anything like your third wife. And you know that. DON'T EVER try bringing me down by bringing me to their level! Ever!" I hung up the phone again.

Sabotage

The next few days I was trying to keep myself busy with working at Eduardo's place. Patrick and I we were still talking over the phone but I kept refusing to see him in person. I was hoping he would get more motivated in finding better and faster ways of first finding and then serving his wife with the petition for the dissolution of their marriage. I thought that if he had the sense of urgency the same way I did that he would be more determined and more committed to this task which successful completion seemed impossible at moments. Her not answering to his emails on purpose and refusing to sign the divorce papers that he had mailed to her mother's address, and for which he had to pay the filing court's fees each time, was more than frustrating. Between what the divorce lawyer had charged him for his services and all the other fees Patrick had spend fifteen hundred dollars without making a single step forward towards achieving the final goal. We had been arguing a lot about how with all that wasted money, which we didn't have any extra of; we could have had the house in Kenya paid off by now. I hated that this woman was causing so much misery in so many lives. Eduardo wasn't making things much easier for me with his statements:

"I'm telling you this game can go on for a very long time. I've been through all that bull shit of getting divorced. Thanks god I don't have to go through this again. I feel bad for you guys. The way things are right now with his ex and all that, I don't think he'll be divorced not even in six months from now. Take my word for it. That divorce lawyer's not doing anything. You guys need to either travel to mainland yourself to take care of it or you'll have to hire a private investigator or something. Why don't you just marry someone else? I know it wouldn't be hard for you to find someone who'd marry you in a spot, just like that. You could have any guy you want and any man would be lucky to have you as his wife. You're not just some pretty girl. You're the type of woman that comes one in a million. Even your face, the type of face you have stands out in a crowd. There is that CHARACTER to it. And you are a real good woman. You don't ask for much, you don't bother anybody, you're a hard worker, the best worker I've ever had and you just wanna live your life peacefully. You should have everything you want and it should be easy for you. Very easy. I'm telling you, you should find a different guy. It'd be a lot easier than what your'e trying to do. Tell me honestly, why don't you find somebody else?"

"Because…"

"Because what?"

"Because this is the guy I want to marry and this is the guy I WILL marry."

"You must really like this guy. Who is this PATRICK guy? How does he look?" Eduardo always looked surprised as if he couldn't believe that I could care that much about a man. I was partially responsible for his confusion because I had told him that I've made a deal with Patrick and that our marriage was going to be nothing else than just "a convenient arrangement". As the emotional and the physical matters kept progressing between my future husband and I, explaining details to others seemed pointless, so I kept my mouth shut. Only my siblings and my mother knew about my developing feelings towards my boyfriend and even they did not know everything that there was to know. I liked keeping my most intimate and private life to myself. Patrick was the only person in the whole world that made me feel like I didn't want to hide any secrets from. It was strange because due to the ever increasing stress from the situation we found ourselves dealing with, the chemistry wasn't always there. However even a single thought of not having this man in my life was not even close to being acceptable. Many times I did wonder whether I was doing the right thing and whether I should have listen to the advice that Linda and Eduardo were offering. The woman was so unhappy with me "stealing" her helpful sweetheart away from all the work that she needed to have done in her place that she even tried sabotaging my relationship with Patrick. He was very upset when he was telling me how she tried to warn him against me. In her words I was probably some Russian prostitute who worked for mafia and who was using children in Africa to collect the money. I confronted her since it wasn't the first time she tried pulling this nonsense on me. She had tried "warning" Eduardo as well before.

"Well Linda, I don't really care if you were joking about it or not when you were saying those things about me but I'm telling you; do not ever try to stab me in the back like this again because it's gonna back fire on you. I mean l like you and I'm grateful that you've introduced me to Eduardo and to Patrick but you cannot continue saying shit like this about me to other people. For god's sake you've contacted me in the first place when I was in Africa because you said you wanted to be my agent and you wanted to promote my book. What kind of promotion is this? I thought you wanted to help me." I had a long conversation over the phone with her and after she realized that it would take more than her words to make a man to give up on me, she tried different approach in splitting Patrick and I. She kept insisting for me to meet with some rich, good looking men that she knew that would be more than willing to marry someone like me.

"Thanks Linda but I already have the man I want. Patrick's the one I'm gonna marry so live with it. Stop obsessing about hooking me up with some rich guys for god's sake. You don't really know me woman, do you? I DO love money, YES, of course, but there are some other things that matter to me more than just being rich. I'd rather be with a man like Patrick than with some rich jerk that may think and act like he owns me." I laughed each time amused by seeing her perplexed look.

"But do you really wanna live like this? Do you wanna have to struggle all your life?" Linda was not the type of person who would give up easily.

"And who said I'm gonna have to? What? You don't think I'm capable of making good money? Why, you don't believe I'm gonna turn my book into a bestseller? Just sit and watch." My response was always the same.

"He must be real good in bed. Am I right?" She asked me one day. I just smiled.

"Oh god. You make me sick." She joked as she often did.

Jail

Patrick had been trying to find reasons to see me. There was always something that couldn't be resolved over the phone. There was his cell phone charger that was left in my place that needed to be picked up. Then there were some papers that also had to be retrieved from the tiny room I was renting. I was very cold and emotionally unavailable to him on purpose each time he came over. I was withdrawing my feelings from him. I was irritated by the sense of being lost that he was exhibiting. I needed for him to be that same strong man that wasn't afraid to literally take bullets while oversees protecting the freedom we all could not live without. Instead it felt like I was dealing with a small boy trapped in a grown man's body who was in desperate need of help and attention. I'd spent hours sometimes staring at an old picture of Patrick wondering what on earth had happened to this man who looked like a completely different person in that photo. His more than well defined muscles were showing off those perfect and ideal shapes through the wet T-shirt that he was wearing in that image. His broad shoulders were not hunched forward and his pushed out chest muscles were creating an illusion of a man who was very confident and proud of himself. His very big arms that in certain points could not even touch the rest of his body because of their muscularity were giving the sensation that this man was not afraid of anything or anyone. The dark "five o'clock shadow" on his serious and determine looking face emphasized how dangerous this man could be and almost served as a warning not to mess with him. His whole silhouette that was emerging from the ocean could serve as an example of a perfect male sex-symbol. He wasn't looking like a pretty boy from some magazine or anything, which was actually making him look that much more manly and therefore that much sexier. He couldn't look more "real" even if he tried to. A real man that besides having a strong looking body had an even stronger character written on his face and in his posture. In that picture he looked like a man by whom I would not want to wait to have my clothes ripped off. And then looking at Patrick in person I wondered what on earth had happened that made him let go of himself so much and in such a short time? His sexy looking muscles were all practically gone and were now replaced with some extra fat. Him being now somewhat overweight gave me the sensation of looking at someone who was trying to hide himself from the world. Almost as if he was afraid to be himself. His hunched body posture made me feel that he doubted himself and more importantly that he didn't feel safe. The look on his face and in his eyes that resembled a look of a little boy who had been hurt real bad and who had been feeling overwhelmed by the pain was making his manly features practically go away at moments. I felt compassion for him then but I could not feel physically attracted to him in those moments.

"When was this picture taken? How long ago?" I asked Patrick unable to even recognize him at first when he showed it to me.

"Just about a year and a half ago. Like right before I went to prison." He explained. I started to understand better than the emotional tall that the incarceration must have had on him was affecting him more than he was ready to admit. I wasn't discussing with him the subject because I didn't feel like I wanted to. As far as I was concerned his past and my past they all belonged in one place and one place only: inside our books. Mine had already three hundred pages. The book had ended at me having abortion with Ahmed's baby and I knew that I still had some more writing to do. I didn't feel like it was OK to disappoint the reader and myself for that matter by not having a more conclusive and happier ending than that. Patrick was just beginning his journey as a writer and so there was still a lot for me to learn about his life. I preferred letting facts about the past to unfold naturally rather than engaging in questioning and cross examining. I could not remain silent and unaffected any longer though when one of these "cold" days versus Patrick I received a call from Linda. She was letting me know that he could be going back to jail.

"What the hell are you talking about?" The concern in my voice was over written by the anger I was feeling.

"Well, he's on probation, didn't he tell you that? He missed his UA this morning. It's a random urine analyses appointment and just for that they can put him back in jail." She explained.

"He doesn't do any drugs for god's sake. He doesn't even smoke or drink alcohol. Why on earth does he have to take some random drug tests? It doesn't make any sense."

"I know but it's part of his probation terms." She explained again.

"So why didn't he take care of that appointment?" I asked.

"We were busy cleaning up the property, we've been working all day long and he just completely forgot about it." She answered.

"So what does this mean? What's gonna happen now?" I asked feeling nervous, concerned, stressed out beyond the limits and angry all at once.

"Well, first thing in the morning he's gonna have to go see his probation officer and even though his drug test will show up negative they still may arrest him for missing the appointment. It's gonna be up to his PO to make that call. If she does send him back to jail then he's gonna have to wait there for the hearing date. And then it's gonna be up to judge. He may decide to keep him in jail or he may decide to release him. Since this would be his first violation of his probation the judge may go easy on him but honestly it's hard to tell what he's gonna do." Linda sounded like she was well informed about the law and about Patrick's case.

"Oh god. I am so freaking angry at him right now it's not even funny. I can't even talk right now. I'll talk to you tomorrow, K? Bye."

Patrick did end up getting arrested the next day after he showed up at his PO's office. I got a call from jail later that evening. He sounded overly calm and even cheerful on the phone, almost as if he was trying to hide the sense of embarrassment. I was infuriated. To get some privacy, I left Eduardo's studio to take the call. I kept yelling at Patrick from the top of my lungs. I told him that he needed to grow up. That he needed to start acting like a responsible grown up man instead of acting like a self-sabotaging needy boy. I was very tough with him. I didn't stop saying the awful and soul-crashing things to him until the pretend cheerfulness in his voice was gone completely. Only then I soften my voice a little bit:

"Look Patrick, just…just do me a favor. Don't ever try telling me that everything's gonna be OK. That just infuriates me. I don't wanna hear those words. I'd rather hear the truth as it is. I want you to stop minimizing things and I need you to stop coming up with all those excuses and rationalizations. All right? Don't think for a moment that I don't see through you. Don't even try to bullshit me 'cause you won't get away with it with me. Stop thinking that if I get to know you well that I will walk away from you. That's not who I am. I don't give up easily. You should know that by now. I have been with you until this point despite everything haven't I? I think I deserve for you to trust me enough to be completely honest with me, don't you agree? So start being painfully honest with yourself and stop self sabotaging your life like you have been doing 'till now."

The House

Two days later Patrick got out from jail. I was still mad at him but not as mad as when he told me that the judge had ordered him to spend weekends locked up for the next two months.

"So what is it mean? You're gonna spend Saturdays and Sundays in jail for the next two months. Oh that's real nice." I tried calming down but not without remaining sarcastic.

"I have to be at triple OC each Friday at 6 p.m. and they'll release me the following Sunday at 6 in the afternoon." He clarified.

With Patrick being gone on the weekends I realized just how much I missed being around him. The anger I was feeling towards him, for whatever reasons, it was always gone, always appearing practically unjustified by the time I received the expected call from the jail. I missed him tremendously when he was gone and by each Sunday I was promising solely to myself that I would stop giving him such a hard time. I would tell myself that it was time for me to stop being so bossy and so demanding. I had some difficulties though with keeping those promises made to myself. I justified in my mind that my inability of letting go of control was caused mainly by the fact that I had to "keep everything in order." I felt as if without my efforts everything would just fall apart. I trusted Patrick and I knew that he was capable of taking care of everything. However I was afraid that his lack of staying completely focused as well as lack of ability to properly prioritize things could in the end cost us more than I was willing to have to pay for later on. I did try cutting him some slack when it came to dealing with the divorce issue. I let him handle it all by himself without trying to nag too much about it. I watched him getting frustrated trying to suppress his anger while looking for ways to make his wife sign the petition. He looked sexy again in my eyes when he was getting mad.

Probably because that face of a lost little boy was replaced with a face of a grown man who was starting to take charge of his life making therefore mine that much easier. I liked seeing him this way. It was turning me on even when he was getting frustrated and mad at me. I could see how he was still struggling internally as if he wasn't completely sure if it was the right thing to do to put himself first before anyone else. He had that attitude that was showing me that he would do just about anything just to see me happy. On my request he started helping out Linda only on days when he didn't have anything else scheduled. Since the demand was high on this more than capable mechanic/electrician/handy man who could do just about anything and who charged way less than most people did, Linda had no choice but to hear "No, I can't help you" more often. I knew she wasn't happy about all that and I knew she was blaming me for her latest inconvenience but I wasn't going to give in to her demands. It wasn't just that she never paid him for all the work he has done for her. Her constant need of assistance was taking the precious time away. I did not like that for occasionally driving Patrick here or there and for using her connections to get him some jobs she felt entitled to everything almost as if she owned him. It drove me crazy to see Patrick allowing others to keep taking advantage of him. As if that wasn't enough those same people were trying to tell me that I was "just using him for papers". Without sugar coating I told Linda that since he had a future wife to take care of that he couldn't afford to be as generous and as giving as he used to be. I know she didn't like me saying it to her but nevertheless she did seem like she wanted to remain friends with us.

Lately Patrick had been doing a lot of work for that old woman that was there with Linda the day when he and I had met. She was a retired immigration officer and she owned few properties, few homes and apartments. She seemed very happy with the jobs Patrick was doing for her these days. She was paying him cash, which was a nice change, as opposed to getting some favors and promises only. I think she was really enjoying Patrick's company and his friendly, modest personality. Knowing how strapped with money he was all the time she even bought some groceries for the two of us from time to time.

"K babe, I'm getting ready to go to finish painting that house for her so we can get some money." Patrick said to me one day.

"How're you gonna get all the way to Waianae? Is she gonna drive you there?" I asked.

"Linda's in town so I'm gonna get a ride with her." He answered.

"You know what? I'm gonna go with you. It'll be a lot faster if there's gonna be two of us painting. I'm not doing anything today anyway so let's go." I put my old clothes that were stained all over with paint that varied in colors. The house was old and as Patrick had informed me was eaten up from inside by termites so badly that it would never pass the inspection. The owner was well aware of the fact that no bank would agree to finance this neglected house that she was trying to short-sale since the mortgage was bringing her budget down. The cleaning up of the land that the house was standing on, was supposed to attract prospective tenants or buyers, whichever came first. After getting tired of stroking the roller covered with pistachio-color paint against the walls I sat down on the dirty floor. I looked around the small living room area that had two very wide windows. While smoking a cigarette I allowed myself to play in my mind the game of what this place would look like if it was mine. I pictured the white frames around each door and each window. In my mind I saw a beautiful wooden floor extending all the way to and through the open kitchen. I imagined gorgeous colorful flowers sneaking their spirit-uplifting heads through the windows. In my mind on the porch there were all sort of pots filled with tomato plants. The green vines were bending due to the weight caused by those ravishing looking delicious and juicy in taste red fruits. I had to stop playing my mental game because it was starting to make me feel depressed.

"What's wrong babe?" Patrick kneeled down in front of me.

"Babe, for how long will I have to keep doing this? How long will I have to watch myself and watch you fixing someone else's place but our own? We'll we ever have a place that we can call home? I'm not asking for that much am I? I mean I could live even in a house like this. I don't even care that it's so old and that it needs so much work. I could live with it. I just wish that we could have a place that's ours, you know what I mean?" I looked nostalgic and depleted from energy. Patrick tried consoling me a little bit and then he went outside. Through the window I saw him talking to someone on his cell phone. He came back shortly after. He had a smile on his face that he tried hiding but without being very successful at it.

"Would you like if we moved in to this house? Would you like if we rented this place?" He asked pretending like he didn't know the answer to that.

"Babe, what're you talking about? You told me she's looking for a tenant that can pay her twenty five hundred a month for this place. You know we could not possibly afford that." I wasn't letting myself to get excited.

"Yeah, but she also plans to do all kinds of repairs first so that someone would be willing to rent this thing. Basically what she said is that we may be able to come up with some agreement that could be good for all of us." He tried explaining.

"What exactly do you mean?" I couldn't wait to hear the answer I thought I was about to hear.

"Well, she said we can start moving in if we want to and that she will deduct my pay for the jobs I'm doing here to cover our rent. AND she said she will charge us only fifteen hundred dollars a month for the first few months instead of twenty five hundred." He explained. I jumped. I started dancing a happy dance. With my arms lifted towards the ceiling I was shaking my hips from side to side. Big wide smile on my previously sad face still had some traces of disbelief. I stopped dancing when I realized that I would get very depressed when after getting used to living in this place and after making all the changes while taking care of it, our landlord would tell us that she finally found someone interested in buying this property. Hearing my legitimate concerns Patrick reassured me that he had already discussed with her the possibility of us buying this place through the owner-financing deal.

"Babe, I'm gonna work as hard as I have to. You know me and you know that working hard is all that I know how to do well. Don't worry, I will secure this place for us OK? I will make sure we'll have enough money to give her the down payment and all that." Seeing a still insecure smile on my face Patrick grabbed my butt and he lifted me. He kept scrolling me in the air until I was laughing at loud again.

"I love you baby. You know I'd do anything to make you happy. I will make sure you'll have everything you've ever wanted. Everything you deserve. You are the most amazing, the most beautiful woman I've ever seen in my life. I can't wait 'till I'll be able to refer to you as my wife." He was looking straight into my eyes. I was afraid he's arms were getting tired of holding me.

"No, no! Don't put me down. Not yet. I like it up here. The world looks a lot more beautiful from here. And I feel a lot less stressed out when you hold me like this." I extended my arms and I tilted my head all the way back as far as I could. I felt like I was a little girl. My legs were hanging loose and I could feel the tension leaving my body. I was feeling loved. I was happy. Finally there seemed to be even if just glimpses of light at the end of the long tunnel called my life. I had a man whom I loved and who was crazy about me. A man, who even though being a human being was full of issues, was treating me like a royal princess. And now I was also allowed to see the beautiful shape that our life together was starting to take.

Surprise

The move to our new place was swift. The girl I was renting the room from was not happy about me leaving before the six month lease expired even though I did find a new roommate for her the same day I left. Few emails going back and forth later she did eventually give me back at least half of my security deposit. Being strapped with money since I wasn't working for Eduardo, at least not on regular basis like I used to, having even two hundred and fifty dollars back made a difference. Patrick and I still didn't have a car and so our mobility was presenting us with lots of challenges. He had his frequent UA (drug test) appointments, meeting with his PO, attending a mandatory weekly therapy class (for which he had no other choice by to pay sixty dollars each week or he'd go back to prison) and of course he had to spend his weekends locked up. In order to get to all the way to Honolulu which was a forty five minutes drive he was arranging rides with Linda and/or our landlord lady at their convenience. I was most of the time at home busy with painting and re-painting our new residence. When I wasn't busy with rearranging and making our new love nest more cozy and livable, I was having coffee and cigarettes with our new neighbors. Linda, since she was living not far away became a frequent guest. I was actually enjoying her company. She brought us some old furniture that she didn't need and she let us borrow few big cushions from some couch so we had something to sleep on. Seeing how modestly we were forced to live she even brought us some pasta and other easily preservable forms of food from time to time.

"I don't want to see you guys starving like this." She'd say in that motherly tone of hers while performing a thorough search through the empty kitchen cabinets. Having this maniac-bipolar-like sometimes but generally funny woman's company was very helpful particularly on the weekends when Patrick was gone. The two of us would drive around sometimes taking care of her errands, sometimes taking care of mine.

"Look! That's a nice jeep over there. I could see you driving that thing." Linda pointed at an old jeep that was parked by the road we were on. It looked abandoned. The bright baby blue color and the black zebra like strikes that was painted in made it look like an adventurous safari vehicle.

"Nice. Definitely nice." I said.

"I know the guy that lives here. He had fixed cars for me before. Let's go talk to him. He may sell this thing to you for like nothing. Patrick will have no problem with making this thing drivable." She sounded excited. We spoke to the guy and he agreed to sell what was pretty much just a shell for two hundred dollars. I paid him a hundred fifty which was all I had and he agreed to wait two more weeks to get the remaining fifty. My new neighbors helped us hauling what turned out to be the original military CJ 5. The owner told us that we could come back if we needed to buy the engine for four hundred dollars from him. I knew that Patrick could make an even better deal by looking at craigslist ads. I was all excited. Even the neighbors seemed all excited with all the commotion that was going on.

"Hey you know what? We should cover it with something so it will be like a surprise when Patrick gets home." I told Linda and she agreed.

"I have some big rapping papers at home. Let's go pick it up so we can wrap it like a gift. And we can write Happy Easter on it. I bet nobody ever had done anything like this for him before. I doubt his ex wives ever made any gesture to make him feel loved. Oh I wanna see the look on his face when he gets back." Her voice sounded all excited as well. We got the wrapping paper and we started taping the jeep. I put different things around it before to camouflage the obvious shape.

"This starts looking like an elephant or something!" I pointed out. We were both laughing. We were having a good time. When we were done with rapping and taping Linda wrote Happy Easter and Patrick's favorite phrases that he liked using with that characteristic accent and slang quite often understandable only to people who grew up in Texas.

"Oh this is nice." She said while looking at the shape of heart and the big letters that I wrote with white paint that said: YOU ARE LOVED. Patrick wasn't coming back home until the next evening. The next day Linda and I went to have lunch at some not expensive dinner. We were having some pasta while talking about everything and anything.

As usual by now Patrick was our favorite topic to discuss. Since Linda really enjoyed talking, our easy going conversation was pretty much me just listening to her. She was going on and on about how Patrick was a great guy, how she didn't like that he allowed people to take advantage of him and how she couldn't understand how he got himself in so much trouble with the law.

"I'm telling you, all those sex assault charges against him sound too fishy to me. There is just too much to this story that makes no sense. I don't believe he had sex with that girl, to be honest with you." She said to me.

"What do you mean? Tell me exactly what you know." I said to Linda.

"Why, you guys don't talk about these things?" She asked.

"Not really. Every time he wants to have a serious conversation I just tell him that I'm not in a mood for it. I just want us to be able to live our life without looking back, without re-evaluating past and all that bull shit."

Linda didn't need the encouragement to talk and so I just sat there with my arms crossed while listening to her version of the story:

"Well, Patrick is a sweetheart but he can also be a real dumbass sometimes. He's biggest problem is that he trusts people way too much and way too easily and that's what's always got him in trouble. Whether it was with his dumbass wives that just used him and then cheated on him when he was serving oversees or this latest fucking bull shit that happened with that business partner of his." As she continued talking she had a noticeable anger not just in her voice but in her facial expressions as well:

"When he got out from the Navy, which was like two years ago, he had this brilliant idea and he started his own business. I guess he still had some money left from his latest deployment to Iraq or Afghanistan which allowed him to get things rolling. He bought all the equipment and he created his own life guard company. His business was providing trained and licensed life guards to some hotels and some military housing that had swimming pools. He had a good number of employees and he was doing real good. He was making fifteen THOUSAND, not hundred, fifteen thousand a month in his salary. He was living a good life. That's how I think he screwed himself over. He HAD TO live in a huge two story house. He absolutely had to drive all those freaking expensive cars and all that. He doesn't freaking understand that some people can get really jealous when you continually flash expensive things in front of them and when they themselves cannot afford any of that. That what makes me so mad at him. Well, anyway. He had a friend that he knew from the time when the two of them were serving overseas. So as naïve as Patrick can be sometimes, of course he makes this guy his business partner because he knows this guy and he's a good guy right? Not only that. He lets this guy, his wife and their fifteen year old daughter move in with him. And that's when the freaking troubles started. Anyway, one day Patrick goes through the papers and he discovers that these people have been forging company's checks and that they had taken over TWENTY THOUSAND dollars from the account. So, he confronts them and guess what happens the very next morning? Patrick gets arrested! Yeap. The police showed up and they took him to prison. He was charged for having sex with that fifteen year old girl; these people's daughter that lived with them. How convenient. These people knew they could be facing jail if they couldn't come up with an explanation where all that missing money went. It doesn't take a genius to figure out that they must have already spent it all. So they came up with a plan and they set up the poor guy without even worrying that he's life would be ruined forever. These fucking mother fuckers, piece of shit, 'cause there's no other way to describe these scumbags should rot in hell for what they did! They must have told that girl: "Hey honey? You need to tell the cops that he had raped you or mommy and daddy will go to prison." If I was in her shoes I'd probably lie too if I knew my parents would go to jail if I didn't. I don't know. This whole thing makes me sick. How can somebody be so cruel? I'm telling you; they were jealous of all the nice things he had so they started stealing from him thinking he wasn't smart enough to find out about it. But when he did and he confronted them, they must have really panicked. I would imagine."

"Oh my goodness." I exhaled while stretching my back. Linda did not only sound convincing; she was actually making a lot of good points. Things she was saying were actually making perfect sense to me. I could see Patrick being able to over-indulge himself in a less than discrete way that would make others hate his guts. I could see him being too trusting and too naïve when it came to dealing with people in general. I did doubt that he did what he was accused of. He was way too much of a gentleman. He had too much respect. Although thoughts of even the slightest possibility of him having a consensual sex with that teenage girl did cross my mind, I did not dwell on it. I knew it wouldn't make a big difference to me whether the prosecutor was right or wrong. By now I would take Patrick's side and I would stand by him no matter what.

"So what happened? Did he get a lawyer or something?" I asked.

"Yeah, and in my opinion that freaking lawyer screwed him big time."

"What do you mean?"

"Well, Patrick has been sitting in that stupid prison for a whole year. They did a DNA test and the results came out negative. All they really had was her words against his. Of course in this country, especially here in Hawaii, this is good enough to keep a man locked up indefinitely. So anyway; while he was sitting in jail his business partner and his "lovely" wife, they took everything he had in that house and they sold it. I mean his flat-screen TV, his computers, his sixty thousand dollars ranger and even the corvette which wasn't even his. He was fixing it for a friend of his. Anyway. Then they just packed up and they left the Island like nothing happened. Then the lawyer when he found out that Patrick had no money to pay him, he just told him: "Take the plea bargain. Physically you do like you could be a criminal and this could hurt you when you'll sit in front of the jury. And if they'd find you guilty, you'd be looking at spending forty years behind the bars. If you take the plea bargain and plead guilty, since you've already spent a year in prison, you'll be free to go and you'll just be on probation for the next four years." Sounds like a sweet deal doesn't it? You tell me. All he has to do is to even just pee in a wrong direction and he's back in jail. Not to mention the criminal record that will hunt him for the rest of his life. He is now a convicted sex offender. Even though they did end up dropping the original rape charges but they still convicted him for having sex with a minor. Still, to the world he's a child molester, a freaking monster! He was STUPID to take that plea, but hey, if that was me sitting in that jail not knowing when the hell I would be able to get out, I don't know. I don't know what I would do." Linda's genuine concern for Patrick was making me like her more.

"Oh god, I don't even wanna think about all this. I think I'm getting a headache." I said.

"Can you imagine this? Can you imagine someone telling you, because you have big muscular body and shaved head, that you fit the profile of a criminal and so you just should accept the guilty plea bargain?" Linda continued. I interrupted her:

"You know what? I need a cigarette. Are you still gonna eat that or can we leave now?" I was overwhelmed.

In the evening Linda pulled over in her truck into our driveway. Patrick was with her. Linda looked like a little girl who couldn't wait for Patrick to notice the weird shaped "package" that was behind the house. When he did finally noticed it he approached it closely to have a better look. He carefully read the writings. He had that same insecure, modesty revealing smile that made me fall in love with him. The look in his eyes was unveiling how touched he was.

"Well open it! Why're you just standing there and keep staring at it?" Linda couldn't control her mouth any longer. The three of us were smiling while Patrick was unwrapping the gift.

"That's what I thought it was." He said after ripping off the first piece of paper. He was smiling now like a little boy who had found under the Christmas tree exactly what he's been asking for in his letters to Santa. It felt good to see the appreciation not just for the gift but for the gesture more than anything. It was more than obvious that this thoughtful and considerate man was not used to receiving this sort of kindness. That was making me sad.

Will You Do Me The Honor...?

Ever since Patrick and I had moved to that old house, even though in such a short time, relationship-wise things were starting to look good. We began to fight less frequently and we started to actually having a good time with each other. In my eyes he was finally looking, sounding and acting more like the man that I knew he was. He was a confident and kind man, no longer hidden underneath numerous layers of unresolved emotional and legal issues. It was finally starting to be obvious to me, and I didn't have to question it anymore, something I hated doing; that he was everything I've been looking for in a man. Patrick had been planning to use his gift-certificate that his mother had sent to him for his birthday to buy some new clothes which he didn't have much of. When he was released from the prison all he had was the pair of shorts and a t-shirt that he was wearing on that day when police arrested him. He hadn't been able to recover any of his belongings that he had left at the house which he was renting prior to his arrest. The friend of his that was letting him live at the boat gave him few old pair of shorts and t-shirts to wear. I knew Patrick wanted to upgrade his wardrobe and so I was encouraging him to do so. One day when I saw him browsing online for woman's jewelry I asked him:

"What're you doing? Why are you wasting your time with these things? You know we couldn't afford any of that right now. What's the point of looking at it? It makes me mad." I complained.

"Yes we can. I can use my gift certificate, remember?" He replied. My eyes got bigger.

"You c-o-o-uld. No. You need some decent clothes more than I need some nice, ver-ry nice, but very unnecessary at this moment jewelry." I kept looking at the internet pages that were luring me with their shiny mood uplifting accessories.

"No. I don't want any of that stuff." I insisted trying not to show how disappointed I was feeling.

"It's my gift certificate and I'll do with it whatever I want." He said firmly. Then he added:

"You can either choose what you want for yourself or you can have me do that for you." All excited since I had none of those things anymore I picked a watch, a set of earrings and a nice necklace.

"Oh that's real nice! Where did you find this one?" I asked while staring at the page on my laptop that was showing an engagement ring.

"So do you like this one?" He asked smiling seeing how content I looked.

"Yeeeah. It's real nice. But that can't be a real diamond. Not for this price and with this size." I noticed.

"No, this ring is made with a synthetic diamond. See this? Read here. It's a lab created diamond. Same properties of a natural diamond are used to compose this stone in a technological environment as oppose to a natural geological one."

"It is very nice. And it comes with a wedding band too. I do like this ring." I said even more with my dreamy eyes than with my words.

"K. This will be the one then." Patrick clicked on the "Add to your cart" link.

Few days later a FedEx truck parked in front of our house. Since all I've been obsessing about was Patrick's divorce, I run out of the house hoping that his legally still considered wife had finally signed the divorce papers.

"*Oh my god, maybe she signed it. Maybe she finally did that. Oh god.*" Thoughts were rushing through my mind while I was approaching the FedEx lady that was getting out of the truck.

"Don't! Don't give that to her! It's not for her! Wait!" The woman and I only now had noticed Patrick running on the street towards the truck. He was coming from the direction of our neighbor's house. I understood then that it was the jewelry package that had arrived and that he was planning to surprise me with it.

"Oh well, your surprise is ruined now." I said to him trying to grab the box out of his hands.

"Nope. You don't get to see it until I say so." He extended his arm away so I couldn't reach it.

"Oh come on! Don't be like that." I complained in a spoiled, girly manner.

"Fine! I don't care." I lied hoping he'd lower his guards but it didn't work. To end the "fight" Patrick grabbed me effortlessly and he threw me like a bag of grain over his shoulder. I started kicking my legs in the air and punching his behind that became my view since my head was hanging in that direction. Other than making a noise while screaming and laughing, I wasn't able to say a word. I was too happy. I went back to painting the kitchen and Patrick went back to fixing the pipes in the bathroom. The day had passed and I already forgot about the jewelry box. I figured Patrick wanted to save up so money so he could take me to a restaurant or something where he could propose to me in a fashionable manner. Covered all over with white paint I went to the bathroom and I looked at my boyfriend who was all sweaty and covered all in dirt himself. I said to him:

"Babe, I don't know about you but I sure could use a nice bath."

"Give me a second babe. Let me scrub this bath tab for you before you get in. It's nasty. Go smoke another cigarette." He answered.

"K. Your bath's ready!" He called me shortly after. I took my dirty clothes of and I submerged my exhausted and aching body into the hot water. The foam from the bubbles exited the half of a regular in size bath tab as I filled it with myself. I did what I normally do first when bathing and I splashed my face with the water.

"Oooh yesss." I moaned.

"Are you coming in or what?" I asked Patrick.

"Yeah, gimme a sec." He answered. He joined me shortly after. He sat behind me wrapping his legs around me. I leaned my head back. I let Patrick's chest support my tired and heavy feeling head. I closed my eyes. I wanted to stop thinking. I didn't even want to think about having thoughts. I wanted to get rid of the weight I've been allowing myself to carry on my shoulders for God only knows how long. I didn't want any more, even if just for short few minutes, to worry about saving the world, saving myself and everybody else who happened to cross their path with me. I wanted to be excused from such self-appointed responsibility. I wanted to be able to see myself as "nobody insignificant". Ironically that was exactly how my subconscious was seeing me and believing in. By now I was well aware of this inner conflict that has been still going on.

"Oh god. I needed this so bad." I said with my eyes still closed. Patrick was washing off the paint that was on my arms. I wasn't moving. I was enjoying the sound of the murmur of the splashing water. The simple act of even keeping my eye lids opened seemed too challenging and not worthy of the effort. I didn't want to look at the beaten up bath tab and the old walls of the small bathroom anyway. I wanted to remain grateful for having a place where I could be this intimate with Patrick without having to worry about curious roommates. These days I could understand more than ever the importance of having privacy in a couple's relationship. Lots of tension and irritability always resulting in fights was resolved automatically by the fact of having our place all to ourselves.

"Babe?" Patrick tried gaining my attention.

"No babe, please don't talk. I just wanna be quiet. I just want us to stay like this for a while." I said to him. My eyes were getting heavier and heavier with each moment. My thoughts could not have control over me. They had no other choice but to keep flowing the way puffy clouds do on the azure sky while the wind of my stilled mind kept blowing them away.

"You know I love you right?" Patrick continued. I was feeling too relaxed to yell at him for not respecting my wish of remaining in silence. I let him talk ignoring completely what he was saying to me. My eyes remained closed the whole time. I let the words of compliments and flatteries addressed towards me go by my ears without paying too much attention. Then when I heard him asking me: "Will you do me the honor of being my wife?" I mistook that for being one of those moments when he liked verbalizing our plans for the future. I felt annoyed and with my eyes still closed I said to him:

"Babe, you know we're not ready for that yet. Come on, stop talking about that already. Come on. You know you're not even divorced yet. I mean it's sweet what you're telling me but…" I opened my eyes surprised to see the ring he was holding in front of me. I couldn't help but to smile.

"Is that a yes?" He asked in nonchalant way.

"Yes. I'll marry you." I smiled even wider. He leaned to kiss me.

"Well put it on!" I freed myself from his lips. I was emotional and all excited. I was happy again. The exhaustion and tiredness were gone in an instant. I watched Patrick sliding the beautiful ring on my finger. He was doing it slowly and tenderly. I didn't know what I wanted to focus on enjoying more; seeing my new engagement ring or seeing happiness and expression of deep love in his face and in his eyes. My head was twisting back and forth between the two. I wasn't just happy. I was utterly ecstatic.

"Wait, this means I am your fiancé now." I said sounding and looking more like a little girl than a grown woman. This new reality seemed starting to sink into my brain, creating new and boosting already existent neurotransmitters.

"Aha! So this is what joy feels like." I kept chatting while enjoying my own happiness and the happiness of Patrick who kept staring at me with amusement. Finally my life was starting to have a shape of a life that I desired to live.

What Do We Do Now?

I was in the middle of our living room. I was standing on a chair while attempting to paint the ceiling fan. I wanted it to match the ceiling itself and the white frames around the doors and the windows that I had painted already. While making strokes with my extended right arm I was holding the cup filled with paint with my left arm. I didn't realize my limitations of multi-tasking until it was too late to change the curse of what happened next. Alert by the feeling of cold on my left shoulder, I looked down only to see that whatever was left in the cup until now; was spreading quickly all over the rest of my body. I stood there motionless staring at the white paint covering entirely the left side of my body. I wasn't sure which reaction I wanted to have more: to cry or to laugh. I was still standing there unwilling to make a move when I saw Patrick coming through the master bedroom's door. He looked like he just saw a ghost and from the look on his face I knew it wasn't because of me. I knew something had to be wrong because the man that I got engaged to would not pass such occasion to laugh and to make jokes about.

"Babe, you may as well stop doing what you're doing." He said in a serious and resigning way.

"Why, what's wrong?" I asked.

"We need to move out. We don't have another choice. She has new tenants and they're moving in tomorrow." He informed me. I got down on the floor dragging the white paint all over.

"I thought you guys were through with discussing this rent thing for the past few days and all that. Last time you spoke with her, didn't she tell you that she'll think about letting us keep renting it?" I asked.

"Yeah, but she makes her point by saying that this guy is willing to pay the twenty five hundred a month and that I on the other hand don't have a steady income and all that. It's done baby. We don't have a choice. We need to start packing."

"Great. And where do you suppose we go from here?" I used cynicism to cope with the anger that was building inside me. The familiar feelings of going through losing a home when I was fifteen were now intensifying my uneasy emotions. The anger I was feeling then towards my mother for losing the legal battle over our home with her brother was now the same kind of anger I was feeling towards my fiancé. I was blaming him for not doing whatever it took to secure our place. I was mad at myself for choosing a man that apparently didn't have what it took to take good care of his woman.

"Please don't tell me that you are thinking about going back to live on that boat."

"That's not gonna happen either." He said with little emotions in his voice.

"Care to elaborate that?" I was getting more and more frustrated and Patrick's slow response was getting on my already shredded nerves.

"I just got a text saying I need to move my shit out of that boat. Apparently if I'm not there all day long fixing it then I'm not welcome to stay there." He answered. I couldn't argue with him about that since I was the one who kept insisting on focusing on doing jobs that he was getting paid for.

"So where do you wanna stay?"

"In the car I guess." He replied. We did have a car now since the landlord lady let Patrick to lease from her an old toyota that she bought with him from craigslist for four hundred dollars. I found out later that she also had offered him that he could live rent free in one of her apartments as long as I wasn't living with him. He turned the offer down. This whole unfriendliness towards me seemed to have started with the day Linda called me asking me for money. She was talking about how she couldn't afford to pay for her cell phone and how because of all that she had done for us so far she was expecting me to convince Patrick in paying for her bill. That just pissed me of.

"Linda, what the hell are you doing asking us for money? And exactly what favors are you talking about here? Didn't Patrick slave for you for free for like a whole month without getting paid? Didn't he fix your and your son's car for free? Besides, can't you see how we live? We sleep on the freaking ground on some cushions and you saw what kind of food we eat. You were the one who brought us food sometimes because we didn't have any for god's sake! Come on, we're friends and we've been helping each other like we suppose to but trying to take advantage is not cool. What makes you think we have any extra money anyway? And in the end you're the one who's richer than we are. I mean you're the one who's buying a house on Big Island and all that. Don't do that BS and ask Patrick to pay for..." I didn't finish my sentence realizing she hung up on me. The following day after that Linda kept leaving messages on Patrick's phone. He kept ignoring them.

"Don't you dare give her any money." I told him.

"I don't intend to." He answered firmly. I knew Patrick liked being generous, even if it had to be on his expense. I didn't want him to think that I was OK with him sacrificing not just himself but me as well. It was obvious that he was lacking assertiveness and that it wouldn't take much for Linda to convince him that it was his "moral" obligation to pay her phone bill. After just a day of unanswered phone calls, Linda showed up in front of our gate that always remained locked throughout the night. We heard the loud and persistent honking and we knew it was her. It was early in the morning and Patrick and I were still totally naked. We were just taking my "cigarette brake" from the love making.

"Come on babe, go open that gate for her." I said to Patrick. As soon as he done that the drama begun. Linda stormed inside the house and while calling me names like: "Russian whore" she started collecting her cushions from the ground.

"Sleep on the naked floor you Russian whore!" She yelled at me with the hatred in her eyes.

"You've got all your pillows? Good. Now, GET THE FUCK OUT OF HERE." I said to her slowly, loud enough but without yelling. I shot the door and I turned the key. Since the old woman who owned the house was a retired INS officer, she informed Patrick that Linda did indeed "made a call to try to get rid of me". Unfortunately for her it didn't work as she was told that as long as my tourist visa remained valid she had no business to be concerned.

"That back stabbing bitch. I don't wanna see her face ever again. I don't care if she comes back apologizing saying that she was just kidding and all that and that she suffers from bi-polar. I've put up with more than enough from her. Some people need to be just kept at a distance. This woman is out of our lives permanently this time." I said to Patrick and he agreed.

Paid Off in Full

Patrick packed everything we owned in some trash bags and he stuffed it all in the car. We had no choice but to leave the old jeep there. We both felt bad about it since it had a sentimental value but there was no room for impracticality.

"What do we do with this poor kitty cat?" He asked me. The cat technically belonged to the landlord lady as it has inhabited the house for a while. While the house was standing empty the neighbors got used to feeding this deformed, sick looking but the sweetest creature ever.

"What do you mean? Of course he's coming with us. I'm not leaving this poor thing here. What if those people won't even feed him? Besides I'm already attached to him." I answered. Patrick didn't look surprised. He was already attached to the kitty himself.

"So I guess I'm gonna have to go back to Eduardo's place. Where the hell are you going to stay?" I asked my fiancé.

"In the car." He's answer irritated me. I knew I was going to ask Eduardo whether Patrick could rent the small room with me but I could not guarantee the results. What was upsetting me even more than then situation itself was Patrick's passiveness about it. I knew he wasn't happy but I wanted him to show more emotions than what he was exhibiting. I expected him to curse, kick the walls even, none of which was happening. The sense of resignation in his body language was driving me nuts. I resented him for not making me feel safe and well taken care of. I blamed him for making me carry the weight of worrying about our stability.

Eduardo had never met Patrick before and so my fiancé waited in the car while I went to talk to him. I explained Eduardo what predicament we found ourselves in.

"He can spend the night in your room. I'm not gonna let the poor guy sleep in the car for god's sake." Eduardo finally offered.

"Thank you so much. There is just one thing you need to know. He's on probation and as one of his conditions he has to let people that he's staying with know about it." I said.

"What is he on probation for?" Eduardo inquired.

"For having sex with a fifteen year old."

"You're not joking?" He looked at me as if expecting me to conform that it was just one of my mental pranks I like to engage in.

"Nope."

"Well, bring the guy in. Don't let him sit in that freaking car. You know where the room is." He said after a short pause.

Both Patrick and Eduardo seemed very uncomfortable at first. The older man fired all kinds of question in the direction of his younger rival. The interrogation and cross examination went on for a while. By then time I finished organizing our stuff in my old room and by the time I decided to join them; the two men looked like were having a good time.

"Where did you find this guy? He's a good man! I'm telling you. You know what we call a guy like Patrick in Italy? We say he's like bread." Eduardo seemed all excited.

"He's like what?" I wasn't sure what he was trying to say.

"Il pane. Haven't you heard of that expression?"

"Noooo." I replied feeling happy that the tension wasn't present anymore.

"Well, don't worry. It means he's a good man. Why don't you go and make us all those nice sandwiches you know how to make. Go in the refrigerator, you know where everything is." Eduardo looked like was having a good time. I was just feeling relieved watching them interacting like they knew each other for some time. I wasn't saying much allowing them to have a good time.

"Tell you what. That small room on the other side of the house, you guys can rent for five hundred bucks a month if you want." Eduardo offered. I could not remain silent:

"Are you serious? Of course! Thanks Eduardo, I really appreciate that."

"You can start paying the rent starting next month. I know you guys don't have any money right now so don't worry about that." The man kept surprising us with his compassion and understanding.

Things were not always going smooth but in general life had improved a little bit for Patrick and I. He was busy working still as a repair man. He wasn't making a lot but we were finally able to send the money for the last payment owned on Fan's house. We both ate very little those days in order to come up with the extra eleven hundred dollars. Patrick did not complain but I sure was tired of the self-imposed sacrifice. I was more than happy knowing that the house in Kenya was finally paid off. I wasn't expecting to spend more than additional hundred bucks for the closing fees but that was when I got surprised.

"No freaking way! She's texting me that it will cost six hundred bucks to transfer the title to her name and all that. This is way too much. I'm not doing it." I was complaining to my future husband. The following weeks I was sending not very pleasant messages to Fan explaining to her that I wasn't going to cover for the closing fees.

"The amount you guys are telling me is close to ten percent of the value of the property. I checked online and it says that in Kenya closing fees on real estate are not more than four percent. So why are you guys telling me it's gonna take six hundred dollars to obtain that title deed? You're on your own. I mean I got you guys the house, take care of the closing fees yourself. Figure something. I'm not doing it." I was very mad at my friend. Sometimes I thought she was lying to me but most of them time I knew it was the local officials who were really behind all that. I felt so frustrated that in order to finish the project completely I had no choice but to let myself feel taken advantage of. Few weeks later I finally gave in.

"You know what babe, let's send that freaking six hundred dollars but that is the last time I'm sending them anything. It's just makes me so freaking mad." I vented to my fiancé. He agreed and we went to Wal-Mart.

"Thaaat's it. Gosh! I'm just glad it's over. Can you hold on to this receipt for me?" I asked Patrick after we were done with sending the money. No matter how upset I was, I was proud of myself for having kept my word. Fan owned the half acre and the house that was on it.

In order to spend more time with Patrick I volunteered to drive with him to work. While he'd crawl underneath people's cars, Nel and I would just sit in the car, waiting. Sometimes I'd take her for a walk around the neighborhood. Sometimes, depends on the costumers, I'd engage in chat with them. Generally speaking it was boring and tiring but I wanted to be around Patrick.

Getting Ready

"Baaabe. Guess what? As of today I am a free man." Patrick said while walking into our tiny room like he was the king of the world. He's face was illuminated with a warm smile. He had that humble yet confident at the same time look on his face which I loved. He's eyes were sparkling with excitement.

"No way! Is the divorce final?" I jumped off the bed, all of a sudden feeling full of energy.

"Yep." He smiled widely now.

"Oh my god! Finally!" I hugged him.

"Lift me. Lift me up!" I commanded with excitement.

"I can't believe we are finally able to get married. I can't believe the nightmare's over." I was just as relieved as excited.

It's been quite some time since my wedding dress, wrapped in a nontransparent bag, has been hanging in our room. While waiting for the divorce to be finalized Patrick and I have been planning our big day impatiently. Originally I gave up the idea of wearing a wedding dress due to our financial struggle but Patrick knowing how much that meant to me, insisted on me going to the store to get one. Since I couldn't have my future husband seeing me wearing it prior to the ceremony, and I didn't have close friends; I went to the bridal store by myself. The pregnant salewoman was very patient while assisting me with the three white dresses that I picked. The one I chose at the end was on sale and cost only three hundred dollars. The dress was all white, simple yet very elegant. It was strapless of course and it had relatively long tail. The top part, after meeting with the store's sawing lady, fit as tight as it could on me. From the waist down the dress was extending giving me the sensation of being a Cinderella ready to go to the ball. The veil I picked was real nice too. It was medium in size and of delicate texture.

"Oh my goodness." I was talking to my own reflection in the big mirror. I was staring at what looked like a live Barbie and I couldn't believe that I've ever questioned my looks before. I kept turning from left to right to see better my profile. I couldn't get enough of what my eyes were seeing. I did not want to get undressed. Ever!

"That's the one. It fits you perfectly." An older woman that was sitting on a chair destructed me with her words. Only now I noticed that she's been observing me the whole time with amusement.

"Thank you. I think so too." I smiled with shyness.

"You look absolutely gorgeous. Like an angel." She added. I did not want to leave the store. I wasn't ready to go back to my ordinary life yet. I wanted to suck in every positive, pleasurable emotion I was deriving for seeing myself as a bride and not bride's made only. Some hour later, still in the dress, parading in front of all the mirrors that the store had, it hit me that it was happening for real.

"Oh my god. I'm getting married." I said to my reflection.

"Ah-ha. So this is why brides often have hard time breathing. It has nothing to do with how uncomfortable the outfit may be." I kept talking to myself while moving my hands fast to generate wind in front of my face. My shortness of breath was a little different from when I had anxiety attacks. This time it was the excitement that was responsible for the quality of my breathing. The positive yet overwhelming feelings were desperately trying to be released. I so wished that my family could be there with me to share my happiness. I tried imagining how we'd all jump and scream while making jokes and while laughing.

"It's all right. We'll have a second wedding when we'll go to Poland. We'll have a big Polish wedding." My thoughts were there to erase the sadness.

Patrick picked for us the place where we'd get married. I had in mind a different beach for that occasion but when he took me to a very isolated place called Eternity Beach, I agreed to follow his lead. I liked how romantic he was while explaining to me that getting married at the Eternity Beach would mean being together for Eternity. The place was absolutely breath taking. It required some serious rock climbing in order to reach it. There was no road that let to it, only a foot-printed passage across the numerous rocks that were spreading everywhere. The different in shapes volcanic stones were dark and sharp looking. On the bottom of

470

the mountain the yellow sand was contrasting with the blue and turquoise water in the ocean. The white waves, without taking a break, were constantly splashing against the dark rocks. In some areas the relentless surf resembled a whales' spout. This horse-shoe shaped valley looked more like it belonged on the moon than earth. In the middle of the mountain there was a cave that added even more romanticism to this piece of paradise. There wasn't much vegetation going on apart from some white birds that liked resting on those big rocks. Also occasional sea turtles would swim near the shore. No doubt the place was magical. It gave you the sensation of being stranded on a very small island in the middle of huge ocean.

Patrick and I got our marriage license the same day he obtained his divorce decree. Which each passing moment one of my life's biggest dream was coming closer to being materialized.

"I don't wanna wait any longer. Let's get married this weekend." I said to him. We had not much but our day was going to be just as magical as the place that we picked for the occasion. I liked how my fiancé was taking our coming wedding so seriously. He was actually in charge of everything and I wasn't allowed to meddle in. Patrick's commitment to organizing everything definitely saved me from becoming one of those bride-zillas.

"What do you mean you haven't found a minister yet?" It was still hard for me to let go of control completely.

"What did I tell you babe? It's not your job. Your job was just to get your dress, which you did, so sit back and relax. Let me handle everything." He sounded almost macho.

"I'm telling you babe, all these ministers are telling you that they're afraid of climbing those rocks because they're chickens. Stop wasting your time and call a minister that's a woman. I guarantee you she won't have a problem with it. Women are not such whiny babies as men are. Find a minister or a reverend or whatever kind of priest that's a woman and she'll climb those rocks, you'll see." I insisted and he finally agreed. I was right.

"We have a reverend. She's not afraid of climbing the rocks. And she's free this Saturday." He informed me after getting off the phone.

The commotion created by the preparations for the wedding spread across the entire "condominium". Eduardo was busy making phone calls inviting everyone. Patrick had asked him to be his best man and the response he got was:

"It will be my honor. Thanks for making me feel special." I was still very surprised when one of those mornings, while having coffee with Eduardo, he announced to me that he'd take care of the reception for us.

"Are you being serious?" I asked in disbelief.

"It will be my wedding gift to you guys," said Eduardo with satisfaction written on his face.

"Wow! That is really generous of you. I don't know what to say other than I really appreciate that." I was feeling very grateful to him. It was so nice to know that our big day wouldn't have to end right after the ceremony.

The few days that were separating me from a long desired happy ending were filled with friendly chaos. Eduardo and Patrick were making numerous trips to the store for food and drinks. The boy that worked for Eduardo was busy cleaning up the whole place. One of the tenants was in charge of getting the flowers. I was mostly lying down on bed while watching TV. I was being a princess. Nobody and nothing could spoil that. This was my time. It was my big moment and I felt like I had earned the special treatment. I sure wasn't going to feel guilty or uncomfortable for enjoying this special time of my life.

The Big Day

"Oh my goodness! I'm getting married today! Is it normal that I feel like I'm about to pass out?" I asked nervously Eduardo's former girl-friend who came for the summer all the way from Europe just the night before.

"It's perfectly normal. It's your big day, of course you're gonna feel a little bit agitated." She was very sweet and I liked her instantly. Helen was my age. Her seven year old son who was also Eduardo's son came to Hawaii with her. Now both of them were also getting ready to attend the ceremony at the Eternity Beach.

"Where is Patrick? Is he getting ready yet?" She asked.

"He's been ready for hours. He's busy making sure that every-thing is in its place." I answered.

"Does this suit make me look alright?" Eduardo seemed almost just as agitated as I was.

"You look very distinguished." Helen complimented him. The excitement, mixed with a little bit of nervousness was in the air. I liked how my big day was on everyone's mind.

"Let's practice the walk one more time," said Eduardo.

"OK. Ready? Tan tan tan tan, tan tan tan tan. Tan tan ta ta ta ta ta ta ta tan." I was singing out loud while walking next to him.

"Don't walk too fast. After each pass we have to make a com-plete stop." I instructed Eduardo.

"Jesus Christ. I'm too old for this." He was complaining but it was obvious to everyone that he enjoyed participating in the wedding.

Only three hours before the ceremony I went to my hairdresser to have my hair styled. When I came back Patrick had already set up the skype for me so I could talk to my family. He had ordered the conference call so I could have four video-calls at the same time.

"Everyone's here! Look Patrick. My sister in Holland, my family in Greece, and everyone in Poland. And here is your mom in Texas." I was shouting excited. I was waving at everyone.

"Nice veil. But where is your dress?" My family wanted to know why I wasn't ready yet.

"I'll be getting dressed on the beach. In the cave. There is no way I'm climbing those rocks in this thing." I explained. I was talking fast. The high excitement's level was making me almost uncomfortable. I wasn't used to feeling so special and so important.

"Look at you guys! You all got dressed up." I was pointing my finger towards the laptop. Patrick was standing behind me. He was enjoying seeing me behave like a little girl.

"Of course. Did you really think we were gonna show up at your wedding in pajamas?"

"Look at Renata's dress! That's a nice dress." I wasn't done being amused.

"Even dad came to your house for this occasion?" I was so pleased to see that my entire family, spread in three different countries, gathered around their computers to participate in my day. They all looked effected by the anticipation the way I did. I so needed to see that.

"It's not every day your daughter gets married. Especially the pickiest one." My mother had that emotional tone so typical for a parent.

"Yeah, this is quite an occasion," Danuta was teasing me.

"The minister's here!" Someone shouted from the porch.

"OK, guys, we're gonna be driving to the beach now. We're taking the laptop with us so if we'll have the signal there you'll be able to watch us. If not, we'll be back in about two hours, OK? See you soon." I said bye to my family. Patrick drove to the beach with a different group of people. He was not allowed to see me in my white dress until the famous wedding march was going to be plaid from the portable stereo.

"Eduardo! Watch out! You just drove pass the red light," we heard Helen screaming. After few seconds of silence we all started to laugh while joking. When we finally arrived we noticed that most guests were already roaming around the parking lot that was above the canyon. The weather was absolutely gorgeous and apart from the gusty wind that was blowing my veil up and down, there was nothing to complain about. The small group of twenty guests was in a relaxed mood. Some tourists were turning their heads. Some of them were taking pictures of me. The passing cars were honking seeing us all marching towards the trail. The professional photographer, who was our wedding gift from Jeff; Eduardo's business partner, was shooting pictures of us descending the mountain. The reverend cut her foot on one of those sharp rocks and Jeff run to assist her. It was very comical and sweet how he was acting as a conductor of the event. He always had a great sense of humor and now it was contributing to this already mellow atmosphere that was present. There still was some shortly lived panicking but it was dissolved quickly by laughter. The beach, the guests, and Nel running around were transmitting an intimate atmosphere. There were no chairs or anything. Everyone was just walking freely around, some tasting the temperature of the water with their bare feet. Jeff was discussing with the reverend the best spa for the ceremony. He was trying to convince her to stand on a flat rock that was partially submerged in the water. She kept expressing her doubts so they finally agreed to have the ceremony on the sand, right next to the water. I went to change inside the cave with Sarah who was my made of honor. She was only few years younger than me. She's been renting one of the rooms in Eduardo's place. Sarah looked very exotic with her dark long hair reaching her waste. The big Hawaiian flower attached above her ear, the lei hanging from her neck and the azure dress accentuating her fragile body made her look like a sea-mermaid. One of our guests was standing in front of the cave's opening to create a sense of privacy. His big arms crossed on his large chest were making him look like a bouncer in front of a night club.

"Is she ready yet?" People were shouting from below. The "bodyguard", without turning his head respectfully, asked about the progress of changing.

"Not yet," Sarah shouted. The cave we were in was dark and narrow. It was hard to maneuver in the big dress.

"Not yet!" The man repeated Sarah's words.

"You look really breath taking. You look like a princess." Sarah's expression on her face and her tone were conforming what she was saying to me.

"I'm having hard time breathing. What if I faint?" I was being serious. I had a sensation of being detached from my body. Everything just seemed surreal. Even though I attempted few times, I was unable to take a deep breath all the way from my stomach. It seemed as if my muscles below the chest decided to get temporarily paralyzed.

"OoooK. I think I'm ready. Let's go before I pass out."

"She's ready! She's coming." Sarah informed the man standing with his back to us.

"Don't forget to take your bouquet." She handed me the orange flowery arrangement.

"She's cooooommming!!!!" The man's loud and deep voice echoed across the beach. Someone hit the play button on the stereo. The sound of the wedding march had to fight with the rumor of the splashing waves and the wind. Eduardo was waiting for me in front of the cave to walk me down. His suit was now decorated with Hawaiian leis. With my bare feet I found it easy to walk over the rocks but I was afraid for Eduardo to lose his balance. He stumbled few times and I couldn't help but to giggle. Everyone was smiling and we all laughed. Walking towards the ocean where all the guests formed a semi-circle, I felt like a member of a royal family. Everyone's sight was fixed on me. The groom and the reverend were standing in the middle of a heart drown in the sand. The reverend was wearing a white toga. Hawaiian leis were handing from her neck as well. She was holding a book. Like me she was bare foot. Patrick was wearing a black suit, white shirt and a silver tie that matched his handkerchief. An orange rose was pinned on the left side of his suit. A gorgeous, very long, green Hawaiian lei was hanging loosely from his neck. It was different than everyone else's. It was made of some exotic leafs and it didn't form a loop. The two separate ends were reaching all the way to his knees. He's head and he's beard were shaved in a manner I liked the most; just enough to see the dark shade of it. He looked very handsome. He was smiling the whole time. He's eyes were piercing me while giving me encouragement. He appeared as calm as a meditating Buddha. Patrick extended his arm and I stood next to him. Everyone's eyes traveled towards Sarah descending from the rocks in the company of the gentleman who earlier served as our privacy screen. The man was holding Nel's leash. My German shepherd was appointed as our ring bearer. She had a small white pillow, decorated with flowers attached to her collar. The rings were tied to the pillow. With unusual strength Nel was pulling on the leash, all excited to be standing next to her momma. I tried not to think about how sad it was making me feel that Rex could not be present with us. I still haven't given up the search for him but I knew that I'd have to change my tactics pretty soon since they weren't producing the desired result.

The reverend blessed the leis that were hanging from her wrist. When she was done with praying she passed the green lei to me and the white one to Patrick. We exchanged those Hawaiian flower-based necklaces by hanging them on each others' necks. After that the reverend opened her book and she begun reciting her speech. I could not understand a single word she was saying. I could not care less about it. I was staring into the grooms eyes and he was staring right back at me. We were both smiling. I was looking at him as if I was seeing for the first time how handsome he was. The insecurities that often made him look more like a boy than a man were completely vanished. I had in front of me a strong man that I've been dreaming about. A manly man, a man that was in total control. There was nothing boyish or immature about him anymore. The confidence he was projecting was giving me a sense of security. He's deep brown eyes and the wrinkles formed around them by the smile were making me feel loved, cherished and protected. I was still having a hard time with digesting the idea that it was me who was about to say: "I do." It still felt too good to be true. The whole time I wasn't breathing well. My legs felt as if they were about to go on strike. Few times the reverend assisted by the groom had to hold my arm so I wouldn't lose my balance. Even the exchange of the rings and the vows did not convince me yet that this was my reality.

"I now pronounce you husband and wife. You can now kiss your bride," the reverend finally announced in her formal tone. Patrick leaned to kiss me. We rapped arms around each other and everyone started to clap.

"You looked absolutely gorgeous! I enjoyed watching you. That was a beautiful wedding," said Helen.

"Are you sure? I didn't look stupid?" I asked her.

"Not at all. You looked very emotional which was very refreshing to watch. It was really nice," she answered.

"OK, it's time for the sand ceremony so let's gather around," announced the reverend. Patrick wanting to add some local tradition to our wedding, he bought special sand and a vase for this occasion. The two bags of sand that he purchased were tinted in two different colors. One was pink and the other white. By pouring the sand into the transparent vase, a design in pink and white would form. The resulting effect of it supposed to symbolize our journey together. Out of respect and to show appreciation we asked Eduardo and Helen to pour the sand before us. When it reached half of the vase Patrick and I took over. After the sand ceremony it was time for pictures to be taken. Some tourists from Japan who were now arriving at the beach asked to have their pictures taken with us. Other foreign visitors who weren't as eager to climb the rocks were waving at us from above. The flash lights indicated that they were taking pictures of us as well.

On the way back to our place, Patrick and I drove together in our beaten up, rusty looking toyota. It didn't really matter to me that it wasn't a luxurious limousine we were in. Nel, Patrick and I, we were all excited and all happy. It was when my newly wedded husband parked the old car in front of Eduardo's house that I was able to take a deep breath. Only then I seemed to fully realize that I was Mrs. Pettingill. Back at home my husband set up the skype connection for me again. It was around two in the morning on the other side of the globe but my family was still awake. Since the portable internet didn't have reception at the beach, I asked the reverend if she could perform the ceremony one more time for my family to see it. She agreed. And so for the second time Patrick and I officially promised each other the eternal love.

The reception went on in just as easy going atmosphere as the wedding did. The guests were busy eating, drinking and chatting. I was having mimosa after mimosa happy to see everyone having a good time but sad at the same time that my family wasn't there with us physically. Eduardo gave a speech and after that the single women gathered to catch the bouquet. Everyone was screaming and laughing with excitement while watching Helen fighting over the bouquet with another guest. For a moment it looked like we were going to witness a "cat fight". Helen being the more determined one won the battle. After that the single men gathered to catch the garter belt that the groom just took of my leg. Men weren't as excited thought over the idea of being the next one in line to tie the knot, as the tradition says, so the piece of the lingerie practically landed on the tallest one. When drummers started to pound rhythmically on their African drums, I started to dance. It was getting dark already and the porch with its exotic pond resembled almost some fairy place. I did not want to have to go to sleep and then to wake up to a regular world again.

Help Me Get My Dog Back

"Is there a way to hack onto that stupid shelter's computer so I can know the name of the person who has Rex?" I asked my husband.

"Or if we could just find someone who'd apply with them as a volunteer and then that person would sneak into their files, that may work…" I've been verbalizing all kinds of ideas these days to Patrick. We had driven around the military base, trying to see behind the tall fences that surrounded the military housings, but with not much luck. I was getting tired of scanning the networking sites on the internet in hopes of seeing the picture of my missing dog that would lead me to his whereabouts. I was tired of asking strangers at dog parks whether they have seen a tall German shepherd.

"What if she doesn't even have him anymore? Or if they had to move and she gave Rex away to some neighbor or something? Or if he run away and someone took him in without bothering to look for his owner?" My husband was used by now hearing the same things from me over and over again. I've been obsessing about Rex so much that I wasn't even too excited about the fact that Patrick and I were planning to move to Big Island. We've been sending the rent money for few months now, hoping to relocate there soon. The rent on Big Island was only three hundred fifty a month. We both were tired of the constant struggle with the lack of money and living on a much less expensive Island seemed to make more sense. The cabin was owned by the same man from whom I rented the primitive shed few years back. The man was desperate to make a sale and so he was willing to owner-finance to us the three acres and the cabin that was on it. Patrick still had to convince his probation officer in submitting the papers for the transfer of his probation to the different county and that wasn't going smooth either. The whole judicial system was getting on my nerves. I was sick and tired of feeling like my life was run by some people, with whom I wished I had nothing to do with, just because I married a man with a criminal record. Frustrated on so many levels I started posting ads on craigslist in the lost and found section. I added Rex's picture to the ads. Some phone calls and some emails later that served only to crash my spirit in the end, I decided that I couldn't take any of that anymore. I decided to share my heartache with the world through facebook. I was a little afraid to be judged and condemn by some insensitive people who liked "stirring shit" just for the heck of it but I was dreading even more the idea of never seeing Rex again. I kept posting Rex's picture and short description of what happened on different groups and pages related to dogs. I was just asking for advice. Most people who stumbled upon my posts were sympathetic to my plea. They were offering some creative ideas like creating a facebook page for Rex. So I crated one. I called it: Help me GET MY DOG BACK (please sign this petition). When one of Rex's supporters suggested that I should write to Penny, who was a German shepherd lover and who was a journalist for an online newspaper, I did that as well. I was surprised to hear back from her. I was filled with lots of hope when Penny wrote to me that she was going to contact the shelter for a statement. I was hoping that they would finally take me seriously understanding that I would never go away and that this time they would do what was necessary to correct the mistake.

I didn't know what was responsible for such big commotions on Rex's page that was going on until I clicked on the link of Penny's article. She gave it a title that said: "Woman fights to find, regain custody of her German shepherd". In her compassionate writing the journalist included the statement that she received from the shelter's Director of Community Relations. The statement made me fully understand that the shelter was never going to do anything to resolve this issue, it gave me a feeling of being dry and rehearsed:

"Thank you so much for your inquiry. What an unfortunate situation. While due to privacy issues we cannot disclose the details of this particular case, I can tell you what our standard process is. If a dog arrives with or without identification, we make every attempt to locate the owner to claim their animal immediately. We may keep the dog for many days while we try to reunite the animal with its owner. If unsuccessful, dogs are made available for adoption. In these rare cases in which the owner comes forward but the pet has already been adopted, we make efforts to contact the new adopter and try to encourage them to relinquish ownership. We also advise the original owner of the subpoena process to obtain our records to recover their dog."

In that statement there was no explanation whatsoever how come Rex wasn't relinquished to Ahmed while still at the shelter and while he went there to retrieve him. Just: "no details due to privacy issues." Over a thousand people joined Rex's page via Penny's article in the next few days and the number kept growing. The supporters, most of which were caring woman in the age range from 35 to 55, were expressing their sympathy. The more enraged ones started to call the shelter demanding a swift action. Some were posting their opinion on the shelter's facebook page but their comments were being quickly deleted and their profile blocked. Mine was blocked too. I was overwhelmed with the response I was getting. People from all over the United States, and some from different countries, where showing their solidarity.

"This is outrageous! The shelter people should be ashamed of themselves! Just give the damn dog back to his rightful owner!" The supporters were posting such comments on my page understanding that the shelter people would be visiting Rex's page. I felt very close, even emotionally attached to all these women. With some of them like Jo Ann, I became close friends with.

"I just got a response from the Animal Advocacy group there in Honolulu. The woman who's in charge of that organization said she'd contact you. Her name is Pamela. I think she may be able to help you," Jo Ann informed me over the phone. Hope inhabited my heart once again. Three days after Penny's article was issued, I received a call from the shelter. Some kind of manager was informing me that the shelter would like to have a meeting with me.

"Why? Do you guys have Rex back with you? Is he coming home with me?" I asked.

"I'm not allowed to discuss any details. All I was told that the directors would like to meet with you." He replied.

"Fine. I'll be there tomorrow then," I responded, knowing what the meeting was going to look like.

"I'm telling you Jo Ann, I feel like this isn't about Rex being returned to me. I have a feeling that this meeting is a set up. I got a comment on Rex's page from some journalist asking if she could participate in the meeting. And yet the shelter told Penny that she could not participate in the conference call."

"I agree with you. This does sound like a set up. They want someone who's on their side to cover the story. They're not interested in doing what's right and giving your Rex back. They seem more interested in looking good in public's opinion, that's for sure. They're gonna try to make you look bad. You know, if you feel that way, you don't have to agree to that meeting," she said.

"No. We'll have that meeting. I don't want them to feel like they didn't have the chance to express their point of view. Even though that's not even the case, because Penny did contact them for a statement."

"You blow my mind girl. You're stronger than anyone I know. You go girl. Give them a rope, let them hang themselves," said Jo Ann.

Pamela from Animal Advocacy agreed to meet my husband and I in front of the shelter prior to the meeting.

"I brought a video camera and audio recorder, and I hope you won't mind me taping the whole thing. I'd like to be able to go back and examine what has been said at this meeting."

"Absolutely," I agreed. The two-hour meeting went just the way I'd expected. The shelter people didn't seem interested in resolving the issue. The two directors and the manager that called me the day before were trying to make things look as if it was me who failed my dog. They were trying to undermine my character by pointing out that I had "questionable" friends and boyfriends.

"We've been informed that you were in an abusive relationship with your ex. That's why we didn't want him to pick up your dog. And your other friend never showed up to take him home. We had no choice but to adopt him out," the director's voice was just as unfriendly as his body posture.

"Let's assume for a moment that was the case. You did know that I was working in Africa, and I could be reached by email. You were informed about that. Why on earth would you not, for example, put Rex in a foster home in the meantime until this would get resolved?" I kept questioning without getting answers that made sense. Toward the end of the meeting, I started to get very emotional. The more I insisted on uncovering the truth, the more uncomfortable the director became.

"What you're saying to me is not clear. Something just doesn't add up here." I finally said while shaking my head.

"What do you want us to do?" he finally asked.

"I want Rex back. I don't want to have to go to court. Can you call this woman one more time and convince her to give me my dog back?"

"I will do that. Even though I told you before that we would not harass her anymore, I will call her again," he answered. My husband wanted to step in with questions, to show that their version of what happened made absolutely no sense, but I interrupted him. I wasn't interested in finding the fault as much as I was interested in getting Rex back.

Naively, I thought the shelter would make a bigger effort to reunite Rex and I, if it was clear to them that that was all I wanted. The next day I got a call from the director. He was telling me that the woman who had Rex said she "would think about it".

"What is there to think about? That's what she said a year ago, when you guys first called her. She didn't even tell you when she'd be done with thinking." I was more than disappointed with that phone call. I felt victimized by both the woman and those shelter people.

"I've been going over the tape and I can tell you that there many inconsistencies in their version of what happened. They keep contradicting themselves. I'm glad we have it on tape. I'm going to try to help you," Pamela told me over the phone.

I called the shelter's director back and told him if they'd return my Rex I'd cancel my appearance on the local radio show that Pamela had planned to get me on.

The next day the journalist, who had a previous working relationship with the shelter, and who participated in the shelter meeting via conference call, published her online article. It was called: "Rex the dog and Elzbieta Trzciak case investigation." The article was written in a manner that was supposed to make it sound like it was laying down the "facts." It depicted me as an irresponsible pet owner, a person of questionable character. It was also focusing on the matter of the domestic violence. The links to this article were being shared at the shelter's facebook page and all over the internet.

I concentrated on working with Carroll, who was the host of a local radio show. Rex and Nel were micro-chipped, and Carroll wanted me to provide him with the official documents from the microchip company which would show that the shelter was not being truthful.

The shelter people claimed during our meeting that they found out Ahmed was "never, ever on the emergency contact list" and that's why they did not have to release Rex to him when he came. The papers I got from the microchip company proved otherwise.

The microchip company's documents stated clearly that Ahmed's name was listed as the emergency contact since 2008 and he, nor his phone number, were ever removed from the emergency contact list. After receiving those documents, Carroll invited me to be a guest on his show. My husband and Pamela were also invited, just as the shelter's directors and "the friend who never showed up to pick up Rex". The last two didn't bother to appear on the show to defend their points of view. Surprisingly, the journalist who previously launched the article depicting me in a less than favorable light joined us over the phone. She was actually on my side this time. She acknowledged that she had written the article in a hurry, unsuspecting that the information the shelter gave to her could be far from the truth. She had even removed her old article and replaced it with a new one that had an apologetic tone.

Also that day Pamela released her article on the Animal Advocacy website. The article was entitled "Where is Rex?" and provided a comprehensive description of the inaccuracies and deception of the directors in that infamous meeting she attended at the shelter.

"I will be filing a formal complaint with the mayor and the city council, and requesting that a thorough investigation of the shelter be performed. Million of taxpayer's money goes to the shelter each year and they need to be held accountable of their actions," she told the listeners.

The following day Penny had published a second article, bringing some more compassionate supporters to Rex's page. The page and the signatures on the petition were growing in numbers.

As promised, the complaint was filed by Pamela and many of Rex's supporters took time to write to the officials demanding that the matter be taken seriously. I also wrote emails to the mayor and the city council. Two weeks later, one of the council members sent a letter to Pamela informing her of the results of their decision. According to the officials the city didn't have spare money for such an investigation and their "initial inquiry" lead them to the conclusion that whatever happened with Rex was "beyond anyone's control."

The shelter seemed to be invincible. All my hopes of seeing my dog again were gone.

Poppy Seeds

While all that was happening, things were heating up in many aspects. The stress was soaring through the roof these days. I was a nervous wreck. Patrick had lost his new job with a company that made modifications and repairs on ships. The primary contractor of that company was military and they had restructured their policy. The new policy no longer allowed anyone with a felony to work as a contractor on base. Along with the stability that this job provided we also lost our health insurance. At home things didn't look good either. Eduardo had told us that we had to move out. The actual reason for his decision remained unknown. There was no real clarity behind his motives and the excuse that he needed the extra room for his guests that were coming for Christmas, seemed just that; an excuse. He claimed that we were welcome back after the holidays. Not surprisingly this turned out to not be the case. Everything we owned, that we had stored under the bed in our room was placed in the driveway for us to pick up a couple of days after we "temporarily" moved out. We had no place to go. With a very limited budget and even more restricting stigma of Patrick's criminal record, we were left with little, if any, options. Part of my husband's probation's requirements was that he had to explain in details to the landlord, or roommates, the legal predicament he was in. The discrimination I've experienced through my husband's situation was a huge eye opener for me. I despised the fact that Eduardo seemed to be indulging himself with unnecessarily sharing Patrick's secret to everyone who stepped their foot on the premises. I discovered that some people loved to know about such "juicy" details as this gave them the illusion of having the upper hand. Having my husband hearing constant remarks from everyone about how I supposedly married him "just for papers" was just as tiring.

A man named Brian came to our rescue. He was friends with Eduardo. Brian was known to Patrick and I, he attended our wedding. Patrick had also worked on his cars before. He was a nice guy. He was a single father of a beautiful four year old daughter. He had an addition being built to his house. It was a work in progress, however, he allowed us to stay there until we could find a better place.

"K guys, as you can see the bathroom is not finished and there is no running water but make yourself comfortable. You can use this mattress here since you don't have a bed." Brian walked us through the place that to me resembled an attic due to exposed beams that weren't covered yet with the dry wall. Later that day Patrick installed a toilet, using a water hose for water.

"Thanks Brian. We really appreciate you rescuing us like this," my husband said to our new landlord. Things were going somewhat smooth again until the day when Patrick got arrested. His drug test came out positive for opiates. There was no doubt in my mind that there had to be some other explanation for it than my husband using. The probation officer, and some other justice system employees that were present, were looking at me as if I was completely crazy while attempting to prevent the arrest. I was never informed by anyone how ridiculously small the amount of the opiate was in the urine, to the point where it should have been ruled out as illegal drug use. I was thinking possible scenarios like the drug reaching the system through the anti-flea products we had been using. I was showing the probation officer the arsenal of flea-killing weapons of mass destruction that we had recently purchased. I was asking her for few extra days, hoping to be able to resolve this mystery. She dismissed my explanations. I had to watch my husband being handcuffed and escorted out by the sheriffs. He spent eight days in the jail awaiting his day in court. I could not understand how the probation officer was getting away with things like, for example, setting his court date eight days later, as opposed to two business days, which was in his rights. The modules in jail were so overfilled that he had to sleep on the floor on some tiny mattress that was less than an inch thick piece of foam. I wasn't even allowed to visit him. Hysterically I called my new friend Jo Ann.

"What do you guys normally eat?" was her first question.

"I don't know, just regular things." I couldn't understand where she was going with that.

"Have you been consuming poppy seeds lately?" she insisted.

"I don't think so. I'm pretty sure that it was some of that flea medicine that caused all this. What are poppy seeds anyway? What does it look like?" I asked while scanning all the items we had in our refrigerator.

"They look like tiny dark dots. They can be on bread or bagels-"

"Oh my god Jo Ann!" I interrupted her.

"Guess what we have in the fridge? Guess what we have been eating lately? Freaking bagels! And they have those dark spots you're talking about!" I yelled.

"Look at the label where it says ingredients." she instructed me.

"Yes! It says here, in black and white, that contains poppy seeds! Oh my god Jo Ann. You just helped me prove my husband's innocents! He's been sitting in that stupid jail for eating a freaking bagel! I'm telling you Jo Ann; I can't take this shit anymore." I was happy and infuriated at the same time.

"Don't throw the package. Make sure you take that with you to the court. Show it to the judge. It should have the date on it from when it was produced."

"Even the receipt is still in the bag." I said to her.

"Take that with you as well. Oh god, I'm telling you girl, you have no idea how often my sister and I, in our line of work, witnessed innocent people being put in jail for eating poppy seeds. You have no idea. This isn't new to me. You know I spoke to my sister, who's a head lab technician by the way, and she said that if the number came below two thousand, that they should have thrown that test away. That is legally a negative result, anything less is most likely consumed. Especially since Patrick has no history of drug abuse whatsoever. Gosh, I'm glad I was able to help. Let me know how the court day goes."

I had asked Pamela, who had been assisting me with Rex's case and with whom I became friends with as well, to accompany me to court. I was a nervous wreck, and to have her there with me meant a lot to me. It had been an incredibly long, hard week.

"OK, why don't we have your wife approach the bench? Can you tell us, without getting into too many details, about what you have discovered? Don't make a speech out of it; just tell us everything in few words." The judge instructed me while I was placing all the evidence on the table. In simple words I told him everything that had transpired. The judge released Patrick that same day. He told him to come back for a follow up hearing in two weeks.

At the follow up hearing Patrick's probation officer explained that the test was most likely a result of the bagels and then proceeded to justify herself as to why she had him arrested even though the numbers were below half of the two thousand cutoff. According to her she didn't trust my husband. This was supposed to be a good enough reason for the arrest. The judge looked at Patrick and stated:

"If you are willing to admit to the violation of probation I am inclined to give you time served." With my over active defensive nature for the ones I love, I almost launched out of my chair, ready to start, what my husband would affectionately call bitching. However Patrick handled it in a much calmer way before I had the chance.

"Excuse me Your Honor, but what exactly would I be saying that I'm guilty of?" Patrick stood up for himself. I was proud of him. The judge announced then that due to the evidence this incident was not a violation of probation.

Somehow the shelter people found out about my husband's sensitive situation, because in that period of time they tried to intimidate me by posting on their facebook page post such as:

"Do you believe that people who have temporary restraining orders against them or those who are on probation for an assault for example, should be allowed to own pets? Tell us what you think?" They didn't go as far with it as they thought they would. Some people would leave comments such as:

"I know people who are doing great because they own pets. Some jails have programs that use dogs to rehabilitate inmates." Also Jo Ann wrote an extensive comment, telling the shelter that she knew what they were trying to do, and to pretty much shove it.

The Lawyer's Office

I've been browsing online these days in search of the best attorney that would take Rex's case. The biggest challenge was that he or she would have to be willing to do the case *pro bono*, as I could not afford the fees for legal representation.

"Get dressed Patrick. We are going to this lawyer's office and I won't leave that place until he takes my case," I said to my husband.

The attorney I picked was no doubt one of the best. He was famous on the island for his "badass" performances in the court of law. We were able to see him but the meeting wasn't going well at all. He didn't seem thrilled whatsoever about taking my case. He kept cross-examining me as if I was on the stand in the courtroom already.

I was fighting the seeming accusations back. Hearing this successful man telling me how busy he was and how he didn't have time for all this, I finally broke down in tears.

"OK, I'll take this case." His words took a tremendous weight off my chest.

"But only because she was the one that cried. If it was you crying I wouldn't take the case." The lawyer cracked a joke while looking at Patrick.

A few days later we went back to his office with copies of all the documents I'd gathered pertaining Rex's case. While waiting in the lobby, I saw a woman who just walked in like she was in a hurry. She was nicely dressed and she gave me a strange sensation of some loving energy emanating from her. It was a pretty strange feeling and I couldn't explain to myself why I noticed her. Later the lawyer introduced that woman as being one of his associates who would work with him on my case. She seemed to have lots of empathy while listening to me and my husband.

"I've dealt with that shelter before. I have some clue what they're like." Her tone was very encouraging. She gave me some papers to fill out explaining what it meant for the case to be taken on a contingency fee basis:

"Basically, whatever you'll be awarded in the final settlement, the law firm gets forty percent of that. You don't pay anything to us before that."

"Thank you God for leading us through this ordeal," I said to my husband back in the car.

"Can you believe this? We've got the best freaking lawyer there is! And we don't have to worry about the money. Rex will be home with us soon." I was smiling the whole time on the way back home.